INTRODUCTION TO SIMULATION
Programming Techniques and Methods of Analysis

McGraw-Hill Computer Science Series

McGraw-Hill Advanced Computer Science Series

INTRODUCTION
TO SIMULATION
Programming Techniques and
Methods of Analysis

James A. Payne

McGraw-Hill Book Company

New York St. Louis San Francisco Auckland Bogotá Hamburg
Johannesburg London Madrid Mexico Montreal New Delhi
Panama Paris São Paulo Singapore Sydney Tokyo Toronto

This book was set in Times Roman by Santype-Byrd.
The editors were James E. Vastyan, James B. Armstrong, and Scott Amerman;
the production supervisor was Leroy A. Young.
New drawings were done by VIP Graphics.

INTRODUCTION TO SIMULATION
Programming Techniques and Methods of Analysis

234567890 HDHD 898765432

ISBN 0-07-048945-9

Library of Congress Cataloging in Publication Data

Payne, James A. (James Andrew), date
    Introduction to simulation.

    (McGraw-Hill computer science series)
    Includes bibliographical references and index.
    1. Digital computer simulation.   I. Title.
II. Series.
QA76.9.C65P39   001.4'34   81-12331
ISBN 0-07-048945-9   AACR2

CONTENTS

PREFACE

Simulation studies represent a widespread and increasingly important area of application for digital computers. As such, simulation is an important topic for students in the computer science discipline. It is also an important topic for students and practitioners in many other disciplines, including engineering, business administration, and the quantitative sciences. Usually the most crucial factor required in applying simulation successfully in a specific problem area is knowledge of that problem area. Thus, the most appropriate person to develop a simulation study is the person most familiar with the system to be studied. However, the development of effective and efficient computer programs can also be critical in these projects. Often this requires the participation of programming specialists as well as subject specialists.

The objective of this textbook is to provide an introduction to the use of digital computers in simulation studies. It is aimed toward upper-division undergraduate students who have completed an introductory programming course and a basic lower-division sequence of mathematics courses, including an introduction to statistics. The topics covered include methods for programming discrete-event model simulations and methods for the analysis of simulation results.

The approach used in this book is to emphasize programming aspects of the simulation process and to cover a few specific examples in detail. Previous experience in teaching simulation-related courses has indicated that many students do not have an intuitive feeling for processes which involve dynamic interaction. Therefore, the approach of going from concrete examples to the more general concepts, rather than vice versa, enables a significantly larger portion of the students to gain a reasonable understanding of the primary ideas which underlie the simulation process.

The selection of topics and the level of presentation are oriented toward making this material accessible to a wide variety of readers and toward providing a basis for further study in this subject area. Thus, more introductory and elementary material in both the programming and the analysis areas are included than will be needed by many readers. This has also led to treating some topics in a somewhat cursory manner, although their importance to and relationship with the subject area have been indicated.

A simulation programming system for discrete event models is developed in Chapter 4. This is intended to demonstrate the basic requirements of such a system as well as to provide a means by which the student can develop nontrivial example programs within the time limits of a single course. I believe this is the most appropriate method for introducing simulation programming, since it provides the proper basis for understanding and learning special-purpose simulation programming languages. This type of extension is considered in Chapter 5. Moreover, there are circumstances for which a general-purpose language is preferred for simulation programming. PL/I is the language primarily used in this book; however, this material has been successfully covered by students with programming experience limited to FORTRAN.

In presenting the analysis methods, I have made an attempt, in each case, to relate their application to the example problems. The methods included are only a small portion of those that have been applied in simulation studies, but they do illustrate most of the "functions" of the analysis required in this process.

The examples for the most part include more details and repetition than are necessary for the reader with a good background in statistics. But often students with only an introductory course in statistics or those who have not used statistics recently need this type of review.

The example programs included in this text are an essential part of the material. In teaching courses, I have made these programs available to the students for use in several of the exercises. One method for doing this with an IBM 360/370 System is outlined in Appendix B. This could also be done with other equipment and with other programming languages, but it would require more effort by the instructor.

This is an introduction to simulation, not a survey of the entire subject area. The programming and mathematical skills common to many undergraduate students are used as the basis for presenting the concepts and procedures used in simulation studies. This book, I hope, will serve the interested reader as a starting point and guide toward the effective use of this very powerful tool.

James A. Payne

ONE

INTRODUCTION AND OVERVIEW

In the movie *The Man with the Golden Gun*, secret agent James Bond escaped one set of pursuers by driving his car up the twisted approach section of a collapsed bridge and jumping it over a canal. After the car left this approach section, it did a complete roll in midair, landed upright on the other side of the canal, and sped off. The screenplay credited this feat to Bond's vast knowledge, skill, and daring, but in reality this stunt was made possible by computer simulation.

The idea of using a curved takeoff ramp to achieve a roll-over jump had occurred to a number of stunt drivers, but the detailed plan for the first successful jump of this type was developed by analysts at the Calspan Corporation. This group derived a set of mathematical equations that describe the motion of an automobile in this type of situation and programmed a digital computer to solve these equations. The program was then used to determine the resulting trajectory, using various shapes for the takeoff ramp and different initial velocities for the car. In this manner, a ramp design was specified and an acceptable range for initial speed was determined. When this scheme was attempted the first time, it worked.

The roll-over jump became a part of the *American Thrill Show* and was later adapted for the film segment in *The Man with the Golden Gun*. A report on this work was presented at a Society of Automotive Engineers meeting in 1976 [7]. As discussed in the report, this work was carried out as part of a long-term project related to safety aspects of highway and roadside design.

The design of this stunt is a novel example of a procedure which has been widely used and is becoming increasingly beneficial in many areas of application. This process is to represent a given situation by mathematical and logical relationships embodied in a computer program and then to study the situation under various conditions by observing the behavior of the computer model. This simulation approach to problem solving has been used with many different types of problems, using a great variety of techniques for implementation.

The range of application areas and procedures used with this approach is too great to cover in any detail in one book. Furthermore, simulation techniques are, to some extent, specialized to specific types of problems or application areas. However, there are some general characteristics of these procedures which are common to and are useful for a wide variety of practical problems.

This book is an introduction to computer methodology for carrying out simulation studies. The emphasis is on programming techniques used with certain studies of this type and on methods required to analyze results obtained from the associated simulations. While computer methodology is only a part of the work required in simulations, these types of projects have given rise to some of the largest and most logically complex computer programs ever developed. This is a major area of computer application. Thus, simulation is an important area of computer science, but it is also a topic that illustrates how computers can interact with many fields of study.

This first chapter includes a discussion of the nature of the simulation process, indicates how it is used, and outlines the topics covered in the book. The objective is to provide a preview of the book's contents and to indicate how this material relates to the practice of applying the simulation approach to problem solving.

1.1 THE SIMULATION PROCESS

Simulation is a method used to study the dynamics of systems. The term *systems* is used here to mean a group of units which operate in some interrelated manner. Often the purpose of system studies is to gain an understanding of the overall operation when a group of well-understood units are connected. Simulation provides a description of system behavior as it evolves over a period of time.

The following definition is given by Shannon [14]:

> Simulation is the process of designing a model of a real system and conducting experiments with this model for the purpose either of understanding the behavior of the system or of evaluating various strategies (within the limits imposed by a criterion or set of criteria) for the operation of the system.

This is typical of the many formal definitions of this term and includes many types of activities not directly covered by the topics in this book.

Here we are primarily concerned with techniques for using general-purpose digital computers in simulations. We choose these topics not because they are the most important or interesting topics in the field of simulation but rather because they are a good starting point for the study of this subject. Our viewpoint is that a certain amount of experience in the practical details of carrying out simulation procedures is necessary in order to properly appreciate the more abstract concepts of a general discussion.

Simulation does not necessarily involve computers. But the availability of these devices has been the impetus to extend the application of simulation to many new areas. This process began with the development of analog computers, which were primarily applied to engineering design problems involving continuous models. Later the development of digital computers led to increased use of simulation in the areas of business and economics where discrete models were prevalent. As digital computing has decreased in cost and become more available, it has become the dominant mode for the simulation of both discrete and continuous models. These factors have led to the increasing use of computer simulation in almost all disciplines of study. In view of anticipated advances in digital computer technology, indications are that this trend will continue.

The simulation approach can be used to study almost any problem. However, it is a reasonable approach only under certain conditions. It requires that a model be constructed that represents system behavior in terms of mathematical and logical relationships between variables. This model must adequately represent the primary effects which relate to the problem being studied. Until such a model is available, simulation cannot be used.

After a computer model of the system is available, simulation is used to investigate the performance of the system. Each simulation run is essentially an experiment on the system. The advantage of simulation is that these experiments can be completely controlled and completely observed.

If the system model can be analyzed using mathematical techniques, this method is generally superior to the simulation method. Analytical solutions are more accurate, provide more information, and are usually more easily obtained than simulation results. Simulation should not be used to replace mathematical analysis. Instead, mathematical analysis should be used to replace simulation to as great a degree as possible.

The primary reason for using simulation is that many models cannot be adequately analyzed by standard mathematical techniques. This is usually the case when the interactions between variables are nonlinear or when random effects are inherent in the system. Systems with waiting lines, or queues, are examples of this situation. Although there are mathematical methods to solve queuing-type problems, the solutions are available only for limited cases and do not provide complete information about system behavior.

Simulation is a very powerful method for solving system problems because of its wide applicability and because it provides a laboratory to study systems without the costs of building or modifying the real systems. The basic method of simulation is easily understood and is simple to apply. However, it is very difficult to draw accurate conclusions from simulation studies. The difficulties are due to problems associated with both developing an effective simulation model and drawing meaningful conclusions from simulation results.

1.2 USES OF SIMULATION

In order to indicate the potential advantages that are offered by simulation, we will discuss a few examples of the type of applications where this method has been useful. This will also help to partially classify the many kinds of problems studied using this approach.

The simulation project for the automobile roll-over jump is an example where the model of the system was represented by a set of differential equations. The technique for describing the motion of a vehicle of this type is provided by the theories or laws of classical mechanics. The proper application of these laws can produce a mathematical model which very accurately and reliably represents the vehicle motion as a function of the external conditions acting upon the vehicle. The advantages of using simulation with this example include:

1. The ability to study the system without the expense and risk of experiments with the real system
2. The ability to determine the ramp shape and driving conditions required to achieve a complete roll before landing
3. The ability to determine the effect of variations from the specified driving conditions on the landing conditions

This is an example of engineering design where the objective is to produce a system that meets certain specifications. There are many areas of engineering where procedures similar to this may be used, and indeed much of the early development of simulation techniques was in these areas. However, the primary characteristics of engineering design models, and hence of their simulation requirements, are determined by the nature of the theories used to describe the physical processes. Thus many of the simulation techniques used in these areas are specialized to certain forms of equations.

Another application area of simulation is in production scheduling. This type of problem may be illustrated by the situation where a fixed number of parts must be produced, which requires the use of machine A and then machine B. Each part requires a specified length of time on each machine type. These times are known but may be different for each part. The problem is to select a sequence in which the jobs are to be run on the machines in order to minimize the time between the start of the first job on machine A and the completion of the last job on machine B. The model required to represent this system in a simulation program consists of the logical operations of selecting the next part to be processed and determining the time at which the processing is completed. The changes in system representation occur only when a part starts or completes processing on a machine; thus, the changes are discrete. A simulation program for this problem would use some rule for specifying the sequence in which parts are processed. The advantages of this approach would include:

1. The ability to compare a large number of parts selection patterns with little human effort

2. The ability to determine the best selection pattern before producing the parts
3. The ability to observe the effects of changes in the selection pattern, which may lead to general rules for specifying parts selection

A production-scheduling problem is typically more complex than this example, involving many operations and more involved relationships between operations. However, the modeling for such problems would be similar to that required for this example. In a production-scheduling problem the model development does not require any theories or special mathematical notation. Only simple arithmetic and logical relationships are needed to represent the system and its operation.

Another production-related example can be used to illustrate a significant aspect of most simulation problems—unpredictable behavior. Consider the case of a shop where 20 tire-building machines are operated by production workers. These machines malfunction from time to time and must be serviced by a repairperson. There are four repairpeople on duty at all times, and the machines are such that only one repairperson can work effectively on them at a time. There is a daily quota of tire production, so any down time above a fixed amount makes overtime work necessary.

Sometimes more than four machines are down, so all the repairpeople are busy and machines are waiting for service. At other times all machines are operating properly and all repairpeople are idle. More often, two or three repairpeople are not occupied. This raises the question of how many repairpeople should there be.

It has been observed that there is one chance in ten that a machine will break down in any given hour. The time required to repair also appears to vary in a random manner but with the following distribution:

40 percent require $\frac{1}{2}$ hour to fix
30 percent require 1 hour to fix
20 percent require $1\frac{1}{2}$ hours to fix
10 percent require 2 hours to fix

In order to simulate the behavior of this system some source of values to represent the chance occurrences is required. If a ten-sided fair die was available, with integers 1 through 10 marking the sides, a series of numbers could be generated by throwing the die repeatedly. This series could then be used to determine if a specific machine failed in a given period and also to determine the time required to repair the machines which did fail.

Using this series of random numbers and a logical model of the shop procedures, a 1-day period of operation could be simulated. The simulation could also be modified for different numbers of repair people, and in each case the cost of overtime operation could be calculated. Such a simulation would represent only a hypothetical day of operation. It would represent what might happen but would not predict the operation for any specific day.

However, if the daily operation were simulated repeatedly, with different random numbers, it would be possible to obtain an average cost of overtime for a given number of repair people. This average cost should be a reasonable prediction for the actual value of this quantity over a long period of operation of the real system. The advantages of an example simulation such as this include:

1. The ability to estimate the long-term or average effects of behavior which can only be described statistically
2. The ability to determine the best number of repair people by comparing changes in overtime costs with costs for increasing or decreasing the number of repair people
3. The ability to recognize the need for idle repair people during much of the period of operation

This is a simplified example which includes using statistical information. In this case, the time of occurrence of machine failures and the time required for repair are not completely known and yet are partially known. Statistical information is, by its nature, partial information. Simulation provides some very useful means for dealing with statistical-type problems, and the systems considered in this book are assumed to include this aspect.

A study of the spare-parts supply operation of the U.S. Army Ordnance Command, conducted by the MIT Operations Research Center [10], illustrates another significant capability of computer-based simulations. The operation of this supply system is fairly simple. Parts are obtained from the manufacturers and placed in main depots at various locations. Then the parts are distributed to smaller depots and then to the supply stations for the various Army units where the parts are used. Certain rules are used to distribute and replenish supplies at the different levels of distribution. The significant characteristic of this system is its size: it must supply thousands of items to all the Army units, which are distributed over much of the world.

This study included the development of a computer program which was used to simulate the demand for parts, the rules for replenishment at each supply level, and the variable time delays in shipment and in factory production. This model was based on the operation and statistics of the real system. The simulation duplicated the past operations in that it showed familiar behavior: depots running out of supplies, recognizable delays in shipment, and so on. The simulation also was used to investigate new rules of operation to see how they reduced the amount of stock-out time and changed the pattern of factory replenishment orders. The advantages achieved by the approach included:

1. The ability to carry out experiments with the model much more quickly and with considerably less trouble than could be done with the real system
2. The ability to demonstrate the results and recommendations of the project to the Army with a realism which no set of equations or other mathematical reasoning could achieve

This example illustrates the ability of simulations to yield valuable insight into complex systems. Even though the operation of individual units is well understood, the interactions between units, with interconnected demands and replenishments, cannot be anticipated without the extensive calculations possible with computers.

These examples should suggest some of the reasons why simulation has been used and why it has potential value in a wide range of applications.

1-3 OUTLINE OF TOPICS

There are many approaches which can be used to introduce the subject of simulation. The method used in this book is to consider specific examples that illustrate the major topics in this field. The objective is to involve the reader in the detail operations required to use the technique. To some extent this means that the material is more oriented toward "how to do it" as contrasted with "what should be done." This is justified by the nature of the simulation process as it is presently used. The successful application of this method is dependent on the skill and imagination of the user. The material here is intended to serve as a basis for developing the primary skills needed to apply this tool.

It is assumed that the reader has experience in both reading and writing computer programs in FORTRAN or a similar, scientifically oriented general-purpose computer language. This type of knowledge is a necessary prerequisite and is exploited as a primary means for presenting information. In Chap. 2, an example simulation program is presented which illustrates the basic properties of the type of problems considered in this book. The example is intended to provide a concrete representation of both the concept of simulation and the programming technique. The program for this example is written in A Programming Language (PL/I). For those readers familiar with FORTRAN but not PL/I, App. A should provide sufficient information to follow the program of Chap. 2.

Mathematical analysis is an essential part of the simulation process. In Chap. 3, the most basic methods of analysis are considered. Statistics is fundamental to all these methods, and this topic is reviewed. Although the material presented is not an adequate introduction to the subject, the reader with some academic background in statistics but with very little experience in using statistics should find it a sufficient reference for the analysis methods covered in this book.

Chapter 4 presents a general approach for programming discrete-event simulation models. The objective is to show how features which are common to these problems can be programmed and included in a programming system that reduces the work required for this task. The emphasis is on the logical operations necessary for these purposes rather than on developing a complete system of programming aids. In this manner, a framework is developed for the presentation of special-purpose simulation languages in Chap. 5. The SIMSCRIPT and GPSS languages introduced there are the most frequently used languages of this type.

The operating of simulation models is essentially equivalent to carrying out statistical experiments. Several techniques for improving the efficiency of these types of procedures are considered in Chap. 6.

The development of models to represent randomly distributed empirical data is considered in Chap. 7. Most of this material is related to sequences of data which exhibit both random and periodic characteristics. Data series of this type are particularly important in simulation problems, and a major objective of this chapter is to provide a better understanding of such series.

The most critical step in a simulation study is the development of the model. The model is a representation of the real system, but never a complete representation. For this reason there are uncertainties as to how closely model behavior corresponds to that of the real system. Techniques for assessing the validity of simulation results are considered in Chap. 8.

The topic of Chap. 9 is a method for combining subsystems modeled by ordinary differential equations into a discrete-event simulation model. Models described by differential equations represent a significant portion of the work which has been done in simulation. Only one solution method for differential equations is presented here, and the emphasis is on the problems relating to including these equations in a discrete-event model simulation program.

The final chapter contains a discussion of some of the achievements and disappointments in the application of computer-based simulations. This is a developing field of study and the material in this chapter presents one viewpoint as to its possible future direction.

1.4 BACKGROUND AND REFERENCES

There is a large body of literature relating to computer simulation. The references given here are primarily introductory textbooks which can provide a logical source for further study. They provide a broader and more extensive presentation of many of the topics covered in this book.

These references are recent books which emphasize the computer-based simulation of discrete-event models. These books vary widely in emphasis and detail, but they all present interesting discussions and examples which help to define the subject of simulation. The books by Mihram [8] and Zeigler [17] cover the more theoretical aspects of model development. The uses of special computer programming languages are given detailed presentation in the books by Gordon [4, 5], Pritsker [11, 12], Schriber [15], and Wyman [16]. Statistical procedures applicable to simulation studies are more thoroughly presented by Fishman [2, 3] and Mihram [8]. Reitman [13] considers engineering system applications as opposed to the business- or economic-oriented examples which tend to predominate in most of the other texts.

REFERENCES

1. Emshoff, J. P., and R. L. Sisson: "Design and Use of Computer Simulation Models," Macmillan, New York, 1970.
2. Fishman, G. S.: "Concepts and Methods in Discrete Event Digital Simulation," Wiley, New York, 1973.

3. Fishman, G. S.: "Principles of Discrete Event Simulation," Wiley, New York, 1978.
4. Gordon, G.: "System Simulation," 2d ed., Prentice-Hall, Englewood Cliffs, N.J., 1978.
5. Gordon, G.: "The Application of GPSS V to Discrete System Simulation," Prentice-Hall, Englewood Cliffs, N.J., 1975.
6. Maisel, H., and G. Gnugnoli: "Simulation of Discrete Stochastic Systems," Science Research Associates, Calif., 1972.
7. McHenry, R. R.: The Astro Spiral Jump—An Automobile Stunt Designed via Computer Simulation, paper no 760339, Society of Automotive Engineers, February, 1976.
8. Mihram, G. A.: "Simulation: Statistical Foundations and Methodology," Academic Press, New York, 1972.
9. Mize, J. H., and J. G. Cox: "Essentials of Simulation," Prentice-Hall, Englewood Cliffs, N.J., 1968.
10. Morse, P. M.: Computers and Operations Research, in W. F. Freiberger and W. Prager (eds), "Applications of Digital Computers," Ginn and Company, New York, 1963, pp. 1–10.
11. Pritsker, A. A. B.: "The GASP IV Simulation Language," Wiley, New York, 1974.
12. Pritsker, A. A. B., and R. E. Young: "Simulation with GASP-PL/I," Wiley, New York, 1975.
13. Reitman, J.: "Computer Simulation Applications," Wiley, New York, 1971.
14. Shannon, R. E.: "System Simulation: The Art and Science," Prentice-Hall, Englewood Cliffs, N.J., 1975.
15. Schriber, T. J.: "Simulation Using GPSS," Wiley, New York, 1974.
16. Wyman, T. P.: "Simulation Modeling: A Guide to Using SIMSCRIPT," Wiley, New York, 1970.
17. Zeigler, B. P.: "Theory of Modelling and Simulation," Wiley, New York, 1978.

TWO

AN INTRODUCTORY EXAMPLE OF A SIMULATION PROGRAM

The primary concepts of the simulation process are easily understood, but the details of a specific application can be complex. A complete program for a fairly simple example is presented in this chapter. The purpose of this material is to illustrate the type of problem and the method of programming emphasized in this book and to show what is required in a simulation program.

This example demonstrates the specification of a discrete model based on observations of a physical system. This is only an elementary model development where many aspects of the system are omitted from the model. But it does illustrate how the physical and logical relationships between elements of the system may be represented in a computer program and used to produce simulated behavior which approximates, to some degree, the behavior of the physical system.

The programming language used for this example is PL/I. This language, rather than FORTRAN, which is more widely known, was chosen for two reasons. PL/I contains a number of built-in functional support features that are very useful in programming simulations. A number of these features are described and used in Chap. 4. The other reason is that PL/I programs are easier to read because of the control structures and the ability to localize the scope of variables. For readers who are familiar with FORTRAN but not PL/I, the material in App. A should provide sufficient background to follow the program in this chapter. Moreover, with a little practice, they should be able to use this language for the programming exercises. PL/I is a very large language, but the features used in this book may be readily considered as extensions of FORTRAN. In fact, the PL/I programs presented here may be converted to FORTRAN programs without great difficulty.

2.1 A CHECKOUT COUNTER PROBLEM

Consider the checkout procedure at a supermarket. After customers have selected the items they wish to purchase, they then proceed to the checkout counters. Except during the busiest periods of the day, some of these counters are not staffed. There always seem to be just enough checkers so that a customer must wait in line for a while before receiving service. The reason for this, in many cases, is a store policy that if the checker has no one to serve, the counter is closed and the checker leaves the area. When the waiting lines reach a certain size, the checker returns and opens a counter.

From the customers' point of view, this policy is an annoyance since it means they will, almost every time, have to wait in line before checking out. But from the point of view of the store's management, it is a desirable policy because if a customer does not have to wait to check out, then for some period of time before that customer arrives at the counter, the checker was not doing any useful work. The management wants to make effective use of the checker's time, either at the checkout counter or in some other activity.

Assume that a manager of a store which has operated with this policy wishes to consider a change. She would like to reduce the customers' waiting time and needs to know how much it would cost in terms of increased checkers' time at the counters. This manager believes that reducing customer waiting time will ultimately result in more customers. She also fears that if she improves service for a short trial period and then, because costs are too high, must go back to the old policy, there is a danger that customers may be lost. Rather than risk this, the manager wishes to determine the effect of a change in policy without changing the actual operation.

We will assume that the approach chosen to investigate this situation is digital computer simulation. That is, a computer program is written which will simulate the process of a customer entering the checkout line, waiting if necessary, and being checked out. The program also is to simulate the activities of the checkers, i.e., checking out customers, opening and closing the counters, and is to compute the time checkers spend away from the counters.

The program will first be developed to reflect the present operation of the store. Then, by comparing the results of the simulation with the observed operation, the computer model can be verified for accuracy. After the program is accurately reflecting the present operation, the policy for checkers will be changed in the simulation. The effects of this change on customer service and checkers' time can then be determined.

2.2 THE SIMULATION PROGRAM

The flowchart for a computer program to simulate the checkout operation is shown in Fig. 2.1. The main procedure of a PL/I program for this simulation is listed in Fig. 2.2. The specific method used in this program is only one of several

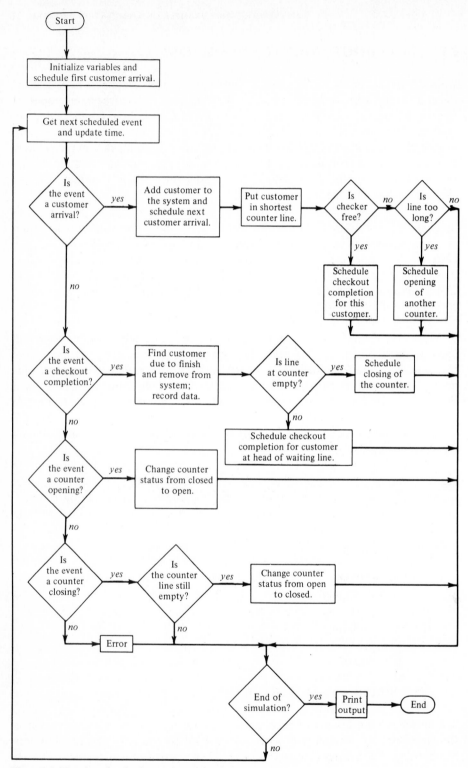

Figure 2.1 Flowchart for checkout counter simulation program.

12

```
          FIRST: PROCEDURE OPTIONS(MAIN);


STMT LEVEL NEST
  1                   FIRST: PROCEDURE OPTIONS(MAIN);
  2     1                 DECLARE(TIME,         /*CURRENT VALUE OF TIME IN THE SIMULATION*/
                              TYPE,             /*CODE NUMBER FOR TYPE OF EVENT SCHEDULED*/
                              SCHEDUL(2,50),    /*LIST OF FUTURE EVENTS*/
                              CUSTOME(6,50),    /*CHARACTERISTICS OF CUSTOMERS PRESENTLY IN THE
                                                   SYSTEM*/
                              COUNTER(8,2),     /*STATUS INFORMATION ON CHECKOUT COUNTERS*/
                              CUST_NO,          /*IDENTIFYING NUMBER GIVEN TO EACH CUSTOMER*/
                              NO_CUST,          /*NUMBER OF CUSTOMERS IN SYSTEM AT PRESENT*/
                              RECORD(35),       /*DATA RECORDED TO BE USED IN RESULTS*/
                              DELAY)            /*TIME BETWEEN COUNTER IDLE AND CLOSING*/
                                            FIXED BINARY(31) EXTERNAL;
  3     1                 DECLARE SEED FIXED BINARY(31) EXTERNAL INITIAL(1956987325); /*RANDOM
                                                   NUMBER GENERATOR SEED*/
  4     1                 DECLARE(SA,SB) FIXED BINARY(31);
                          /* INITIALIZE SYSTEM*/
  5     1                     DELAY = 5;
  6     1                     ENDTIME= 3600; /*END SIMULATION AT TIME = 3600*/
  7     1                     DO I = 1 TO 6; COUNTER(I,1) = 0; END;  /*OPEN COUNTERS 1-6*/
 10     1                     DO I = 7 TO 8; COUNTER(I,1) =-1; END;  /*CLOSE COUNTERS 7-8*/
 13     1                     SA = 1;       SB = 1;
 15     1                     CALL SCHED(SA,SB); /*SCHEDULE ARRIVAL OF FIRST CUSTOMER AT TIME=1*/
                          /*EXECUTE EVENTS*/
 16     1                 DO WHILE (TIME < ENDTIME);
 17     1   1                 CALL EVENT(TIME,TYPE);          /*GET NEXT EVENT*/
 18     1   1                 IF TYPE = 1 THEN CALL ARRIVE;   /*NEW CUSTOMER ARRIVES*/
 20     1   1                     ELSE
 20     1   1                     IF TYPE = 2 THEN CALL DEPART;   /*CUSTOMER LEAVES*/
 22     1   1                         ELSE
 22     1   1                         IF TYPE = 3 THEN CALL OPEN;   /*OPEN ANOTHER COUNTER*/
 24     1   1                             ELSE
 24     1   1                             IF TYPE = 4 THEN CALL CLOSE;   /*CLOSE A COUNTER*/
 26     1   1                                 ELSE PUT LIST('ERROR');
 27     1   1                 END;
 28     1                     CALL OUTPUT;   /*PRINT RESULTS*/
 29     1                 END FIRST;                                 /*STOP SIMULATION*/
```

Figure 2.2 Main procedure for the checkout counter program.

approaches which could be used. It is an example of the discrete-event scheduling method in which the program executes the actions that occur when a particular event which alters the status of the system takes place.

In the problem the scheduled events are: (1) customer arrives, (2) customer finishes checkout, (3) a counter opens, and (4) a counter closes. There are other events which occur in the process, but they occur as the result of and at the same time as the scheduled events. Counters are scheduled to be opened when the size of the lines at the already-open counters exceeds some specified value, but the opening actually occurs after a time delay. Similarly, counter closings are scheduled when a line becomes empty, but the closing occurs after a time delay. If a customer arrives at the counter before this delay is over, the customer receives service and the scheduled closing is cancelled.

The second statement in the program of Fig. 2.2 declares the variables used to maintain information on the status or state of the system at any particular point in time. An example of this information is shown in Fig. 2.3, which represents the state of the system when 1396 time units, which represent seconds, have elapsed since the simulation started. In this period of time, 145 customers have entered the counter area and all but 7 have completed checkout. At this time the SCHEDUL array contains six future events. The next event which will occur in the system is a customer arrival (TYPE = 1) at 3 time units from the present (TIME = 1399). There is also a counter-closing event (TYPE = 4) and four customer departures (TYPE = 2) scheduled.

TIME | 1396 |

CUST_NO | 145 |

NO_CUST | 7 |

SCHEDUL			COUNTER	
TIME	TYPE		NUMBER IN LINE	TIME DUE TO CLOSE
1399	1		2	37
1401	4		2	0
1447	2		2	84
1452	2		1	83
1462	2		0	1401
1463	2		−1	1394
0	0		−1	1385
↓	↓		−1	1266

CUSTOME

CUST NO	ARRIVAL TIME	COUNTER	POSITION IN LINE	TIME DUE TO COMPLETE	TIME WAITING ENDED
134	1283	4	1	1452	1363
136	1313	1	1	1463	1376
141	1361	2	1	1447	1370
142	1365	3	1	1462	1382
143	1373	2	2	0	0
144	1377	1	2	↓	↓
145	1387	3	2		
0	0	0	0		
↓	↓	↓	↓		

Figure 2.3 Information on the state of the system.

The first column of the COUNTER array gives the number of customers in line at each of eight different counters or contains −1 if the corresponding counter is closed. The second column of this array gives the time at which the counters are scheduled to close. Note that counter 5 has an empty line and is scheduled to close in the future. However, since the next event is a customer arrival which will occur before the scheduled closing time, the counter will not be closed at TIME = 1401.

The CUSTOME array contains data on customers presently in the system. The 134th customer arrived in the system at time 1283, is at counter 4, is first in line at that counter (i.e., is being checked out), is due to complete checkout at time 1452, and started checkout at time 1363. The last customer to arrive (cus-

```
                   SCHED: PROCEDURE(LS,MS);    /*SCHDULE EVENT TYPE MS AT TIME LS*/

STMT LEVEL NEST
   1                       SCHED: PROCEDURE(LS,MS);   /*SCHDULE EVENT TYPE MS AT TIME LS*/
   2     1                 DCL(SCHEDUL(2,50)) BINARY FIXED(31) EXTERNAL;
   3     1                 DCL (JS(2), KS(2),LS, MS) FIXED BINARY(31);
   4     1                     JS(1) = LS;     JS(2) = MS;
   6     1                 DO I = 1 TO 50;
   7     1    1               IF SCHEDUL(1,I) = 0
   8     1    1               THEN DO;  /*ADD NEW EVENT AT END OF LIST*/
   9     1    2                   SCHEDUL(*,I) = JS;    RETURN;
  11     1    2                   END;
  12     1    1               IF SCHEDUL (1,I) > JS(1)
  13     1    1               THEN DC L = I TO 50; /*INSERT EVENT INTO PROPER POSITION*/
  14     1    2                   KS = SCHEDUL(*,L);
  15     1    2                   SCHEDUL(*,L) = JS;
  16     1    2                   IF KS(1) = 0 THEN RETURN; /*STOP AT END OF LIST*/
  18     1    2                   JS = KS;
  19     1    2                   END;
  20     1    1               END;  PUT LIST('SCHEDULE FULL');   RETURN;
  23     1                 EVENT: ENTRY(LS,MS);         /*GET NEXT SCHEDULED EVENT*/
  24     1                     LS = SCHEDUL(1,1);     MS = SCHEDUL(2,1);
  26     1                     DO I = 1 TO 50; SCHEDUL(*,I) = SCHEDUL(*,I+1);
  28     1    1                   IF SCHEDUL(1,I) = 0 THEN RETURN;
  30     1    1                   END;
  31     1                 END SCHED;
```

Figure 2.4 The SCHED and EVENT procedures for the checkout counter example.

tomer 145) is second in line at counter 3 and does not have a completion time since he is still waiting for service.

The RECORD array contains data gathered during the simulation which will be used in calculating the results printed out after the simulation is completed. This data includes information on the time customers wait before receiving service and total time spent at the counters. Average values and histograms for this data are presented in the output. This array also maintains data on how long each counter is open and the period of time during which the counters are open but no customers are in line, i.e., the period of time when checkers are idle.

At the start of program execution, the system is initialized by specifying the length of time to be simulated and the status of the counters at the start of simulation and by scheduling the arrival of the first customer by a call to procedure SCHED which is listed in Fig. 2.4. The scheduling of customer arrivals after the first one is a part of the ARRIVE event routine, Fig. 2.5, which simulates the arrival of a customer. Empirical data relating to the time between successive customers is used to schedule the arrival of the next customer, at some future time, when the simulation is at the time of the present customer arrival.

After initialization, the program cycles through a loop which increments TIME to the next scheduled event and obtains the type of that event (by a call to EVENT, Fig. 2.4), then carries out the proper procedure required by that type event. This loop continues until TIME equals or exceeds the value specified to end the simulation.

The first step of the ARRIVE procedure is to schedule the arrival of the succeeding customer. This operation is actually accomplished by a separate procedure labeled GENARIV. The next steps of the ARRIVE procedure enter data into the CUSTOME array that represents the characteristics of the new customer. This data includes a unique customer number, the arrival time, the counter line entered, and the position in this line. The method used to choose the

```
          ARRIVE: PROCEDURE;      /*ARRIVAL OF CUSTOMER EVENT*/

STMT LEVEL NEST
  1                      ARRIVE: PROCEDURE;        /*ARRIVAL OF CUSTOMER EVENT*/
  2     1                 DCL(TIME, SCHEDUL(2,50),CUSTOME(6,50),COUNTER(8,2), CUST_NO, NO_CUST)
                            FIXED BINARY(31) EXTERNAL;
  3     1                 DCL(SA,SB) FIXED BINARY(31);
  4     1                 CALL GENARIV; /*GENERATE NEXT CUSTOMER ARRIVAL*/
  5     1                 CUST_NO = CUST_NO + 1;
  6     1                 NO_CUST = NO_CUST + 1;
  7     1                 CUSTOME(1,NO_CUST) = CUST_NO;
  8     1                 CUSTOME(2,NO_CUST) = TIME;
                        /*FIND SHORTEST WAITING LINE OF LENGTH M AT COUNTER N*/
  9     1                 M = 10;
 10     1                 DO I = 1 TO 8 WHILE(M¬=0);
 11     1    1               IF COUNTER(I,1) = 0    /*CHECK FOR EMPTY LINE*/
 12     1    1                  THEN DO;  M = 0;  N=I;  END;
 16     1    1               IF COUNTER(I,1) > 0    /*CHECK FOR CLOSED LINES*/
 17     1    1                  THEN IF COUNTER(I,1) < M
 18     1    1                          THEN DO;  M = COUNTER(I,1);  N = I;  END;
 22     1    1               END;
 23     1                 COUNTER(N,1) = COUNTER(N,1) + 1;
 24     1                 CUSTOME(3,NO_CUST) = N;
 25     1                 CUSTOME(4,NO_CUST) = M + 1;
 26     1                 IF M = 0 THEN DO; /*CHECKER IS READY*/
 28     1    1                          CALL GENCOC(NO_CUST);    /*SCHEDULE CHECKOUT*/
 29     1    1                          END;
 30     1                    ELSE IF M > 2
 31     1                              THEN DO I = 1 TO 50 WHILE(SCHEDUL(2,I)¬=3);
                                   /*SCHEDUAL OPENING OF ANOTHER COUNTER*/
                                   /* IF NOT ALREADY SCHEDULED*/
 32     1    1                          IF SCHEDUL(1,I) = 0
 33     1    1                             THEN DO;
 34     1    2                                 SA = TIME + 120;     SB = 3;
 36     1    2                                 CALL SCHED(SA,SB);   RETURN;
 38     1    2                                 END;
 39     1    1                          END;
 40     1               END ARRIVE;
```

Figure 2.5 The ARRIVE procedure for the checkout counter example.

counter is to find the one with the shortest line and add the new customer to it. If the customer is added to an empty line, this means that checking can begin immediately, so a checkout completion event for this customer is scheduled by a call to the GENCOC procedure. If the shortest line is found to be greater than two, i.e., if there are at least three customers at every open counter, then a counter-opening event is scheduled. The counter will be scheduled to open 120 time units in the future unless an event of this type is already on the schedule of future events. The 120 s represents the time required for a checker to reach the counter and open it after being summoned.

The procedures GENARIV and GENRND are shown in Fig. 2.6. GENARIV generates the simulated time between customer arrivals by using a uniformly distributed random number obtained from GENRND to choose an integer from 1 to 16. The next customer arrival is scheduled to occur at 2-times-this-integer time units in the future. Before justifying this step, we will first consider the source of our random numbers.

As an intuitive explanation of the random-number algorithm, consider a modified version of GENRND, as in Fig. 2.7, in which the variable SEED has a length of 6 binary bits and the multiplier in statement 3 is 37. Note that in this statement if the results of the multiplication overflow the space allocated to SEED, no action is taken and the overflow is lost. Now if the initial value of SEED was 1, the sequence of successive values obtained from GENRND would be as shown in Fig. 2.7.

```
          GENARIV: PROCEDURE;     /*SCHEDULE NEXT CUSTOMER ARRIVAL*/


STMT LEVEL NEST
  1                     GENARIV: PROCEDURE;     /*SCHEDULE NEXT CUSTOMER ARRIVAL*/
  2     1               DCL(TIME) FIXED BINARY(31) EXTERNAL;
  3     1                 DCL(SA,SB) FIXED BINARY(31);
  4     1               DCL FNC(16) FLOAT INITIAL(.18,.33,.45,.56,.64,.71,.77,.82,.86,.89,
                                               .92,.94,.96,.98,.99,1.00) STATIC;
  5     1                 CALL GENRND(X);  /*GENERATE UNIFORMILY DISTRIBUTED NUMBER X*/
  6     1                 DO I = 1 TO 16;  IF X<FNC(I)
  8     1     1                 THEN DO;
  9     1     2                     SA = TIME + 2*I;    SB = 1;
 11     1     2                     CALL SCHED(SA,SB);
 12     1     2                     RETURN;
 13     1     2                     END;
 14     1     1           END;   END GENARIV;
```

```
          GENRND: PROCEDURE(W);    /*GENERATE A RANDOM NUMBER*/


STMT LEVEL NEST
  1                     GENRND: PROCEDURE(W);    /*GENERATE A RANDOM NUMBER*/
  2     1               DCL(SEED) FIXED BINARY(31) EXTERNAL;
  3     1               (NOFIXEDOVERFLOW): SEED = SEED*65533;
  4     1                 IF SEED < 0 THEN SEED = SEED+2147483647+1;
  6     1               W = SEED;     W = W*0.465661E-9;
  8     1               RETURN; END GENRND;
```

Figure 2.6 The GENARIV and GENRND procedures of the checkout counter example.

The sequence of Fig. 2.7 repeats after 16 values, and these values include every fourth integer from 1 through 61, but there does not appear to be any particular pattern in the manner in which successive values appear. If the numbers of this sequence were divided by 64, they would have something like a uniform distribution in the range between 0 and 1 and a random order.

X	Decimal equivalent
000001	1
100101	37
011001	25
011101	29
110001	49
010101	21
001001	9
001101	13
100001	33
000101	5
111001	57
111101	61
010001	17
110101	53
101001	41
101101	45
000001	1

Figure 2.7 Modified version of the GENRND algorithm. Let X be a binary integer of length 6 bits. A new value of X is obtained by multiplying X by $100101_2 = 37_{10}$, with overflow ignored. If, initially, $X = 1$, the sequence shown is obtained.

For the 6-bit example, one-fourth of all possible integers were generated before the sequence repeated. For the 31-bit case of the GENRND procedure, if one-fourth of all possible integers were generated, the length of the sequence would be 536,870,912 before it starts repeating. As we will see later, this will be the case under certain conditions. So it seems reasonable to assume that GENRND will generate a sequence of values for W which closely approximates the operation of randomly sampling from a uniform distribution of range 0 to 1.

Assume that the time between customer arrivals at the checkout counters of the store was measured for 100 customers during a moderately busy period of a typical day. The results of these measurements are given in Fig. 2.8, where the times between arrivals are given to the nearest even second. That is, 18 customers arrived approximately 2 s after the customer immediately preceding them, 15 customers arrived approximately 4 s after the customer immediately preceding them, etc.

Each call to GENRND from the GENARIV procedure will return a value for x which is essentially equally likely to be any value in the range from 0 to 1. Thus, the probability that the value of x will be less than .64 but greater than or equal to .56 is .08. Thus the probability of the value I being 5 in statement 9 is 8 percent, which is the probability that the next customer arrival will be scheduled to occur 10 s in the future. Similarly, the values selected for all customer interarrival times will have the same distribution as the data of Fig. 2.8.

Figure 2.9 gives a histogram of measured data for times required by the checkout process of 100 customers and the corresponding cumulative distribution of this data. Procedure GENCOC, shown in Fig. 2.10, will schedule checkout

Interarrival time	Number of customers	Cumulative fraction of customers
2	18	.18
4	15	.33
6	12	.45
8	11	.56
10	8	.64
12	7	.71
14	6	.77
16	5	.82
18	4	.86
20	3	.89
22	3	.92
24	2	.94
26	2	.96
28	2	.98
30	1	.99
32	1	1.00
	100	

Figure 2.8 Observations of time between customer arrivals.

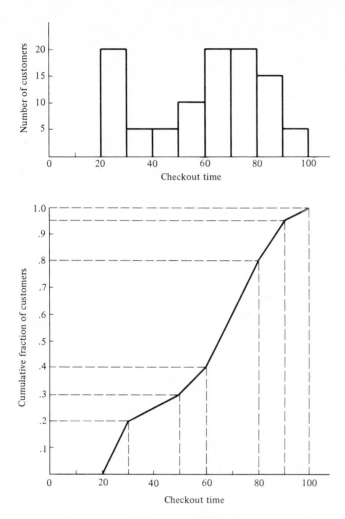

Figure 2.9 Distribution of customer checkout times.

completions after a time delay which is a random value having the same distribution as the data of Fig. 2.9. It is readily seen that the value of x returned to the GENCOC procedure by GENRND will lie in the range 0 to .2, 20 percent of the time, and this will result in a value of Z in the range of 20 to 30. This is consistent with the histogram data.

The technique used to generate a specified distribution by use of uniformly distributed random numbers and the cumulative distribution function is a general approach which can be used with any distribution. It is usually an efficient method in terms of computer execution time requirements, but it is not always the best approach to use. The reason for this has to do with the statistical properties of the sequence of numbers and will be considered in the next chapter.

```
        GENCOC: PROCEDURE(M);      /*SCHEDULE CHECKOUT COMPLETION*/


STMT LEVEL NEST
  1                   GENCOC: PROCEDURE(M);      /*SCHEDULE CHECKOUT COMPLETION*/
  2     1               DCL(TIME,CUSTOME(6,50)) FIXED BINARY(31) EXTERNAL;
  3     1               DCL(M,SA,SB) FIXED BINARY(31);
  4     1               DCL FUNC(8,2) FLOAT INITIAL(0,20,,2,30,,3,50,,4,60,,6,70,,8,80,
                                    ,95,90,1.0,100) STATIC;
                        /*FIND TIME REQUIRED FOR CHECKOUT*/
  5     1               CALL GENRND(X);    SA = 0;
  7     1               DO I = 2 TO 8 WHILE(SA=0);
  8     1   1             IF X <= FUNC(I,1)
  9     1   1               THEN DO;    SA = 1;
 11     1   2               Z = FUNC(I-1,2) + (FUNC(I,2)-FUNC(I-1,2))*(X-FUNC(I-1,1))
                                   /(FUNC(I,1) - FUNC(I-1,1));
 12     1   2             END;
 13     1   1           END;    SA = TIME + Z;    SB = 2;
 16     1               CALL SCHED(SA,SB);    /*SCHEDULE CHECKOUT*/
 17     1               CUSTOME(5,M) = SA;    CUSTOME(6,M) = TIME;
 19     1             END GENCOC;
```

Figure 2.10 The GENCOC procedure for the checkout counter example.

The customer-departure event procedure, DEPART, is listed in Fig. 2.11. In this procedure, column 5 of array CUSTOME is used to identify which customer is due to leave. This step is required since more than one departure event may be scheduled. The customer due to depart is removed from the CUSTOME array, and any other customer waiting in the same line is moved up one position in line. The data for the customer completing checkout is recorded by a call to procedure STAT. If the line at the counter which the customer left is empty, the closing of

```
        DEPART: PROCEDURE;     /*CUSTOMER DEPARTURE EVENT*/


STMT LEVEL NEST
  1                   DEPART: PROCEDURE;     /*CUSTOMER DEPARTURE EVENT*/
  2     1               DCL(TIME,CUSTOME(6,50),COUNTER(8,2),NO_CUST,DELAY)
                                         FIXED BINARY(31) EXTERNAL;
  3     1               DCL(IR(6),P,SA,SB,N) FIXED BINARY(31);
                        /*FIND CUSTOMER DUE TO FINISH AND REMOVE FROM LIST*/
  4     1               DO I = 1 TO NO_CUST;
  5     1   1             IF CUSTOME(5,I) = TIME     /*FIND CUSTOMER DUE TO FINISH*/
  6     1   1               THEN DO; IR = CUSTOME (*,I);
  8     1   2                 COUNTER(IR(3),1) = COUNTER(IR(3),1) - 1;
  9     1   2                 DO J = I TO NO_CUST;
 10     1   3                   CUSTOME(*,J) = CUSTOME(*,J+1);
 11     1   3                   IF CUSTOME (3,J) = IR(3)   /*MOVE UP IN COUNTER LN*/
 12     1   3                     THEN CUSTOME(4,J) = CUSTOME(4,J) - 1;
 13     1   3                 END;
 14     1   2                 GO TO RCD;
 15     1   2             END;
 16     1   1           END;
 17     1               PUT EDIT('ERROR - DID NOT FIND CUSTOMER DUE TO FINISH') (SKIP,A);
 18     1               RCD:NO_CUST = NO_CUST - 1;
 19     1               P = IR(3);
 20     1               CALL STAT(IR);    /*RECORD DATA FOR CUSTOMER THAT FINISHED*/
 21     1               IF COUNTER(P,1) = 0    /*CHECK FOR EMPTY LINE AT COUNTER*/
 22     1                 THEN DO;
 23     1   1               SA = TIME + DELAY;    SB = 4;
 25     1   1               CALL SCHED(SA,SB); /*SCHEDULE CLOSING*/
 26     1   1               COUNTER(P,2) = TIME + DELAY;
 27     1   1             END;
 28     1                 ELSE                  /*GET NEXT CUSTOMER IN LINE TO START
                                                 CHECKOUT*/
 28     1               DO N = 1 TO NO_CUST;
 29     1   1             IF(CUSTOME(3,N) = P)&(CUSTOME(4,N) = 1)
 30     1   1               THEN DO;
 31     1   2                 CALL GENCOC(N);   /*SCHEDULE CHECKOUT COMPLETION*/
 32     1   2                 RETURN;
 33     1   2               END;
 34     1   1           END;
 35     1             END DEPART;
```

Figure 2.11 The DEPART procedure for the checkout counter example.

```
        STAT: PROCEDURE(IS);


STMT LEVEL NEST
   1                      STAT: PROCEDURE(IS);
   2     1                  DCL(TIME,COUNTER(8,2),RECORD(35)) FIXED BINARY(31) EXTERNAL;
   3     1                  DCL IS(6) BINARY FIXED(31);
   4     1                  RECORD(1) = RECORD(1) + 1;  /*NUMBER CHECKED OUT*/
   5     1                     IS(1) = TIME - IS(2);     IS(3) = IS(6) - IS(2);
   7     1                  RECORD(2) = RECORD(2) + IS(1);   /*TOTAL TIME IN THE SYSTEM*/
   8     1                  RECORD(3) = RECORD(3) + IS(3);   /*TOTAL WAITING TIME*/
   9     1                     IS(4) = TIME - IS(6);
  10     1                  RECORD(34) = RECORD(34) + IS(4);   /*TOTAL SERVICE TIME*/
                            /*RECORD TIME COUNTERS ARE BUSY*/
  11     1                  IF (RECORD(35) = 0) THEN RECORD(35) = TIME;
  13     1                  INT = TIME - RECORD(35);   RECORD(35) = TIME;
  15     1                  DO I = 1 TO 8;
  16     1    1               IF COUNTER(I,1) ¬<0 THEN RECORD(I+3) = RECORD(I+3) + INT;
  18     1    1             END;
  19     1                     J = 1;   K = 32;   L = 50;   M = 35;   N = 11;
  24     1                  CALL HIST;
  25     1                     J = 3;   K = 33;   L = 1;   M = 30;   N = 21;
  30     1                  CALL HIST;
  31     1                  RETURN;
  32     1                  HIST: PROCEDURE;              /*ENTER HISTOGRAM POINT*/
  33     2                  IF IS(J) > RECORD(K) THEN RECORD(K) = IS(J);
  35     2                  LA = L;     JA = 0;
  37     2                  DO I = 1 TO 9 WHILE(JA=0);
  38     2    1             IF IS(J) < LA THEN DO;   RECORD(I+N) = RECORD(I+N) + 1;   JA =1;
  42     2    2                         END;         LA = LA + M;
  44     2    1             END;   IF JA = 0 THEN RECORD(N+10) = RECORD(N+10) + 1;
  47     2                  END HIST;
  48     1                END STAT;
```

Figure 2.12 The STAT procedure for the checkout counter example.

that counter is scheduled to occur after a time delay. If the line is not empty, a checkout completion is scheduled for the customer who is now at the head of the line.

Procedure STAT, shown in Fig. 2.12, updates the values for the number of customers checked out, total time in the system for these customers, and total waiting time and service time. It also records the total time each counter is open and updates the histogram data for system time and waiting time.

The counter-opening and -closing event procedures are listed in Fig. 2.13.

```
        OPEN: PROCEDURE;   /*OPEN COUNTER EVENT*/


STMT LEVEL NEST
   1                  OPEN: PROCEDURE;   /*OPEN COUNTER EVENT*/
   2     1               DCL(TIME,COUNTER(8,2)) FIXED BINARY(31) EXTERNAL;
   3     1               J = 0;
   4     1                      DO I = 1 TO 8 WHILE(J=0);
   5     1    1                   IF COUNTER(I,1) < 0  /*FIND CLOSED COUNTER*/
   6     1    1                   THEN DO;
   7     1    2                      COUNTER(I,1) = 0;  /*OPEN IT*/
   8     1    2                      J = 1;  /*EXIT LOOP*/
   9     1    2                      END;
  10     1    1                   END;
  11     1               RETURN;
  12     1               CLOSE: ENTRY;      /*CLOSE COUNTER EVENT*/
  13     1                      DO I = 1 TO 8;
  14     1    1                   IF COUNTER(I,2) = TIME  /*FIND COUNTER DUE TO CLOSE*/
                                  THEN
  15     1    1                      IF COUNTER(I,1) = 0  /*IF LINE STILL EMPTY*/
  16     1    1                      THEN COUNTER(I,1) = -1; /*CLOSE COUNTER*/
  17     1    1                   END;
  18     1               RETURN;
  19     1             END OPEN;
```

Figure 2.13 The OPEN and CLOSE procedures for the checkout counter example.

```
        OUTPUT: PROCEDURE;


STMT LEVEL NEST
  1                      OUTPUT: PROCEDURE;
  2      1              DCL(TIME,CUST_NO,RECORD(35),DELAY) FIXED BINARY(31) EXTERNAL;
  3      1                 PUT PAGE LIST('OUTPUT FOR CHECKOUT COUNTER SIMULATION');
  4      1                 PUT SKIP(3);
  5      1                 PUT EDIT('COUNTER CLOSING DELAY',DELAY,
                               'TOTAL TIME OF SIMULATION', TIME,
                               'NUMBER OF CUSTOMER ARRIVALS', CUST_NO,
                                'NUMBER OF CUSTOMERS CHECKED OUT', RECORD(1))
                               (SKIP(1), A, X(5), F(5));
  6      1              X = RECORD(1);        Y = RECORD(2);       Z = RECORD(3);
  9      1                 PUT EDIT ('AVERAGE TIME IN LINE', Y/X,
                               'AVERAGE WAITING TIME', Z/X)
                               (SKIP, A, X(5), F(8,2));
 10      1                 PUT EDIT ('PERCENTAGE OF TIME COUNTER OPEN') (SKIP(2),A);
 11      1              Z = 0;
 12      1              DO I = 1 TO 8;
 13      1    1            Y = RECORD(I+3);       Z = Z + Y;
 15      1    1            PUT EDIT( I,Y/TIME)
                               (SKIP, X(3), F(1), X(5), F(6,4));
 16      1    1         END;
 17      1              Y = Z - RECORD(34);
 18      1                 PUT EDIT('TOTAL TIME CHECKERS IDLE',Y)(SKIP(2),A,X(5),F(6));
 19      1                 PUT EDIT('TIME IN LINE   DISTRIBUTION')(SKIP(2), A);
 20      1                 PUT EDIT('    TIME <= ', 'NUMBER', 'PERCENT')
                               (SKIP(2), A, X(5), A, X(5), A);
 21      1              IP = 50;
 22      1              DO I = 1 TO 10;  IF I ¬= 10 THEN Z = IP;   ELSE Z = RECORD(32);
 26      1    1            Y = RECORD(I+11);
 27      1    1            PUT EDIT( Z, Y, 100.*Y/X)   (SKIP, X(4),
                               F(5), X(9), F(3), X(8), F(6,2));
 28      1    1         IP = IP + 35;
 29      1    1         END;
 30      1                 PUT EDIT('WAITING TIME DISTRIBUTION')(SKIP(2), A);
 31      1                 PUT EDIT('    TIME <= ', 'NUMBER', 'PERCENT')
                               (SKIP(2), A, X(5), A, X(5), A);
 32      1              IP = 0;
 33      1              DO I = 1 TO 10;  IF I ¬= 10 THEN Z = IP;   ELSE Z = RECORD(33);
 37      1    1            Y = RECORD(I+21);
 38      1    1            PUT EDIT( Z, Y, 100.*Y/X)   (SKIP, X(4),
                               F(5), X(9), F(3), X(8), F(6,2));
 39      1    1         IP = IP + 30;
 40      1    1         END;   END OUTPUT;
```

Figure 2.14 The OUTPUT procedure for the checkout counter example.

Note that a counter-closing event is cancelled if a customer has arrived in the DELAY period since the closing was scheduled.

At the end of the specified simulation time, the OUTPUT procedure of Fig. 2.14 is called, which produces the report shown in Fig. 2.15.

While this example uses a quite simple model and the program is not a particularly efficient one, it does present a basic approach to programming discrete-event simulations and does illustrate the primary features of this technique.

2.3 USE OF THE SIMULATION

The first step in using the simulation program is to verify that the results agree with the actual operation of the store. Assume that when the data used to specify the interarrival times and the checkout times was collected, the data on waiting times was also collected. Then, by comparing the output data of Fig. 2.15 with the actual data, we can check the agreement between our computer model and the real system.

Assume that this comparison shows that the average waiting time given by the simulation is a few seconds low and that the distribution of waiting times has a higher percentage of customers with 0 waiting time but also a higher percentage of customers with long waiting times. This raises a question as to the cause of these differences; is it due to the model used or is it merely due to random effects? The model is clearly not an exact replication of the system operation. Two obvious differences are that customers will change lines from one counter to another at times and do not necessarily go to the shortest line if some customers already in the shortest line appear to have a large number of purchases. But it is also true that random effects occur in the store operations. If the same measurements were repeated, they would not duplicate the previous results. This means that not only values for interarrival, service, and waiting time must be measured but also their variability must be estimated.

One approach to estimating variability is simply to repeat a process several times and observe the range of values obtained. When the simulation program is run for 10 h of simulated time, but the output data is calculated for each hour, these results will show considerable variability. For example, the 10 values calcu-

```
OUTPUT FOR CHECKOUT COUNTER SIMULATION


COUNTER CLOSING DELAY        5
TOTAL TIME OF SIMULATION     3605
NUMBER OF CUSTOMER ARRIVALS       354
NUMBER OF CUSTOMERS CHECKED OUT       336
AVERAGE TIME IN LINE       154.93
AVERAGE WAITING TIME       96.56

PERCENTAGE OF TIME COUNTER OPEN
   1      0.9925
   2      0.9232
   3      0.9925
   4      0.7451
   5      0.6929
   6      0.5459
   7      0.1981
   8      0.4860

TOTAL TIME CHECKERS IDLE       491

TIME IN LINE   DISTRIBUTION

   TIME <=      NUMBER      PERCENT
      50          14          4.17
      85          42         12.50
     120          56         16.67
     155          61         18.15
     190          67         19.94
     225          39         11.61
     260          29          8.63
     295          19          5.65
     330           6          1.79
     414           3          0.89

WAITING TIME DISTRIBUTION

   TIME <=      NUMBER      PERCENT
       0          29          8.63
      30          29          8.63
      60          55         16.37
      90          57         16.96
     120          54         16.07
     150          39         11.61
     180          34         10.12
     210          20          5.95
     240          12          3.57
     341           7          2.08
```

Figure 2.15 Report produced by the checkout counter simulation program.

lated for average customer waiting time will range from 74 to 99 s. The actual values observed lie well within this range, so the results of the simulation may be consistent with the observations.

If we assume that several observations of actual store operation were made and compared with several simulation runs, and that this data seems to approximately agree in both values and variability, then we can accept the simulation program as a reasonable model of the system. Note that it is not necessary that the model replicate exactly what happens in the physical process as long as the quantities being measured follow the same pattern.

The purpose of this example was to study the tradeoff between customer waiting time and checker counter-open time. The model of present operation assumed that when a line became empty, the counter would close if another customer did not arrive within a 5-s period. To investigate an improved service model, we will assume that the policy will be to keep counters open for a longer period of time before closing. The only program modification required for this is to change the values for the DELAY variable. When this is done, the results are that average waiting time is reduced and checker idle time increases as the value of DELAY increases. This is not true for each 1-h simulation, but if simulations of 10-h duration are used, the changes are fairly smooth as functions of DELAY time.

Figure 2.16 gives the results obtained for customer waiting time and checker idle time for a 5-s counter-closing delay, representing present operation, and for a 45-s delay, representing a new policy. This data shows that by increasing the period of time checkers are at the counters by about $2\frac{1}{2}$ h over a 10-h period, the average waiting time for customers can be reduced by over 45 s. Since there were approximately 3600 customers checked out in this period, the tradeoff is $2\frac{1}{2}$ h of extra checker time that resulted in a reduction of 45 h of customer time.

These results also show that about 25 percent of the customers did not wait

(a) Counter-closing delay: 5 s Total time checkers idle: 2270 s Average customer waiting time: 106.13 s		(b) Counter-closing delay: 45 s Total time checkers idle: 11,258 s Average customer waiting time: 59.22 s	
Distribution time < =	Percent	Distribution time < =	Percent
0	5.47	0	24.92
30	9.49	30	15.24
60	14.55	60	18.31
90	21.00	90	18.99
120	13.32	120	8.04
150	12.76	150	5.64
180	9.13	180	3.70
210	5.28	210	1.89
240	3.97	240	1.75
649	5.03	419	1.52

Figure 2.16 Customer waiting time results from two simulations, 10 h in length.

at all with the new policy and that the longest waiting time was reduced from 649 to 419 s. In addition, the percentage of customers who must wait over 180 s is reduced from 14.28 to 5.16.

The significance of these results is dependent upon a subjective evaluation by the management of the store. A decision to change the store policy will be made on the basis of an estimate as to what effect this would have on customer behavior in response to this change. This was not part of the simulation model, so for this case there is very little to be gained by determining precise values for the simulation results.

2.4 EXTENSION OF THE APPROACH

The approach used to study the checkout counter problem can be extended to a wide variety of systems. It is limited, however, to what are often called *discrete-event systems*. These systems are represented by some set of data, called the *system state*, which remains unchanged until some *event* occurs which causes a discrete change in the state. The state contains all the information required to characterize the system at one point in time.

The state representation for the checkout counter is the information shown in Fig. 2.3. This information changes discretely each time that any one of the four event types occurs. Note that changes in the state occurred with no elapsed time because of the manner in which we chose to model the system, not because customer movement or counter changes are physically instantaneous. Indeed, most systems can be modeled as discrete-event processes, although this approach may not necessarily produce a good model.

To develop a discrete-event model for a system, we must select certain objects of interest in a system. These items are referred to as *entities*. The characteristics of an entity are called its *attributes*. The interactions between entities are called *activities*, and these activities cause the events to occur when certain conditions are met.

In the checkout counter example, the entities were the customers and the counters. The attributes for these entities are shown as the elements of the CUSTOME and COUNTER arrays of Fig. 2.3. The activities in this example are the processes of checking out and waiting. These activities give rise to three of the events: customer departure, counter opening, and counter closing. The customer arrival event is caused by conditions external to the model, so it is referred to as an *exogenous event*, in distinction from the three *endogenous events*.

There is no systematic procedure for model development which will guarantee successful simulation. As with any complex system, there are many different models possible. For the exercises in this book, almost any reasonable representation can be used to find the solutions, although some are better than others. For more realistic problems, the nature of the model may be critical to a successful solution.

Model development is usually the most important aspect in a simulation study but also the least well defined in terms of techniques. The process depends on the experience and intuition of the modeler and usually involves data gathering and several trial models before an adequate representation is obtained. The type of model chosen is also influenced by the simulation techniques used. Throughout this book a number of example models and techniques for modeling will be considered, but the general problem of model development will be discussed only in the final chapter.

The program used for the checkout counter example can be used as a basis for computer simulation of any discrete-event model. The main procedure of Fig. 2.2 illustrates the *event-scheduling approach* to programming this type of simulation. This approach emphasizes a detailed description of the steps that occur when an individual event takes place. These descriptions are contained in the four event procedures: ARRIVE, DEPART, OPEN, and CLOSE. Other models can be simulated by properly defining alternate event procedures and with minor changes to the remaining procedures.

More general program procedures for use with the event-scheduling approach will be presented in Chap. 4. While this is the programming approach emphasized in this book, it should be noted that it is not the only programming approach possible nor is it necessarily the most convenient method available for programming simulations. The approach was selected in order to provide a clear understanding of the steps involved in simulation programming and should provide an adequate foundation for further study and use of alternate approaches and specialized simulation programming utilities.

2.5 BACKGROUND AND REFERENCES

The example given in this chapter is one of the types of problems considered in the field of study called *operations research*. This subject area primarily concerns problems relating to the control of systems which involve both people and machines, and simulation is an important tool for workers in this field. The text by Ackoff and Sasieni [1] contains a discussion of the general aspects of formulating problems and constructing models as well as other major topics in operations research. Several prototype problems to which much of the work in this subject area is devoted are also described in this text, as are the principal mathematical techniques employed.

A major goal of operations research is to apply science to the executive function of management. The executive function is that of integrating the control of diverse operating tasks so that they serve efficiently the interests of the whole organization. This implies that the executive function requires that management consider an organization to be what we have labeled a *system*.

The systems approach [2] is a concept rather than a method. The idea is to study overall system performance rather than to concentrate on investigating the components. This attitude usually becomes important when the relationship between component performance and a well-defined system objective is not well understood. To illustrate this in terms of our example, we may assume that from the viewpoint of management, the objective of the supermarket system is to maximize the profit earned over a given period of time. This is a well-defined objective, but the relationship between the policy used to open and close checkout counters and this profit is neither known nor easily determined. The main purpose of the example simulation was to provide a better understanding of one aspect of this relationship.

As systems become larger, the need for this approach increases, and it is particularly important when human behavior or processes occurring in nature are included in the system model. Although most of the successful practical applications of simulation are related to engineering or to artificial systems, much of the current interest and activity in simulation are directed toward accurate modeling for natural systems and for human behavior and organizations. The primary difficulty in modeling systems of this type is due to the fact that these systems cannot, in general, be subjected to controlled experimentation.

REFERENCES

1. Ackoff, R. L., and M. W. Sasieni: "Fundamentals of Operations Research," Wiley, New York, 1968.
2. Hall, A. D.: "A Methodology for Systems Engineering," Van Nostrand-Reinhold, Princeton, N.J., 1962.

EXERCISES

Exercises 2.1 to 2.6 assume that the subprocedures used with the example program of this chapter have been stored in a computer system for use by the student. An example of job control language which may be used with System 360/370, OS/VS, computer systems for these exercises is shown in App. B.

2.1 Modify the main procedure of Fig. 2.2 to represent the situation where two customers are checking out at the start of the simulation.

2.2 Modify the SCHED procedure of Fig. 2.4 so that one or more events can be scheduled to occur when TIME $= 0$.

2.3 Modify the ARRIVE procedure of Fig. 2.5 so that if all counters are busy and the shortest line is available at two or more counters, a customer will choose one of these counters in some random fashion.

2.4 Add the following capabilities to the example program:

   (*a*) A check of the average value over the complete simulation of the values returned by the calls to the GENRND procedure

   (*b*) A check of the interarrival times generated in the complete simulation to compare with Fig. 2.8

   (*c*) A check of the checkout times generated by the GENCOC procedure to compare with Fig. 2.9

2.5 An alternate policy for staffing the checkout counters would be to open enough counters to service the customers and keep these counters open throughout the period of operation. Figure 2.15 shows that the average number of counters open at one time is approximately 5.6. Modify the example program to simulate the case of seven open counters with no opening or closing events. Compare the average customer waiting time and checker idle time with the results using the original policy.

2.6 Simulate the checkout counter example for the case of only one counter, always open, and with one-seventh of the original customer arrival rate. Compare the results with those of Exercise 2.5.

2.7 Assume that we wish to run the simulation program for a period of time and then later restart the simulation with the conditions which existed at the end of the initial run. What variables must be recorded at the end of the first period and used to initialize the second run?

2.8 Describe a discrete-event model for the operation of a gas station. Specify a system state, a set of events, entities, attributes, and activities.

THREE

BASIC ANALYSIS TECHNIQUES

Problems which are studied by means of simulation are, almost always, not amenable to analytic or closed-form solutions. Simulation is an alternative to the usual mathematical methods of analysis. This does not mean that simulation should be used to replace analysis, but rather to extend it. A good simulation study makes use of all the appropriate analysis techniques which are available.

The type of simulation studies we are considering involves the determination of system behavior over a period of time and includes random effects in the model. Simulation of this type is equivalent to a sampling experiment; i.e., our results are actually a sample value obtained from an underlying statistical distribution. Thus, we will need statistical procedures to interpret the results or outputs of simulation programs.

Statistical notation and nomenclature differ in many areas of application. In order to provide a definition of the notation used in this book, and to review some of the basic statistical methods used later, this chapter includes a brief presentation of some of the concepts of probability and statistical inference. After that, we consider the problem of generating random numbers. Although this operation was introduced in the checkout counter example, a more general approach is presented here; and we also consider what checks should be made to validate the results from one of these generators.

Three methods for analyzing problems closely associated with simulations are also discussed in this chapter. *Queuing theory* provides a method for solving certain simplified versions of a class of problems often studied by means of simulation. This theory can sometimes provide approximate solutions for complex models and often is helpful in verifying simulation programs. The second method, *time series analysis*, is concerned with correlated data which often arises in simulation studies. Another approach, the *regenerative state method*, illustrates one technique for obtaining uncorrelated measurements from sequences of correlated data.

3.1 BRIEF REVIEW OF RANDOM VARIABLES AND PROBABILITY DISTRIBUTIONS

A random variable is a numerically valued function of a chance event. For example, if numerical values are associated with obtaining a head or a tail from tossing a coin, then this numerical value is a random variable while the result of tossing the coin is the chance event. Thus, any numerically valued chance event is a random variable, and any function of a random variable is also a random variable.

3.1.1 Discrete Random Variables

Consider a variable x which can take on the discrete values $x_1, x_2, \ldots, x_m$. The function $f(x_i)$, which gives the probability associated with each x_i, is defined to be the *probability density function* of the discrete random variable x. The term *probability mass function* is also used for this function when x takes on only discrete values. For example, the result of rolling a single fair die has

$$f(x_i) = \frac{1}{6} \qquad x_i = 1, 2, \ldots, 6$$

The *cumulative distribution function*, denoted by $F(x_i)$, is defined to be the probability that x is less than or equal to x_i. Thus, for a discrete random variable

$$F(x) = \sum_{x_i \leq x} f(x_i)$$

Probability density functions can have almost any form, subject to the restrictions that $f > 0$ and $F(\infty) = 1$. But if the random variables arise from similar physical situations, the probability density functions will have a similar form. We next consider two special forms of discrete probability distributions and the physical situations they represent.

Consider a random variable x which is the number of successes in independent trials where the probability of success per trial is a constant value p. For example, in the case of the checkout counter model, if we assume that the probability of any customer using a credit card is equal to a constant, say, .38, then x is the number of credit card transactions for n customers checked out. The probability distribution associated with this random variable is known as the *binomial distribution*.

By the multiplication law, the probability of a specific sequence of x successes and $n - x$ failures in n independent trials, with p the probability of success at each trial, is

$$p^x(1 - p)^{n-x}$$

From the law of combinations, it can be shown that there are

$$\frac{n!}{x!(n - x)!} \overset{s}{=} \binom{n}{x}$$

equally likely sequences in which x successes and $n - x$ failures can occur. So, by the addition law, the probability of exactly x successes in n trials, given p, is

$$f(x) = \binom{n}{x}p^x(1 - p)^{n-x} \qquad 0 \le p \le 1 \tag{1}$$

Furthermore,

$$F(x) = \sum_{k=0}^{x} \binom{n}{k}p^k(1 - p)^{n-k} \tag{2}$$

gives the probability of x or fewer successes in n trials. Thus, (1) and (2) are, respectively, the probability density functions and the cumulative distribution function for any random variable that fits a binomial distribution model.

The *Poisson distribution* is an appropriate model for the number of events that occur in an interval of time, assuming that the events happen independently at a constant average rate. Assume that the constant λ is the mean number of customer arrivals per unit time. The actual number of arrivals in an interval of time t is a random variable. The probability of x arrivals occurring in an interval of length t is given by

$$f(x) = \frac{(\lambda t)^x}{x!} e^{-\lambda t} \tag{3}$$

This density function is the limiting case of the binomial density function, (1), as n approaches infinity. That is, as n becomes arbitrarily large and p becomes arbitrarily small, with np remaining constant, then the binomial distribution approaches the Poisson distribution with $\lambda = np$. This means that if customers are assumed to come from an infinite population in a completely random manner subject only to a constant mean number of arrivals per unit time, then the Poisson distribution is an appropriate model for the number of customers which arrive in an interval of time.

Figure 3.1 shows the density and distribution function for a Poisson distribution with an average of two events per unit time. There is a finite probability that more than six events will occur in a unit of time, but the values are too small to show on the scale of this figure.

3.1.2 Continuous Random Variables

Consider a variable x which can take on any value in some interval, e.g., $0 \le x \le 1$ or $-5 \le x < \infty$. The cumulative distribution function $F(u)$ of a

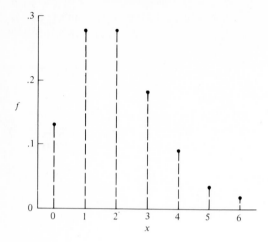

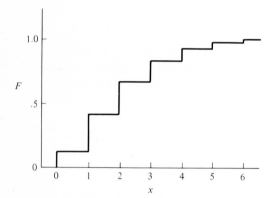

Figure 3.1 Poisson distribution ($\lambda t = 2$).

continuous random variable x is defined as the probability that the variable takes a value equal to or less than some specified value a,

$$F(a) = \text{Prob } [x \leq a]$$

The probability density function for a continuous random variable x is defined as

$$f(x) = \lim_{\Delta x \to 0} \frac{\text{Prob } [a \leq x \leq a + \Delta x]}{\Delta x}$$

$$= \lim_{\Delta x \to 0} \frac{F(a + x) - F(a)}{\Delta x} = \frac{dF(x)}{dx} \qquad (4)$$

Therefore,

$$F(a) = \int_{-\infty}^{a} f(x) \, dx \qquad (5)$$

As an example of a continuous random variable, consider a uniformly distributed variable in the range 0 to 1, i.e., a variable that has equal probability of having any value in the range 0 to 1. For this *uniform distribution*

$$f(x) = \begin{cases} 1 & 0 < x < 1 \\ 0 & \text{otherwise} \end{cases}$$

or, more general

$$f(x) = \begin{cases} \dfrac{1}{\beta - \alpha} & \alpha < x < \beta \\ 0 & \text{otherwise} \end{cases} \tag{6}$$

The *exponential distribution* is an appropriate model for the time between occurrences of independent random events. It may, for example, represent the interarrival times for customers arriving at a service facility when the time of the next arrival is independent of the previous arrival. This is the same physical situation represented by the Poisson distribution; the two distributions are connected in that they describe different aspects of the same process. If λ is the mean number of arrivals per unit time, the exponential probability density function is

$$f(t) = \lambda e^{-\lambda t} \qquad 0 \leq t \tag{7}$$

and its cumulative distribution function is

$$F(x) = 1 - e^{-\lambda x} \tag{8}$$

There is a class of distribution functions named after A. K. Erlang, who found these distributions to be representative of certain types of telephone traffic [3]. The probability density function for an *Erlang distribution* with parameter m is

$$f(t) = (m\lambda)^m \left(\frac{e^{-m\lambda t}}{(m-1)!} \right) t^{m-1} \tag{9}$$

where λ is a constant representing the mean number of arrivals per unit time and m is a positive integer greater than 0. The cumulative distribution is given by

$$F(t) = 1 - e^{-m\lambda t} \left(\sum_{k=0}^{m-1} (mt)^k / k! \right) \tag{10}$$

When $m = 1$, the Erlang distribution becomes the exponential distribution; and as m increases and approaches infinity, the Erlang distribution approaches a constant value.

Erlang distributions can be given a simple physical interpretation. Suppose the counter checkout operation consists of three operations carried out in sequence. For example, the operations could be: (1) checking the packages, (2) making the payment, and (3) sacking the packages. If, for each of these three operations, the time required is an exponentially distributed random variable with equal average times, then the total time to check out would be Erlang-distributed with the parameter m equal to 3 and the average time equal to 3 times the average time for each operation. Thus, the Erlang distribution can be interpreted as the description of a physical process where the random variable is the result of summing m exponentially distributed random variables from a single population.

Figure 3.2 shows density and distribution functions for the exponential, Erlang-2, Erlang-5, and a uniform distribution with λ equal to 1. The Erlang distribution with parameter ∞ corresponds to a constant value which would be an impulse in the f plot and a step in the F plot at $t = 1$.

The Erlang distribution is itself a special case of a more general family of distributions. These are the *gamma distributions*, whose probability density function differs from that of the Erlang distributions in that m is not restricted to integers but can be any positive number.

The *normal* (or *gaussian*) *distribution* is the most important statistical model.

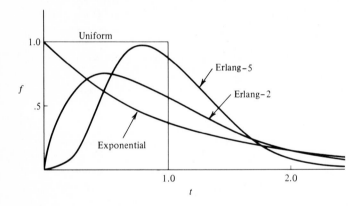

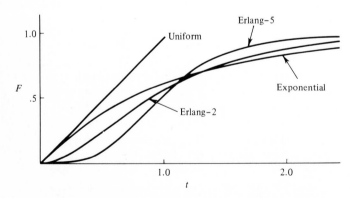

Figure 3.2 Some examples of continuous density and distribution functions.

Its probability density function is

$$f(x) = \frac{1}{\sigma\sqrt{2\pi}} \, e^{-(x-\mu)^2/2\sigma^2} \tag{11}$$

where μ and σ are parameters of the distribution, and its cumulative distribution is

$$F(x) = \frac{1}{\sqrt{2\pi}} \int_{-\infty}^{(x-\mu)/\sigma} e^{-t^2/2} \, dt \tag{12}$$

Note that if x is normally distributed with parameters μ and σ, then

$$y = \frac{x - \mu}{\sigma} \tag{13}$$

is normally distributed with $\mu = 0$ and $\sigma = 1$. These parameter values are associated with what is called the *standard normal distribution*.

Empirical evidence has shown that the normal distribution provides a good representation for many physical measurements such as the heights of a group of adults and the temperature at various locations in a given region. Of course, most physical variables have upper and lower limits, and the range of a normally distributed variate is from minus infinity to plus infinity. Even so, the normal distribution is often a good approximation.

The physical situation that gives rise to a normally distributed variable is one in which a large number of independent chance events occur and each contributes to the resulting numerical value. This interpretation is based on the central-limit theorem, which is discussed along with sampling properties of the normal distribution in Sec. 3.2.

A table of values for the standard cumulative normal distribution is given in App. C. This appendix also contains tables for the student's t distribution, chi-square distribution, and F distribution, which are related to the normal distribution.

3.1.3 Characteristic Measurements for Probability Distributions

It is often useful to be able to characterize a statistical distribution by a few numbers which summarize the most basic information about the distribution. We now define some of these measurements.

The *expected value* of a random variable x, denoted by $E[x]$, or of any function of a random variable $g(x)$, denoted by $E[g(x)]$, is the average value of the function over all possible values of the variable. Thus, if f denotes the probability density function for x,

$$E[x] = \begin{cases} \displaystyle\sum_{i=1}^{n} x_i f(x_i) & \text{if } x \text{ is discrete} \\[4mm] \displaystyle\int_{-\infty}^{\infty} x f(x) \, dx & \text{if } x \text{ is continuous} \end{cases}$$

Similarly,

$$E[g(x)] = \begin{cases} \sum_{i=1}^{n} g(x_i)f(x_i) \\ \int_{-\infty}^{\infty} g(x)f(x)\, dx \end{cases}$$

The expected value of x is the center of gravity of the density function of x and is frequently called the *arithmetic average* or the *arithmetic mean*. This is the point on which the distribution is centered and is known as a *measure of central tendency*.

Other measures of central tendency are the *median* and the *mode* of a distribution. For a continuous random variable, the median is that value of c such that

$$\int_{-\infty}^{c} f(x)\, dx = .5$$

and the mode is the value at which $f(x)$ attains its maximum value. If a unique maximum exists, it may be found by using

$$\frac{df(x)}{dx} = 0 \quad \text{and} \quad \frac{d^2f(x)}{dx^2} < 0$$

In general, these measures of central tendency are different; but for the normal distribution, they are the same and are equal to the parameter μ of the distribution.

Characteristics of a distribution other than the central value may be described by the use of the distribution's *moments*. The Kth moment is defined to be

$$\mu_K = E[x^K]$$

and frequently the mean $E[x]$ is denoted by μ_1.

The *variance* of a distribution is a measure of the dispersion or spread of the distribution about its mean. The variance is defined as

$$\text{var}(x) = E[(x - \mu_1)^2]$$

and is sometimes referred to as the *second moment* of a distribution about its mean. The relationship between the variance and the second moment of a distribution is found as follows:

$$\begin{aligned} \text{var}(x) &= E[x^2 - 2x\mu_1 + \mu_1^2] \\ &= E(x^2) - 2\mu_1 E(x) + \mu_1^2 \\ &= \mu_2 - \mu_1^2 \end{aligned}$$

For the normal distribution, it can be shown that the variance is equal to the parameter σ^2 of the distribution function.

The variance of a distribution is equal to the square of the *standard deviation* of the distribution. For a set of discrete values x_i, the standard deviation σ_x is the root-mean-square deviation of the values and can be calculated by the formula:

$$\sigma_x = \sqrt{\sum_{i=1}^{n}\left[x_i - \left(\sum_{i=1}^{n}x_i\right)\Big/N\right]^2 \Big/ N}$$

The relation between the variance, second moment, and mean, together with

$$\text{var}(x) = \sigma_x^2$$

provides an alternate method for calculating the standard deviation.

Higher moments may be calculated and used as simple descriptors of distributions. The values of these moments are related to the shape of the density function and may be given physical interpretations.

Another way of summarizing information about a distribution is by use of its *fractiles*. The αth fractile is the value of the random variable that has a proportion α of the cumulative distribution below it. Thus, for a continuous random variable with probability density function $f(x)$, the αth fractile is that value of c such that

$$\int_{-\infty}^{c} f(x)\, dx = \alpha$$

The .1, .2, .3, etc., fractile points are often referred to as the 10, 20, 30, etc., *percentile points*. Note that the median of a distribution is the 50 percentile point.

Figure 3.3 shows a density function for a normal distribution. Note that

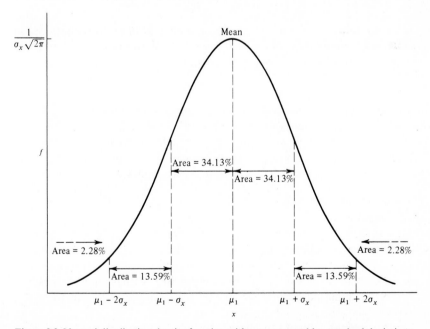

Figure 3.3 Normal distribution density function with areas covered by standard deviations.

$x = \mu_1$ is the 50 percentile point, $x = \mu_1 + \sigma_x$ is the 84.13 percentile point, and $x = \mu_1 + 2\sigma_x$ is the 97.72 percentile point.

3.2 SAMPLING, ESTIMATION, AND INDUCTIVE INFERENCE

Samples are observations of particular values of a variable. They correspond to whatever values are available or will be obtained for a random variable.

Consider the problem of developing a statistical model for some system. Assume that on the basis of physical considerations, a particular probability density function is selected for the model. The values of x with the true distribution $f(x)$ are the *population*. The samples are members of the population. The constants of the distribution are called *parameters*; e.g., μ and σ are parameters of the normal distribution. A *statistic* is a number calculated from the samples. A statistic used to approximate an unknown parameter is called an *estimator*.

Using the observed data, we wish to draw certain conclusions about the population. This sort of extension from the particular to the general is called *inductive inference*. Exact inductive inference is not possible; however, uncertain inferences can be made and the degree of uncertainty can be measured if the samples satisfy a certain condition. That condition is: the samples must be chosen from the population in a random manner.

The parameter estimation problem may be stated as follows: we are interested in a population having a density function represented as

$$f(x; \theta_1, \theta_2, \ldots, \theta_k)$$

where x is the variable and $\theta_1, \theta_2, \ldots, \theta_k$ are parameters of the distribution. On the basis of random samples $x_1, x_2, \ldots, x_n$, we wish to estimate one or more of the parameters. The problem is to find functions of the observations (estimators)

$$\hat{\theta}_i(x_1, x_2, \ldots, x_n) \qquad i = 1, \ldots, k$$

which will be good approximations to the true values of the parameters θ_i.

Intuitively it is clear what is meant by "good"—the distribution of the estimator should be concentrated near the true parameter value θ_i. But to choose among possible estimators we need certain criteria by which to judge them. Some of the criteria that have been developed for evaluating estimators are:

1. *Unbiased.* If an estimator $\hat{\theta}$ for a parameter θ is such that $E[\hat{\theta}] = \theta$, then $\hat{\theta}$ is said to be unbiased.
2. *Consistent.* If the estimator comes closer to the parameter value as the number of samples increases without limit, then $\hat{\theta}$ is said to be a consistent estimate of θ.
3. *Minimum variance.* If the estimator is more precise, i.e., has smaller variance, than any other unbiased estimate from the same sample, it is said to be the *minimum variance estimator*.
4. *Sufficient.* An estimator is said to be sufficient if it contains all the information

in the sample regarding the parameter. That is, no other function of x_i can provide any more information about θ.

It would be desirable for an estimator to have all these properties, but unfortunately they do not exist except in certain special cases. We must use estimators which can be obtained using some type of working rules. The method of maximum likelihood is one such procedure.

3.2.1 Maximum-Likelihood Estimators

The likelihood L of a particular set of observed values is the probability of obtaining such values based on a given theoretical model with specified parameters $\theta_1, \theta_2, \ldots, \theta_k$. The maximum-likelihood estimators $\hat{\theta}_1, \hat{\theta}_2, \ldots, \hat{\theta}_k$ are those values of the specified parameters θ_i which maximize the likelihood, i.e., those values for the θ_i's which appear most likely on the basis of the given data.

To illustrate the procedure for calculating maximum-likelihood estimates, we consider the following example [11]. In a life test of batteries, results were:

1 battery failed after 10 h
1 battery failed after 40 h
1 battery failed after 60 h
1 battery was tested 70 h without failure

From previous experience with batteries, it is known that a reasonable assumption is that the time to failure will be exponentially distributed. If we let $\theta = 1/\lambda$, then we have the density function

$$f(x) = \frac{1}{\theta} e^{-x/\theta}$$

Since the observations are independent, their likelihood, or probability, is the product of their individual probabilities. So,

$L =$ (probability of first battery failing at 10 h)
    $\times$ (probability of second battery failing at 40 h)
    $\times$ (probability of third battery failing at 60 h)
    $\times$ (probability of fourth battery surviving 70 h)

$$L = f(10)f(40)f(60)\left[1 - \int_0^{70} f(x)\, dx\right]$$

$$= \left(\frac{1}{\theta} e^{-10/\theta}\right)\left(\frac{1}{\theta} e^{-40/\theta}\right)\left(\frac{1}{\theta} e^{-60/\theta}\right)\left(1 - \int_0^{70} \frac{1}{\theta} e^{-x/\theta}\, dx\right)$$

$$= \frac{1}{\theta^3} e^{-180/\theta}$$

The maximum-likelihood estimator $\hat{\theta}$ is that value of θ which maximizes L, or equivalently $\ln L$, where

$$\ln L = -3 \ln \theta - \frac{180}{\theta}$$

To find this value let

$$\frac{d(\ln L)}{d\theta} = -\frac{3}{\theta} + \frac{180}{\theta^2} = 0$$

so

$$\hat{\theta} = 60 \text{ h}$$

Actually, in this example, the density function values should be multiplied by some small value of Δx. But Δx is not a function of θ; so it will not change the results. The maximum-likelihood estimate for any arbitrary combination of failure and survival times, presuming an exponential model for time to failure, could also be obtained using this method.

A procedure similar to that shown above may be used to derive the *maximum-likelihood estimators for the parameters of the normal distribution.* Let $x_1, x_2, \ldots, x_n$ represent the values of a sample of independent observations from a normal distribution. Then, the likelihood function is

$$L = \prod_{i=1}^{n} \frac{1}{\sigma\sqrt{2\pi}} e^{-(x_i - \mu)/(2\sigma^2)}$$

$$= \left(\frac{1}{2\pi\sigma^2}\right)^{n/2} e^{-(1/2\sigma^2)(\Sigma/i = 1n/(x_i - \mu)2)}_{i=1}$$

and

$$\ln L = -\frac{n}{2} \ln 2\pi - \frac{n}{2} \ln \sigma^2 - \frac{1}{2\sigma^2} \sum_{i=1}^{n} (x_i - \mu)^2$$

We compute

$$\frac{\partial(\ln L)}{\partial \mu} = \frac{1}{\sigma^2} \sum_{i=1}^{n} (x_i - \mu)$$

$$\frac{\partial(\ln L)}{\partial \sigma^2} = -\frac{n}{2}\frac{1}{\sigma^2} + \frac{1}{2\sigma^4} \sum_{i=1}^{n} (x_i - \mu)^2$$

and by setting these derivatives equal to 0 and solving the resulting equations for μ and σ^2, we find the maximum-likelihood estimators

$$\hat{\mu} = \frac{1}{n} \sum_{i=1}^{n} x_i = \bar{x} \tag{1}$$

$$\hat{\sigma}^2 = \frac{1}{n} \sum_{i=1}^{n} (x_i - \bar{x})^2$$

The estimator $\hat{\mu}$, the average sample value, is unbiased; but $\hat{\sigma}^2$ is not, since

$$E[\hat{\sigma}^2] = \frac{n-1}{n} \sigma^2$$

The estimator

$$\hat{\sigma}^2 = \frac{1}{n-1} \sum_{i=1}^{n} (x_i - \bar{x})^2 = S^2 \tag{2}$$

is an unbiased estimator for the variance of a normal distribution.

Maximum-likelihood estimators are consistent and have minimum variance. They are not necessarily unbiased but usually can be slightly modified so that they are. Not all parameters have sufficient estimators, but if a parameter does have sufficient estimators, it can be shown that the maximum-likelihood estimator will be a sufficient estimator. Thus, this method gives estimators which have desirable properties and, moreover, these estimators can be obtained.

3.2.2 Sampling Properties of the Normal Distribution

Let $x_1, \ldots, x_n$ be independent samples from a common population having a mean μ_1 and a finite variance σ_x^2. Then, as n increases, the average sample value $\bar{x}$ tends toward μ_1 and the variance of $\bar{x}$ is equal to σ_x^2/n. This is true no matter what the distribution of the underlying population is. A more precise statement of this property is given by the *central-limit theorem*:

> **Theorem** If a population has a finite variance σ^2 and mean μ, then the distribution of the sample mean approaches the normal distribution with variance σ^2/n and mean μ as the sample size n increases.

Although the central-limit theorem is concerned with large samples, the sample mean tends to be normally distributed even for relatively small values of n and even for samples from different distributions. This result is extremely important and provides the basis for normal sampling theory. Even when the samples are not, the sample means are approximately normally distributed.

Properties of samples from normal distributions follow. If $x_1, \ldots, x_n$ are random samples from a normal distribution with mean μ and variance σ^2, then:

1.
$$\bar{x} = \frac{1}{n} \sum_{i=1}^{n} x_i$$

is normally distributed with mean μ and variance σ^2/n.

2.
$$\left(\frac{n-1}{\sigma^2}\right) S^2 = \sum_{i=1}^{n} (x_i - \bar{x})^2$$

has the chi-square distribution with $n - 1$ degrees of freedom.

3.
$$t = \frac{\bar{x} - \mu}{S/(n)^{1/2}}$$

has the student's t distribution with $n - 1$ degrees of freedom.

Degrees of freedom refers to the number of independent components into which a random variable may be decomposed. In the second property above there are n squares in the summation which would be independent if the population mean μ had been used rather than the sample mean $\bar{x}$. It is sometimes said that 1 degree of freedom is used up in estimating the mean.

Another distribution of considerable practical interest is that of the ratio of two quantities independently distributed by chi-square laws. If U and W are independently distributed with chi-square distributions having k and m degrees of freedom, respectively, then

$$\mathscr{F} = \frac{U/k}{W/m}$$

has the F distribution with k and m degrees of freedom.

These properties provide the basis for extending sampling estimates for the purpose of inductive inference.

3.2.3 Confidence-Interval Estimation

An estimate of the value of a parameter will not, in general, be the true value. Such an estimate is not very meaningful without some measure of the possible error in the estimate. This is given by a statistical confidence interval.

Definition A *confidence interval* is a random interval whose end points β and γ are functions of the observed random variables such that the probabilities that the inequality

$$\beta < \theta < \gamma \qquad \beta < \gamma$$

are satisfied is a predetermined number $1 - \alpha$. θ is the parameter whose value is estimated.

This may be interpreted as meaning that, on the average, one would be correct $(1 - \alpha) \times 100$ percent of the time in saying that θ lies in the range from β to γ. The value $1 - \alpha$ is called the *confidence level*.

If a sample of n independent values $x_1, x_2, \ldots, x_n$ are obtained from a normally distributed population with unknown parameters μ and σ, and if we compute $\bar{x}$ and S^2 by (1) and (2), then the random variable

$$t_v = \frac{\bar{x} - \mu}{S/\sqrt{n}}$$

is distributed according to the student's t distribution. The subscript v refers to the degrees of freedom and equals $n - 1$.

Let $t_{\alpha/2,v}$ and $t_{1-\alpha/2,v}$ represent the values of the t_v distribution which have, respectively, $(\alpha/2) \times 100$ percent and $(1 - \alpha/2) \times 100$ percent of the area of the distribution to their left, as shown in Fig. 3.4. Then,

$$\text{Prob } [t_{\alpha/2,v} < t_v < t_{1-\alpha/2,v}] = 1 - \alpha$$

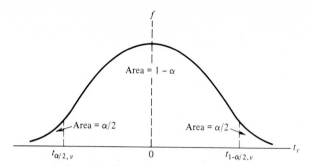

Figure 3.4 Percentile value for student's t distributions.

and since, by symmetry,

$$-t_{\alpha/2,v} = t_{1-\alpha/2,v}$$

we have

$$\text{Prob}\ [x - (t_{1-\alpha/2,v})(S/\sqrt{n}) < \mu < \bar{x} + (t_{1-\alpha/2,v})(S/\sqrt{n})] = 1 - \alpha \qquad (3)$$

Now $\bar{x}$, S, and n can be found from the given data; and $t_{1-\alpha/2,v}$ can be found from tables of percentile values for the student's t cumulative distribution as given in App. C. Thus Eq. (3) provides a means by which a confidence interval for the estimate of the mean of a normal distribution can be determined.

From Eq. (3), it can be seen that the size of the confidence interval depends upon (1) the standard deviation of the data S, (2) the confidence level $1 - \alpha$, and (3) the sample size n. The size of the confidence interval increases with increases in S and $1 - \alpha$ and decreases as n increases.

To illustrate the use of confidence intervals, we will use some results from the checkout counter example, which were summarized in Fig. 2.16. By using the results, for average customer waiting time, for each hour of the 10-h period, we can calculate the estimates of the mean and variance using Eqs. (1) and (2) as shown in Table 3.1.

If we assume that the values are independent and normally distributed, then the 90 percent confidence interval for the 5-s delay case is

$$\text{Prob}\ [\bar{x} - t_{.95,9}(S/\sqrt{10}) < \mu < 88.36 + (1.833)(2.516)] = 1 - .1$$

$$\text{Prob}\ [83.75 < \mu < 92.97] = .9$$

Thus, under this assumption, we may say that the average value for customer waiting time, with a 5-s delay in counter closing, lies in the range of 83.75 to 92.97 s with a 90 percent confidence level. Similarly the 90 percent confidence interval for the 45-s delay is found to be 52.33 to 58.79 s.

From the tables in App. C, it may be noted that as the number of degrees of freedom increases, the student's t distribution approaches the standard normal distribution. Thus, for large samples the standard normal distribution may be used to give approximate values for calculating confidence intervals.

Table 3.1

Hour	Average customer waiting time	
	5-s delay	45-s delay
1	85.66	51.03
2	99.03	54.45
3	99.32	59.90
4	89.34	43.69
5	78.04	57.84
6	74.61	60.13
7	87.62	51.89
8	87.78	57.87
9	94.02	56.04
10	88.19	62.79
$\bar{x} = \dfrac{1}{n} \sum\limits_{i=1}^{n} x_i$	88.36	55.56
$S^2 = \dfrac{1}{n-1} \sum\limits_{i=1}^{n} (x_i - \bar{x})^2$	63.30	30.99

One-sided confidence intervals In some cases, instead of being interested in a confidence interval, we may desire only an upper or lower bound. Such a region, e.g., $(-\infty, \beta)$, is called a *one-sided confidence interval*. The equation corresponding to (3) for this case is

$$\text{Prob}\ [\mu < \bar{x} + t_{1-\alpha,v}(S/n)] = 1 - \alpha \qquad (4)$$

For example, using Table 3.1 data for average customer waiting time, in the 5-s delay case, we have

$$\text{Prob}\ [\mu < 88.36 + (1.383)(2.516)] = .9$$

$$\text{Prob}\ [\mu < 91.84] = .9$$

Thus, we can say that the mean value is less than 91.84 s with a 90 percent confidence level. Similarly, this relation indicates that the average customer waiting time in this case is greater than 84.88 s with a 90 percent confidence level. This result is, of course, dependent on the assumption of normally distributed data.

A different type of interval, called a *tolerance interval*, can also be found which gives a probability statement about the range within which a certain portion of the population is located.

Results similar to the above case can be found for samples from certain probability functions other than the normal distribution.

3.2.4 Hypothesis Testing

A major area of statistical inference is the testing of hypotheses. These are statistical procedures used to evaluate a specific question or, more correctly, to determine if a statement of hypothesis is correct or not on the basis of available data. The general procedure for hypothesis testing is as follows:

1. Some "statement of hypothesis" relevant to the problem is made.
2. A "statistical significance level," such as 1, 5, or 10 percent, is chosen. This value, known as the *Type I error probability*, is the chance one is ready to take of incorrectly rejecting the hypothesis, i.e., of concluding the hypothesis to be false when in fact it is true.
3. Some specified function of the observed data is calculated. This is a random function whose distribution is known. By comparing the calculated value with the significance level value for the known distribution, one of the following conclusions can be drawn:
   (*a*) The hypothesis is rejected as being incorrect.
   (*b*) The data provides no evidence to reject the hypothesis.

Note that it is possible to disprove a hypothesis (in the probability sense) but that a hypothesis can never be proved correct.

Establishing statistical significance depends upon the amount of data available. Thus, with a small amount of data, large differences may not make a statistically significant difference; while with a large amount of data, very small differences may lead to statistically significant differences. Hence, statistical significance does not necessarily mean practical significance.

The significance analysis may be made more meaningful by designating an allowable Type II error probability, i.e., the chance one is ready to take of wrongly failing to reject the stated hypothesis when a difference of practical significance actually exists.

Although Type II error is a significant aspect of hypothesis testing, it will not be included in the tests used in this book in order to keep the formulas relatively simple and the statistical procedures straightforward. Moreover, in simulation studies, while it is desirable to keep the number of samples small, this is not a restriction, and additional samples can be obtained if needed for a statistical decision.

To illustrate the procedures of hypothesis testing, we will consider a few of the more common problems that arise in practice.

(i) Tests of the mean of a normal population Suppose that we have samples x_1, $x_2, \ldots, x_m$ from a normally distributed population with mean μ and variance σ^2. We wish to test the hypothesis

$$H: \quad \mu = c$$

when c is some constant. That is, we wish to test if the population mean is equal to a given value.

The procedure in this case is to construct a confidence interval for the population mean. If c lies in the confidence interval, accept H. If c does not lie in the confidence interval, the hypothesis H is rejected. Thus, if c lies within a 90 percent confidence interval for μ, we are not able to reject the hypothesis that $\mu = c$ with a 10 percent significance level.

A more usual test is for the hypothesis that the mean is greater than or equal to a given value:

$$\text{H:} \quad \mu \geq c$$

For this case the one-sided confidence interval is used. The hypothesis is rejected if c is greater than the upper bound of the confidence interval.

As an example of these hypothesis tests we can use the confidence interval values already calculated for the average customer waiting time data. Consider the hypothesis that the average customer waiting time (5-s delay) is equal to 93 s:

$$\text{H:} \quad \mu = 93$$

This hypothesis may be rejected at the 10 percent significance level since this value lies outside the 90 percent confidence interval. However, the hypothesis

$$\text{H:} \quad \mu = 92$$

cannot be rejected since it lies within this interval. The hypothesis that the average customer waiting time is greater than or equal to 92 s:

$$\text{H:} \quad \mu \geq 92$$

can be rejected at the 10 percent significance level since this value lies above the upper bound of the one-sided confidence interval (91.84).

(ii) Tests of the means of two normal populations Suppose that we have samples $x_1, x_2, \ldots, x_{n_1}$ and $y_1, y_2, \ldots, y_{n_2}$ from two normally distributed populations with means μ_1 and μ_2, and variances σ_1^2 and σ_2^2, respectively. We wish to test the hypothesis

$$\text{H:} \quad \mu_1 = \mu_2$$

under the assumption that

$$\sigma_1^2 = \sigma_2^2$$

We compute

$$t_{ii} = \frac{\bar{x} - \bar{y}}{\sqrt{S_{ii}^2(n_2 + n_1)/(n_1 n_2)}}$$

where

$$S_{ii}^2 = \frac{\sum_{i=1}^{n_1} x_i^2 - n_1(\bar{x})^2 + \sum_{i=1}^{n_2} y_i^2 - n_2(\bar{y})^2}{n_1 + n_2 - 2}$$

$$= \frac{(n_1 - 1)S_x + (n_2 - 1)S_y}{n_1 + n_2 - 2}$$

Table 3.2

i	x_i	y_i
1	20.38	25.68
2	27.51	42.58
3	30.42	40.94
4	35.76	31.22
5	36.46	32.53
6	25.82	34.33
7	28.66	34.80
8	32.27	31.33
9	32.99	32.70
10	23.82	25.68

The hypothesis is accepted at the α significance level if

$$t_{\alpha/2,(n_1+n_2-2)} < t_{ii} < t_{(1-\alpha/2),(n_1+n_2-2)}$$

where $t_{\alpha/2,(n_1+n_2-2)}$ is the $(\alpha/2)$th fractile of the student's t distribution function with $n_1 + n_2 - 2$ degrees of freedom.

If the hypothesis is

$$H: \quad \mu_1 \geq \mu_2$$

then this hypothesis is accepted at the α significance level if

$$t_{ii} > t_{\alpha,(n_1+n_2-2)}$$

As an example of this test, consider the set of values in Table 3.2. These values give

$$\bar{x} = 29.409 \qquad \bar{y} = 33.179$$

$$\Sigma x_i^2 = 8890.7835 \qquad \Sigma y_i^2 = 11{,}281.402$$

Thus,

$$S_{ii}^2 = \frac{8890.7835 - 10\,(29.409)^2 + 11{,}281.402 - 10\,(33.179)^2}{10 + 10 - 2}$$

$$= 28.6018$$

and

$$t_{ii} = \frac{29.409 - 33.179}{[2(28.6018)/10]^{1/2}} = -1.576$$

If we wish to test the hypothesis that the mean of x is equal to the mean of y, we find from the table in App. C,

$$t_{.1,18} = -1.330$$

$$t_{.05,18} = -1.734$$

This implies that we would reject the hypothesis of equal means at the 20 percent significance level but would accept it at the 10 percent significance level. Or, alternately, we may state this result as: the hypothesis of equal means could be rejected with a 80 percent confidence level but could not be rejected with a 90 percent confidence level.

If the hypothesis were

$$H: \quad \mu_x \geq \mu_y$$

we could reject the hypothesis at the 10 percent significance level but not at the 5 percent significance level.

(iii) Tests of the variance of a normal population Given samples $x_1, x_2, \ldots, x_n$ from a normally distributed population, we wish to test the hypothesis that the population variance σ^2 is equal to some specified value c:

$$H: \quad \sigma^2 = c$$

The procedure is to compute the quantity

$$U = \frac{\sum\limits_{i=1}^{n} (x_i - \bar{x})^2}{c}$$

This statistic has the chi-square, χ^2, distribution with $n - 1$ degrees of freedom. The value of U which cuts off an area of $\alpha/2$ at the right-hand tail of the χ^2 distribution (i.e., the $1 - \alpha/2$ fractile point) for $n - 1$ degrees of freedom is denoted by $\chi^2_{[1-(\alpha/2)],(n-1)}$. The hypothesis is accepted at the $1 - \alpha$ significance level if

$$\chi^2_{(\alpha/2),(n-1)} < U < \chi^2_{(1-\alpha/2),(n-1)}$$

For the one-sided hypothesis,

$$H: \quad \sigma^2 \leq c$$

the same quantity U is calculated. This hypothesis is accepted at the $1 - \alpha$ significance level if

$$U < \chi^2_{(1-\alpha),(n-1)}$$

(iv) Comparison of the variances of two normal populations Given samples $x_1, x_2, \ldots, x_{n_1}$ and $y_1, y_2, \ldots, y_{n_2}$ from two normal distributions, we wish to test the hypothesis that the variances of the two populations are equal:

$$H: \quad \sigma_1^2 = \sigma_2^2$$

The procedure is to calculate the quantity

$$F = \frac{\left(\sum\limits_{i=1}^{n_1} (x_i - \bar{x})^2\right) \Big/ (n_1 - 1)}{\left(\sum\limits_{i=1}^{n_2} (y_i - \bar{y})^2\right) \Big/ (n_2 - 1)} = \frac{S_x^2}{S_y^2}$$

This statistic has the F distribution with $\gamma_1 = n_1 - 1$ and $\gamma_2 = n_2 - 1$ degrees of freedom.

The hypothesis is accepted at the $1 - \alpha$ significance level if

$$F_{(\alpha/2),\,(\gamma_1,\gamma_2)} < F < F_{(1-\alpha/2),\,(\gamma_1,\gamma_2)}$$

using notation analogous to that for the χ^2 distribution.

3.2.5 Distribution-Free Methods

In the previous two subsections we assumed that the probability distributions for the variables of interest were known. In fact, it was implied that enough data would be obtained so that by use of the central-limit theorem, normally distributed values would be obtained. This is a valid approach when sufficient data is available, but often in simulation, primarily because of computer time costs, we must use small amounts of data. In such cases we may have no knowledge as to the distribution of these values.

Techniques have been developed for estimating parameters and testing hypotheses which require no assumptions as to the form of the probability distribution. These techniques are referred to as *nonparametric methods* or *distribution-free methods*.

In this section sample values are interpreted in a different manner. Previously, when denoting n samples by $x_1, x_2, \ldots, x_n$, it was meant that x_1 was the first observation, x_2 the second, and so on. For distribution-free methods the samples are ordered. That is, we will denote the observation with the smallest value by x_1; x_2 will represent the second smallest; and so on up to x_n, the largest value. Most distribution-free methods use these ordered observations, which are also called *order statistics*.

Distribution-free methods are based on a simple property of order statistics; namely, the distribution of the area under the density function between any two ordered observations is independent of the form of the density function. To illustrate this property, consider the case where five samples are chosen from an arbitrary distribution as shown below:

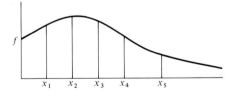

These samples would divide the area under the probability density function into six parts. The total area in any one part could vary from almost zero to almost 1, but the expected value or most likely value for the area of each part is 1/6. Since the area under $f(x)$ for a given range of x is equal to the probability that x will be in that range, it should be intuitively clear that the expected area between any two ordered samples should be the same. This property holds regardless of what shape the probability density function has.

This general property, which can be proven mathematically [19], may be stated as follows: For any distribution $f(x)$ and n ordered samples $x_1, x_2, \ldots, x_n$, the expected value of the probability density function between x_i and x_{i+1} is equal to $1/(n + 1)$. In terms of the cumulative distribution $F(x)$, this may be written

$$F(x_{i+1}) - F(x_i) = \frac{1}{n + 1}$$

With distribution-free methods, the center of a distribution is denoted by the median (symbolically, $\mu_{.5}$) rather than by the arithmetic mean; i.e.,

$$F(\mu_{.5}) = \int_{-\infty}^{\mu_{.5}} f(x)\, dx = .5$$

The estimate for the sample median is the middle observation if the number of observations is odd or the average of the two middle observations if the sample size is even. That is,

$$\hat{\mu}_{.5} = \begin{cases} x_{k+1} & \text{if } n = 2k + 1 \\ \frac{1}{2}(x_k + x_{k+1}) & \text{if } n = 2k \end{cases}$$

A confidence interval for the median can be constructed by use of the binomial distribution. Note that the probability that any one observation falls below or above $\mu_{.5}$ is equal to one-half in either case. Thus, the probability that exactly l observations fall below (or above) $\mu_{.5}$ is equal to

$$\binom{n}{l}\left(\frac{1}{2}\right)^n$$

since there are $\binom{n}{l}$ different ways this may occur. For the ith order sample, the probability that x_i exceeds $\mu_{.5}$ is equal to the sum of the probabilities that there are $0, 1, 2, \ldots, i - 1$ observations below $\mu_{.5}$, so

$$\text{Prob}\,[x_i > \mu_{.5}] = \sum_{l=0}^{i-1}\binom{n}{l}\left(\frac{1}{2}\right)^n$$

Similarly, the probability that x_j is less than $\mu_{.5}$ is the sum of the probabilities that there are $j, j + 1, \ldots, n$ observations above $\mu_{.5}$, so

$$\text{Prob}\,[x_j < \mu_{.5}] = \sum_{l=j}^{n}\binom{n}{l}\left(\frac{1}{2}\right)^n$$

Now if $i < j$, we have

$$\text{Prob}\,[x_i < \mu_{.5} < x_j] = 1 - \text{Prob}\,[x_i > \mu_{.5}] - \text{Prob}\,[x_j < \mu_{.5}]$$

$$= \sum_{l=i}^{j-1}\binom{n}{l}\left(\frac{1}{2}\right)^n$$

This last expression provides a confidence interval for $\mu_{.5}$.

To illustrate this, the data from Table 3.3 will be used as an example. There are 10 observations of x and when placed in order they become

$$x_1, x_2, \ldots, x_{10} = 20.38, 23.82, 25.82, 27.51, 28.66, 30.42, 32.27,$$

$$32.99, 35.76, 36.48$$

Thus the sample median is

$$\hat{\mu}_{.5} = \tfrac{1}{2}(28.66 + 30.42) = 29.54$$

The confidence-interval levels in this example, and for any other case where there are 10 observations are

$$\text{Prob } [x_5 < \mu_{.5} < x_6] = \sum_{l=5}^{5} \binom{10}{l}\left(\frac{1}{2}\right)^{10} = \left(\frac{10!}{5!5!}\right)\left(\frac{1}{2}\right)^{10} = .2461$$

$$\text{Prob } [x_4 < \mu_{.5} < x_7] = .6562$$

$$\text{Prob } [x_3 < \mu_{.5} < x_8] = .8906$$

$$\text{Prob } [x_2 < \mu_{.5} < x_9] = .9785$$

$$\text{Prob } [x_1 < \mu_{.5} < x_{10}] = .9980$$

Using these results, we may specify a 89 percent confidence interval for the median as the interval from x_3 to x_8, or

$$(25.82, 32.99)$$

These results compare with the previously calculated arithmetic mean value of 29.41 and corresponding 90 percent confidence interval of

$$(27.229, 31.589)$$

In a manner similar to the above, confidence intervals for percentages of a population and tests of hypothesis can be developed based on the binomial distribution. With a slight change these methods also apply to the case where the sampled population has a discrete distribution.

For small sample size, distribution-free methods are often preferred for making statistical inference since they are more widely applicable than distribution-dependent methods. However, these methods still require the assumption that the sample values are randomly chosen from some underlying population. Also, the power of nonparametric tests is less, or, in other words more conservative results are obtained than with the parametric-based tests.

3.3 GENERATING AND TESTING RANDOM NUMBERS

The example of Chap. 2 demonstrated the need for random numbers in simulations and included an intuitive explanation of how the algorithm used there results in a succession of values that appear to be independent random samples from a uniform distribution. In this section, the random-number generating techniques used with that example are discussed further, and the important concept of testing properties of these numbers is introduced.

Random-number generation by means of digital computers is a topic that has received a great deal of attention by many investigators [18]. Many useful results have been established and many algorithms have been developed for this purpose. This subject is considered further in App. D. But no matter how good the procedure for generating random numbers is, certain subsets of these numbers may exhibit undesirable statistical characteristics. For this reason, it is always desirable that in any simulation, the properties of the random variables actually used be recorded and tested.

Only the most elementary tests on random numbers are included in this section. The objective is to introduce the nature of these tests and, in addition, to introduce the concept of autocovariance.

3.3.1 Uniform Distribution

The most popular algorithm presently used for this task is referred to as a *multiplicative congruential pseudorandom number generator*. For a k-digit binary arithmetic process, this type of generating algorithm may be represented by

$$x_{n+1} = \rho x_n (\text{mod } 2^k)$$

The notation $(\text{mod } 2^k)$ means that x_{n+1} is congruent to x_n modulo 2^k; i.e.,

$$x_{n+1} = \rho x_n - \left[\frac{\rho x_n}{m}\right] m \qquad m = 2^k$$

where the brackets indicate the largest integer of the enclosed quantity. The procedure illustrated in Fig. 2.7 is an example of this type of generator, where $k = 6$, $\rho = 37$, and $x_0 = 1$. Note that the $(\text{mod } 2^k)$ operation is accomplished merely by neglecting overflow in the multiplication operation.

It is clear from the example given in Fig. 2.7 that the numbers generated by this type of process are completely determined by the preceding numbers and that any sequence of numbers is determined by the initial number. Moreover, after a certain number of values have been generated, the same sequence of values will be repeated. In Fig. 2.7, the sequence repeats after 16 values are generated and is said to have a period of 16.

Even though the multiplicative congruential generator gives numbers which are deterministic, in many cases the numbers are sufficiently varied to give a practical approximation to random numbers. The generated numbers are called *pseudorandom numbers* to emphasize the fact that they are not truly random.

The most important property of multiplicative congruential generators based on binary arithmetic is contained in the following theorem:

Theorem For k-bit length numbers, if we choose

$$\rho = 8t - 3$$

where t is some integer, then the period of the generated sequence is $2^{(k-2)}$, and the sequence is some permutation of

$$1, 5, \quad 9, \ldots, 2^k - 3 \qquad \text{if } x_0 \equiv 1 \ (\text{mod } 4)$$

$$3, 7, 11, \ldots, 2^k - 1 \qquad \text{if } x_0 \equiv 3 \ (\text{mod } 4)$$

The integer t is usually selected to give ρ a value sufficiently large so that when a small value of x occurs, the multiplication operation will cause overflow to occur within two or three iterations so that a small value of x will not be followed by several more relatively small values.

For the GENRND procedure, used in the checkout counter example program, the period of the sequence generated is $2^{29} = 538,870,912$. The floating-point values w are equally spaced in the interval from 0 to 1, and if the complete sequence of values were generated, the distribution of w would be a close approximation to the uniform distribution from 0 to 1. We hope that any part of the sequence would also be a close approximation to the uniform distribution, but this is not necessarily true.

Many other procedures for generating pseudorandom numbers have been used. Some are considerably more sophisticated and have been shown, by example, to generate sequences of uniform and independent numbers. However, there is no guarantee that a specific sequence of the numbers will have the desired random character needed for a particular simulation application. The numbers used in a simulation should be tested to verify that the assumed random nature is present.

3.3.2 Testing Uniform Variates

There are a large number of test procedures which have been developed for verifying the randomness of a sequence of numbers. We will consider two of these tests in order to illustrate the major purpose of these procedures. As in hypothesis testing, it is not possible to prove the conjecture that a sequence is truly random, but we can show, to some level of confidence, that it does have certain characteristics of random numbers.

The primary criteria for random sequences are that they be uniform and independent. By uniformity we mean that if we assume a sequence is uniformly distributed in, for example, an interval (0, 1), then any subsequence of these numbers is also uniformly distributed in (0, 1). The random variables x_i and x_j are considered independent if when x_i occurs before x_j, then x_j is in no way statistically dependent on the value assumed by x_i and vice versa.

(i) Chi-square goodness-of-fit test Assume that we have observations $x_1, x_2, \ldots, x_n$ produced by a uniform random-number generator with interval (0, 1). We divide the unit interval into k equal subintervals. Then, under the hypothesis of uniformity, the probability that a number x_i falls in a particular interval is $1/k$, and the expected number of observations in each interval is n/k.

Let f_j be the frequency with which the observations fall in the jth interval, i.e., have values in the range $[(j - 1)/k, j/k]$. Then if the sequence $\{x_i\}$ is made up of uniformly distributed random values, the statistic

$$U = \frac{k}{n} \sum_{j=1}^{k} \left(f_j - \frac{n}{k} \right)^2$$

has a distribution that converges to that of chi-square with $k - 1$ degrees of freedom as n becomes large. Usually if $n > 5k$, we may consider n sufficiently large. Thus,

$$\text{Prob} \left[U < \chi^2_{(1 - \alpha),(k - 1)} \right] = 1 - \alpha$$

and we may use this relation to test the hypothesis of independence and uniformity at a given level of confidence. Alternatively, we may use

$$\text{Prob} \left[U > \chi^2_{(1 - \alpha),(k - 1)} \right] = \alpha$$

to estimate the probability of obtaining a particular value of U.

As an example of this test, a total of 100 samples were obtained from the uniform random-number generator GENRND of Fig. 2.6. For 10 intervals of length .1, the frequencies were found to be

f	14	10	11	10	8	5	11	13	11	7
j	1	2	3	4	5	6	7	8	9	10

This gave a value for U of 6.6. Now since $\chi^2_{.9, 9} = 14.7$, we cannot reject the hypothesis that the distribution is uniform with a confidence level of 90 percent. From tables of the cumulative chi-square distribution in App. C, we also find that

$$\text{Prob} [U > 5.90] = .75$$

$$\text{Prob} [U > 8.34] = .50$$

Thus we can say that the probability of getting this large a value for U, 6.6, assuming a uniform distribution, is between 50 and 75 percent. This implies that sample frequencies f_i in this example deviate from the nominal value of 10 less than would usually be expected.

(ii) Test of correlation If random variables are not independent, it is necessary to know the conditional probability density function relating these variables in order to describe their jointly dependent behavior. Generally, we do not know the conditional probability density function, and it is not practical to obtain estimates for these functions. Because of this, dependence is usually estimated by use of measures of correlation.

The *covariance* between two variables x_i and x_j is defined as

$$\text{cov} (x_i, x_j) = E[(x_i - E[x_i])(x_j - E[x_j])]$$

$$= E[x_i x_j] - E[x_i]E[x_j]$$

$$\overset{s}{=} R_{ij}$$

If x_i and x_j are independent, $E[x_i x_j] = E[x_i]E[x_j]$, and their covariance is equal to 0. Note that R_{ii} is the variance of x_i.

If $R_{ij} > 0$, then we say that x_i and x_j are positively correlated. This may be interpreted to mean that on average a deviation in x_i above its mean value occurs when a deviation in x_j above its mean value occurs, or values below the mean values tend to occur together. If $R_{ij} < 0$, then x_i and x_j are negatively correlated, and values of x_i and x_j which are on opposite sides of their means tend to occur together.

The *correlation coefficient* is defined as

$$r_{ij} = \frac{R_{ij}}{\sqrt{R_{ii}R_{jj}}}$$

and it can be shown that

$$-1 \le r_{ij} \le 1$$

The larger $|r_{ij}|$ is, the greater the correlation between x_i and x_j.

If we consider a sequence of random numbers $x_1, x_2, \ldots, x_n$ from a particular random variable, then the covariance between the ith and jth numbers, R_{ij}, is called the *autocovariance* between the ith and jth events. If the sequence meets certain conditions, then the autocovariance of any two events depends only upon their separation in the series; e.g.,

$$R_{1,5} = R_{2,6} = \cdots = R_{i,i+4}$$

The required conditions are that the series be strictly stationary, which may be interpreted as meaning that the distribution of the series does not change as the index changes. For example, if the index is related to time, the series must be independent of time. The autocovariance functions are often denoted by a single lag subscript,

$$R_k = R_{i,i+k}$$

If we assume that a sequence of observations $x_1, x_2, \ldots, x_n$ are independent and uniformly distributed in the range $(0, 1)$, then we may estimate the auto-covariance functions by

$$\hat{R}_k = \frac{1}{n-k} \sum_{j=1}^{n-k} [(x_j - \tfrac{1}{2})(x_{j+k} - \tfrac{1}{2})]$$

The mean value for $\hat{R}_k$ is

$$E[\hat{R}_k] = \frac{1}{n-k} \sum_{j=1}^{n-k} E[(x_j - \tfrac{1}{2})(x_{j+k} - \tfrac{1}{2})]$$

$$= \frac{1}{n-k} \sum_{j=1}^{n-k} \{E[x_j x_{j+k}] - \tfrac{1}{2}E[x_j] - \tfrac{1}{2}E[x_{j+k}] + \tfrac{1}{4}\}$$

but

$$E[x_j] = \tfrac{1}{2} \quad \text{for} \quad j = 1, 2, \ldots, n$$

and since x_i are independent,

$$E[x_j x_{j+k}] = E[x_j]E[x_{j+k}] \qquad \text{if} \quad k \neq 0$$

so

$$E[\hat{R}_k] = 0 \qquad \text{for} \quad k > 0$$

Since

$$E[x_j^2] = 1/3 \qquad \left(= \int_0^1 x^2 f(x)\, dx, \ f(x) = \begin{cases} 1 & 0 < x < 1 \\ 0 & \text{elsewhere} \end{cases} \right.$$

for $\hat{R}_0$, we have

$$E[\hat{R}_0] = \frac{1}{12}$$

Similarly, we can show that

$$E[\hat{R}_k^2] = \frac{1}{144(n-k)} \qquad \text{for} \quad k > 0$$

As n increases, the distribution of

$$(\sqrt{n-k})\,\hat{R}_k$$

converges to the normal distribution with mean 0 and variance 1/144. Thus, we compute the autocovariance functions for a sequence and test the hypothesis,

$$R_k = 0 \qquad k = 1, 2, 3, \ldots, L$$

provided that $n \gg L$. In this case, we may use the statistic

$$S_k = 12(\sqrt{n-k})\,\hat{R}_k$$

and a table of the cumulative normal distribution to test the hypothesis. For example,

$$\text{Prob}\,[\,|S_k| < x] = \int_{-x}^{x} \left[\frac{(e^{-t^2/2})}{\sqrt{2\pi}} \right] dt$$

$$\text{Prob}\,[\,|S_k| < 1.282] = .80$$

and

$$\text{Prob}\,[\,|S_k| < 1.645] = .90$$

Thus in order to reject the hypothesis with a confidence level of 90 percent, the magnitude of S_k must be greater than 1.645. Or we may reject the hypothesis with 80 percent confidence if $|S_k|$ exceeds 1.282.

As an illustration, values of the first 10 autocovariances for sequences of length 100 and 1000, produced by GENRND using an initial value of SEED = 961871201, are shown, together with the corresponding values of S_k:

K	n = 100		n = 1000	
	$\hat{R}_k$	S_k	$\hat{R}_k$	S_k
1	0.00611	0.729	−0.00188	−0.712
2	0.00122	0.144	−0.00282	−1.068
3	0.00137	0.162	−0.00093	−0.351
4	0.00306	−0.454	0.00399	1.512
5	0.00597	0.698	−0.00075	−0.283
6	−0.00546	−0.635	−0.00016	−0.060
7	0.00616	0.713	−0.00058	−0.221
8	0.01638	1.886	−0.00298	−1.127
9	−0.01207	−1.382	−0.00120	−0.455
10	0.00307	0.349	0.00240	0.904

The fact that we can reject the hypothesis

$$\hat{R}_8 = 0$$

in the short sequence, with a high level of confidence does not imply that the random-number generator produces values with a consistent autocorrelation with lag 8, as shown by the results for the longer sequence. But it does indicate that if this type of autocorrelation would produce significant effects in a particular simulation, then this specific sequence of random numbers should not be used.

If the sequence does have correlation, this implies that the events of the sequence are dependent. However, 0 correlation does not guarantee independence.

There is no objective measure as to how random random numbers must be for use in a simulation. In the final analysis, this should be determined by how they are to be used.

3.3.3 Nonuniform Distributions

Thus far we have only considered generating uniformly distributed numbers, but in fact the uniform distribution can be used to generate random numbers from any distribution. This is due to the following property: if x_i is a sequence of random numbers which are uniformly distributed in the interval (0, 1) and if y has the probability density function $f(y)$ and cumulative distribution function $F(y)$, then the sequence of random numbers y_i generated by the operation

$$y_i = F^{-1}(x_i) \tag{1}$$

has the density function f. For example, to generate an exponentially distributed sequence, i.e.,

$$f(y) = \frac{1}{\alpha} e^{-y/\alpha}$$

$$F(y) = 1 - e^{-y/\alpha}$$

then we may use (1) in the form

$$F(y_i) = x_i$$

or

$$1 - e^{-y_i/\alpha} = x_i$$

$$e^{-y_i/\alpha} = 1 - x_i$$

$$y_i = -\alpha \log (1 - x_i) \tag{2}$$

Thus, formula (2) will generate the desired sequence. Note that if x_i is uniformly distributed in the range 0 to 1, so is $1 - x_i$. Thus in using (2), it is not necessary to subtract the random value from 1.

Algorithms have been developed to accomplish transformation of uniformly distributed random numbers to almost all the theoretical distributions. Several of these are given in App. D. This same type of inverse transformation can also be used for empirical distributions.

The GENCOC subroutine of the checkout counter example illustrates a general technique for generating empirical distributions. Figure 2-9 illustrates the procedure for going from a frequency distribution table to a continuous distribution function. Figure 2-9 also provides an intuitive explanation as to why this transformation works. If we assume that the uniformly distributed numbers are points on the abscissa and the desired numbers are the corresponding ordinate points of the curve, it is clear that 20 percent of the generated numbers will lie in the range from 20 to 30, 10 percent will be in the range (30, 40), and so on.

This method for generating empirical distributions is essentially a table look-up procedure and can be used to generate any distribution. For example, the GENARIV procedure of the checkout counter example generates a sequence which is a close approximation to the exponential distribution. Furthermore, the table look-up procedure is often more efficient in computations than the transformations based on theoretical distributions. However, there is an advantage to using theoretical distributions.

Consider the case of sample data from a real system. If we use an empirical distribution based on the samples, then we can, at best, reproduce the statistical behavior reflected in the samples. But if there is a theoretical distribution which is appropriate for the physical process which produced the samples and fits the sample data with properly chosen parameters, it should be used in the simulation. In this manner, the statistical characteristics of the parent population are represented rather than those of the sample which represents only a part of the actual population.

3.4 QUEUING THEORY

The checkout counter model of Chap. 2 is an example of a queuing situation. A *queue* arises whenever a customer or user arrives at a service facility and, finding it busy, is forced to wait. Queuing theory is a recently developed branch of probability theory which studies processes involving queues and provides analytical or closed-form solutions in certain cases. The theory has progressed to the point where tractable solutions are available for a number of idealized systems but not for the more complex cases. Because of this, simulation is often used to study more realistic models of queuing systems than those which can be analyzed mathematically. In fact, a quite large proportion of simulation studies involve queuing situations in some form.

Queuing theory is often used to solve idealized systems which are combined to approximate a more realistic model. The more general nature of these solutions may serve for developing insight into the character of congestion problems, can be helpful in providing upper bounds for certain effects, and may be very useful in checking accuracy and reasonableness of simulation results.

Figure 3.5 is a schematic representation of a simple queuing system. The input traffic represents the arrival of customers to the system. It is assumed that the customers are drawn from a population of potential customers in some random manner. The important characteristics that determine the input traffic are the size of the population and the arrival rate of customers from the population to the system. The service facility is made up of one or more "servers" in parallel, and each server can service only one customer at a time. The chief characteristic of a server is the time required to service a customer, which is usually described by a probability distribution. After being served, the customer leaves the system. A waiting line forms whenever a customer arrives and cannot be served. There are two characteristics to consider in the organization of a waiting line. One of these is the possibility of a finite-sized waiting area which will cause customers to be turned away if the waiting line is at its maximum length. The rule by which the server picks the next customer to be served from the waiting line is called the *queue discipline*. The most familiar pattern is "first in, first out," but many other patterns such as "last in, first out" order, service by priority, and service with interrupts also occur.

The following parameters are used to describe basic characteristics of queuing systems:

T_a = mean interarrival time between customers

λ = mean arrival rate of customers, $\lambda = 1/T_a$

T_s = mean service time

μ = mean service rate, $\mu = 1/T_s$

U = traffic intensity, $U = T_s/T_a = \lambda T_s = \lambda/\mu$

ρ = server utilization, the fraction of time that a single server is busy

Figure 3.5 Representation of a single-server queuing system.

The following distributions give a dynamic picture of system performance:

$$P_k(t) = \text{Prob } [k \text{ customers are in the system at time } t]$$

$$Q(t) = \text{Prob } [\text{queuing time} < t]$$

$$W(t) = \text{Prob } [\text{waiting time} < t]$$

Note that queuing time represents the total time a customer is in the system, while waiting time represents the time a customer spends in the waiting line. In many cases these distributions are difficult to obtain, and so their mean values and variances are used. Symbolic representation of these variables are

Variable	Mean value	Variance
Number of customers in the system	L_q	σ^2_{Lq}
Number of customers in the waiting line	L_w	σ^2_{Lw}
Queuing time	T_q	σ^2_{Tq}
Waiting time	T_w	σ^2_{Tw}

3.4.1 Single-Server Queues

We first consider the case of only one server in a system and assume customers arrive from an infinite source so that arrivals do not cause a depletion in the source. We also assume that the waiting line length is not restricted so that no customers are lost to the system.

(i) Random arrivals/random service In this case the arrival rate is described by the Poisson distribution, or equivalently, the interarrival times are exponentially distributed. Similarly the length of time required to service a customer is exponentially distributed. Thus, we have

$$\text{Prob } [\text{interarrival time for a customer} < t] = 1 - e^{-\lambda t}$$

$$T_a = 1/\lambda$$

$$\sigma^2_{Ta} = T_a^2$$

$$\text{Prob } [\text{service time for a customer} < t] = 1 - e^{-\mu t}$$

$$T_s = 1/\mu$$

$$\sigma^2_{Ts} = T_s^2$$

since

$$P_k = \text{probability that the number of customers in the system equals } K$$

then P_0 is the probability that the system is idle. Now over a long period of time T_L the number of customers arriving at the system will be

$$n = T_L/T_a$$

and for these customers, the total service time will be $n(T_s)$. Thus the fraction of time that the server is busy is

$$\rho = n\left(\frac{T_s}{T_L}\right) = \frac{n(T_s)}{n(T_a)} = \frac{T_s}{T_a}$$

But when the server is not busy, the system is idle, so

$$P_0 = 1 - \rho = 1 - T_s/T_a \tag{1}$$

This result assumes that over a long period of time the fraction of time that the system is idle will equal the probability that the system is idle.

In order to consider the probability that the system is idle at some specific time t_1, we must analyze how it can reach the idle state. Assume that

$$t_1 = t_0 + h$$

where h is some short period of time. Then the probability that the system is idle at t_1 is equal to the sum of:

1. The probability the system was idle at t_0 and no customers arrived during the period h, and
2. The probability the system had one customer at t_0 and one customer departed during the period h.

The probability that no customer arrives in the period h can be found by using the Poisson distribution, but this value can be approximated by a series expansion in powers of h; and if h is sufficiently small, all terms with h^2 and higher power can be neglected. This gives

$$\text{Prob [no customers arrive in period } h] = 1 - \frac{h}{T_a}$$

Similarly we may use the approximation

$$\text{Prob [one customer departs in period } h] = \frac{h}{T_s}$$

Using these expressions, we have

$$P_0(t_1) = \left(1 - \frac{h}{T_a}\right)P_0(t_0) + \left(\frac{h}{T_s}\right)P_1(t_0) \tag{2}$$

or

$$\frac{P_0(t_0 + h) - P_0(t_0)}{h} = -\frac{P_0(t_0)}{T_a} + \frac{P_1(t_0)}{T_s}$$

The right-hand side of this equation, as h goes to 0, is the derivative of P_0 with respect to time. If we assume that we are interested in steady-state values for the various P_K's, then their derivatives will be 0. The term *steady state* is defined as the time period after any initial transient in the system has been damped out so that there is no change of the state probabilities with time.

Therefore,

$$P_1 = \frac{T_s}{T_a} P_0 \tag{3}$$

For any other system state j, $j > 0$, an expression similar to (2) may be developed which includes the three possibilities of no arrivals or departures, one arrival, or one departure:

$$P_j(t + h) = \left[1 - \left(\frac{1}{T_a} + \frac{1}{T_s} \right) h \right] P_j(t) + \left(\frac{1}{T_a} \right) h P_{j-1}(t) + \left(\frac{1}{T_s} \right) h P_{j+1}(t)$$

Thus,

$$\frac{P_j(t + h) - P_j(t)}{h} = - \left(\frac{1}{T_a} + \frac{1}{T_s} \right) P_j(t) + \left(\frac{1}{T_a} \right) P_{j-1}(t) + \left(\frac{1}{T_s} \right) P_{j+1}(t)$$

and for steady-state conditions

$$P_{j+1} = \frac{T_a + T_s}{T_a} P_j - \frac{T_s}{T_a} P_{j-1} \tag{4}$$

Using (1) and (2) with Eq. (4) gives the solution

$$P_K = \left(\frac{T_s}{T_a} \right)^K P_0 \qquad K > 1 \tag{5}$$

This development is intended to give a plausible argument for the result (5), which can be rigorously derived [2].

We can now write

$$P_k = \rho^K (1 - \rho)$$

and using this expression for P_k we can find the mean queue size and its variance in terms of ρ

$$L_q = \sum_{k=0}^{\infty} k\, P_k = \frac{\rho}{1 - \rho}$$

$$\sigma_{Lq}^2 = \sum_{k=0}^{\infty} k^2\, P_k - L_q^2 = \frac{\rho}{(1 - \rho)^2}$$

Similarly, the mean size of the waiting line and its variance are

$$L_w = \sum_{k=1}^{\infty} (k - 1)\, P_k = \frac{\rho^2}{1 - \rho}$$

$$\sigma_{Lw}^2 = \sum_{k=1}^{\infty} (k - 1)^2\, P_k - L_w^2 = \frac{\rho^2(1 + \rho - \rho^2)}{(1 - \rho)^2}$$

Note that the mean waiting line length differs from the mean queue size by the quantity ρ

$$L_q = L_w + \rho$$

This is due to the fact that L_w is one customer shorter than L_q when the server is busy. The system is busy a fraction of the total time equal to ρ. When the system is idle, L_w and L_q are both 0, so

$$L_q = \rho(L'_q)$$

$$L_w = \rho(L'_q - 1) = L_q - \rho$$

where L'_q is the mean value of the queue size when the server is busy. This result is true for any single-server queue, regardless of the type of arrival or service distribution.

The distribution for total time spent in this type of system can be shown to be

$$\text{Prob [queuing time} < t] = Q(t) = 1 - e^{-(1-\rho)t/T_s}$$

The mean queuing time and its variance are

$$T_q = \int_0^\infty t\, dQ(t) = \frac{T_s}{1 - \rho}$$

$$\sigma^2_{Tq} = \int_0^\infty (t - T_q)^2\, dQ(t) = \frac{T_s^2}{(1-\rho)^2}$$

The distribution for waiting time is found to be

$$\text{Prob [waiting time} < t] = W(t) = 1 - \rho e^{-(1-\rho)t/T_s}$$

and

$$T_w = \int_0^\infty t\, dW(t) = \frac{\rho T_s}{1 - \rho} \qquad \sigma^2_{Tw} = \int_0^\infty (t - T_w)^2\, dW(t) = \frac{(2-\rho)\rho T_s^2}{(1-\rho)^2}$$

Note that

$$T_q = T_w + T_s$$

and

$$\sigma^2_{Tq} = \sigma^2_{Tw} + \sigma^2_{Ts}$$

(ii) Random arrivals/general service This case generalizes the assumption regarding the distribution of service times. We assume only that there is a service time distribution denoted by $H(t)$ which has moments b_n:

$$\text{Prob [service time} < t] = H(t)$$

$$b_n = \int_0^\infty t^n\, dH(t)$$

This case was first analyzed by Pollaczek and Khintchine, and the formulas for the mean values of the system parameters are usually known by their names. The mean and variance of the queue statistics depend only on the first three statistical moments of the service distribution so they may be used when only an approximation for this distribution is known.

The input in this case is Poisson with mean arrival rate λ. The server utilization is then given as

$$\rho = \lambda T_s = \lambda b_1$$

The distributions for queue size (P_k) and waiting time $W(t)$ are not known in the general case but the moments of these distributions can be found.

The formulas for mean queue size, mean queuing time, mean waiting time, and their variances, in terms of the service time moments b_n, are

$$L_q = \frac{\lambda^2 b_2}{2(1-\rho)} + \rho \qquad \sigma_{Lq}^2 = \frac{\lambda^3 b_3}{3(1-\rho)} + \frac{\lambda^4 b_2^2}{4(1-\rho)^2} + \frac{\lambda^2(3-2\rho)b_2}{2(1-\rho)} + \rho(1-\rho)$$

$$T_q = \frac{\lambda b_2}{2(1-\rho)} + b_1 \qquad \sigma_{Tq}^2 = \frac{\lambda b_3 + 3b_2}{3(1-\rho)} + \frac{\lambda^2 b_2^2}{2(1-\rho)^2} - T_q^2$$

$$T_w = \frac{\lambda b_2}{2(1-\rho)} \qquad \sigma_{Tw}^2 = \frac{\lambda b_3}{3(1-\rho)} + \frac{\lambda^2 b_2}{2(1-\rho)^2} - T_w^2$$

We next consider three special cases where the service time has constant, exponential, or Erlang distributions and compute their moments.

1. *Constant service time*:

$$H(t) = \begin{cases} 0, & \text{when } 0 < t < T_s \\ 1, & \text{when } t \geq T_s \end{cases}$$

$$b_n = \int_0^\infty t^n \, dH(t) = \int_0^\infty t^n \, \delta(t - T_s) \, dt = T_s^n$$

2. *Exponential service time*:

$$H(t) = 1 - e^{-t/T_s}$$

$$b_n = \int_0^\infty t^n (e^{-t/T_s}/T_s) \, dt = n! \, T_s^n$$

3. *Erlang distribution with parameter* m *service time*:

$$H(t) = 1 - e^{-mt/T_s} \left(\sum_{k=0}^{m-1} \frac{(mt)^k}{k!} \right)$$

$$b_n = \frac{(n+m-1)!}{(m-1)!} \left(\frac{T_s}{m} \right)^n$$

These three special cases provide a range of solutions which cover most service time distributions of interest with simple queuing systems. The constant service time provides a lower bound for the average time delay, and the exponential case provides the upper bound. The Erlang distributions cover the range between the other two. Note that for $m = 1$, the Erlang is the exponential distribution, and as m increases and approaches infinity, the Erlang distribution approaches a constant. Figure 3.6 shows plots of the normalized mean queuing time T_q/T_s versus the service utilization ρ for these cases.

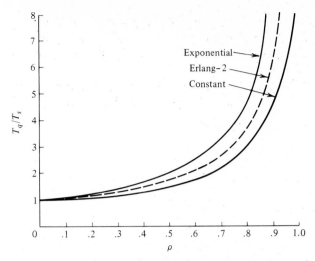

Figure 3.6 Comparison of normalized mean queuing time.

There are other distributions which cause greater degradation in queuing systems than the exponential. Generally these are distributions which exhibit a bimodal density function, such as the hyperexponential distribution [3].

Example To illustrate the use of the formulas and the source of Fig. 3.6, we consider the following example. Let the mean interarrival time be 5 s and the mean service time be 3 s. Then the server utilization is

$$\rho = T_s/T_a = .6$$

and for the cases of (a) constant service time, (b) exponential service time, and (c) service time with an Erlang-2 distribution, we have

(a) $b_1 = T_s = 3$

$b_2 = T_s^2 = 9$

$$T_q = \frac{\lambda b_2}{2(1 - \rho)} + b_1 = \frac{(1/5)9}{2(1 - .6)} + 3 = 5.25$$

(b) $b_1 = T_s = 3$

$b_2 = 2T_s^2 = 18$

$T_q = 7.5$

(c) $b_1 = \frac{(1 + 2 - 1)!}{(2 - 1)!}\left(\frac{T_s}{2}\right)^1 = \frac{2!}{1!}\frac{T_s}{2} = T_s$

$b_2 = \frac{(2 + 2 - 1)!}{(2 - 1)!}\left(\frac{T_s}{2}\right)^2 = \frac{3!}{1!}\frac{T_s^2}{2^2} = \frac{3.2}{2.2}T_s^2 = 1.5T_s^2 = 13.5$

$T_q = 6.375$

The values of T_q are normalized by dividing by T_s to obtain the points given in Fig. 3.6. Note that the Erlang-2 curve is midway between the exponential and the constant service time curves. As the parameter m of the Erlang distribution increases the corresponding curve approaches that for constant service time.

3.4.2 Multiserver Queues

We now consider the case where the queuing system has several service facilities in parallel. The service facilities are assumed to be identical, and there is one common waiting line. Figure 3.7 is a schematic representation of this system for the case of three servers.

For this model it is assumed that both the interarrival times and the service times are exponentially distributed. If there are m servers, the average server utilization or the system utilization, denoted by ρ_s, is the product of the average service time and the mean arrival rate divided by the number of servers,

$$\rho_s = \lambda T_s / m$$

The following equation has been shown to apply for the probability that k customers are in the system:

$$P_k = \begin{cases} \dfrac{(\lambda T_s)^k}{k!} P_0 & \text{if } k < m \\[2em] \dfrac{(\lambda T_s)^k}{m!\, m^{(k-m)}} P_0 & \text{if } k \geq m \end{cases}$$

where P_0 is the probability that no customers are in the system. Using the law of total probabilities

$$\sum_{k=0}^{\infty} P_k = 1$$

it can be shown that

$$P_0 = \left[\left(\sum_{k=0}^{m-1} \frac{(\lambda T_s)^k}{k!} \right) + \frac{m}{m - \lambda T_s} \frac{(\lambda T_s)^m}{m!} \right]^{-1}$$

The probability that all servers are busy is

$$P_f = \text{Prob } [k \geq m] = \sum_{k=m}^{\infty} P_k = 1 - \sum_{k=0}^{m-1} P_k$$

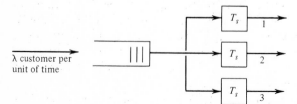

λ customer per unit of time

Figure 3.7 A multiserver queuing system.

The waiting time distribution has been found to be

$$W(t) = \text{Prob [waiting time} < t] = 1 - P_f \, e^{-(m - \lambda T_s)t/T_s}$$

The formulas for the mean waiting line length and mean waiting time and their variances are

$$L_w = \sum_{k=m}^{\infty} (k - m)P_k = \frac{\rho_s}{1 - \rho_s} P_f$$

$$\sigma_{Lw}^2 = \sum_{k=m}^{\infty} (k - m)^2 P_k - L_w^2 = \frac{\rho_s P_f(1 + \rho_s - \rho_s P_f)}{(1 - \rho_s)^2}$$

$$T_w = \frac{P_f T_s}{m(1 - \rho_s)}$$

$$\sigma_{Tw}^2 = \frac{(2 - P_f)P_f \, T_s^2}{m^2(1 - \rho_s)^2}$$

For example, consider a system as shown in Fig. 3.7 with three servers, with exponentially distributed service times having an average value of 2 min and customer interarrival times with exponential distribution and mean of 1 min; i.e.,

$$m = 3 \qquad T_s = 2 \qquad T_a = 1$$

Then the probability of no customers in the system is

$$P_0 = \left[\frac{(2)^0}{0!} + \frac{(2)^1}{1!} + \frac{(2)^2}{2!} + \frac{3}{3 - 2}\left(\frac{(2)^3}{3!}\right) \right]^{-1} = \frac{1}{9}$$

and the probabilities P_k are

$$P_1 = 2/9$$

$$P_2 = 2/9$$

$$P_3 = \left(\frac{2}{3}\right)\left(\frac{2}{9}\right) = \frac{4}{27}$$

$$\vdots$$

$$P_k = \left(\frac{\lambda T_s}{m}\right)P_{k-1} = \left(\frac{2}{3}\right)^{k-2} P_2 = \left(\frac{2}{3}\right)^{k-2}\left(\frac{2}{9}\right)$$

The probability that all servers are busy is

$$P_f = 1 - (P_0 + P_1 + P_2) = 1 - \frac{5}{9} = \frac{4}{9}$$

and the average waiting time for each customer is

$$T_w = \frac{(4/9)(2)}{3[1 - (2/3)]} = \frac{8}{9}$$

We can compare the performance of multiserver queues with that of single-server queues by modifying this example. If we assume that the customers were being served by three single-server queues and that each of these queues had one-third the customer arrival rate, but with the exponential distribution, then the average customer waiting time would be

$$T_w = \frac{\rho T_s}{1 - \rho} = \frac{(2/3)(2)}{1 - (2/3)} = 4$$

Thus by combining the three waiting lines and placing the servers in parallel, the average customer waiting time was reduced from 4 min to $53\frac{1}{3}$ s.

It is a general result that by placing servers in parallel, the level of customer service is increased. The larger the number of servers, the greater the relative increase in performance. If the servers are in close physical proximity, but have separate waiting lines, the system will approach the performance of the common waiting line system. This assumes that if one server becomes idle, and one or more customers are waiting in another line, someone will move to the idle service facility. If so, the average customer waiting time of the system will be the same as that of the common waiting line system. However, the variance of the waiting times will be greater.

3.4.3 Queuing Disciplines

Up to this point we have assumed that the queuing discipline was first in first out (FIFO). This is the situation where service is in order of arrival; i.e., the next customer to be served is the one who has waited the longest. If the customers are people, this is the common procedure and is usually necessary. But if the customers are things, such as messages, parts, etc., other disciplines may be convenient or even advantageous.

Priority service We will consider one type of non-FIFO queuing, where customers have priority levels. Suppose each customer coming into a single-server system has a priority classification value, $1, 2, \ldots, l$ where 1 is the highest priority and l the lowest. A customer of class j will be served ahead of customers with priority $j + 1, j + 2, \ldots, l$, and customers of the same class are served FIFO. Assume that the arrivals in each class are independent and with Poisson distribution and arrival rate of $\lambda_1, \lambda_2, \ldots, \lambda_l$. The total mean arrival rate to the queue is

$$\lambda = \lambda_1 + \lambda_2 + \cdots + \lambda_l$$

If the service time distribution for customers in class j is $H_j(t)$, then the overall service time distribution is

$$H(t) = \frac{\lambda_1}{\lambda} H_1(t) + \frac{\lambda_2}{\lambda} H_2(t) + \cdots + \frac{\lambda_l}{\lambda} H_l(t)$$

Similarly, the mean and second moment of service times for class j are denoted by

$b_{1,j}$ and $b_{2,j}$. For the overall service time,

$$b_1 = \frac{\lambda_1}{\lambda} b_{1,1} + \frac{\lambda_2}{\lambda} b_{1,2} + \cdots + \frac{\lambda_l}{\lambda} b_{1,l}$$

$$b_2 = \frac{\lambda_1}{\lambda} b_{2,1} + \frac{\lambda_2}{\lambda} b_{2,2} + \cdots + \frac{\lambda_l}{\lambda} b_{2,l}$$

The fraction of server utilization due to traffic from class j is

$$\rho_j = \lambda_j b_{1,j}$$

The total server utilization will be denoted by I_l:

$$I_l = \rho_1 + \rho_2 + \cdots + \rho_l$$

The cumulative server utilization due to classes 1 through j will be denoted by I_j:

$$I_j = \rho_1 + \rho_2 + \cdots + \rho_j \qquad j < l$$

Nonpreemptive case If customers are not interrupted once their service starts, then the mean waiting time for class j customers is given by

$$T_{w,j} = \frac{\lambda b_2}{2(1 - I_{j-1})(1 - I_j)} \qquad I_0 = 0$$

The average waiting time for all customers is

$$T_w = \frac{\lambda_1}{\lambda} T_{w,1} + \frac{\lambda_2}{\lambda} T_{w,2} + \cdots + \frac{\lambda_l}{\lambda} T_{w,l}$$

The mean queuing time for class j customers is

$$T_{q,j} = T_{w,j} + b_{1,j}$$

and the overall average queuing time is

$$T_q = T_w + b_1$$

Preemptive case Consider the situation where higher-priority customers can interrupt the service of lower-priority customers; i.e., during the service of a class j customer, if a customer from class i ($i < j$) arrives, the service of the class j customer is interrupted and delayed until service to the customer from class i is completed, provided no new arrivals with higher priority have occurred. This case is referred to as a *preemptive-resume priority scheme*. The mean queuing time for a class j customer to get through this system is given by

$$T_{q,j} = \frac{1}{(1 - I_{j-1})} \left[b_{1,j} + \frac{\sum_{i=1}^{j} \lambda_i b_{2,i}}{2(1 - I_j)} \right] \qquad I_0 = 0$$

The average queuing time for all customers is

$$T_q = \frac{\lambda_1}{\lambda} T_{q,1} + \frac{\lambda_2}{\lambda} T_{q,2} + \cdots + \frac{\lambda_l}{\lambda} T_{q,l}$$

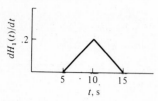 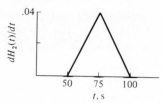

Figure 3.8 Distribution of service times.

Example As an example of priority queuing disciplines, the following model can be considered. A computer is sequentially processing two types of jobs. The distribution of computer time required by these two types of jobs is given in Fig. 3.8. The arrival rate for the short type 1 job is on the average, one job every 25 s and for the larger type 2 jobs, one every 250 s. The arrivals are assumed to be independent and with an exponential distribution for each type. Thus we have

$$\lambda_1 = .04 \quad s^{-1}$$
$$\lambda_2 = .004 \; s^{-1}$$

The mean service times are

$$b_{1,1} = 10 \text{ s}$$
$$b_{1,2} = 75 \text{ s}$$

The second moments are obtained from

$$b_{2,1} = \int_5^{10} (.04)t^2(t-5) \, dt + \int_{10}^{15} (.04)t^2(15-t) \, dt = 104.167$$

$$b_{2,2} = \int_{50}^{75} (.0016)t^2(t-50) \, dt + \int_{75}^{100} (.0016)t^2(100-t) \, dt = 5729.167$$

The overall first and second moments and the system utilization are

$$b_1 = \frac{.04}{.044}(10) + \frac{.004}{.044}(75) = 15.91 \text{ s}$$

$$b_2 = \frac{.04}{.044}(104.167) + \frac{.004}{.044}(5729.167) = 615.53 \; s^2$$

$$I_2 = \lambda b_1 = (.044)(15.91) = .70$$

(a) If we first assume that the computer does not use a priority system for these jobs, then the overall mean waiting time and mean queuing time are given by

$$T_w = \frac{\lambda b_2}{2(1 - I_2)} = \frac{(.044)(615.53)}{2(1 - .70)} = 45.14 \text{ s}$$

$$T_q = T_w + b_1 = 61.05 \text{ s}$$

The mean queuing time for the type 1 and type 2 jobs are

$$T_{q,1} = T_w + b_{1,1} = 55.14 \text{ s}$$

$$T_{q,2} = T_w + b_{1,2} = 120.14 \text{ s}$$

(b) Next we assume that the short type 1 jobs have priority over the longer type 2 jobs but do not preempt type 2 jobs which have started processing. The cumulative utilizations are

$$I_1 = \lambda_1 b_{1,1} = .04(10) = .4$$

$$I_2 = \lambda_1 b_{1,1} + \lambda_2 b_{1,2} = .04(10) + .004(75) = .7$$

For this case, the mean waiting times for type 1 jobs and for type 2 jobs are given by

$$T_{w,1} = \frac{\lambda b_2}{2(1 - I_1)} = \frac{.044(615.53)}{2(1 - .4)} = 22.57 \text{ s}$$

$$T_{w,2} = \frac{\lambda b_2}{2(1 - I_1)(1 - I_2)} = \frac{.044(615.53)}{2(1 - .4)(1 - .7)} = 75.23 \text{ s}$$

The corresponding queuing times are

$$T_{q,1} = T_{w,1} + b_{1,1} = 32.57 \text{ s}$$

$$T_{q,2} = T_{w,2} + b_{1,2} = 150.23 \text{ s}$$

The overall mean waiting time and mean queuing time are

$$T_w = \frac{\lambda_1}{\lambda} T_{w,1} + \frac{\lambda_2}{\lambda} T_{w,2} = \frac{.04(22.57)}{.044} + \frac{.004(75.23)}{.044} = 27.36 \text{ s}$$

$$T_q = T_w + b_1 = 43.27 \text{ s}$$

(c) If we assume that the type 1 jobs have priority and may interrupt the type 2 jobs, then the mean queuing times for the two job types are given by

$$T_{q,1} = b_{1,1} + \frac{\lambda_1 b_{2,1}}{2(1 - I_1)} = 10 + \frac{.04(104.167)}{2(1 - .4)} = 13.47 \text{ s}$$

$$T_{q,2} = \frac{1}{(1 - I_1)} \left[b_{1,2} + \frac{(\lambda_1 b_{2,1} + \lambda_2 b_{2,2})}{2(1 - I_2)} \right] = 200.23 \text{ s}$$

and the corresponding waiting times are

$$T_{w,1} = T_{q,1} - b_{1,1} = 3.47 \text{ s}$$

$$T_{w,2} = T_{q,2} - b_{1,2} = 125.23 \text{ s}$$

The overall mean waiting time and mean queuing time is

$$T_w = \frac{\lambda_1}{\lambda} T_{w,1} + \frac{\lambda_2}{\lambda} T_{w,2} = 14.54 \text{ s}$$

$$T_q = T_w + b_1 = 30.45 \text{ s}$$

This example shows that priority schemes can reduce the overall mean waiting time for a system. Of course, this reduction was achieved by reducing the waiting time for the more numerous type 1 jobs and increasing the waiting times of type 2 jobs. So the improved average system performance was achieved at the expense of the service to type 2 jobs.

3.5 TIME SERIES ANALYSIS

The type of simulations we are considering involve the study of systems as they change over a period of time. Generally, the same approach is valid if some other, monotonically increasing quantity is used as the independent variable, but it is convenient to think of the processes as developing as time progresses. Thus when we consider a sequence of successive observations $\{X_i\}$ of some variable X, this sequence is a discrete time series. If a system evolves in time according to probabilistic laws, it is called a *stochastic process*; and the sequence of observations of any state variable of the system is a *statistical time series*. The time series we consider here are assumed to arise from a stochastic process.

To illustrate the type of process we are considering, we use the following hypothetical example. The average number of units produced by a crew of workers in a certain manufacturing operation is 100 units per day. The actual number· produced each day varies because of certain random effects. The variation from the mean value each day is composed of two components. One of these components is a normally distributed random variable with a mean of 0 and a variance of 25 units. This component is assumed to be created by daily differences in the performance of the equipment used in the manufacturing operation. The second component of daily variation is equal to one-half the value of the first component of variation for the previous day. That is, if during the previous day the equipment performed less (more) effectively than usual, the crew will work proportionally slower (faster) than usual during the present day. A mathematical model for this process is

$$X_i = 100 + e_i + .5e_{i-1} \tag{1}$$

where X_i is the number of units produced during day i and e_i is a sample from a normal distribution with $\mu = 0$ and $\sigma^2 = 25$.

An example of a time series generated by the model (1) for a specific set of random variations is shown in Fig. 3.9. Figure 3.9 also shows the sequence of random numbers e_i used, and a time series generated by the model,

$$X_i = 100 + e_i - .5e_{i-1} \tag{2}$$

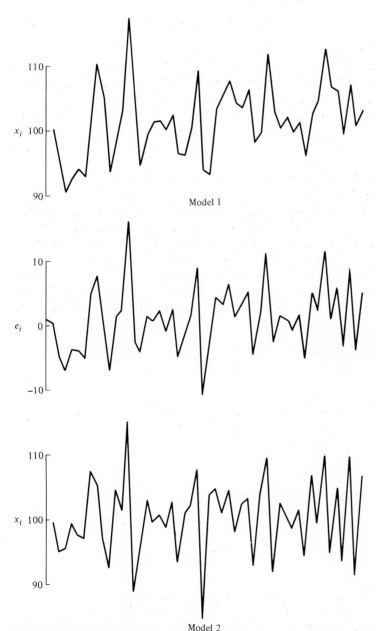

Figure 3.9 Example of an autocorrelated time series.

using the same values for e_i. This model, (2), may be interpreted as assuming that the effect of equipment performance on one day influences worker performance the next day in an opposite manner than that assumed for model (1).

Comparing the curves in Fig. 3.9, which were obtained by connecting the X_i and e_i points with straight lines, shows that the effect of the $+.5e_{i-1}$ term in model (1) is to smooth out the variations somewhat and to cause some brief trends in the evolution of X. The effect of the similar term in model (2) is to cause variations in X to be somewhat more rapid than in the purely random behavior of e.

If a time series is not affected by a change in time, i.e., if the statistical properties relating X_i, X_{i+1}, ..., X_{i+k} are the same for any value of i, then the stochastic process underlying these values is said to be *strictly stationary*. A stationary process has a constant mean and variance and autocovariances which are functions only of the separation between pairs of observations (X_i, X_{i+k}) or what we have called lag k.

3.5.1 Autocovariance and Autocorrelation Functions

Given a theoretical model, as, for example, Eq. (1), we may calculate the mean, variance, and autocovariances as follows:

$$\mu = E[X_i] = E[100] + E[e_i] + .5E[e_{i-1}] = 100$$

$$\sigma^2 = E[(X_i - \mu)^2] = E[(e_i + .5e_{i-1})^2]$$

$$= E[e_i^2] + E[e_i e_{i-1}] + .25E[e_{i-1}^2] = 31.25$$

$$R_k = E[(x_i - \mu)(X_{i+k} - \mu)]$$

$$= E[e_i e_{i+k}] + .5E[e_i e_{i+k-1}]$$

$$+ .5E[e_{i-1}e_{i+k}] + .25E[e_{i-1}e_{i+k-1}]$$

Thus,

$$R_1 = .5(25) = 12.5$$

$$R_k = 0 \qquad k = 2, 3, 4, \ldots$$

Note that $R_0 = \sigma^2$.

The corresponding autocorrelation coefficients are

$$r_1 = R_1/R_0 = .4$$

$$r_k = 0 \qquad k > 1$$

and, of course, $r_0 = 1$. The results for model (2) differ only in the signs of R_1 and r_1.

The plot of R_k versus the lag k is called the *autocovariance function of a process*. Similarly, the plot of r_k versus k is referred to as the *autocorrelation function*. These plots are useful in determining how much the value of a time series at time t depends on its value at some previous time. Thus, these plots provide a measure of the "memory" of a stochastic process in the sense of how long the result of a disturbance to the system at some point in time will affect the state of the system in the future. This aspect of system behavior is somewhat analogous to the inertia of mechanical systems.

For the example series of Fig. 3.9, using the estimators

$$\bar{x} = (1/n) \sum_{i=1}^{n} x_i \tag{3}$$

$$S^2 = [1/(n-1)] \sum_{i=1}^{n} (x_i - \bar{x})^2 \tag{4}$$

$$\hat{R}_k = [1/(n-k)] \sum_{i=1}^{n-k} (x_i - \bar{x})(x_{i+k} - \bar{x}) \tag{5}$$

the following values were obtained using 100 sample values:

	Model (1)	Model (2)
$\bar{x}$	101.09	100.41
S^2	27.79	33.93
$\hat{R}_1$	9.41	-16.99
$\hat{R}_2$	0.23	4.22
$\hat{R}_3$	1.69	-4.69
$\hat{R}_4$	6.22	6.30
$\hat{R}_5$	3.78	-0.97

This example illustrates a major difficulty in using covariance functions. If the theoretical model is not known, the true form of the function is not readily available from the computed estimates. It is possible to statistically test the sample values against a proposed model. In the case of the above computed values, it can be shown $\hat{R}_2$, $\hat{R}_3$, $\hat{R}_4$, $\hat{R}_5$ lie within a 90 percent confidence interval for the true zero values of the autocovariance function of the systems defined by Eqs. (1) and (2). The basic idea of this test is similar to the test of correlation discussed in Sec. 3.3.2. A method to carry out this procedure will be covered when we consider techniques for model development in Chap. 7.

3.5.2 Autocorrelation Effects in Queuing Systems

Consider the simulation of a single-server queuing system with Poisson distributed arrivals, exponentially distributed service times, and first in–first out queue discipline. This is the case considered in Sec. 2.4.1(i) of the queuing theory discussion. Suppose the objective of the simulation is to determine the mean waiting time. An analytic solution for T_w and its variance is available in terms of the server utilization ρ and the mean service time T_s.

For a specific example, take the case where $\rho = .75$ and $T_s = 1$, then the mean waiting time and its variance are

$$T_w = \frac{\rho T_s}{1 - \rho} = 3$$

$$\sigma_{tw}^2 = \frac{(2 - \rho)\rho T_s^2}{(1 - \rho)^2} = 15$$

A simulation of this example was carried out using the estimators given in Eqs. (3) and (4). Figure 3.10 shows the results obtained for T_w and σ_{tw}^2 as a function of the length of the simulation. The estimate obtained for T_w is close to the correct

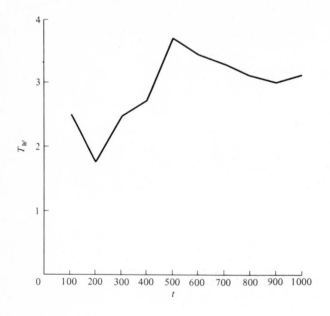

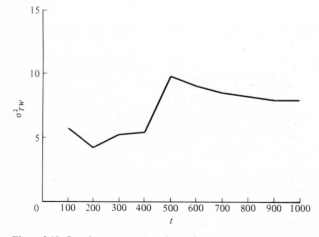

Figure 3.10 Queuing system example results.

value 3 and can be improved by a longer simulation run. The estimate for the variance is low compared with the correct value and does not improve with longer simulation runs.

The reason that the simulation does not give a good estimate for the variance is that the observations of waiting times for entities in the system are not independent. When a queue forms, the waiting time for any specific arrival is clearly related to the waiting time of its predecessors. Figure 3.11 gives an example of waiting times for a sequence of arrivals from the simulation results. The length of the queue at the arrival time for each entity is also shown. This figure illustrates the typical queuing system behavior where the length of the queue tends to build up and then decrease to 0, periodically. Thus, the observations of the waiting time in a queue are autocorrelated.

For autocorrelated variables, the variance of the observations is not simply related to the variance of the mean value of the observations. To find the variance of the mean value of a series of observations, we may write

$$\text{var}(\bar{x}) = E[(\bar{x} - \mu)^2]$$

$$= E\left[\left(\frac{1}{n}\sum_{i=1}^{n}(x_i - \mu)\right)^2\right] = \frac{1}{n^2}E\left[\left(\sum_{i=1}^{n}(x_i - \mu)\right)\left(\sum_{k=1}^{n}(x_k - \mu)\right)\right]$$

$$= \frac{1}{n^2}\sum_{i=1}^{n}\sum_{k=1}^{n}E[(x_i - \mu)(x_k - \mu)]$$

$$= \frac{1}{n^2}\sum_{i=1}^{n}\sum_{k=1}^{n}R_{k-i}$$

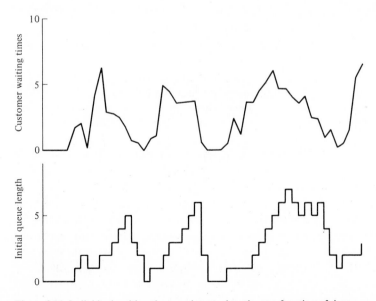

Figure 3.11 Individual waiting times and queue lengths as a function of time.

The double summation may be simplified to give

$$\text{var}\,(\bar{x}) = \frac{1}{n^2} \sum_{k=1-n}^{n-1} (n - |k|)R_k$$

and, since $R_k = R_{-k}$, we have

$$\text{var}\,(\bar{x}) = \frac{1}{n}\left[R_0 + 2\sum_{k=1}^{n-1}\left(1 - \frac{k}{n}\right)R_k \right] \tag{6}$$

For uncorrelated observations, the variance of the mean is equal to σ^2/n, which corresponds to the first term in this expression.

Equation (6) includes n autocovariances which cannot all be determined accurately. But if these terms decrease to zero beyond some index m, ($R_k = 0$ for $k > m$) where $m \ll n$, then this relation may provide an efficient technique for estimating var $(\bar{x})$.

Another approach to measuring the sample variance of autocorrelated data is based on the central limit theorem. If the observations are grouped into subintervals of length m, then the means of these subintervals,

$$\bar{x}_j = \frac{1}{m}\sum_{i=1}^{m} x_{i+m(j-1)} \qquad \begin{aligned} &j = 1, 2, \ldots, k \\ &k = n/m \end{aligned}$$

will be normally distributed if m is sufficiently large. Then the variance can be estimated by

$$S^2 = \frac{1}{k-1}\sum_{j=1}^{k}\left(\bar{x}_j - \frac{1}{k}\sum_{l=1}^{k}\bar{x}_l\right)^2 \tag{7}$$

This estimate can be used to establish a confidence interval for the mean value. This approach is often referred to as the *batch-mean method*.

The difficulty with the batch-mean approach is in determining an acceptable value for m. The value for m should be large enough to include the queue buildup cycles. But since the length of these cycles is random, it is not possible to establish a value for m which is large enough to ensure independence of the mean values and small enough to make efficient use of the data. The usual procedure is to choose a value of m, obtain the batch means $\bar{x}_j$, and then test for correlation in these values.

The relative efficiency of the autocovariance method and the batch-mean method is dependent on the nature of the observations. The choice of m is a similar problem in both techniques.

We may apply these procedures for estimating variance to the checkout counter example of Chap. 2. Clearly that model is a queuing system and autocorrelation should be expected. However, the values used in our previous confidence-interval calculation for mean customer waiting time were mean values averaged over a 1-h simulation time period. Thus, we have already used the batch-mean method for estimating the variance. But it remains to be determined whether or not the choice of a 1-h interval is adequate.

The first five autocorrelation coefficients for the 10 values given in Sec. 3.2.3, which are each based on 1 h of simulated operation, are

$$r_1 = +.417$$

$$r_2 = -.274$$

$$r_3 = -.766$$

$$r_4 = -.485$$

$$r_5 = +.113$$

These values tend to indicate that the batch means are not independent. This also indicates that conditions at one point in the simulation may affect the waiting time results several hours in the future. In view of this, additional results should be obtained for this model.

When the checkout counter program is run for a simulated time period of 100 h, the results differ considerably from those obtained in the first 10 h. In particular, the mean value for customer waiting time after 100 h of operation is 108 s. This clearly indicates that the calculations of Sec. 3.2.3 are not applicable to the longer run and demonstrates the difficulty in detecting convergence of statistical quantities.

Observation of the additional results suggests that the values obtained in the first 10 h were influenced by the initial conditions used at the beginning of the simulation. That is, because the lines were empty at the start of the simulation but not at any later point, the first several hours gave a lower average waiting time. The presence of bias in answers because of nontypical initial conditions is a common occurrence in simulation problems. It can be eliminated by deleting data obtained in the early parts of a simulation run from the values used to compute overall averages. However, in the checkout counter simulation, this would not be an appropriate procedure.

The arrival rate used with the checkout counter model was based on a period of relatively rapid customer arrivals. Such a period would not normally follow several hours of similar activity. This means that to improve the accuracy of our results, the simulations should use variable initial conditions based on observed values and fixed run length, rather than merely extending the length of the run.

3.5.3 Spectrum and Spectral Density Functions

An alternate approach to studying covariance between events in a sequence is based on representing the time series as the sum of a number of sinusoidal waves of different frequency. This method uses the same information as is used to produce the autocovariance function but gives a different interpretation for the results. As we will see later, the usefulness of the different types of interpretations depends upon the nature of the time series, but in general, much is to be gained by using both methods of analysis.

Assume that we have N observations of a series $\{x_i\}$. Here we assume, for simplicity, that the observations are equally spaced in time and that N is even. We wish to represent this data as a Fourier series:

$$\hat{x}_i = \alpha_0 + \sum_{j=1}^{N/2} [\alpha_j \cos(i\omega_j) + \beta_j \sin(i\omega_j)] \tag{8}$$

where

$$\omega_j = 2\pi j/N$$

The best least-squares estimates for the coefficients α_j and β_j are given by

$$\alpha_0 = \frac{1}{N} \sum_{i=1}^{N} x_i = \bar{x}$$

$$\left. \begin{array}{l} \alpha_j = \dfrac{2}{N} \displaystyle\sum_{i=1}^{N} x_i \cos(i\omega_j) \\[2mm] \beta_j = \dfrac{2}{N} \displaystyle\sum_{i=1}^{N} x_i \sin(i\omega_j) \\[2mm] \alpha_{N/2} = \dfrac{1}{N} \displaystyle\sum_{i=1}^{N} (-1)^i X_i \end{array} \right\} \quad j = 1, 2, \ldots, (N/2 - 1) \tag{9}$$

$$\beta_{N/2} = 0$$

This procedure consists of approximating the time series by a weighted sum of sine and cosine waves having frequencies $f_j = j/N$. The lowest frequency $f_1 = 1/N$ has one cycle over the total period of the observations, and the highest frequency term $f_{N/2} = \frac{1}{2}$ has one-half cycle per time interval of the observations.

A simple example of approximating a series of six observations by a Fourier series is illustrated in Fig. 3.12. This figure includes the continuous curves for the sines and cosines used in the approximation and the resulting continuous version of the approximation $\hat{x}$.

Using the results from (9), we may compute the values of

$$I_j = \frac{2}{N} (\alpha_j^2 + \beta_j^2) \qquad j = 1, 2, \ldots, N/2 \tag{10}$$

which are referred to as the *intensity of the series* $\{x_i\}$ at frequency f_j. The plot of I_j as a function of j is called the *periodogram for the series* $\{x_i\}$.

If the frequencies used in the Fourier approximation included all possible values in the range $(f = 0, f = .5)$, i.e., if f varied continuously in this range, we could define a function

$$I(f) = \frac{2}{N} (\alpha_f^2 + \beta_f^2) \qquad 0 \le f \le \frac{1}{2} \tag{11}$$

which is called the *sample spectrum*. Like the periodogram, the sample spectrum would indicate the amplitude of a frequency component in a series but would not be limited to the frequencies which are related by integers to the length of the series of observations. To carry out this approximation would require continuous

For the series of observations

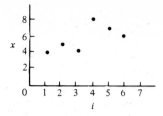

the approximation function

$$x_i = \alpha_0 + \sum_{j=1}^{3} (\alpha_j \cos (2\pi\, ij/6) + \beta_j \sin (2\pi\, ij/6))$$

uses the sinusoidal functions

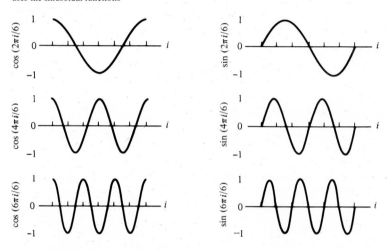

Using Eq. (9) gives the estimates

$$\alpha_0 = 5\tfrac{2}{3},\ \alpha_1 = \tfrac{1}{3},\ \alpha_2 = -\tfrac{2}{3},\ \alpha_3 = \tfrac{2}{3},$$
$$\beta_1 = -\sqrt{3},\ \beta_2 = 0,\ \beta_3 = 0$$

The corresponding continuous approximation function is

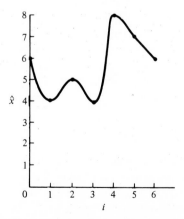

Figure 3.12 Approximating a discrete series by a Fourier series.

measurement of $X(t)$, which is not possible; but by using many sets of observations and carrying out the Fourier approximation for various frequencies, an estimate for $I(f)$ could be obtained from the mean value of these observations.

It may be shown that the sample spectrum and the estimates for the autocovariances are related by the equation

$$I(f) = 2\left[\hat{R}_0 + 2\sum_{k=1}^{n-1} \hat{R}_k \cos (2\pi f \cdot k)\right] \qquad 0 \le f \le \frac{1}{2} \qquad (12)$$

Thus the sample spectrum is the Fourier cosine transform of the estimated autocovariance function. Similarly, the power spectrum, defined by

$$P(f) = 2\left[R_0 + 2\sum_{k=1}^{\infty} R_k \cos (2\pi f \cdot k)\right] \qquad 0 \le f \le \frac{1}{2} \qquad (13)$$

is the Fourier cosine transform of the autocovariance function. $P(f)$ is often called the *spectrum of a series*, and this function contains information which is mathematically equivalent to the information contained in the autocovariance function and vice versa.

The spectral density function

$$g(f) = 2\left[1 + 2\sum_{k=1}^{\infty} r_k \cos (2\pi f \cdot k)\right] \qquad 0 \le f \le \frac{1}{2} \qquad (14)$$

is defined in terms of the autocorrelation function and is simply $P(f)/R_0$. Since $g(f)$ is positive for all f, and

$$\int_0^{1/2} g(f)\, df = 1$$

the spectral density function has the same properties as an ordinary probability density function.

The spectrum cannot be adequately estimated by direct use of Eq. (12). The variation of the sample spectrum about the theoretical spectrum is too large to give a reasonable approximation. This is due to the fact that the sample spectrum uses a frequency interval which is too small. This is analogous to using too small a group interval for a histogram when estimating an ordinary probability distribution. There are techniques for modifying the sample spectrum estimate [Eq. (12)] that do produce improved estimates for the spectrum. In addition, more convenient estimates for the spectrum can be obtained by using an autoregressive model for the time series, or by use of special Fourier transform algorithms.

3.5.4 Interpretation of Autocorrelation and Spectral Density Functions

The autocorrelation and spectral density functions are useful in analyzing the output of simulations. In many cases, a primary objective of a simulation is to provide insight into the operation of a system, and properly interpreted, these functions may be used for this purpose.

To illustrate the nature of these functions, we will use the two time series models given by Eq. (1) and (2) and a third model given by:

$$X_i = 100 + e_i - 5 \cos\left(2\pi \frac{i}{5}\right) \tag{15}$$

This model is assumed to represent the same situation as do the first two models. Again e_i represents variations due to equipment performance, but now the variations in worker efficiency are represented by the term $-5 \cos(2\pi i/5)$. Points of this function are plotted in Fig. 3.13 and may be interpreted to represent variations in worker efficiency as a function of the day in a week. If we assume that $i = 1, 6, 11, 16, \ldots$ corresponds to a Monday, $i = 2, 7, 12, 17, \ldots$ to Tuesday, etc., then we are assuming that worker performance varies periodically, with a period of 1 week.

For the first two models, the spectral density function can be readily obtained by using Eq. (14). For the third model, the autocovariances are given by

$$R_k = E[(x_i - \bar{x})(x_{i+k} - \bar{x})] \qquad k = 1, 2, \ldots$$

$$= 25E\left[\cos\frac{2\pi i}{5} \cos\frac{2\pi(i + k)}{5}\right]$$

In this case, the autocorrelation function is an oscillating function and does not go to 0 as k increases. The spectral density function for the third model is not readily available in a closed form but can be approximated and tends toward an impulse function at $f = .2$, which is 1 divided by the period of the variations in worker efficiency, and an impulse at $f = 0$.

These results for the autocorrelation function and spectral density function for each of the three models are shown in Fig. 3.14.

Output results from a simulation can be used to construct estimates for the autocorrelation and spectral density functions. The autocorrelation function can then be used to estimate how some event in a simulation will influence future output values. The spectral density function may be used to identify cyclic behavior in the simulated system.

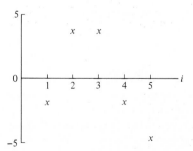

Figure 3.13 Points on the function: $-5 \cos(2\pi i/5)$

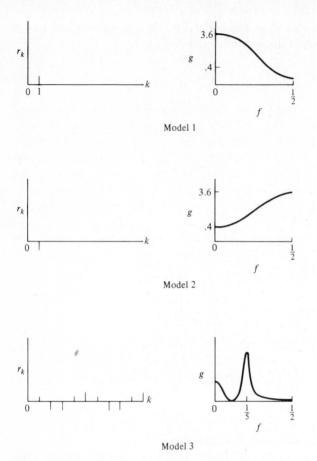

Model 1

Model 2

Model 3

Figure 3.14 Examples of autocorrelation and spectral density functions.

3.6 REGENERATIVE STATE METHOD

In the previous section, we saw that the existence of statistical dependence between observations on successive entities in a simulation leads to complications in the analysis of these variables. The use of regenerative states is a recently developed approach which avoids the necessity of time series analysis.

The basic concept of this approach can be illustrated by considering a simple queuing system. In Fig. 3.11, the waiting times and corresponding queue lengths at arrival for several entities to a single-server queuing system are shown. This figure was used to illustrate the dependence between these values for successive entities. The basic behavior of the queue length variable L_q is that it tends to build up from a 0 value and at some later time returns back to the 0 value. The length of time between the zero values is random as is the manner in which the variable fluctuates during this period. However, if we consider the situation at the zero value points, i.e., when the system is empty and idle, there the future behavior of L_q is affected by the fact that the system is in the idle state, but it is not affected by how the system reached the idle state. Thus, the behavior of the system as it goes from an idle state and then eventually returns to the idle state is not dependent on the previous sequences of this type. These sequences are referred to as *tours, cycles,* or *epochs*; and observations made on separate sequences are statistically independent and come from a common distribution.

To show how the characteristics of a queuing system can be estimated using measures over an epoch, we will consider a single-server queuing system. Let t_{ij} denote the length of time during which the system contained i entities or customers, measured in epoch j. We will refer to this as the time in which the system was in state i during epoch j. Then the total length of time for epoch j is

$$p_j = \sum_{i=0}^{\infty} t_{ij}$$

and the total length of time the server is busy during this epoch is

$$b_j = \sum_{i=1}^{\infty} t_{ij}$$

The measure

$$l_j = \sum_{i=0}^{\infty} it_{ij}$$

is the time-integrated value of the queue length during epoch j, and

$$w_j = \sum_{i=2}^{\infty} (i-1)t_{ij}$$

is the total time spent waiting by all the customers during epoch j. Figure 3.15 illustrates an example of one epoch for a single-server queuing system.

Using these measurements and that of n_j, the number of customers processed during an epoch, we may estimate several of the queuing system parameters. For example, after a total of J epochs, the server utilization estimate is

$$\hat{\rho} = \left(\sum_{j=1}^{J} b_j \right) \bigg/ \left(\sum_{j=1}^{J} p_j \right) \tag{1}$$

The mean queue length estimate is

$$\hat{L}_q = \left(\sum_{j=1}^{J} l_j \right) \bigg/ \left(\sum_{j=1}^{J} p_j \right) \tag{2}$$

and the average waiting time is estimated by

$$\hat{T}_w = \left(\sum_{j=1}^{J} w_j \right) \bigg/ \left(\sum_{j=1}^{J} n_j \right) \tag{3}$$

The advantage of this technique is that the measurements made in separate epochs may reasonably be assumed to be independent samples from common distributions. Thus, the methods of classical statistical analysis can be used for

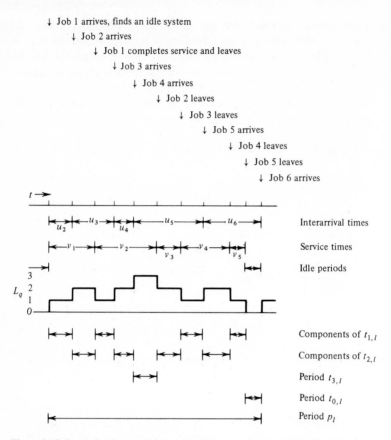

↓ Job 1 arrives, finds an idle system
↓ Job 2 arrives
↓ Job 1 completes service and leaves
↓ Job 3 arrives
↓ Job 4 arrives
↓ Job 2 leaves
↓ Job 3 leaves
↓ Job 5 arrives
↓ Job 4 leaves
↓ Job 5 leaves
↓ Job 6 arrives

Figure 3.15 Example of one epoch in a single-server queuing system.

deriving estimators and drawing inferences. In general, the underlying distributions from which the samples are drawn are not normal. For example, we would expect the period of the epochs p_j to have a relatively large number of short values, corresponding to those cases where successive jobs arrive to find an idle system.

Equations (1), (2), and (3) are ratio estimators; and although we are assuming that the sequences of measurements $\{p_j\}$, $\{b_j\}$, $\{l_j\}$, and $\{n_j\}$ will not be auto-correlated, they do exhibit correlation between sequences. Because of this, these estimators are biased. However, unbiased estimators can be developed and analyzed using statistical theory. For example, in the case of estimating mean waiting time, the following results have been developed.

Let

$$\bar{n} = \frac{1}{J} \sum_{j=1}^{J} n_j$$

$$\bar{w} = \frac{1}{J} \sum_{j=1}^{J} w_j$$

then calculate the covariance terms,

$$S_{ww} = \frac{1}{J-1} \sum_{j=1}^{J} (w_j - \bar{w})^2$$

$$S_{wn} = \frac{1}{J-1} \sum_{j=1}^{J} (w_j - \bar{w})(n_j - \bar{n})$$

$$S_{nn} = \frac{1}{J-1} \sum_{j=1}^{J} (n_j - \bar{n})^2$$

The estimate for mean waiting time

$$\hat{T}_w = \bar{w}/\bar{n}$$

is biased, but the estimate

$$\tilde{T}_w = \hat{T}_w \left[1 + \left(\frac{S_{wn}}{\bar{w}\bar{n}} - \frac{S_{nn}}{\bar{n}^2} \right) \bigg/ J \right]$$

is unbiased. Also, an estimate for the variance of $\hat{T}_w$ is given by

$$\text{var} \, (\hat{T}_w) = \hat{T}_w^2 \left(\frac{S_{ww}}{\bar{w}^2} - 2 \frac{S_{wn}}{\bar{w}\bar{n}} + \frac{S_{nn}}{\bar{n}^2} \right) \bigg/ J$$

Moreover,

$$\text{Prob} \, [\hat{T}_w(B - C) < T_w < \hat{T}_w(B + C)] = 1 - \alpha$$

where

$$B = \frac{J - (t_{(1-\alpha/2),\infty})^2 \dfrac{S_{wn}}{\bar{w}\bar{n}}}{J - (t_{(1-\alpha/2),\infty})^2 \dfrac{S_{nn}}{\bar{n}^2}} \qquad C^2 = B^2 - \frac{J - (t_{(1-\alpha/2),\infty})^2 \dfrac{S_{ww}}{\bar{w}^2}}{J - (t_{(1-\alpha/2),\infty})^2 \dfrac{S_{nn}}{\bar{n}^2}}$$

Thus we can compute a confidence interval for the mean waiting time.

A very desirable aspect of this approach is that the simulations start and stop with the same state conditions. When a specified time period or a fixed number of job completions are used to determine the length of a simulation, biases are introduced because of different final state conditions. The regenerative state approach eliminates both initial and final state bias.

This technique is appropriate for standard-type queuing systems, and most applications to date have centered on these problems. However, the technique is not limited to only these systems. The principal assumption required for this method is that the behavior of a system in a period between leaving one specified state and return to that state is independent of its behavior in similar periods. Thus in a simulation, any system state which periodically recurs and for which future system behavior is independent of prior behavior can be used as the regenerative state. That is, any regenerative state may replace the idle state used in the above discussion.

The primary advantage of this method, as compared with the time series approach, is that the statistical analyses of the estimates obtained from the data are theoretically justified. This is not the case when, for example, using batch means or autocorrelation estimates to determine variances of time series data.

3.7 BACKGROUND AND REFERENCES

The topics introduced in this chapter are the subjects of a very large body of literature. There are many books and professional journals devoted to these fields of study. The references included at the end of this chapter are not intended to cover these subjects but should give the interested reader a starting point for further study.

References [10], [12], and [19] are textbooks which are often used in introductory courses on probability and statistics. The book by Guttman, Wilks, and Hunter is at a somewhat less advanced mathematical level than the other two and is oriented toward applications of statistics. The book by Mood, Graybill, and Boes includes more material on applications than that by Hogg and Craig.

The book by Johnson and Leone [15] provides more extensive material on application techniques than the introductory texts, and gives more interpretation as to the physical basis for certain statistical distributions. The four-volume series by Johnson and Kotz [14] is devoted to discussing the properties and uses of statistical distributions. These are not introductory-level books, but they can be very valuable in developing a more intuitive understanding of the basis for many distribution functions.

Knuth's book [18] is the most extensive single reference on the subject of generating and testing pseudorandom numbers. More recent articles and references in this area can be found in the various publications of the Association for Computing Machinery.

Cox and Smith [2] give a brief, concise survey of queuing theory including applications. A more recent and extensive coverage of the topic is provided by the books by Kleinrock [17].

A good introduction to time series analysis is the book by Kendall [16]. More detailed presentations of techniques in this area are covered by Box and Jenkins [1] and Jenkins and Watts [13].

References [3], [4], [6], and [7] introduce the statistical analysis of estimators using regenerative state measurements. These references present results primarily for general input, general service time, and multiple-server queuing systems and include several example applications. The basic concepts of this approach are discussed in sec. 10.16 of the textbook by Fishman [8], and a monograph devoted to this topic has recently been published [5].

REFERENCES

1. Box, G. E. P., and G. M. Jenkins: "Time Series Analysis Forecasting and Control," rev. ed., Holden-Day, Inc., Publisher, San Francisco, 1976.
2. Cox, D. R., and W. L. Smith: "Queues," Wiley, New York, 1961.

3. Crane, M. A., and D. I. Iglehart: Simulating Stable Stochastic Systems, I: General Multiserver Queues, *Journal of the ACM*, vol. 21, no. 1, pp. 103–113, January 1974.
4. Crane, M. A., and D. I. Iglehart, Simulating Stable Stochastic Systems, II: Markov Chains, *Journal of the ACM*, vol. 21, no. 1, pp. 114–123, January 1974.
5. Crane, M. A., and A. J. Lemoine, "An Introduction to the Regenerative Method for Simulation Analysis," Springer-Verlag, New York, 1977.
6. Fishman, G. S.: Statistical Analysis for Queueing Simulations, *Management Science*, vol. 20, no. 3, pp. 363–369, November 1973.
7. Fishman, G. S.: Estimation in Multiserver Queueing Simulation, *Operations Research*, vol. 22, no. 1, pp. 72–78, January–February 1974.
8. Fishman, G. S.: "Concepts and Methods in Discrete Event Digital Simulation," Wiley, New York, 1973.
9. Gordon, G.: "System Simulation," Prentice-Hall, Englewood Cliffs, N.J., 1969.
10. Guttman, I., S. S. Wilks, and J. S. Hunter: "Introductory Engineering Statistics," 2d ed., Wiley, New York, 1971.
11. Hahn, G. J.: Probability and Statistics, in H. Chestnut, "Systems Engineering Tools," Chap. 6, Wiley, New York, 1965.
12. Hogg, R. V., and A. T. Craig: "Introduction to Mathematical Statistics," 3d ed., Macmillan, Toronto, 1970.
13. Jenkins, G. M., and D. G. Watts: "Spectral Analysis and Its Application," Holden-Day, Inc., Publishers, San Francisco, 1968.
14. Johnson, N. L., and S. Kotz: "Distribution in Statistics," Series in Applied Probability and Statistics, four volumes, Wiley, New York, 1969–1972.
15. Johnson, N. L., and F. C. Leone: "Statistics and Experimental Design in Engineering and the Physical Sciences," 2d ed., vols. I and II, Wiley, New York, 1977.
16. Kendall, M. G.: "Time-Series," Griffin, London, 1973.
17. Kleinrock, L.: "Queuing Systems," vols. 1 and 2, Wiley, New York, 1975–1976.
18. Knuth, D. E.: "The Art of Computer Programming, vol. 2: Semi-numerical Algorithms," Addison-Wesley, Reading, Mass., 1969.
19. Mood, A. M., F. A. Graybill, and W. C. Boes: "Introduction to the Theory of Statistics," 3d ed., McGraw-Hill, New York, 1974.

EXERCISES

3.1 If a hunter can hit a bear with a probability of .6 for each shot, and the probability that any hit will kill a bear is .7, how many bullets should the hunter carry in order to have 99 percent confidence that he will kill a bear given enough opportunities?

3.2 Find the expected value, variance, and standard deviation of the following distribution:

x_i	1	3	4	5
f_i	.4	.1	.2	.3

3.3 Let x be a continuous random variable with probability density function

$$f(x) = \begin{cases} x/k & 0 \leq x \leq 3 \\ 0 & \text{elsewhere} \end{cases}$$

What is the probability that x will be greater than 2?

3.4 Determine the expected number of boys in a family with six children, assuming girls and boys are equally likely. What is the probability that the expected number of boys does occur?

3.5 Suppose the weights of 1000 students are normally distributed with mean of 140 lb and standard deviation of 20 lb. How many students weigh

(*a*) Between 120 and 140 lb?

(*b*) Over 180 lb?

3.6 Suppose 500 misprints are distributed randomly throughout a 300-page book. Find the probability that a given page contains

    (*a*) No misprints

    (*b*) Three or more misprints

3.7 Consider the data given in Table 3.1. Assume these values are from normally distributed populations having the same variance. Can we reject, at the 1 percent significance level, the hypothesis that the use of a 45-s delay, rather than a 5-s delay, results in a higher average customer waiting time?

3.8 Assume that in a simulation experiment we are trying to find the parameter value X that gives a maximum value for an output variable Z. If the following results are obtained:

X	$\bar{Z}$	S_z^2	n
20	50.83	.47	30
30	51.78	.58	20

where S_z^2 is the estimated variance of Z. Can we say that $X = 30$ is a better choice than $X = 20$ with a confidence level of 95 percent, or do we need more simulation runs?

3.9 Assume that 30 values of some variable x have been obtained from a simulation. These values appear to be approximately normally distributed and have an average value of 13.85 and a standard deviation of 4.43. If we wish to determine the correct value of x to within an accuracy of 1.00 at a 90 percent confidence level, how many more values of x need to be generated in the simulation?

3.10 Generate 1000 uniformly distributed random numbers using the GENRND procedure of Chap. 2 and the initial seed value of

    (*a*) 1956987325

    (*b*) 1156987325

    (*c*)   990496323

    For each sequence, test for uniformity and independence, by using the chi-square goodness-of-fit test and by testing the first 10 autocovariances.

3.11 Customers arrive at a service facility with a Poisson-distributed arrival rate with a mean value of 45 per hour. The service time is exponentially distributed with a mean of 1 min.

    (*a*) What is the average value and the variance of the time a customer is at this facility?

    (*b*) What is the average value and the variance of the number of customers at this facility?

    (*c*) Ninety percent of the customers at this facility will receive service after waiting less than how long?

3.12 Consider a single-server queuing system where arrivals are Poisson distributed with an average of 20 arrivals per minute. The distribution of service times in this system is given by the following histogram:

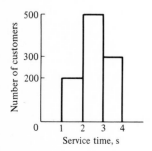

What is the mean waiting time for customers in this system?

3.13 Assume that during a particular hour of the week, a reservation center receives, on the average, 120 telephone calls. The average length of the conversations is 1 min. Assume that calls, interarrival times, and conversations lengths are exponentially distributed.

(a) If there are four operators on duty, what percentage of callers must wait more than 10 s for an operator?

(b) What percentage of the time are the operators busy?

3.14 Assume that last week the average number of jobs printed out at a computer center during a typical hour was 100 and that the average time required to print a job was 35 s. Assuming the jobs arrive at the printer queue with a Poisson distribution and that the print times are exponentially distributed, how long did the jobs wait to be printed out? What would the average waiting time have been if a second, similar speed, printer had been used in parallel with the present one?

3.15 Assume that a computer processes three types of jobs, A, B, and C. Priority without interrupt is used, with type A highest priority and type C lowest. The interarrival times for each type job are exponentially distributed with mean values of 5 s, 30 s, and 2 min for types A, B, and C, respectively. The process time required by the jobs are Type A = constant time of 2 s, Type B = exponential distribution of time with mean of 6 s, Type C = Erlang-3 distribution with mean time of 24 s

(a) What is the average waiting time for all jobs?

(b) What is the average waiting time for jobs of each type?

3.16 Consider the following models for a process:

(a) $x_t = \frac{1}{2}x_{t-1} + e_t$

(b) $x_t = \frac{3}{4}x_{t-1} - \frac{1}{2}x_{t-2} + e_t$

(c) $x_t = e_t - \frac{3}{2}e_{t-1} - \frac{1}{4}e_{t-2}$

(d) $x_t = \frac{1}{2}x_{t-1} + e_t - \frac{1}{2}e_{t-1}$

where e_t is a normally distributed random variable with mean of 0 and variance of 1.

Generate a time series for each of these models and plot 50 points. Use a table look-up and interpolating procedure to generate the random values for e_t.

3.17 For the models of Exercise 3.16, use the batch-mean method to estimate the variance of x. Try several lengths, and check to see if the variance converges to one value for each model. Note that the variance of the means is equal to the variance of x divided by the number of observations used to compute the means.

FOUR

PROGRAMMING TECHNIQUES

The computer program for every simulation study will be different. But there are many procedures which are common to large classes of models. Because of this it is possible to provide software tools to assist in preparing computer simulation programs.

There are two common forms for these software tools: (1) a library of computer routines which can be either incorporated into a simulation program or used to generate parts of a computer program or (2) computer languages which have a vocabulary and a syntax that can be used to describe models and simulation procedures.

Simulation languages offer significant advantages in terms of reducing the time and effort required to program a problem. This advantage is available, of course, only after learning the language. There is also an advantage in using the model structures which are built into these languages. This structure can help in formulating the model by having certain operations or processes built into the language vocabulary. This is also an advantage in communicating a model to others since the model description is much simpler than it would be in a general-purpose computer language.

The advantages of simulation languages are obtained at the expense of flexibility in programming and efficiency of execution of the program. Usually the most important disadvantage of these languages is that the built-in model structure can tend to restrict the direction of model development.

The most frequently used simulation languages, at the present time, are GPSS and SIMSCRIPT. These languages can be used to simulate almost any discrete-event model, but they are better suited to certain types of problems than to others. The relationship between them is that GPSS is more easily programmed for problems to which it is well suited than is SIMSCRIPT, and SIMSCRIPT is more easily applied to a wider range of problems than is GPSS. In general, the more specialized a language is, the more convenient it can be. Because of this relationship, a large number of simulation languages have been developed and many are specialized to particular types of problems.

In this chapter a number of software tools for simulation programming will be developed as library routines. These routines will not be as extensive as many others which are available and are not as convenient to use as are many simulation languages. But they do illustrate the basic operations common to programming simulations and should provide an understanding of the fundamental operations which are built into simulation languages.

4.1 GENERAL ROUTINES

The requirements of a computer program for carrying out discrete-event simulations can be divided into three main tasks. The first task is to represent a model and initialize it. This representation includes some set of variables which corresponds to the system state and a set of event routines which represents the activities that result in changes to the system state. The second main task is to control the cycle of actions required to simulate the system dynamics. This control program can be a general routine, but it should be based on some particular simulation algorithm. The third task is the generation of an output report which presents the results of the simulation. This report usually requires collection of statistics and often makes use of some data analysis routines.

In this section, several program procedures will be presented which can be used in the simulation program for almost any discrete-event model. In following sections, the use and extension of these procedures will be illustrated by considering a number of example simulation problems.

4.1.1 Linked Lists

The system state is a set of data elements that provides characteristics of the objects in a model and of the relationships among these objects. The event routines involve some changes or manipulations of this state. A computer program for simulation must include some realization of these features. In this section, we will consider a method for accomplishing this which is an alternative to the simple arrays used with the checkout counter example.

To introduce the idea of linked lists, we will consider the SCHEDUL array used in the checkout counter example. Assume that there is a second array, called

LINK, and that for every entry in SCHEDUL, there is an associated entry in LINK. A possible set of data for these arrays might be

SCHEDUL(*,1)	1452	2	LINK(1)	4
SCHEDUL(*,2)	1401	4	LINK(2)	6
(*,3)	1463	2	(3)	0
(*,4)	1462	2	(4)	3
(*,5)	1399	1	(5)	2
(*,6)	1447	2	(6)	1
(*,7)	0	0	(7)	—

with a variable named HEAD equal to 5. This version of SCHEDUL contains the same data as is shown in Fig. 2.3, but the sequence of the values is different. Even though the physical sequence in this array is different, the logical sequence is the same as that of Fig. 2.3 since the number stored in LINK (I) represents the index of the next entry in the schedule. The variable HEAD points to the first element in the logical sequence of the schedule list which is index 5 where TIME = 1399. The next logical element is given by LINK(5), which points to index 2 where the value of TIME = 1401. In this manner, the elements of the schedule can be obtained in their logical order with the last element indicated by an associated link value of 0.

An advantage of this type of data structure is that if a new event is to be added to the schedule, it can be inserted by changing one link value and it is not necessary to move any elements in the SCHEDUL array.

To illustrate this difference, assume that the event scheduled to occur at TIME = 1399, a customer arrival, is executed and results in a new customer arrival event scheduled to occur at TIME = 1409. Using the version of the SCHED procedure listed in Fig. 2.4, this operation would require, first, removing the event scheduled for TIME = 1399 from the SCHEDUL array and moving the other five events up one position in the array and then, second, inserting the new event into the second position in the array and moving the four events scheduled to occur later down one position. But if a procedure was available which used linked lists, the only changes necessary to the structure shown above would be, first, the value of HEAD would be changed to 2 and, second, the new event would be placed in the fifth position with the corresponding link value of 6 and the value of LINK(2) changed to 5. That is, the data array shown above would be changed to be

SCHEDUL(*,1)	1452	2	LINK(1)	4
SCHEDUL(*,2)	1401	4	(2)	5
(*,3)	1463	2	(3)	0
(*,4)	1462	2	(4)	3
(*,5)	1409	1	(5)	6
(*,6)	1447	2	(6)	1
(*,7)	0	0	(7)	—
HEAD = 2				

Thus, by using the linked-list technique a number of data moves are avoided.

The use of linked lists requires extra storage space for the link information and added operations to update this information. But for any large list, the savings in data movements make linked lists more efficient than reordering arrays. This advantage increases with the size of the list.

An example of a procedure using a linked-list version of the schedule is shown in Fig. 4.1. This procedure performs the same function as that of Fig. 2.4, but the SCHEDUL array has been changed to a PL/I record structure with the link variable included. In order to know what positions in the structure are available for storing data, the variable AVAILABLE is set equal to the index of the first element in the structure not being used. The lists of these available elements are linked in a similar manner, as are the elements used in the list of future events.

It is necessary to initialize this SCHEDUL record prior to the first call to SCHED. This can be accomplished by the following statements:

```
HEAD = 0;   AVAILABLE = 1;
DO I = 1 TO 49;   SC_LINK(I) = I + 1;
END;      SC_LINK(50) = 0;
```

The record structure used for SCHEDUL provides space for a data matrix of 50 rows and 3 columns. The columns can be referred to by name, i.e., SC_TIME, SC_TYPE, or SC_LINK; and these names can be used with subscripts to denote the row. An advantage of the record structure is that the type of data can be different in each column. For example, SC_TIME could be declared as a floating-point variable if desired.

The operation carried out by statements 10 to 13 of the procedure in Fig. 4.1 is to place a new event in the first available storage space. Statement 14 checks to see if the list is empty or if the time required for the new event is less than that for the event at the head of the list. If so, the new event becomes the new head of the list; if not, the list is searched in logical order until the proper position for the new event is found. At this point, the link for the preceding element IS is set to the index of the new event JS, and the link for the new event is set to the index of the former successor to IS, which is KS.

To remove the next event from the schedule, the element with index HEAD provides the time and type information, and its link value becomes the new HEAD value. This element then becomes the first element of the list of available spaces.

The procedure of Fig. 4.1 does eliminate the data movements of the previous version, but it increases the storage requirements of the structure SCHEDUL. It is usually possible to reduce the storage requirements for data lists by making use of the "based storage" features of PL/I. This feature enables the programmer to use only the amount of storage needed at any particular time rather than maintaining a constant-sized space throughout the entire execution period.

To introduce the concept of based storage, we will briefly review the storage allocation procedure of PL/I. Program variables actually represent locations in

```
                SCHED: PROCEDURE(LS,MS);     /*SCHEDULE EVENT TYPE MS AT TIME LS*/


STMT LEVEL NEST
   1                      SCHED: PROCEDURE(LS,MS);     /*SCHEDULE EVENT TYPE MS AT TIME LS*/
   2      1                 DCL   1 SCHEDUL(5C)   EXTERNAL,
                                    2 SC_TIME   FIXED BINARY(31),
                                    2 SC_TYPE   FIXED BINARY(31),
                                    2 SC_LINK   FIXED BINARY(31);
   3      1                 DCL (HEAD, AVAILAB)   EXTERNAL FIXED BINARY(31);
   4      1                 DCL (LS, MS, IS, JS, KS) FIXED BINARY(31);
   5      1                 IF AVAILAB   = 0 THEN DO;   /*NO SPACE AVAILABLE*/
   7      1    1              PUT LIST('SCHEDULE FULL');   END;
   9      1                 ELSE DO;   /*STORE NEW EVENT*/
  10      1    1              JS = AVAILAB ;     AVAILAB   = SC_LINK(JS);
  12      1    1              SC_TIME(JS) = LS;    SC_TYPE(JS) = MS;
  14      1    1              IF (HEAD = 0 | LS<SC_TIME(HEAD) )
  15      1    1                THEN DO;   /*PUT NEW EVENT AT HEAD OF LIST*/
  16      1    2                  SC_LINK(JS) = HEAD;    HEAD = JS;    END;
  19      1    1                ELSE DO;   /* FIND PLACE OF NEW EVENT */
  20      1    2                  IS = HEAD;    KS = SC_LINK(HEAD);
  22      1    2                  DO WHILE(KS¬=C & LS>SC_TIME(KS));
  23      1    3                    IS = KS;    KS = SC_LINK(IS);    END;
  26      1    2                  SC_LINK(IS) = JS;    SC_LINK(JS) = KS;    END;
  29      1    1                END;
  30      1                 RETURN;
  31      1                 EVENT: ENTRY(LS,MS);   /*GET NEXT SCHEDULED EVENT*/
  32      1                 LS = SC_TIME(HEAD);    MS = SC_TYPE(HEAD);
  34      1                 /* RESET THE LINKS*/   IS = HEAD;    HEAD = SC_LINK(IS);
  36      1                 SC_LINK(IS) = AVAILAB ;    AVAILAB   = IS;    RETURN;
  39      1                 END SCHED;
```

Figure 4.1 Example of using a linked list.

main storage where the data values are recorded. When a location in main storage has been associated with a variable name, the storage is said to be *allocated*. The storage class of a variable determines the manner in which main storage is allocated.

Unless declared to have another storage class, all variables will be of the AUTOMATIC class, i.e., the default attribute for storage class. For variables of this class, storage is allocated during the execution of the procedures in which the variable appears. The storage remains allocated as long as the procedure remains active but is released when the procedure becomes inactive. For example, all the variables of the MAIN procedure (FIRST) of Fig. 2.2 are allocated storage space at the start of execution of the program. When the procedure SCHED is called (statement 15), then space is allocated for the variables unique to SCHED; e.g., space will be allocated for the array JS. After the return from SCHED, the space in main storage used for JS is freed and becomes available for other uses. During the execution of the SCHED procedure, the space allocated to TIME, TYPE, etc., is not freed, since FIRST is the calling procedure and remains active. This means that all variables declared in the MAIN procedure will be allocated throughout the program execution, and if they have the EXTERNAL attribute, they are available to any other procedure.

There are times when the dynamic storage allocation of AUTOMATIC variables is not convenient. Such a case is the variable array FNC of the GENARIV procedure shown in Fig. 2.6. If FNC were AUTOMATIC, the values stored there initially would be lost after the completion of the first call to GENARIV. Because of this, FNC was declared to have the STATIC storage class. For variables of this class, storage is allocated before execution of the program and remains allocated throughout the entire execution of the program.

The BASED storage class gives the programmer a greater degree of control over the allocation of storage that is available with AUTOMATIC or STATIC variables. Storage for a BASED variable can be allocated by the ALLOCATE statement and freed by the FREE statement.

With based storage, the address of the storage space associated with a variable is contained in a pointer variable. A *pointer variable* is a special type of variable which can be used to locate data in storage, that is, to "point" to data in storage. Thus, a pointer variable can be thought of as an address.

Figure 4.2 is a listing of a procedure which uses based storage and pointer variables in the SCHED procedure. The structure SCHEDUL is declared to have based storage with its address determined by the contents of the pointer variable JS. Note that in this version SCHEDUL is not given a subscript. Also note that HEAD, SC_LINK, IS, JS, and KS are declared to be pointer variables.

Execution of the allocate statement (statement 6) causes some available space in main storage to be allocated to a data item with the structure of SCHEDUL and the address of this space is placed in the pointer JS. The assignment statement

$$JS \rightarrow SC\_TIME = LS;$$

can be interpreted to mean: place the contents of the variable LS into the SC_TIME item of the SCHEDUL structure pointed to by the variable JS. Since SCHEDUL is declared as based on the variable JS, the use of JS as the pointer is not necessary; i.e., SC_TIME = LS; would also accomplish the same operation. However, other pointer variables must be included; e.g., IS→ could not be omitted in statement 21.

NULL is a PL/I built-in function which returns a special pointer value that points nowhere. This value is not zero but rather is a unique value that can be

```
          SCHED: PROCEDURE(LS,MS);    /*SCHEDULE EVENT TYPE MS AT TIME LS*/

STMT LEVEL NEST
  1                         SCHED: PROCEDURE(LS,MS);    /*SCHEDULE EVENT TYPE MS AT TIME LS*/
  2      1                  DCL  1 SCHEDUL      BASED(JS),
                                 2 SC_TIME    FIXED BINARY(31),
                                 2 SC_TYPE    FIXED BINARY(31),
                                 2 SC_LINK    POINTER;
  3      1                  DCL HEAD EXTERNAL POINTER;    DCL (LS,MS) FIXED BINARY(31);
  5      1                  DCL (IS,JS,KS) POINTER;
  6      1                  ALLOCATE SCHEDUL;    /*PROVIDE SPACE FOR NEW EVENT AT JS*/
  7      1                  JS->SC_TIME = LS;    JS->SC_TYPE = MS;
  9      1                  IF (HEAD = NULL | LS<HEAD->SC_TIME)
 10      1                     THEN DO;   /*PUT NEW EVENT AT HEAD OF LIST*/
 11      1     1                JS->SC_LINK = HEAD;    HEAD = JS;    END;
 14      1                     ELSE DO;   /*FIND PLACE OF NEW EVENT*/
 15      1     1                IS = HEAD;    KS = HEAD->SC_LINK;
 17      1     1                DO WHILE (KS ¬= NULL & LS > KS->SC_TIME);
 18      1     2                  IS = KS;    KS = IS->SC_LINK;    END;
 21      1     1                IS->SC_LINK = JS;    JS->SC_LINK = KS;    END;
 24      1                  RETURN;
 25      1                  EVENT: ENTRY(LS,MS);    /*GET NEXT SCHEDULED EVENT*/
 26      1                  LS = HEAD->SC_TIME;    MS = HEAD->SC_TYPE;    IS = HEAD;
 29      1                  HEAD = IS->SC_LINK;    FREE IS->SCHEDUL;
 31      1                  RETURN;
 32      1                  END SCHED;
```

Figure 4.2 The example using pointers.

```
        INITLST:   PROCEDURE(NAME,ORDER,INDEX);   /*ROUTINE TO INITIALIZE LIST*/


STMT LEVEL NEST
  1                    INITLST:   PROCEDURE(NAME,ORDER,INDEX);    /*ROUTINE TO INITIALIZE LIST*/
  2      1             DCL  1 FOR_EACH_LIST   BASED(PN),
                         2 FIRST           POINTER,
                         2 LAST            POINTER,
                         2 ACCESS          CHARACTER(4),
                         2 PRIO_INDEX      FIXED BINARY(15);
  3      1             DCL  1 LIST_CONTENTS  BASED(PD),
                         2 ITEM(5)         FLOAT,
                         2 NEXT_ELEMENT POINTER;
  4      1             DCL NAME POINTER,INDEX FIXED BINARY(15), ORDER CHAR(4);
  5      1                ALLOCATE FOR_EACH_LIST;   /*ALLOCATE SPACE FOR LIST INFORMATION*/
  6      1                NAME = PN;    ACCESS = ORDER;   PRIO_INDEX = INDEX;
  9      1                FIRST = NULL;    LAST = NULL;
 11      1                RETURN;
 12      1             FREELST: ENTRY(NAME);   /*ROUTINE TO DELETE A LIST*/
 13      1                DCL PX POINTER;
 14      1                PD = NAME->FIRST;
 15      1                DO WHILE (PD ¬= NULL);
 16      1     1            PX = PD->NEXT_ELEMENT;
 17      1     1            FREE LIST_CONTENTS;   PD = PX;    END;
 20      1                PN = NAME;   FREE FOR_EACH_LIST;
 22      1                RETURN;
 23      1             END INITLST;
```

Figure 4.3 Procedure to initialize lists.

tested. Note that this version of SCHED requires that the external pointer variable HEAD be initialized to equal NULL.

The form of the procedure of Fig. 4.2 is similar to that of Fig. 4.1 but with pointer operations replacing subscript operations. The advantage of the based storage version is that space in main storage will be used for a copy of the SCHEDUL structure for each future event that is on the schedule at any point in simulated time and that the storage used for each event will be freed when that event occurs.

The procedure of Fig. 4.2 is a typical file-manipulation routine. It maintains a list or file of entries with a particular ordering and provides for adding to and deleting from this file. This type of operation is a common requirement in simulation programs, not only for the event-scheduling file but also for handling elements of the system-state description. For example, the CUSTOME array of the checkout counter simulation program could have used a very similar procedure to add and delete elements in the present customer file.

Lists are a very effective method for handling manipulations of system state representations, and a generalized version of these operations can be a convenient tool in developing simulation programs. A set of routines which can be used for this purpose is shown in Figs. 4.3 to 4.6.

The procedure of Fig. 4.3 is used to initialize a list. Each call to this procedure will allocate space for four data elements which characterize a particular list. These elements consist of a pointer to the first element of the list, a pointer to the last element of the list, a string of four characters which denote the type of ordering in the list, and the index of the data item used for the ordering. The following statement

CALL INITLST(LINE_3,'PRIO',K)

will initialize a list where the ordering of elements will be based on the value of the Kth data element, low value first. The data characterizing this list will be pointed to by the variable LINE_3 which can be considered to be the name of the list. In this procedure, the data elements of the list will consist of five floating-point data items and a pointer to the next element of the list.

To insert an element into lists of this type, the procedure of Fig. 4.4 may be used. Note that there are two special cases for the access method. If the access character string is FIFO, then the list is a queue and the new element is placed at the bottom of the list; while if it is LIFO, then the list is a stack and the new element is placed at the top. For these cases, the PRIO_INDEX value is not used.

The procedure of Fig. 4.5 provides a means for removing an element from a list. The three entry points enable the removal of the top element, the bottom element, or a specific element for which a pointer is provided. The pointer required for the last type of deletion can be obtained by using the procedure FINDELE, shown in Fig. 4.6. FINDELE makes it possible to find an element in the list which has a particular value for a data item (to within .01 percent tolerance), a value greater or less than some specified value, or the element which has the largest or smallest value for a particular item. The use of these procedures will be illustrated in example simulation programs later in this chapter.

```
          ADDTO: PROCEDURE(NAME,DATA);    /*ADD ELEMENT TO LIST*/

STMT LEVEL NEST
  1                    ADDTO: PROCEDURE(NAME,DATA);    /*ADD ELEMENT TO LIST*/
  2     1             DCL  1 FOR_EACH_LIST  BASED(PN),
                             2 FIRST          POINTER,
                             2 LAST           POINTER,
                             2 ACCESS         CHARACTER(4),
                             2 PRIO_INDEX     FIXED BINARY(15);
  3     1             DCL  1 LIST_CONTENTS  BASED(PC),
                             2 ITEM(5)        FLOAT,
                             2 NEXT_ELEMENT POINTER;
  4     1             DCL (NAME,IS) POINTER, DATA(5) FLOAT, ID FIXED BINARY(15);
  5     1             ALLOCATE LIST_CONTENTS;   ITEM = DATA;
  7     1             IF NAME->FIRST = NULL THEN   /*LIST EMPTY*/
  8     1               DO; NAME->FIRST = PD;   NEXT_ELEMENT = NULL;
 11     1    1           NAME->LAST = PD;    END;
 13     1             ELSE IF NAME->ACCESS = 'FIFO' THEN    /* LIST IS A QUEUE*/
 14     1               DO;   IS = NAME->LAST;   IS->NEXT_ELEMENT = PD;
 17     1    1           NAME->LAST = PD;    PD->NEXT_ELEMENT = NULL;    END;
 20     1             ELSE IF NAME->ACCESS = 'LIFO' THEN    /* LIST IS A STACK */
 21     1               DO;     PD->NEXT_ELEMENT = NAME->FIRST;
 23     1    1           NAME->FIRST = PD;    END;
 25     1             ELSE DO;    /*INSERT ELEMENT ON BASIS OF PRIORITY
                                   PARAMETER, LOW VALUE FIRST*/
 26     1    1           ID = NAME->PRIO_INDEX;    IS = NAME->LAST;
 28     1    1           IF DATA(ID) >= IS->ITEM(ID) THEN /*PUT AT BOTTOM*/
 29     1    1             DO;   IS->NEXT_ELEMENT = PD;   PD->NEXT_ELEMENT =
 32     1    2             NULL;    NAME->LAST = PD;    END;
 34     1    1           ELSE DO;
 35     1    2             IS = NAME->FIRST;
 36     1    2             IF DATA(ID) < IS->ITEM(ID) THEN /*PUT AT TOP*/
 37     1    2               DO;   NEXT_ELEMENT = IS;    NAME->FIRST = PD;
 40     1    3               END;
 41     1    2             ELSE DO;
 42     1    3               JS = IS->NEXT_ELEMENT;
 43     1    3               DO WHILE (DATA(ID) ¬< JS->ITEM(ID));
 44     1    4                 IS = JS;    JS = IS->NEXT_ELEMENT;
 46     1    4                 END;
 47     1    3               IS->NEXT_ELEMENT = PD;
 48     1    3               PD->NEXT_ELEMENT = JS;    END;
 50     1    2             END;
 51     1    1           END;
 52     1             RETURN;
 53     1             END ADDTO;
```

Figure 4.4 Procedure to add elements to a list.

```
        GETTOP: PROCEDURE(NAME,DATA);    /*REMOVE TOP ELEMENT FROM LIST*/

STMT LEVEL NEST
  1                    GETTOP: PROCEDURE(NAME,DATA);    /*REMOVE TOP ELEMENT FROM LIST*/
  2     1             DCL   1 FOR_EACH_LIST  BASED(PN),
                              2 FIRST           POINTER,
                              2 LAST            POINTER,
                              2 ACCESS          CHARACTER(4),
                              2 PRIO_INDEX      FIXED BINARY(15);
  3     1             DCL   1 LIST_CONTENTS  BASED(PC),
                              2 ITEM(5)         FLOAT,
                              2 NEXT_ELEMENT  POINTER;
  4     1             DCL (NAME,IS,POINT) POINTER, DATA(5) FLOAT;
  5     1             PD = NAME->FIRST;
  6     1             IF PD = NULL THEN    /*LIST EMPTY*/
  7     1                 DATA = 0;
  8     1             ELSE DO;    DATA = PD->ITEM;   /*GET DATA*/
 10     1    1            NAME->FIRST = PD->NEXT_ELEMENT;   /*SET POINTERS*/
 11     1    1            FREE LIST_CONTENTS;   END;   /*RELEASE STORAGE SPACE*/
 13     1             RETURN;
 14     1             GETBOT: ENTRY(NAME,DATA);   /*REMOVE BOTTOM ELEMENT FROM LIST*/
 15     1             PD = NAME->LAST;
 16     1             IF PD = NULL THEN   DATA = 0;   /*LIST EMPTY*/
 18     1             ELSE DO;    DATA = PD->ITEM;
 20     1    1            IS = NAME->FIRST;
 21     1    1            DO WHILE (IS->NEXT_ELEMENT ¬= PD);
 22     1    2               IS = IS->NEXT_ELEMENT;   END;
 24     1    1            IS->NEXT_ELEMENT = NULL;
 25     1    1            NAME->LAST = IS;
 26     1    1            FREE LIST_CONTENTS;   END;
 28     1             RETURN;
 29     1             GETELE: ENTRY(NAME,DATA,POINT);   /*REMOVE SPECIFIC ELEMENT OF LIST*/
 30     1             PD = POINT;    DATA = PD->ITEM;   /*GET DATA AT POINT*/
 32     1             IF POINT = NULL THEN DO;   DATA = 0;   RETURN;   END;
 37     1             IF NAME->FIRST = PD THEN   /*WAS TOP ELEMENT*/
 38     1                                NAME->FIRST = PD->NEXT_ELEMENT;
 39     1             ELSE DO;   IS = NAME->FIRST;
 41     1    1            DO WHILE (IS->NEXT_ELEMENT ¬= PD);
 42     1    2               IS = IS->NEXT_ELEMENT;   END;
 44     1    1            IF PD->NEXT_ELEMENT = NULL THEN
 45     1    1               DO;    IS->NEXT_ELEMENT = NULL;
 47     1    2               NAME->LAST = IS;    END;
 49     1    1            ELSE IS->NEXT_ELEMENT = PD->NEXT_ELEMENT;
 50     1    1            END;
 51     1             FREE LIST_CONTENTS;
 52     1             RETURN;
 53     1             END GETTOP;
```

Figure 4.5 Procedure to remove elements from a list.

4.1.2 A Simulation Control Program—Preprocessing

The function of a simulation control program is basically to advance the simulation time variable. This requires that the proper order of execution be maintained for the various program segments which represent the component operations of the system. The control program can be considered as the top level of a hierarchically structured simulation program. As such, it is responsible for the overall simulation operations.

The nature of the control program depends upon the approach used to perform the simulation. Here we will consider an example based on the event-scheduling approach. The basic operations of a simulation program using event scheduling are shown in Fig. 4.7. This is the same approach as was used with the checkout counter example of Chap. 2.

A possible control program for this type of simulation is shown in Fig. 4.8. This procedure assumes that an OPTIONS MAIN procedure is used to call CONTROL and that TIME, ENDTIME, and STOP are declared as external variables in that procedure. In addition to external procedures for each of the

```
            FINDELE:  PROCEDURE(NAME,INDEX,REL,VALUE,PCINT);     /*FIND ELEMENT*/

STMT LEVEL NEST
  1                          FINDELE: PROCEDURE(NAME,INDEX,REL,VALUE,POINT);    /*FIND ELEMENT*/
  2     1                    DCL (NAME,POINT) POINTER,  INDEX FIXED BINARY(15),  REL CHAR(3),
                                 VALUE FLOAT;
  3     1                    DCL  1 FOR_EACH_LIST   BASED(PN),
                                    2 FIRST          POINTER,
                                    2 LAST           POINTER,
                                    2 ACCESS         CHARACTER(4),
                                    2 PRIO_INDEX     FIXED BINARY(15);
  4     1                    DCL  1 LIST_CONTENTS   BASED(PC),
                                    2 ITEM(5)        FLOAT,
                                    2 NEXT_ELEMENT   PCINTER;
  5     1                    IS = NAME->FIRST;
  6     1                    IF (IS = NULL) THEN DO;   PCINT = NULL;   RETURN;   END;
 11     1                    IF REL = 'EQU' THEN    /*FIND DATA VALUE EQUAL WITHIN TOLERANCE*/
 12     1                      DO;   TOL = .0001*ABS(VALUE);
 14     1    1                  VAL = ABS(IS->ITEM(INDEX));
 15     1    1                  DO WHILE((VAL > VALUE + TOL | VAL < VALUE - TOL)
                                         & (IS ¬= NULL));
 16     1    2                    IS = IS->NEXT_ELEMENT;
 17     1    2                    VAL = ABS(IS->ITEM(INDEX));   END;
 19     1    1                  PCINT = IS;
 20     1    1                END;
 21     1                    ELSE IF (REL='LST' | REL='GRT') THEN   /*FIND DATA VALUE < OR > */
 22     1                      DO;   DO WHILE(((IS->ITEM(INDEX) ¬< VALUE & REL='LST') |
                                              (IS->ITEM(INDEX) ¬> VALUE & REL='GRT')) &
                                              IS->NEXT_ELEMENT ¬= NULL);
 24     1    2                    IS = IS->NEXT_ELEMENT;   END;
 26     1    1                  IF IS->NEXT_ELEMENT ¬= NULL THEN POINT = IS;
 28     1    1                  ELSE IF (IS->ITEM(INDEX) < VALUE & REL='LST') |
 29     1    1                          (IS->ITEM(INDEX) > VALUE & REL='GRT') THEN POINT=IS;
 30     1    1                  ELSE POINT = NULL;
 31     1    1                END;
 32     1                    ELSE IF (REL='MAX' | REL='MIN') THEN   /*FIND MAX OR MIN VALUE*/
 33     1                      DO;   VALUE = IS->ITEM(INDEX);   POINT = IS;
 36     1    1                  IS = IS->NEXT_ELEMENT;
 37     1    1                  DO WHILE (IS ¬= NULL);
 38     1    2                    IF ((VALUE < IS->ITEM(INDEX) & REL='MAX') |
                                     (VALUE > IS->ITEM(INDEX) & REL='MIN')) THEN
 39     1    2                      DO;   VALUE = IS->ITEM(INDEX);
 41     1    3                        POINT = IS;   END;
 43     1    2                    IS = IS->NEXT_ELEMENT;   END;
 45     1    1                END;
 46     1                    RETURN;
 47     1                 END FINDELE;
```

Figure 4.6 Procedure to find a specific element in a list.

events, external procedures are assumed to be available to initialize the system, collect statistics, and produce the output report.

The program of Fig. 4.8 assumes the use of the general file-handling routines for the schedule file. This means that either the MAIN or INITIAL procedure will include the statement

CALL INITLST(SCHEDUL, 'PRIO',K)

where K is equal to 1, and will include at least one call to ADDTO to schedule the first event. Other events are presumably added to the schedule in the various

This version of the control program assumes that there are five events in the simulation program and requires that several of the procedures used in the simulation have specific names. Although this is acceptable for simple systems, it does not provide an adequate general routine for a control program.

One method for developing a more generalized version of the control program is to make use of the preprocessor facilities of the PL/I compiler. The

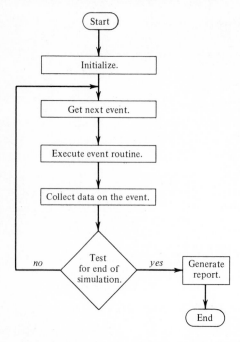

Figure 4.7 General flowchart for event-scheduling simulation programs.

function of the compiler is to accept a *source module*, which consists of PL/I statements, and produce a set of machine-language instructions, called an *object module*. The processor stage of the compiler translates PL/I source statements into machine-language instructions. The preprocessor stage scans the source program; and if this contains preprocessor statements, the original source program is

```
            CONTROL: PROCEDURE;    /*TIMING ROUTINE FOR EVENT SCHEDULING SIMULATIO*/


STMT LEVEL NEST
  1                      CONTROL: PROCEDURE;    /*TIMING ROUTINE FOR EVENT SCHEDULING SIMULATIO*/
  2      1                 DCL (TIME,ENDTIME) FLOAT EXTERNAL, STOP FIXED BINARY(31) EXTERNAL;
  3      1                 DCL SCHEDUL POINTER EXTERNAL;
  4      1                 DCL INFO(5) FLOAT;
  5      1                 CALL INITIAL;    /*INITIALIZE THE SYSTEM*/
  6      1                 DO WHILE (TIME < ENDTIME & STOP = 0);
  7      1    1              CALL GETTOP(SCHEDUL,INFO);
  8      1    1              A = 0.;    DO I = 1 TO 5;
 10      1    2                A = A + ABS(INFO(I));    END;
 12      1    1              IF A = 0. THEN STOP = 1;
 14      1    1              ELSE DO;    TIME = INFO(1);    TYPE = INFO(2);
 17      1    2                IF TYPE = 1 THEN CALL EVENT1;
 19      1    2                ELSE
 19      1    2                IF TYPE = 2 THEN CALL EVENT2;
 21      1    2                ELSE
 21      1    2                IF TYPE = 3 THEN CALL EVENT3;
 23      1    2                ELSE
 23      1    2                IF TYPE = 4 THEN CALL EVENT4;
 25      1    2                ELSE
 25      1    2                IF TYPE = 5 THEN CALL EVENT5;
 27      1    2                END;
 28      1    1              CALL STAT;    /*COLLECT STATISTICS*/
 29      1    1              END;
 30      1                 CALL OUTPUT;    /*PRINT REPORT*/
 31      1                 RETURN;
 32                   END CONTROL;
```

Figure 4.8 An example control procedure for event-scheduling simulation.

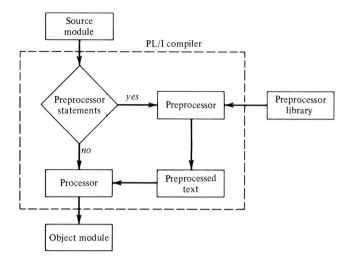

Figure 4.9 A flowchart for the PL/I compiler preprocessor operation.

modified as directed by the preprocessor statements, and an altered version of the PL/I source text is used as the input to the processor stage. This relationship is illustrated by the flowchart shown in Fig. 4.9.

Preprocessor statements are identified by a leading percent sign. Examples of such statements are shown in Fig. 4.10. The %DECLARE statements are used to specify preprocessor variables. The only attributes which these variables may have are CHARACTER or FIXED. The %ASSIGNMENT statements (statements 2, 3, 4, 6, 7) are used to assign character strings or fixed decimal numbers to the previously declared preprocessor variables. The %INCLUDE statement (8) retrieves source text from a library and incorporates it in a PL/I program. In this case, CONTROL is the name of a member of a library set of PL/I source text. The contents of the library member CONTROL are shown in Fig. 4.11. Note that this procedure contains several preprocessor statements in its text.

The operation of the preprocessor is as follows. The PL/I source program is scanned, as a character string, one character at a time. Regular PL/I statements are copied with no changes. Copying is interrupted when a preprocessor statement is encountered. Instead of being copied, the preprocessor statement is

```
          %DECLARE(EVENT1,EVENT2,EVENT3) CHARACTER;

COMPILE-TIME MACRO PROCESSOR
MACRO SOURCE2 LISTING

   1       %DECLARE(EVENT1,EVENT2,EVENT3) CHARACTER;
   2       %EVENT1    = 'SALE';
   3       %EVENT2    = 'INVTORY';
   4       %EVENT3    = 'RECEIVE';
   5       %DECLARE(J,L) FIXED;
   6       %J = 5;
   7       %L = 3;
   8       %INCLUDE CONTROL;
```

Figure 4.10 Source module deck.

```
INCLUDED TEXT FOLLOWS FROM DD.MEMBER =   SYSLIB   .CONTROL

 9      CONTROL: PROCEDURE; /*TIMING ROUTINE*/
10          DCL (TIME,ENDTIME,TYPE) FLOAT EXTERNAL,  STOP FIXED BIN(31) EXTERNAL;
11          DCL SCHEDUL POINTER EXTERNAL;
12          DCL INFO(J) FLOAT EXTERNAL;
13              CALL INITIAL;   /*INITIALIZE THE SYSTEM*/
14              DO WHILE (TIME < ENDTIME & STOP = 0);
15              CALL GETTOP(SCHEDUL,INFO);
16              A = 0;   DO I = 1 TO J;
17                      A = A + ABS(INFO(I));    END;
18              IF A = 0 THEN STOP = 1;
19              ELSE DO;   TIME = INFO(1);   TYPE = INFO(2);
20                  %DECLARE K FIXED;
21                  %K=L;
22                  IF TYPE = 1 THEN CALL EVENT1;
23                  %IF K = 1 %THEN %GO TO OVER;
24                  ELSE;
25                  IF TYPE = 2 THEN CALL EVENT2;
26                  %IF K = 2 %THEN %GO TO OVER;
27                  ELSE;
28                  IF TYPE = 3 THEN CALL EVENT3;
29                  %IF K = 3 %THEN %GO TO OVER;
30                  ELSE;
31                  IF TYPE = 4 THEN CALL EVENT4;
32                  %IF K = 4 %THEN %GO TO OVER;
33                  ELSE;
34                  IF TYPE = 5 THEN CALL EVENT5;
35                  %IF K = 5 %THEN %GO TO OVER;
36                  ELSE;
37                  %OVER:;
38                  END;
39              CALL STAT;   /*COLLECT STATISTICS*/
40              END;
41          CALL OUTPUT;   /*PRINT REPORT*/
42          RETURN;
43      END CONTROL;
```

Figure 4.11 Contents of the preprocessor library module member CONTROL.

executed. This execution can alter the manner in which subsequent statements are formulated by the preprocessor. If a preprocessor statement assigns a value to an identifier, then the subsequent occurrence of that identifier in a non-preprocessor statement will result in the identifier being replaced by its currently

```
                %DECLARE(EVENT1,EVENT2,EVENT3) CHARACTER;

                      SOURCE LISTING.


STMT LEVEL NEST
  1                    CONTROL: PROCEDURE; /*TIMING ROUTINE*/                                      9
  2      1             DCL (TIME,ENDTIME,TYPE) FLOAT EXTERNAL, STOP FIXED BIN(31) EXTERNAL;       10
  3      1             DCL SCHEDUL POINTER EXTERNAL;                                              11
  4      1             DCL INFO(     5 ) FLOAT EXTERNAL;                                         12 1
  5      1                 CALL INITIAL;   /*INITIALIZE THE SYSTEM*/                              13
  6      1                 DO WHILE (TIME < ENDTIME & STOP = 0);                                  14
  7      1      1          CALL GETTOP(SCHEDUL,INFO);                                             15
  8      1      1          A = 0;   DO I = 1 TO     5 ;                                          16 1
 10      1      2                  A = A + ABS(INFO(I));    END;                                  17
 12      1      1          IF A = 0 THEN STOP = 1;                                                18
 14      1      1          ELSE DO;   TIME = INFO(1);   TYPE = INFO(2);                           19
 17      1      2              IF TYPE = 1 THEN CALL   SALE ;                                    22 1
 19      1      2              ELSE;                                                              24
 20      1      2              IF TYPE = 2 THEN CALL   INVTORY ;                                 25 1
 22      1      2              ELSE;                                                              27
 23      1      2              IF TYPE = 3 THEN CALL   RECEIVE ;                                 28 1
 25      1      2              END;                                                               38
 26      1      1          CALL STAT;   /*COLLECT STATISTICS*/                                    39
 27      1      1          END;                                                                   40
 28      1                 CALL OUTPUT;   /*PRINT REPORT*/                                        41
 29      1                 RETURN;                                                                42
 30      1             END CONTROL;                                                               43
```

Figure 4.12 The preprocessed text, input to the PL/I compiler processor.

```
            RND: PROCEDURE(I) RETURNS(FLOAT);

STMT LEVEL NEST
  1                    RND: PROCEDURE(I) RETURNS(FLOAT);
  2      1               DCL SEED(8) FIXED BINARY(31) EXTERNAL;
  3      1               (NOFIXEDOVERFLOW): SEED(I) = SEED(I)*65539;
  4      1                   IF SEED(I) < 0 THEN SEED(I) = SEED(I)+2147483647+1;
  6      1               W = SEED(I);  W = W*0.4656613E-9;
  8      1               RETURN(W);
  9      1             END RND;
```

Figure 4.13 Procedure to generate random numbers with a uniform distribution.

assigned value in the preprocessed text. Preprocessor statements are never copied into the preprocessed text.

This operation of the preprocessor is illustrated by the preprocessed text of Fig. 4.12, which was generated by the source module of Fig. 4.10. Note that the dimension of INFO, J in the PL/I text of CONTROL, has been replaced by 5 and EVENT1 has been replaced by SALE. Also the preprocessor %IF statements in CONTROL caused the elimination of the calls to EVENT4 and EVENT5, which were not needed in this procedure.

There are other ways in which the preprocessor can alter the formation of the preprocessed text. These include causing scanning to continue from a different point in the source program, which may involve rescanning of the source text and the use of preprocessor function procedures.

Preprocessor libraries can be used to retrieve standard procedures and data declarations to ease the task of creating programs. They also allow a source program to be designed so that it is easily modified with a minimum number of changes in the source program. This can be of great help in reducing errors during program development, testing, and modification.

4.1.3 Random-Number Generators

There are a large number of probability distribution functions which are useful in simulation problems. A collection of these routines, which have been extensively tested and carefully coded for efficient execution, is an important part of any simulation programming system. Several routines of this type are given in App. D, and many more may be found in the references.

At this point in developing a simulation programming system, we will include only a few simplified procedures for random-variate generations. The procedures included are shown in Figs. 4.13, 4.14, and 4.15, which are used to generate uniform, exponential, and normal distributions, respectively. These procedures are included as compiled object modules in the programming system.

The function procedure RND is the same uniform distribution generator used in Chap. 1 but with SEED changed to an array. This change makes it possible to use different streams of random numbers for various functions in a simulation. The reason for this feature will be discussed in Chap. 6.

The RNEXP function procedure uses the inverse transformation derived in Sec. 3.3.3. The RNNORM function procedure also uses an inverse transformation

```
         RNEXP: PROCEDURE(I,U) RETURNS(FLOAT);


STMT LEVEL NEST
  1                    RNEXP: PROCEDURE(I,U) RETURNS(FLOAT);
  2     1                DCL SEED(8) FIXED BINARY(31) EXTERNAL;
  3     1                  (NOFIXEDOVERFLOW): SEED(I) = SEED(I)*65539;
  4     1                      IF SEED(I) < 0 THEN SEED(I) = SEED(I)+2147483647+1;
  6     1                  W = SEED(I);   W = W*0.4656613E-9;
  8     1                  V = -U * LOG(W);
  9     1                  RETURN(V);
 10     1              END RNEXP;
```

Figure 4.14 Procedure to generate random numbers with an exponential distribution.

procedure, one developed by Marsaglia and Bray [9]. The parameters I, U, and S in these functions refer to the stream number, the mean value, and the standard deviation, respectively.

4.2 AN INVENTORY SYSTEM SIMULATION

An inventory is a stock of items being held for future use or sale. In a typical operation, items are removed from the inventory at a rate which is a stochastic variate. Then, periodically, the size of the inventory is counted, and if this is less than some reorder point, an order is placed for enough items to bring the inventory up to some stock control level. The time delay between placing this order and receipt of the items may also be a stochastic variate.

There are costs associated with having items in an inventory, with counting the size of the inventory and placing an order, and with failing to have an item in stock when there is a demand for the item. The objective of studying an inventory system is to determine the best operating rules that minimize these costs. For the system described in the previous paragraph, these rules would be to set the time period for counting the inventory, the reorder point, and the stock-control level.

Inventory control is a significant problem in most production and distribution operations. The models used in various situations differ in many details

```
         RNNORM: PROCEDURE(I,U,S) RETURNS(FLOAT);


STMT LEVEL NEST
  1                    RNNORM: PROCEDURE(I,U,S) RETURNS(FLOAT);
  2     1                DCL SEED(8) FIXED BINARY(31) EXTERNAL;
  3     1                  T = 2.;
  4     1                  DO WHILE (T>1.);
  5     1     1              X = RN(I);    Y = 2.*RN(I) - 1.;
  7     1     1              XS = X*X;    YS = Y*Y;    T = XS + YS;
 10     1     1            END;
 11     1                  R = SQRT(-2.*LOG(RN(I)))/T;
 12     1                  V = U + (XS - YS)*R*S;
 13     1                  RETURN(V);
 14     1                  RN: PROCEDURE(I) RETURNS(FLOAT);
 15     2                    (NOFIXEDOVERFLOW): SEED(I) = SEED(I)*65539;
 16     2                        IF SEED(I) < 0 THEN SEED(I) = SEED(I)+2147483647+1;
 18     2                    W = SEED(I);   W = W*0.4656613E-9;
 20     2                    RETURN(W);
 21     2                  END RN;
 22     1              END RNNORM;
```

Figure 4.15 Procedure to generate random numbers with a normal distribution.

but are similar to the simplified case described here. This is an area where the application of computer-based simulation has been found to be a useful and effective tool.

We will use a simplified inventory system problem to illustrate the use of the general routines of Sec. 4.1 in developing a simulation program. The operation to be simulated is a retail store which sells units of a single product from an inventory and obtains replacements from a wholesale supplier.

For this example, the following program variables will be used to represent the state of the system:

STOCK = number of units on hand at the present time
ONORDER = number of units that have been ordered but not yet delivered
SALES = total number of units supplied from inventory since the start of the simulation
LOSTSLS = total number of times units have been requested from inventory but were not supplied because the inventory was depleted
NOORDER = number of times orders have been placed
NOINVT = number of times an inventory of the stock has been taken

Two lists will be used: one, the schedule of next events, and the other, a record of orders which have been placed but not filled by the supplier. Each entry in both lists will have two data items. For the schedule, the data items are (1) time of occurrence and (2) type of event. For the list of orders, the data items are (1) time of receipt of order and (2) the number of items in the order.

The following program variables are used as parameters of the model:

INVTPRD = length of period between taking inventory of stock
INVTLEV = stock control level used to determine the size of orders
DELTIME = time delay between placing an order and receipt of the units

In this example, the model has been simplified by using a fixed value for DELTIME and no reorder point is used; i.e., orders are always placed if the size of the stock plus the outstanding orders are less than INVTLEV.

The assumed values for costs in this model are: $50 to count the number of items in stock and to process the paperwork associated with this operation and placing an order; $15 for handling the receipt of an order; $10 for each sale lost due to no stock available; and $.03 per day, per unit, in stock-carrying cost to maintain the inventory. It is also assumed that a $20 profit is realized on each sale.

In order to calculate the carrying costs, it is necessary to have the time-integrated value of the stock level. This value is obtained by adding an increment each time the stock level changes. This increment is the stock level before the change multiplied by the time interval since the last change. For example, in the sketch below, the time-integrated value of x is 2, 6, 8, 14 at time equals 1, 2, 4, 6, respectively. In the program, the three-element array **STKLEV** is used to store the data needed for this operation, and

$$STKLEV(1) = \text{time-integrated value of the stock level}$$
$$STKLEV(2) = \text{value of the stock level prior to present change}$$
$$STKLEV(3) = \text{time of the stock level change prior to the present one}$$

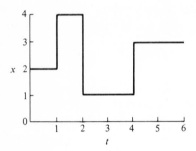

The events which are used in this model are as follows:

Type	Name	Function
1	SALE	The event of selling one unit which is removed from the inventory.
2	INVTORY	The event of counting the stock and placing an order if required.
3	RECEIVE	The event of receiving units of an order.

The program statements for all these events are included in one procedure, as shown in Fig. 4.16. In this procedure, the variables and parameters of the model and the pointers to the two lists used, SCHEDUL and ORDERS, are declared as EXTERNAL variables. Additions to and deletions from the lists use the general procedures of Sec. 4.1.1. These general procedures are also used in the INITIAL procedure (Fig. 4.17) to initialize the lists and to schedule the first sale and the first inventory.

The CONTROL procedure of Fig. 4.12 is used with this example. The main procedure, shown in Fig. 4.18, serves to declare the EXTERNAL variables, to set parameters' values, and to call the CONTROL routine.

The procedure STAT (Fig. 4.19) calculates the time-integrated value of the stock level when a SALE or RECEIVE event occurs and counts the number of inventories taken and the number of orders received. This data is used, together with the values for the number of sales and lost sales, in the OUTPUT procedure (Fig. 4.20), to calculate the profit realized during the simulation. The time unit of

```
            SALE: PROCEDURE;    /*SELL ONE UNIT*/


STMT LEVEL NEST
  1                    SALE: PROCEDURE;    /*SELL ONE UNIT*/
  2       1                DCL (TIME,ENDTIME,TYPE) FLOAT EXTERNAL, STOP FIXED BIN(31) EXTERNAL;
  3       1                DCL (STOCK,SALES,ONORDER,LOSTSLS) FLOAT EXTERNAL;
  4       1                DCL (INVTPRD,INVTLEV,DELTIME,NOORDER,NOINVT) FLOAT EXTERNAL;
  5       1                DCL (ORDERS,SCHEDUL) POINTER EXTERNAL;
  6       1                DCL A(2) FLOAT;
  7       1                   I = 1;   X = 5.;
  9       1                   A(1) = TIME + RNEXP(I,X);   A(2) = 1.;
  11      1                CALL ADDTO(SCHEDUL,A);   /*SCHEDULE NEXT SALE*/
  12      1                IF STOCK > 0. THEN   /*STOCK AVAILABLE*/
  13      1                   DO;   SALES = SALES + 1.;   STOCK = STOCK - 1.;   END;
  17      1                ELSE LOSTSLS = LOSTSLS + 1.;
  18      1                RETURN;
  19      1                INVTORY: ENTRY;   /*TAKE INVENTORY OF STOCK*/
  20      1                   A(1) = TIME + INVTPRD;   A(2) = 2;
  22      1                CALL ADDTO(SCHEDUL,A);   /*SCHEDULE NEXT INVENTORY*/
  23      1                IF (STOCK + ONORDER) < INVTLEV THEN
  24      1                   DO;   A(1) = TIME + DELTIME;   A(2) = 3;
  27      1    1              CALL ADDTO(SCHEDUL,A);   /*SCHEDULE RECEIPT OF ORDER*/
  28      1    1              A(2) = INVTLEV - (STOCK + ONORDER);
  29      1    1              CALL ADDTO(ORDERS,A);
  30      1    1              ONORDER = ONORDER + A(2);   END;
  32      1                RETURN;
  33      1                RECEIVE: ENTRY;   /*RECEIVE STOCK ORDER*/
  34      1                   CALL GETTOP(ORDERS,A);
  35      1                STOCK = STOCK + A(2);   ONORDER = ONORDER - A(2);
  37      1                RETURN;
  38      1                END SALE;
```

Figure 4.16 The event routines for the inventory control example.

```
            INITIAL: PROCEDURE;


STMT LEVEL NEST
  1                    INITIAL: PROCEDURE;
  2       1                DCL (ORDERS,SCHEDUL) POINTER EXTERNAL;
  3       1                DCL A(2) FLOAT;
  4       1                   I = 1;   CALL INITLST(SCHEDUL,'PRIO',I);
  6       1                             CALL INITLST(ORDERS,'PRIO',I);
  7       1                   A(1) = 2.;   A(2) = 1.;   CALL ADDTO(SCHEDUL,A);
  10      1                   A(1) = 9.;   A(2) = 2.;   CALL ADDTO(SCHEDUL,A);
  13      1                RETURN;
  14      1                END INITIAL;
```

Figure 4.17 The INITIAL procedure for the inventory control example.

```
            INVENEX: PROCEDURE OPTIONS(MAIN);


            SOURCE LISTING.


STMT LEVEL NEST
  1                    INVENEX: PROCEDURE OPTIONS(MAIN);                                      1
  2       1                DCL (TIME,ENDTIME,TYPE) FLOAT EXTERNAL, STOP FIXED BIN(31) EXTERNAL;  2
  3       1                DCL (STOCK,SALES,ONORDER,LOSTSLS) FLOAT EXTERNAL;                   3
  4       1                DCL (INVTPRD,INVTLEV,DELTIME,NOORDER,NOINVT) FLOAT EXTERNAL;        4
  5       1                DCL (ORDERS,SCHEDUL) POINTER EXTERNAL;                              5
  6       1                DCL STKLEV(3) FLOAT EXTERNAL;                                       6
  7       1                DCL SEED(8) FIXED BINARY(31) EXTERNAL INITIAL(1956987325,1156987325, 7
                           1908986925,1508586121,1468582113,1472622913,1480662953,1521070957);  8
  8       1                   TIME = 0.;   ENDTIME = 1200.;   STOP = 0;                       9
  11      1                INVTPRD = 120.;   INVTLEV = 30.;   DELTIME = 60.;                  10
  14      1                STOCK = 30.;   CALL CONTROL;                                       11
  16      1                END INVENEX;                                                       12
```

Figure 4.18 The main procedure for the inventory control example.

```
          STAT: PROCEDURE;

STMT LEVEL NEST
  1                         STAT: PROCEDURE;
  2     1                     DCL (STOCK,SALES,ONORDER,LOSTSLS) FLOAT EXTERNAL;
  3     1                     DCL (TIME,ENDTIME,TYPE) FLOAT EXTERNAL, STOP FIXED BIN(31) EXTERNAL;
  4     1                     DCL (INVTPRD,INVTLEV,DELTIME,NOORDER,NOINVT) FLOAT EXTERNAL;
  5     1                     DCL STKLEV(3) FLOAT EXTERNAL;
  6     1                     IF TYPE = 1 THEN
  7     1                        DO;    STKLEV(1) = STKLEV(2)*(TIME - STKLEV(3)) + STKLEV(1);
  9     1    1                      STKLEV(2) = STOCK;   STKLEV(3) = TIME;   END;
 12     1                     ELSE IF TYPE = 2 THEN NOINVT = NOINVT + 1;
 14     1                         ELSE IF TYPE = 3 THEN
 15     1                            DO;    STKLEV(1) = STKLEV(2)*(TIME - STKLEV(3))
                                                  + STKLEV(1);
 17     1    1                         STKLEV(2) = STOCK;   STKLEV(3) = TIME;
 19     1    1                         NOORDER = NOORDER + 1;   END;
 21     1                     RETURN;
 22     1                   END STAT;
```

Figure 4.19 Data-collection procedure for the inventory control example.

this simulation is one day, and the output report, as shown in Fig. 4.21, includes an average weekly profit based on a 5-day week.

From the results shown in Fig. 4.21, it is evident that the number of lost sales, 36, is high compared with total sales of 197. This could be reduced by either increasing the stock control level to above 30 or reducing the time between inventories from 120 days. The function of the simulation program is to study how changes in these parameters will affect the average weekly profit.

4.2.1 The Programming Process

The simulation program for this example uses some of the procedures discussed in Sec. 4.1. It is assumed that these general routines have been developed for

```
          OUTPUT: PROCEDURE;

STMT LEVEL NEST
  1                         OUTPUT: PROCEDURE;
  2     1                     DCL (STOCK,SALES,ONORDER,LOSTSLS) FLOAT EXTERNAL;
  3     1                     DCL (TIME,ENDTIME,TYPE) FLOAT EXTERNAL, STOP FIXED BIN(31) EXTERNAL;
  4     1                     DCL (INVTPRD,INVTLEV,DELTIME,NOORDER,NOINVT) FLOAT EXTERNAL;
  5     1                     DCL STKLEV(3) FLOAT EXTERNAL;
  6     1                     PROFIT = SALES*20. - STKLEV(1)*.03 - LOSTSLS*10. - NOINVT*50.
                                       - NOORDER*15.;
  7     1                     PUT EDIT('TOTAL PROFIT = ',PROFIT,'NUMBER OF SALES = ',SALES,
                                      'NUMBER OF LOST SALES = ',LOSTSLS,'AVERAGE STOCKLEVEL = ',
                                      STKLEV(1)/TIME,'TIME PERIOD = ',TIME,'AVERAGE WEEKLY PROFIT = '
                                      ,PROFIT* 5./TIME) (SKIP,A,F(8.2));
  8     1                     RETURN;
  9     1                   END OUTPUT;
```

Figure 4.20 Procedure for generating the inventory control example output report.

```
TOTAL PROFIT =  2638.33
NUMBER OF SALES =   208.00
NUMBER OF LOST SALES =    51.00
AVERAGE STOCKLEVEL =    10.02
TIME PERIOD = 1202.60
AVERAGE WEEKLY PROFIT =    10.97
```

Figure 4.21 Output of the inventory system simulation program.

use in many different simulation programs and that they exist as data sets stored in an on-line random-access device.

The additional programming required for this inventory system simulation consists of the procedures shown in Figs. 4.16 to 4.20 and the source module shown in Fig. 4.10.

The usual approach in developing the simulation program for a specific example is to start by defining the variables required to describe the state of the system. Recall that these variables must include all the quantities necessary to completely specify the system at one point in time. The next step is to program the event routines which accomplish the changes to the system state at the occurrence of each discrete event. After these procedures are developed, the INITIAL, CONTROL, STAT, OUTPUT, and main procedures are written.

In developing simulation programs, it is advisable to make use of the facilities of the computer operating system to divide the programming effort into easily manageable small components. The specific routines required for this purpose depend on the computer system used. Examples of procedures of this type for use with the IBM 360/370 OS/VS operating system are presented in App. B.

4.3 SIMULATION OF A TIMESHARING COMPUTER SYSTEM

We will consider, as a second example of developing a simulation program, a computer system which provides service to 12 terminals which are being operated in an interactive mode. That is, the terminal operators send in a command to the computer, wait for a response from the computer, then, after some delay, send in their next command.

The terminal operation characteristics are as follows. The length of the input messages from the terminals is a random number with a uniform distribution from 5 to 80 characters in length. After a response is received from the computer, the time delay until the next input is exponentially distributed. In 80 percent of the cases, the mean value of this delay is 5 s; in the other 20 percent, the mean value is 30 s.

The computer operation is composed of two phases: polling and execution. At 1-s intervals, the computer checks each terminal to see if there is input waiting to be read from the terminal. If there is, the input message is read in at a rate of 300 characters per second. The polling of each terminal requires .01 s in addition to the transmission time. Any time during each 1-s interval which is not required for polling and input operations is available for use in an execution phase. During the execution phase, the computer executes programs required to service the input commands and sends reply messages to the terminals.

In the execution phase, the terminals are serviced in order. If a program execution is required, a period of .01 s is devoted to this operation for each terminal sequentially. If an output message is ready for a terminal, it is sent out at a rate of 300 characters per second until completed or until it is time for the next polling phase. A message output operation requires .01 s to establish contact with a terminal, in addition to the transmission time. Service to the terminals continues during the execution phase until no further service is needed or until the next polling time.

The distribution of program execution time required by the input command is assumed to be given by the following discrete-frequency distribution:

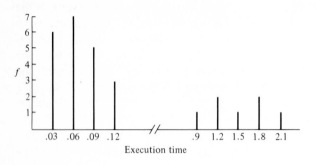

```
              POLL: PROCEDURE;      /*POLLING EVENT*/

STMT LEVEL NEST
   1                      POLL: PROCEDURE;    /*POLLING EVENT*/
   2      1                 DCL (TIME,ENDTIME,TYPE) FLOAT EXTERNAL, STOP FIXED BIN(31) EXTERNAL;
   3      1                 DCL INFO(5) FLOAT EXTERNAL;
   4      1                 DCL (SCHEDUL,TERM) POINTER EXTERNAL;
   5      1                 INFO(1) = TIME + 1.0;    INFO(2) = 1.;
   7      1                 X = TIME;    Y = INFO(1);    Z = TIME;
  10      1                 CALL ADDTO(SCHEDUL,INFO);    /*SCHEDULE NEXT POLLING*/
  11      1                 CALL GETTOP(TERM,INFO);
  12      1                 DO I = 1 TO 12 WHILE((Y - X - .01) > INFO(2)/300.);
  13      1    1               IF (INFO(1) ¬= 1) THEN X = X + .01;    /*.01 IS POLLING TIME*/
  15      1    1               ELSE DO;    X = X + .01 + INFO(2)/300.;
  17      1    2                  INFO(1) = 2;    INFO(2) = 0;    END;
  20      1    1               CALL ADDTO(TERM,INFO);    CALL GETTOP(TERM,INFO);    END;
  23      1                 CALL ADDTO(TERM,INFO);
  24      1                 INFO(1) = X;    INFO(2) = 2;
  26      1                 INFO(3) = Y - X;    /*TIME AVAILABLE FOR EXECUTION*/
  27      1                 INFO(4) = X - Z;    /*TIME REQUIRED FOR POLLING*/
  28      1                 CALL ADDTO(SCHEDUL,INFO);    /*SCHEDULE EXECUTION*/
  29      1                 RETURN;
  30      1                 EXECU: ENTRY;    /*EXECUTE PROGRAM STEPS EVENT*/
  31      1                 X = TIME;    Z = TIME;    Y = INFO(3) + X;    /*TIME OF NEXT POLLING*/
  34      1                 XL = 0.;
  35      1                 DO WHILE (XL ¬= X);    XL = X;
  37      1    1               DO I = 1 TO 12 WHILE((Y - X - .01) >= 0.);
  38      1    2                  CALL GETTOP(TERM,INFO);
  39      1    2                  IF INFO(1) = 3. THEN    /*OUTPUT TO TERMINAL*/
  40      1    2                     DO;    IF (Y - X - .01) > (INFO(3)/ 300.) THEN
  42      1    3                        DO;    X = X + .01 + INFO(3)/ 300.;
  44      1    4                           INFO(1) = X;    INFO(2) = 3.;
  46      1    4                           CALL ADDTO(SCHEDUL,INFO);    /*SCHEDULE REPLY*/
  47      1    4                           INFO(1) = 4.;    END;
  49      1    3                        ELSE DO;    W = (Y - X - .01)* 300.;
  51      1    4                           INFO(3) = INFO(3) - W;    X = Y;    END;
  54      1    3                     END;
  55      1    2                  ELSE IF INFO(1) = 2.  THEN    /*EXECUTE PROGRAM*/
  56      1    2                     DO;    X = X + .01;    INFO(4) = INFO(4) - 1.;
  59      1    3                        IF INFO(4) = 0 THEN INFO(1) = 3.;
  61      1    3                     END;
  62      1    2                  CALL ADDTO(TERM,INFO);    END;
  64      1    1               END;
  65      1                 INFO(4) = X - Z;    /*TIME REQUIRED FOR EXECUTION*/
  66      1                 END POLL;
```

Figure 4.22 The POLL and EXECU event routines for the computer system example.

This implies relatively short execution times for 75 percent of the commands and relatively long times for 25 percent of the commands.

The distribution of the reply messages is assumed to be 10, 20, 30, 100, or 150 characters in length, with each length having a 20 percent probability of occurring.

In order to characterize the state of this system, we need to know the state of each terminal at any point in time. This information is maintained in a list with the name TERM. The data items included for each terminal are

INFO(1) denotes the status of the terminal.

> INFO(1) = 0 if the terminal is idle, i.e., has received a reply but
> does not yet have an input ready
> = 1 if the terminal has an input ready for the computer
> = 2 if program to service terminal is in execution
> = 3 if output message is ready to be sent to this terminal
> = 4 at the time terminal receives a message

INFO(2) is length of input command from the terminal.
INFO(3) is length of output message to the terminal.
INFO(4) is time required to execute program required by command, in units of
.01 time periods.
INFO(5) is the identifying number for the terminal, i.e., 1, 2, 3, ..., 12.

The events used in this model are

Type	Name	Function
1	POLL	The event of polling the terminals for inputs to the computer.
2	EXECU	Simulates execution phase where computer executes programs and sends output messages to the terminals.
3	REPLY	The event of a terminal receiving a reply from the computer.
4	REQUEST	Operator command input event (provides parameters of the processing of the command).

The event procedures for POLL and EXECU are shown in Fig. 4.22. In the POLL procedure, the first step is to schedule the next polling event at a time 1 s in the future. Then each of the terminals is polled in order and input commands read in until all 12 terminals have been polled or until time for the next polling event. At the conclusion of the polling event, an execution event is scheduled. The SCHEDUL list uses the third data item INFO(3) to specify the time available for the execution phase.

The execution event services terminals in order either until no further service is required or until no time is left for execution. If a complete message is sent to a terminal, a reply event is scheduled. Note that the fifth data item, INFO(5),

```
                REPLY: PROCEDURE;   /*REPLY TO TERMINAL FRCM COMPUTER EVENT*/

STMT LEVEL NEST
  1                     REPLY: PROCEDURE;    /*REPLY TO TERMINAL FROM COMPUTER EVENT*/
  2    1                    DCL (TIME,ENDTIME,TYPE) FLOAT EXTERNAL, STOP FIXED BIN(31) EXTERNAL;
  3    1                    DCL (SCHEDUL,TERM) POINTER EXTERNAL;
  4    1                    DCL INFO(5) FLOAT EXTERNAL;
  5    1                    DCL PNT POINTER, N FIXED BINARY(31);
  6    1                    I = 1;
  7    1                    IF (RND(I) < .8) THEN X = 5.;
  9    1                    ELSE X = 30.;
 10    1                    I = 2;
 11    1                    INFO(1) = TIME + RNEXP(I,X);   INFO(2) = 4.;
 13    1                    CALL ADDTO(SCHEDUL,INFO);   /*SCHEDULE NEXT REQUEST*/
 14    1                    RETURN;
 15    1                 REQUEST: ENTRY;   /*INPUT FROM TERMINAL TO COMPUTER EVENT*/
 16    1                    X = INFO(5);
 17    1                    N = 5.;    CALL FINDELE(TERM,N,'EQU',X,PNT);
 19    1                    CALL GETELE(TERM,INFO,PNT);
 20    1                    INFO(1) = 1.;   I = 1;   X = RND(I)*75.;   I = X;   INFO(2) = I+5;
 25    1                    INFO(3) = FNCOTL;   INFO(4) = FNCEXL;
 27    1                    CALL ADDTO(TERM,INFO);    RETURN;
 29    1                 FNCOTL: PROCEDURE RETURNS(FLOAT);
 30    2                    DCL C(5,2) FLOAT STATIC INITIAL(.2,10,.4,20,.6,30,.8,100,1,150);
 31    2                    I = 1;   X = RND(I);
 33    2                    DO WHILE (X > C(I,1));
 34    2   1                   I = I + 1;   END;
 36    2                    RETURN(C(I,2));
 37    2                 END FNCOTL;
 38    1                 FNCEXL: PROCEDURE RETURNS(FLOAT);
 39    2                    DCL B(9,2) FLOAT STATIC INITIAL(6,3,13,6,18,9,21,12,22,90,24,120,
                                                       25,150,27,180,28,210);
 40    2                    I = 1;   X = RND(I)*28.;
 42    2                    DO WHILE (X > B(I,1));
 43    2   1                   I = I + 1;   END;
 45    2                    RETURN(B(I,2));
 46    2                 END FNCEXL;
 47    1                 END REPLY;
```

Figure 4.23 The REPLY and REQUEST event routines for the computer system example.

placed in the SCHEDUL list at this point is the identification number for the terminal receiving the reply.

The event procedures for REPLY and REQUEST are shown in Fig. 4.23. The function of the reply event is to schedule the next request event at the appropriate future time. The request event uses the FINDELE procedure to find the terminal which is due to have a new input command and then updates the status data for this particular terminal.

```
                STAT: PROCEDURE;

STMT LEVEL NEST
  1                     STAT: PROCEDURE;
  2    1                    DCL (TIME,ENDTIME,TYPE) FLOAT EXTERNAL, STOP FIXED BIN(31) EXTERNAL;
  3    1                    DCL INFO(5) FLOAT EXTERNAL;
  4    1                    DCL B(12) FLCAT STATIC;
  5    1                    IF TYPE = 1 THEN   /*RECORD POLLING TIME*/
  6    1                        DO;   I = 1;   CALL OBSERV(I,INFO(4));   END;
 10    1                    ELSE
 10    1                    IF TYPE = 2 THEN   /*RECORD EXECUTION TIME*/
 11    1                        DO;   I = 2;   CALL OBSERV(I,INFO(4));   END;
 15    1                    ELSE
 15    1                    IF TYPE = 3 THEN   /*RECORC WAITING TIME FOR REPLY*/
 16    1                        DO;   I = INFO(5);   X = TIME - B(I);
 19    1   1                    CALL HISTO(I,X);   END;
 21    1                    ELSE
 21    1                    IF TYPE = 4 THEN   /*STORE TIME OF REQUEST*/
 22    1                        DO;   I = INFO(5);   B(I) = TIME;   END;
 26    1                 END STAT;
```

Figure 4.24 The STAT procedure for the computer system example.

Data on the timesharing computer system is collected in the procedure STAT (shown in Fig. 4.24). Specifically, time spent by the computer in the polling and execution phases is recorded, and time intervals between input commands and computer replies for each terminal are entered into histograms. There are two data collection routines, OBSERV and HISTO (shown in Fig. 4.25), which are used to record this data. The procedure used to print out this collected data is

```
        %DECLARE(K,L,M) FIXED;


COMPILE-TIME MACRO PROCESSOR
MACRO SOURCE2 LISTING

    1       %DECLARE(K,L,M) FIXED;
    2       %K = 2;    %L = 13;    %M = 11;
    3       %INCLUDE OBSERV;


INCLUDED TEXT FOLLOWS FROM DD.MEMBER =  SYSLIB  .OBSERV

    4       OBSERV: PROCEDURE(I,X);
    5         DCL OBSVDAT(K,3) FLOAT EXTERNAL;
    6         Y = 1.;   DO J = 1 TO 3;
    7               OBSVDAT(I,J) = OBSVDAT(I,J) + Y;   Y = Y*X;   END;
    8       RETURN;
    9       HISTO: ENTRY(I,X);
   10         DCL (HISTPAR( L,3),HISTDAT( L, M)) FLOAT EXTERNAL;
   11       /* HISTPAR(*,1) = UPPER LIMIT OF FIRST INTERVAL
   12          HISTPAR(*,2) = SIZE OF INTERMEDIATE INTERVALS
   13          HISTPAR(*,3) = NUMBER OF INTERVALS LESS ONE */
   14         JA = 0;   Y = HISTPAR(I,1);
   15         DO J = 1 TO HISTPAR(I,3) WHILE (JA = 0);
   16           IF X <= Y THEN
   17             DO; HISTDAT(I,J) = HISTDAT(I,J) + 1;   JA = 1;   END;
   18           Y = Y + HISTPAR(I,2);   END;
   19         IF JA = 0 THEN
   20           DO;   N = HISTPAR(I,3) + 1;   HISTDAT(I,N) = HISTDAT(I,N) + 1;
   21           END;
   22       END OBSERV;


NO ERROR OR WARNING CONDITION HAS BEEN DETECTED FOR THIS MACRO PASS.
```

```
        %DECLARE(K,L,M) FIXED;


        SOURCE LISTING.


STMT LEVEL NEST
   1              OBSERV: PROCEDURE(I,X);                                          4
   2      1         DCL OBSVDAT(      2 ,3) FLOAT EXTERNAL;                        5  1
   3      1         Y = 1.;   DO J = 1 TO 3;                                       6
   5      1    1          OBSVDAT(I,J) = OBSVDAT(I,J) + Y;   Y = Y*X;   END;       7
   8      1         RETURN;                                                        8
   9      1         HISTO: ENTRY(I,X);                                            9
  10      1           DCL (HISTPAR(      13 ,3),HISTDAT(      13 ,      11 )) FLOAT   10 1
                    EXTERNAL;                                                     10
                  /* HISTPAR(*,1) = UPPER LIMIT OF FIRST INTERVAL                 11
                     HISTPAR(*,2) = SIZE OF INTERMEDIATE INTERVALS               11
                     HISTPAR(*,3) = NUMBER OF INTERVALS LESS ONE */               11
                                                                                 13
  11      1         JA = 0;   Y = HISTPAR(I,1);                                   14
  13      1         DO J = 1 TO HISTPAR(I,3) WHILE (JA = 0);                      15
  14      1    1       IF X <= Y THEN                                            16
  15      1    1         DO; HISTDAT(I,J) = HISTDAT(I,J) + 1;   JA = 1;   END;    17
  19      1    1       Y = Y + HISTPAR(I,2);   END;                              18
  21      1         IF JA = 0 THEN                                               19
  22      1           DO;   N = HISTPAR(I,3) + 1;   HISTDAT(I,N) = HISTDAT(I,N) + 1;   20
  25      1    1       END;                                                      21
  26      1         END OBSERV;                                                  22
```

Figure 4.25 The source, library, and preprocessed text for the OBSERV procedure.

```
        %DECLARE(K,L,M) FIXED;


COMPILE-TIME MACRO PROCESSOR
MACRO SOURCE2 LISTING

   1       %DECLARE(K,L,M) FIXED;
   2       %K = 2;   %L = 13;   %M = 11;
   3       %INCLUDE PRNTOBS;


INCLUDED TEXT FOLLOWS FROM DD.MEMBER =  SYSLIB   .PRNTOBS

   4    PRNTOBS: PROCEDURE(I,NAME);
   5       DCL OBSVDAT(K,3) FLOAT EXTERNAL;
   6       DCL NAME CHARACTER(40) VARYING;
   7       IF (OBSVDAT(I,1) = 0) THEN
   8          DO;   PUT EDIT(NAME,' HAD NO OBSERVATIONS') (SKIP,A,A);
   9          RETURN;   END;
  10       IF (OBSVDAT(I,1) = 1) THEN
  11          DO;   PUT EDIT(NAME,' ONLY OBSERVATION WAS',OBSVDAT(I,2))
  12          (SKIP,A,A,F(9,5));   RETURN;   END;
  13       Y = OBSVDAT(I,2)/OBSVDAT(I,1);
  14       Z = SQRT((OBSVDAT(I,3) - OBSVDAT(I,2)**2/OBSVDAT(I,1))
  15          /(OBSVDAT(I,1) - 1));
  16       PUT EDIT(NAME,' MEAN = ',Y,' STD DEV = ',Z,' OBSERVATIONS = ',
  17          OBSVDAT(I,1)) (SKIP(2),A(40),A,F(9,5),X(6),A,F(9,5),
  18          X(6),A,F(5,0));
  19       RETURN;
  20    PRNTHIS: ENTRY(I,NAME);
  21       DCL (HISTPAR( L,3),HISTDAT( L, M)) FLOAT EXTERNAL;
  22       PUT EDIT(NAME) (SKIP(3),A);
  23       IN = HISTPAR(I,3) + 1;   X = 0;
  24       DO J = 1 TO IN;   X = X + HISTDAT(I,J);   END;
  25       IF X = 0 THEN
  26          DO;   PUT EDIT('NO OBSERVATIONS') (SKIP,A);   RETURN;   END;
  27       PUT EDIT(' UPPER LIMIT','OBSERVATIONS','PERCENTAGE')
  28          (SKIP(2), 3 (A,X(8)));
  29       UL = HISTPAR(I,1);
  30       DO J = 1 TO IN;   Y = HISTDAT(I,J);
  31       PUT EDIT(UL,Y,Y/X) (SKIP,F(9,2),X(15),F(5,0),X(15),F(7,5));
  32          UL = UL + HISTPAR(I,2);   END;
  33    END PRNTOBS;


NO ERROR OR WARNING CONDITION HAS BEEN DETECTED FOR THIS MACRO PASS.
```

```
        %DECLARE(K,L,M) FIXED;


        SOURCE LISTING.


STMT LEVEL NEST
   1                PRNTOBS: PROCEDURE(I,NAME);                                        4
   2    1              DCL OBSVDAT(       2 ,3) FLOAT EXTERNAL;                        5  1
   3    1              DCL NAME CHARACTER(40) VARYING;                                 6
   4    1              IF (OBSVDAT(I,1) = 0) THEN                                      7
   5    1                 DO;   PUT EDIT(NAME,' HAD NO OBSERVATIONS') (SKIP,A,A);      8
   7    1    1          RETURN;   END;                                                9
   9    1              IF (OBSVDAT(I,1) = 1) THEN                                     10
  10    1                 DO;   PUT EDIT(NAME,' ONLY OBSERVATION WAS',OBSVDAT(I,2))   11
  12    1    1          (SKIP,A,A,F(9,5));   RETURN;   END;                           12
  14    1              Y = OBSVDAT(I,2)/OBSVDAT(I,1);                                 13
  15    1              Z = SQRT((OBSVDAT(I,3) - OBSVDAT(I,2)**2/OBSVDAT(I,1))         14
                          /(OBSVDAT(I,1) - 1));                                       15
  16    1              PUT EDIT(NAME,' MEAN = ',Y,' STD DEV = ',Z,' OBSERVATIONS = ', 16
                          OBSVDAT(I,1)) (SKIP(2),A(40),A,F(9,5),X(6),A,F(9,5),        17
                          X(6),A,F(5,0));                                             18
  17    1              RETURN;                                                        19
  18    1           PRNTHIS: ENTRY(I,NAME);                                           20
  19    1              DCL (HISTPAR(      13 ,3),HISTDAT(      13 ,     11 )) FLOAT    21  1
                       EXTERNAL;                                                      21
  20    1              PUT EDIT(NAME) (SKIP(3),A);                                    22
  21    1              IN = HISTPAR(I,3) + 1;   X = 0;                                23
  23    1              DO J = 1 TO IN;   X = X + HISTDAT(I,J);   END;                 24
  26    1              IF X = 0 THEN                                                  25
  27    1                 DO;   PUT EDIT('NO OBSERVATIONS') (SKIP,A);   RETURN;   END; 26
  31    1              PUT EDIT(' UPPER LIMIT','OBSERVATIONS','PERCENTAGE')           27
                          (SKIP(2), 3 (A,X(8)));                                      28
  32    1              UL = HISTPAR(I,1);                                             29
  33    1              DO J = 1 TO IN;   Y = HISTDAT(I,J);                            30
  35    1    1         PUT EDIT(UL,Y,Y/X) (SKIP,F(9,2),X(15),F(5,0),X(15),F(7,5));    31
  36    1    1            UL = UL + HISTPAR(I,2);   END;                              32
  38    1           END PRNTOBS;                                                     33
```

Figure 4.26 The source, library, and preprocessed text for the PRNTOBS procedure.

```
          TSSEX: PROCEDURE OPTIONS(MAIN);


               SOURCE LISTING.


STMT LEVEL NEST
  1               TSSEX: PROCEDURE OPTIONS(MAIN);                                    1
  2     1           DCL (TIME,ENDTIME,TYPE) FLOAT EXTERNAL, STOP FIXED BIN(31) EXTERNAL;   2
  3     1           DCL (SCHEDUL,TERM) POINTER EXTERNAL;                             3
  4     1           DCL INFO(5) FLOAT EXTERNAL;                                      4
  5     1           DCL SEED(8) FIXED BINARY(31) EXTERNAL INITIAL(1956987325,1156987325,   5
                      1908986925,1508586121,1468582113,1472622913,1480662953,1521070957);   6
  6     1           DCL (OBSVDAT(2,3),HISTPAR(12,3),HISTDAT(12,10)) FLOAT EXTERNAL;  7
  7     1             HISTPAR(*,1) = 1.;    HISTPAR(*,2) = 1.;    HISTPAR(*,3) = 10.;  8
 10     1             CALL CONTROL;                                                  9
 11     1           END TSSEX;                                                      10
```

Figure 4.27 The main procedure for the computer system example.

```
     %DECLARE(EVENT1,EVENT2,EVENT3,EVENT4) CHARACTER;


               SOURCE LISTING.


STMT LEVEL NEST
  1                CONTROL: PROCEDURE; /*TIMING ROUTINE*/                          6
  2     1           DCL (TIME,ENDTIME,TYPE) FLOAT EXTERNAL, STOP FIXED BIN(31) EXTERNAL;   7
  3     1           DCL SCHEDUL POINTER EXTERNAL;                                  8
  4     1           DCL INFO(       5 ) FLOAT EXTERNAL;                          9  1
  5     1            CALL INITIAL;  /*INITIALIZE THE SYSTEM*/                     10
  6     1            DO WHILE (TIME < ENDTIME & STOP = 0);                        11
  7     1    1       CALL GETTOP(SCHEDUL,INFO);                                   12
  8     1    1       A = 0;   DO I = 1 TO         5 ;                           13  1
 10     1    2            A = A + ABS(INFO(I));    END;                           14
 12     1    1       IF A = 0 THEN STOP = 1;                                      15
 14     1    1       ELSE DO;    TIME = INFO(1);    TYPE = INFO(2);               16
 17     1    2            IF TYPE = 1 THEN CALL  POLL ;                         19  1
 19     1    2            ELSE;                                                   21
 20     1    2            IF TYPE = 2 THEN CALL  EXECU ;                        22  1
 22     1    2            ELSE;                                                   24
 23     1    2            IF TYPE = 3 THEN CALL  REPLY ;                        25  1
 25     1    2            ELSE;                                                   27
 26     1    2            IF TYPE = 4 THEN CALL  REQUEST ;                      28  1
 28     1    2            END;                                                    35
 29     1    1       CALL STAT;   /*COLLECT STATISTICS*/                          36
 30     1    1       END;                                                         37
 31     1           CALL OUTPUT;    /*PRINT REPORT*/                             38
 32     1           RETURN;                                                       39
 33     1          END CONTROL;                                                   40
```

Figure 4.28 The CONTROL procedure for the computer system example.

```
          INITIAL: PROCEDURE;


STMT LEVEL NEST
  1               INITIAL: PROCEDURE;
  2     1           DCL (TIME,ENDTIME,TYPE) FLOAT EXTERNAL, STOP FIXED BIN(31) EXTERNAL;
  3     1           DCL (SCHEDUL,TERM) POINTER EXTERNAL;
  4     1           DCL INFO(5) FLOAT EXTERNAL;
  5     1           DCL (OBSVDAT(2,3),HISTPAR(12,3),HISTDAT(12,11)) FLOAT EXTERNAL;
  6     1             HISTDAT = 0.;    OBSVDAT = 0.;    TIME = 0.;    ENDTIME = 150.;
 10     1             I = 1;    CALL INITLST(SCHEDUL,'PRIO',I);
 12     1                  CALL INITLST(TERM,'FIFO',I);
 13     1             INFO(1) = 0;    INFO(2) = 1.;    CALL ADDTO(SCHEDUL,INFO);
 16     1             DO I = 1 TO 12;
 17     1    1             INFO(5) = I;    CALL ADDTO(TERM,INFO);
 19     1    1             CALL REQUEST;    END;
 21     1          END INITIAL;
```

Figure 4.29 The INITIAL procedure for the computer system example.

```
          OUTPUT: PROCEDURE;

STMT LEVEL NEST
  1                    OUTPUT: PROCEDURE;
  2      1                 DCL TIME FLOAT EXTERNAL;
  3      1                 DCL NAME CHARACTER(40) VARYING;
  4      1                 PUT EDIT(' INTERACTIVE SYSTEM PERFORMANCE') (PAGE,A);
  5      1                 PUT SKIP(5);
  6      1                 PUT EDIT(' SIMULATION TIME PERIOD',TIME)
                              (SKIP,A,X(5),F(7,2));
  7      1                 I = 1;    CALL PRNTOBS(I,'POLLING TIME');
  9      1                 I = 2;    CALL PRNTOBS(I,'EXECUTION TIME');
 11      1                 PUT EDIT('TERMINAL WAIT TIME DISTRIBUTIONS') (SKIP(5),A);
 12      1                 DO I = 1 TO 12;   NAME = 'TERMINAL'||I;
 14      1      1              CALL PRNTHIS(I,NAME);   END;
 16      1             END OUTPUT;
```

Figure 4.30 The OUTPUT procedure for the computer system example.

shown in Fig. 4.26. These procedures utilized members of the preprocessor library.

The main procedure for this example is shown in Fig. 4.27, and as in the previous example, is used to declare variables, set parameter values, and call CONTROL. The CONTROL routine is shown in Fig. 4.28. This procedure was generated in a similar manner as in the case shown in the previous example. The INITIAL procedure is shown in Fig. 4.29. In addition to initializing the lists and scheduling the first polling event, it also provides initial conditions for the TERM list. The OUTPUT procedure is shown in Fig. 4.30. It uses the PRNTOBS and PRNTHIS routines of the procedure shown in Fig. 4.26 to print the contents of the data-collection arrays. A portion of the output generated by this example is shown in Fig. 4.31.

4.4 AN ELEVATOR SYSTEM EXAMPLE

Consider an elevator system with two cars operating in two adjacent shafts in a building with 11 floors. Passengers arrive at the elevator entrance at some floor and request service by pressing the up or down call button.

The logic of the elevator car movement is as follows. A car traveling up continues in that direction as long as some passenger on board has a destination floor above the car's present position or if a potential passenger is waiting at a higher floor to go up. If neither of these conditions exists, the car will try to serve potential passengers waiting to go down, with priority given to those waiting at the highest floor. If no one is waiting to go down, the car will try to find passengers waiting below its present position seeking to go up, with priority given to those waiting at the lowest floor. If no passengers remain in the car or are waiting for service, the car remains idle until a call for service occurs. The logic for a car when moving down is similar but with opposite directions of motion.

Assume it has been observed that during periods of heavy use, the two cars tend to move in the same direction the majority of the time. On the basis of this observation, it has been suggested that service could be improved by modifying

INTERACTIVE SYSTEM PERFORMANCE

SIMULATION TIME PERIOD   150.00

POLLING TIME   MEAN =   0.27057   STD DEV =   0.15854   OBSERVATIONS =   151

EXECUTION TIME   MEAN =   0.67574   STD DEV =   0.21864   OBSERVATIONS =   150

TERMINAL WAIT TIME DISTRIBUTIONS

TERMINAL   1

UPPER LIMIT	OBSERVATIONS	PERCENTAGE
1.00	1	0.09091
2.00	3	0.27273
3.00	1	0.09091
4.00	0	0.00000
5.00	1	0.09091
6.00	0	0.00000
7.00	1	0.09091
8.00	1	0.09091
9.00	0	0.00000
10.00	1	0.09091
11.00	2	0.18182

TERMINAL   2

UPPER LIMIT	OBSERVATIONS	PERCENTAGE
1.00	2	0.10526
2.00	7	0.36842
3.00	4	0.21053
4.00	2	0.10526
5.00	0	0.00000
6.00	0	0.00000
7.00	1	0.05263
8.00	0	0.00000
9.00	0	0.00000
10.00	0	0.00000
11.00	3	0.15789

TERMINAL   3

UPPER LIMIT	OBSERVATIONS	PERCENTAGE
1.00	3	0.27273
2.00	3	0.27273
3.00	1	0.09091
4.00	0	0.00000
5.00	1	0.09091
6.00	0	0.00000
7.00	0	0.00000

Figure 4.31 Sample of output from the computer system example program.

the logic for car movement during periods of heavy traffic. The purpose of this simulation example is to investigate that suggestion.

As with the previous examples, the process for developing the system model and simulation program starts by defining the state variables for the system. Next the system events are specified, and then the event routines are programmed.

In order to specify the system state, it is necessary to describe the pertinent information on all passengers in the system. The following variables are used to maintain this data:

ITEM(1) = arrival time in the system, i.e., time passenger arrived at elevator door area

ITEM(2) = floor at which passenger arrived

ITEM(3) = destination floor for the passenger
ITEM(4) = time passenger got on elevator car

This data is maintained in one of the following lists:

WAITING is the list of all passengers waiting for an elevator car.
CAR1 is the list of all passengers on board car 1.
CAR2 is the list of all passengers on board car 2.
OUT is the list of all passengers who exited car during present event (used to pass data to the STAT procedure).

The array FLOOR is used to store the number of passengers waiting at each floor:

FLOOR(1, J) = number of passengers at floor J to travel up
FLOOR(2, J) = number of passengers at floor J to travel down

The data representing the state of the elevator cars is stored in the following arrays:

P(I) is the present position (floor number) of elevator I (equals 0 if the car is moving).
D(I) is the direction of travel for elevator I.

D(I) = 1, indicates elevator is traveling in up direction
= 2, indicates elevator is traveling in down direction
= 3, indicates elevator is idle

S(I, J) is the destination requests of passengers on board elevator I.

S(I, J) = 1, indicates stop at floor J has been requested
= 0, indicates no stop request for floor J

The events used in this model are

Type	Name	Function
1	CALL	Passenger arrives at elevator door area and places call for service.
2	ARRIVE	Elevator car stops at a floor, unloads and loads passengers.
3	LEAVE	Elevator leaves one floor, starts moving toward another.

The event-schedule information is

INFO(1) is the time of scheduled event.
INFO(2) is the type of scheduled event.
INFO(3) is the number of the car scheduled to arrive or leave.

INFO(4) is the destination floor for car scheduled to arrive.

INFO(5) is the direction that caller wishes to travel if idle elevator is sent to caller.

Figure 4.32 is a functional block diagram for the CALL event procedure. For each block, the program statement number of the first operation is shown at the block entry point. A program listing of the CALL procedure is shown in Fig. 4.33.

The passengers are assumed to arrive with exponentially distributed interarrival time. The average interarrival time (AVIAT), used to schedule the next passenger, is read in from a data card by the INITIAL procedure. The arrival and destination floor numbers for each passenger are assigned using an internal

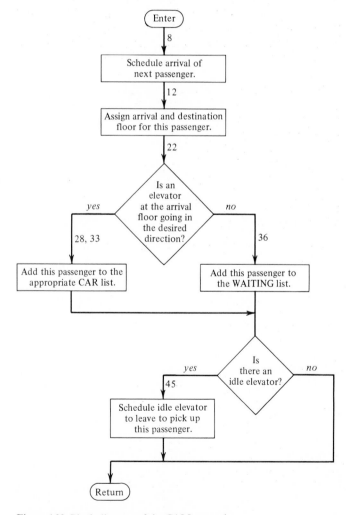

Figure 4.32 Block diagram of the CALL procedure.

```
                    CALL: PROCEDURE;    /*PASSENGER REQUEST ELEVATOR SERVICE*/

STMT LEVEL NEST
 1                              CALL: PROCEDURE;    /*PASSENGER REQUEST ELEVATOR SERVICE*/
 2     1                          DCL (TIME,ENDTIME,TYPE) FLOAT EXTERNAL, STOP FIXED BIN(31) EXTERNAL;
 3     1                          DCL (FLOOR(2,11),D(2),S(2,11),P(2)) FIXED BIN(15) EXTERNAL;
 4     1                          DCL (SCHEDUL,CAR1,CAR2,WAITING,OUT) POINTER EXTERNAL;
 5     1                          DCL INFO(5) FLOAT EXTERNAL;
 6     1                          DCL (AVIAT,B(11,2),C(11,2)) FLOAT EXTERNAL;
 7     1                          DCL A(5) FLOAT;
 8     1                          I = 1;
 9     1                          A(1) = TIME + RNEXP(I,AVIAT);    A(2) = 1;
11     1                          CALL ADDTO(SCHEDUL,A);    /*SCHEDULE NEXT PASSENGER*/
12     1                          A(1) = TIME;    J = 11;    I = 2;
15     1                          A(2) = DFNC(B,J,I);    /*WAITING FLOOR*/
16     1                          A(3) = A(2);    DO WHILE (A(3) = A(2));
18     1     1                        A(3) = DFNC(C,J,I);    END;    /*DESTINATION FLOOR*/
20     1                          INFO(2) = A(2);    INFO(3) = A(3);
                                  /*CHECK IF ELEVATOR AT THIS FLOOR GOING IN DESIRED DIRECTION*/
22     1                          IF A(3) > A(2) THEN DIREC = 1; ELSE DIREC = 2;
25     1                             A(4) = TIME;
26     1                             IF (P(1) = A(2) & (D(1) = DIREC | D(1) = 3.)) THEN
27     1                                DO;    CALL ADDTO(CAR1,A);    S(1,A(3)) = 1;    END;
31     1                             ELSE
31     1                             IF (P(2) = A(2) & (D(2) = DIREC | D(2) = 3.)) THEN
32     1                                DO;    CALL ADDTO(CAR2,A);    S(2,A(3)) = 1;    END;
36     1                             ELSE DO;    /*ADD THIS PASSENGER TO FLOOR ARRAY*/
37     1     1                          FLOOR(DIREC,A(2)) = FLOOR(DIREC,A(2)) + 1;
38     1     1                          CALL ADDTO(WAITING,A);    /*ADD TO LIST WAITING*/
39     1     1                          END;
                                  /*CHECK FOR IDLE ELEVATOR*/
40     1                          IF D(1) = 3 THEN ELNUM = 1;
42     1                          ELSE IF D(2) = 3 THEN ELNUM = 2;
44     1                             ELSE ELNUM = 0;
45     1                          IF ELNUM ¬= 0 THEN    /*SCHEDULE ELEVATOR TO LEAVE*/
46     1                             DO;    A(1) = TIME;    IF A(2) = P(ELNUM) THEN A(4) = A(3);
50     1     1                             ELSE A(4) = A(2);
51     1     1                          IF A(2) < A(3) THEN A(5) = 1;    ELSE A(5) = 2;
54     1     1                          A(2) = 3;    A(3) = ELNUM;    CALL ADDTO(SCHEDUL,A);    END;
58     1                          DFNC: PROCEDURE(Y,N,I) RETURNS(FLOAT);
59     2                             DCL Y(11,2) FLOAT, (N,I) FIXED BIN(15);
60     2                             K = 1;    X = RND(I);
62     2                             DO WHILE (X > Y(K,1) & K < N);
63     2     1                          K = K + 1;    END;
65     2                             RETURN(Y(K,2));
66     2                          END DFNC;
67     1                       END CALL;
```

Figure 4.33 The CALL event routine for the elevator example.

procedure named DFNC. This procedure selects 1 of 11 discrete values randomly. For this example, the probability of arrival and destination for each floor are as follows:

Floor number	Percentage of passenger arrivals	Percentage of passenger destinations
1	20	11
2	22	31
3	4	5
4	11	10
5	7	7
6	7	7
7	7	7
8	7	7
9	6	6
10	5	5
11	4	4

The input data for the DFNC procedure, arrays B and C, are cumulative distribution functions of these frequency distributions. The data for B and C is read in by the INITIAL procedure, and the input data cards are
For B,

.2, 1, .42, 2, .46, 3, .57, 4, .64, 5, .71, 6, .78, 7, .85, 8, .91, 9,

.96, 10, 1, 11

For C,

.11, 1, .42, 2, .47, 3, .57, 4, .64, 5, .71, 6, .78, 7, .85, 8, .91, 9,

.96, 10, 1, 11

A block diagram for the ARRIVE event procedure is given in Fig. 4.34, and

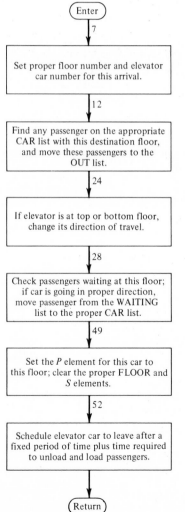

Figure 4.34 Block diagram for the ARRIVE procedure.

Fig. 4.35 is the corresponding program listing. The basic operations in this event are moving passengers out of and into the elevator car. The delay between arrival and scheduled leaving is intended to approximate the time an elevator spends stopped at a floor, although this time is actually a random variable in the real system.

The LEAVE event procedure in functional block diagram form is shown in Fig. 4.36 and is listed in Fig. 4.37. The number of the elevator scheduled to leave is passed to this procedure by the INFO(3) variable, and the number of the floor from which it is leaving is obtained from the *P* array. If the elevator car is idle at the time this event occurs, the car is sent immediately to the last caller, and its arrival at the caller's floor is scheduled as a future event.

If the car scheduled to leave is not idle, then it is necessary to determine which floor will be its next stop. At this point in the simulation (program statement 15), alternative scheduling strategies for the elevator system can be introduced. In this example, one alternate operating rule is included and is implemented in a procedure named ALTSTG.

Statements 17 to 67 of procedure LEAVE serve to carry out the original elevator scheduling rule. If the elevator is going up and has a scheduled stop at a higher floor, or if a passenger at a higher floor is going up, then the variable OVR

```
      ARRIVE: PROCEDURE;    /*ELEVATOR ARRIVES AT A FLOOR*/

STMT LEVEL NEST
 1                          ARRIVE: PROCEDURE;    /*ELEVATOR ARRIVES AT A FLOOR*/
 2     1                    DCL (TIME,ENDTIME,TYPE) FLOAT EXTERNAL, STOP FIXED BIN(31) EXTERNAL;
 3     1                    DCL (FLOOR(2,11),D(2),S(2,11),P(2)) FIXED BIN(15) EXTERNAL;
 4     1                    DCL (SCHEDUL,CAR1,CAR2,WAITING,OUT) POINTER EXTERNAL;
 5     1                    DCL INFO(5) FLOAT EXTERNAL;
 6     1                    DCL (CAR,PNTR) POINTER;
 7     1                       FLNUM = INFO(4);    ELNUM = INFO(3);
 9     1                       IF ELNUM = 1 THEN CAR = CAR1;    ELSE CAR = CAR2;
12     1                       I = 3;    NUMEX = 0;
14     1                    CALL FINDELE(CAR,I,'EQU',FLNUM,PNTR);
15     1                    IF (PNTR ¬= NULL) THEN    /*UNLOAD PASSENGERS*/
16     1                       DO;
17     1     1                 DO WHILE(PNTR ¬= NULL);
18     1     2                 CALL GETELE(CAR,INFO,PNTR);    NUMEX = NUMEX + 1;
20     1     2                 CALL ADDTO(OUT,INFO);    /*PUT DEPARTING PASSENGERS INTO OUT*/
21     1     2                 CALL FINDELE(CAR,I,'EQU',FLNUM,PNTR);    END;
23     1     1                 END;
24     1                    IF FLNUM = 1 THEN D(ELNUM) = 1;
26     1                    IF FLNUM = 11 THEN D(ELNUM) = 2;
28     1                    NUMWT = FLOOR(D(ELNUM),FLNUM);    J = 2;
30     1                    IF (NUMWT ¬= 0) THEN    /*LOAD WAITING PASSENGERS*/
31     1                       DO;    I = 1;
33     1     1                 DO WHILE(I ¬> NUMWT);    /*MOVE FROM WAITING LIST TO CAR*/
34     1     2                 CALL FINDELE(WAITING,J,'EQU',FLNUM,PNTR);
35     1     2                 CALL GETELE(WAITING,INFO,PNTR);
36     1     2                 IF INFO(2) < INFO(3) THEN DIREC = 1;    ELSE DIREC = 2;
39     1     2                 IF D(ELNUM) = DIREC THEN
40     1     2                    DO;    INFO(4) = TIME;    CALL ADDTO(CAR,INFO);
43     1     3                    S(ELNUM,INFO(3)) = 1;    I = I + 1;    END;
46     1     2                 ELSE CALL ADDTO(WAITING,INFO);
47     1     2                 END;
48     1     1                 END;
49     1                    P(ELNUM) = FLNUM;    /*CLEAR ARRAYS FOR THIS FLOOR*/
50     1                    FLOOR(D(ELNUM),FLNUM) = 0;    S(ELNUM,FLNUM) = 0;
52     1                    INFO(1) = TIME + .5 + NUMEX + NUMWT;
53     1                    INFO(2) = 3;    INFO(3) = ELNUM;
55     1                    CALL ADDTO(SCHEDUL,INFO);    /*SCHEDULE DEPARTURE*/
56     1                    RETURN;
57     1                    END ARRIVE;
```

Figure 4.35 The ARRIVE event routine for the elevator example.

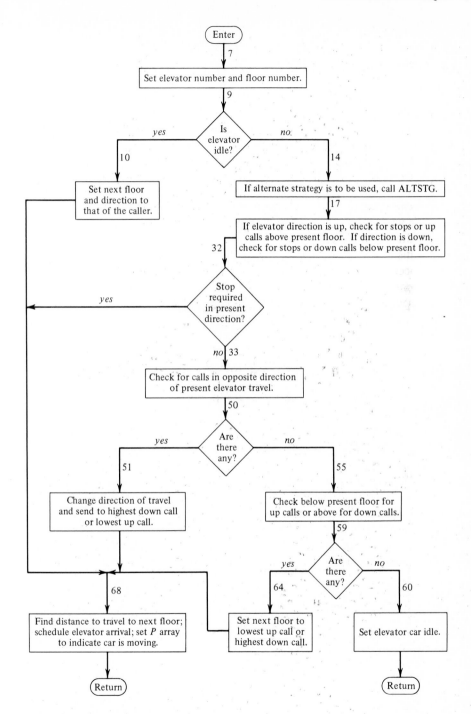

Figure 4.36 Block diagram for the LEAVE procedure.

```
          LEAVE: PROCEDURE;

STMT LEVEL NEST
   1                 LEAVE: PROCEDURE;
   2    1                DCL (TIME,ENDTIME,TYPE) FLOAT EXTERNAL, STOP FIXED BIN(31) EXTERNAL;
   3    1                DCL (FLOOR(2,11),D(2),S(2,11),P(2),ALT) FIXED BIN(15) EXTERNAL;
   4    1                DCL (SCHEDUL,CAR1,CAR2,WAITING,OUT) POINTER EXTERNAL;
   5    1                DCL INFO(5) FLOAT EXTERNAL;
   6    1                DCL A(5) FLOAT, (ELNUM,FLNUM,CVR) FIXED BIN(15);
   7    1                ELNUM = INFO(3);    FLNUM = P(ELNUM);
   9    1                IF D(ELNUM) = 3 THEN    /*SEND TO CALLER*/
  10    1                    DO;   NXFL = INFO(4);   D(ELNUM) = INFO(5);    END;
  14    1                ELSE   /*FIND NEXT STOP*/
  14    1                DO;   IF ALT = 1 THEN CALL ALTSTG(ELNUM,FLNUM);
  17    1    1          OVR = 0;    NXFL = FLNUM;
  19    1    1          IF D(ELNUM) = 1 THEN M = 1;    ELSE M = -1;
  22    1    1          IF D(ELNUM) = 1 THEN N = 1;    ELSE N = 2;
  25    1    1          DO WHILE((NXFL + M) < 12 & (NXFL + M) > 0 & OVR = 0);
  26    1    2              NXFL = NXFL + M;    IF FLOOR(N,NXFL) ¬= 0 THEN OVR = 1;
  29    1    2              IF (S(ELNUM,NXFL) = 1) THEN OVR = 1;    END;
  32    1    1          IF OVR = 0 THEN    /*NO MORE STOPS IN THIS DIRECTION*/
  33    1    1              DO;   IF D(ELNUM) = 1 THEN   /*CHECK FOR DOWN CALLS*/
  35    1    2                  DO;   L = 2;    I = 11;    K = -1;    J = 1;    END;
  41    1    2              ELSE   /*CHECK FOR UP CALLS*/
  41    1    2                  DO; L = 1;    I = 1;    K = 1;    J = 11;    END;
  47    1    2              DO WHILE(FLOOR(L,I) = 0 & I ¬= J);
  48    1    3                  I = I + K;    END;
  50    1    2              IF I ¬= J THEN   /*CHANGE DIRECTION OF TRAVEL*/
  51    1    2                  DO;   D(ELNUM) = L;    NXFL = I;    END;
  55    1    2              ELSE   /*CHECK FOR PASSENGERS BELOW GOING UP OR ABOVE GOING DOWN*/
  55    1    2                  DO;   /*I IS NOW 1 OR 11*/
  56    1    3                      DO WHILE(FLOOR(N,I) = 0 & I ¬= FLNUM);
  57    1    4                          I = I + M;    END;
  59    1    3                      IF I = FLNUM  THEN   /*SET ELEVATOR IDLE*/
  60    1    3                          DO;   D(ELNUM) = 3;    RETURN;    END;
  64    1    3                      NXFL = I;    END;
  66    1    2              END;
  67    1    1          END;
  68    1              DIST = ABS(NXFL - FLNUM);
  69    1              IF DIST = 0 THEN A(1) = TIME - 5;    /*ELIMINATE EXTRA DOOR OPEN*/
  71    1              ELSE A(1) = TIME + 5 + DIST;
  72    1              A(2) = 2;    A(3) = ELNUM;    A(4) = NXFL;
  75    1              CALL ADDTO(SCHEDUL,A);    /*SCHEDULE NEXT ARRIVAL*/
  76    1              P(ELNUM) = 0;
  77    1              RETURN;
  78    1          END LEAVE;
```

Figure 4.37 The LEAVE event routine for the elevator example.

is set to 1 and the next floor is set to the lowest floor number which is a scheduled stop or has a waiting passenger going up. For an elevator car going down, a similar result occurs. If OVR is not set to 1, this indicates the elevator has no scheduled stops, i.e., is empty of passengers. In this case, the FLOOR array is searched to find where the waiting passenger with top priority is located.

The listing for the procedure ALTSTG is given in Fig. 4.38. When this alternate strategy is used, if both elevator cars are moving in the up direction,

```
          ALTSTG: PROCEDURE(ELNUM,FLNUM);

STMT LEVEL NEST
   1                 ALTSTG: PROCEDURE(ELNUM,FLNUM);
   2    1                DCL (D(2),S(2,11)) FIXED BIN(15) EXTERNAL;
   3    1                DCL (ELNUM,FLNUM) FIXED BIN(15);
   4    1                IF (FLNUM < 5 | D(1) ¬= 1 | D(2) ¬= 1) THEN RETURN;   /*CHECK
                             THAT BOTH ARE GOING UP AND THAT ELEVATOR IS LEAVING AN
                             UPPER FLOOR*/
   6    1                J = 0;   /*CHECK IF ANY ONBOARD PASSENGERS ARE GOING UP*/
   7    1                DO I = FLNUM TO 12;    IF S(ELNUM,I) = 1 THEN J = 1;    END;
  11    1                IF J = 1 THEN RETURN;
  13    1                ELSE D(ELNUM) = 2;   /*IF NOT, SET ELEVATOR TO GO DOWN*/
  14    1             END ALTSTG;
```

Figure 4.38 Alternate strategy procedure for the elevator example.

and the car scheduled to leave is departing from floor 5 or higher but has no onboard passengers going up, its direction of travel is changed to down. This strategy is used to prevent the two cars from moving in a synchronized fashion.

The main procedure, LIFT, and the INITIAL, STAT, and OUTPUT procedures for this example are listed in Figs. 4.39 to 4.42. The procedures CONTROL, OBSERV, and PRNTOBS were generated using the preprocessor library in a manner similar to that of the previous example. .

Note that this example uses input data cards for establishing the number of repetitions of the simulation run as well as for the average passenger interarrival time and distributions for arrival and destination floors. The number of runs is read in by the main procedure and appears once on a data card. The other information is read by the INITIAL procedure on each run so that it may vary from one run to another. Input data should usually be read in by either the main procedure or the INITIAL procedure. The choice between these two for locating the input statements is dependent on how repetitive simulation runs are to be carried out.

Portions of sample outputs of this example program are shown in Figs. 4.43

```
        LIFT: PROCEDURE OPTIONS(MAIN);

STMT LEVEL NEST
   1              LIFT: PROCEDURE OPTIONS(MAIN);
   2      1       DCL (TIME,ENDTIME,TYPE) FLOAT EXTERNAL, STOP FIXED BIN(31) EXTERNAL;
   3      1       DCL INFO(5) FLOAT EXTERNAL;
   4      1       DCL (SCHEDUL,CAR1,CAR2,WAITING,OUT) POINTER EXTERNAL;
   5      1       DCL (FLOOR(2,11),D(2),S(2,11),P(2),ALT) FIXED BIN(15) EXTERNAL;
   6      1       DCL SEED(8) FIXED BINARY(31) EXTERNAL INITIAL(1956987325,1156987325,
                    1908986925,1508586121,1468582113,1472622913,1480662953,1521070957);
   7      1       DCL OBSVDAT(2,3) FLOAT EXTERNAL;
   8      1       DCL (HISTPAR(13,3),HISTDAT(13,11)) FLOAT EXTERNAL;
   9      1       DCL (AVIAT,B(11,2),C(11,2)) FLOAT EXTERNAL;
  10      1         HISTPAR(*,1) = 1.;    HISTPAR(*,2) = 1.;   HISTPAR(*,3) = 10.;
  13      1         HISTPAR(12,1) = 60.;  HISTPAR(12,2) = 30.;  HISTPAR(12,3) = 10.;
  16      1         HISTPAR(13,1) = 60.;  HISTPAR(13,2) = 30.;  HISTPAR(13,3) = 10.;
  19      1         ALT = 0;
  20      1         GET LIST(NO_RUNS);
  21      1         DO I = 1 TO NO_RUNS;   CALL CONTROL;   END;
  24      1       END LIFT;
```

Figure 4.39 Main procedure for the elevator example.

```
        INITIAL: PROCEDURE;

STMT LEVEL NEST
   1              INITIAL: PROCEDURE;
   2      1       DCL (TIME,ENDTIME,TYPE) FLOAT EXTERNAL, STOP FIXED BIN(31) EXTERNAL;
   3      1       DCL (FLOOR(2,11),D(2),S(2,11),P(2)) FIXED BIN(15) EXTERNAL;
   4      1       DCL (SCHEDUL,CAR1,CAR2,WAITING,OUT) POINTER EXTERNAL;
   5      1       DCL (AVIAT,B(11,2),C(11,2)) FLOAT EXTERNAL;
   6      1       DCL A(5) FLOAT;
   7      1         GET LIST(TIME,ENDTIME,STOP);
   8      1         GET LIST (AVIAT,B,C);
   9      1         I = 1;   CALL INITLST(SCHEDUL,'PRIO',I);
  11      1                  CALL INITLST(WAITING,'FIFO',I);
  12      1                  CALL INITLST(CAR1,'FIFO',I);
  13      1                  CALL INITLST(CAR2,'FIFO',I);
  14      1                  CALL INITLST(OUT,'FIFO',I);
  15      1         A(1) = 1;   A(2) = 1;   CALL ADDTO(SCHEDUL,A);
  18      1         FLOOR = 0;   D = 3;   S = 0;   P = 1;
  22      1         RETURN;
  23      1       END INITIAL;
```

Figure 4.40 The INITIAL procedure for the elevator example.

```
        STAT: PROCEDURE;

STMT LEVEL NEST
   1                     STAT: PROCEDURE;
   2      1                 DCL (TIME,ENDTIME,TYPE) FLOAT EXTERNAL, STOP FIXED BIN(31) EXTERNAL;
   3      1                 DCL (SCHEDUL,CAR1,CAR2,WAITING,OUT) POINTER EXTERNAL;
   4      1                 DCL INFO(5) FLOAT EXTERNAL;
   5      1                 IF TYPE = 1 THEN    /*RECORD DESTINATION FOR EACH FLOOR*/
   6      1                    DO;    I = INFO(2);    Z = INFO(3);
   9      1    1                CALL HISTO(I,Z);    END;
  11      1                 ELSE
  11      1                 IF TYPE = 2 THEN    /*RECORD PASSENGER WAITING AND SYSTEM TIMES*/
  12      1                    DO;    CALL GETTOP(OUT,INFO);
  14      1    1                DO WHILE(SUM(INFO) ¬= 0);
  15      1    2                  I = 1;    Z = TIME - INFO(1);    CALL OBSERV(I,Z);
  18      1    2                  J = 12;    CALL HISTO(J,Z);
  20      1    2                  I = 2;    Z = INFO(4) - INFO(1);    CALL OBSERV(I,Z);
  23      1    2                  J = 13;    CALL HISTO(J,Z);
  25      1    2                  CALL GETTOP(OUT,INFO);    END;
  27      1    1                END;
  28      1                 END STAT;
```

Figure 4.41 The STAT procedure for the elevator example.

```
        OUTPUT: PROCEDURE;

STMT LEVEL NEST
   1                     OUTPUT: PROCEDURE;
   2      1                 DCL (TIME,ENDTIME,TYPE) FLOAT EXTERNAL, STOP FIXED BIN(31) EXTERNAL;
   3      1                 DCL ALT FIXED BIN(15) EXTERNAL;
   4      1                 DCL NAME CHARACTER(40) VARYING;
   5      1                 PUT EDIT('ELEVATOR SYSTEM PERFORMANCE') (PAGE,A);
   6      1                 PUT SKIP(4);
   7      1                 PUT EDIT('STRATEGY USED IN THIS RUN,  ',ALT) (A,F(3));
   8      1                 PUT EDIT('SIMULATION TIME PERIOD',TIME) (SKIP,A,X(5),F(7,2));
   9      1                 PUT SKIP(2);
  10      1                 I = 1;    CALL PRNTOBS(I,'TOTAL TIME IN SYSTEM');
  12      1                 J = 12;    CALL PRNTHIS(J,'DISTRIBUTION');
  14      1                 PUT SKIP(2);
  15      1                 I = 2;    CALL PRNTOBS(I,'WAITING TIME');
  17      1                 J = 13;    CALL PRNTHIS(J,'DISTRIBUTION');
  19      1                 PUT PAGE;
  20      1                 PUT EDIT('DESTINATION FLOOR DISTRIBUTIONS') (SKIP(5),A);
  21      1                    DO I = 1 TO 11;    NAME = 'ORIGIN FLOOR '||I;
  23      1    1                CALL PRNTHIS(I,NAME);    END;
  25      1                 END OUTPUT;
```

Figure 4.42 The OUTPUT procedure for the elevator example.

and 4.44, which correspond to the original and to the alternate elevator scheduling strategy, respectively. These results do indicate a significant change in average waiting time for the passengers of approximately 25 s. By printing out a plot of the elevator car positions versus time, it can be shown that the original strategy does result in the two cars tending to move together when a relatively large number of passengers are waiting for service. The alternate strategy does reduce this tendency, which accounts for the better service.

4.5 BACKGROUND AND REFERENCES

The programming system of this chapter is similar in approach to the GASP system developed by Pritsker [10]. The GASP system is more comprehensive, most notably in that standard input and output capabilities and also debugging facilities are included.

```
ELEVATOR SYSTEM PERFORMANCE


STRATEGY USED IN THIS RUN.     0
SIMULATION TIME PERIOD     1805.60


TOTAL TIME IN SYSTEM      MEAN = 147.61101      STD DEV =   77.60287      OBSERVATIONS =    343


DISTRIBUTION

 UPPER LIMIT          OBSERVATIONS           PERCENTAGE
     60.00                48                   0.13994
     90.00                42                   0.12245
    120.00                56                   0.16327
    150.00                37                   0.10787
    180.00                36                   0.10496
    210.00                39                   0.11370
    240.00                29                   0.08455
    270.00                33                   0.09621
    300.00                17                   0.04956
    330.00                 6                   0.01749
    360.00                 0                   0.00000


WAITING TIME             MEAN =  97.35011      STD DEV =   69.36748      OBSERVATIONS =    343


DISTRIBUTION

 UPPER LIMIT          OBSERVATIONS           PERCENTAGE
     60.00               124                   0.36152
     90.00                46                   0.13411
    120.00                44                   0.12828
    150.00                31                   0.09038
    180.00                38                   0.11079
    210.00                43                   0.12536
    240.00                17                   0.04956
    270.00                 0                   0.00000
    300.00                 0                   0.00000
    330.00                 0                   0.00000
    360.00                 0                   0.00000
```

Figure 4.43 Sample output for the elevator example, using the original strategy.

The event-scheduling approach used here is also the basic modeling technique used with the SIMSCRIPT simulation language [1, 8]. Programming a simulation in SIMSCRIPT includes writing event routines that have the same function as those in this chapter. These event routines are written using FORTRAN-like statements, but SIMSCRIPT provides many special "commands" and other facilities not available in FORTRAN. The special features of SIMSCRIPT greatly simplify the simulation programming task.

The event-scheduling approach is not the only way to model and program discrete-event processes. The GPSS simulation language [2, 3] uses the process interaction approach, which emphasizes the progress of an entity through a system from its arrival event to its departure event. Programming in this language requires describing the paths through a system which the entities traverse in terms of the activities which act on the entities. These activities are specified by special terms called *block types*. A major goal of this language is to permit the user to describe a system in terms of block diagrams and to convert this diagram directly into a program.

```
ELEVATOR SYSTEM PERFORMANCE


STRATEGY USED IN THIS RUN.    1
SIMULATION TIME PERIOD    1801.98


TOTAL TIME IN SYSTEM          MEAN = 120.93823     STD DEV =   67.62662     OBSERVATIONS =    351

DISTRIBUTION

  UPPER LIMIT         OBSERVATIONS           PERCENTAGE
     60.00                70                  0.19943
     90.00                63                  0.17949
    120.00                66                  0.18803
    150.00                43                  0.12251
    180.00                42                  0.11966
    210.00                21                  0.05983
    240.00                21                  0.05983
    270.00                16                  0.04558
    300.00                 8                  0.02279
    330.00                 1                  0.00285
    360.00                 0                  0.00000


WAITING TIME                  MEAN =  72.33264     STD DEV =   57.21825     OBSERVATIONS =    351

DISTRIBUTION

  UPPER LIMIT         OBSERVATIONS           PERCENTAGE
     60.00               177                  0.50427
     90.00                53                  0.15100
    120.00                46                  0.13105
    150.00                36                  0.10256
    180.00                18                  0.05128
    210.00                15                  0.04274
    240.00                 5                  0.01425
    270.00                 1                  0.00285
    300.00                 0                  0.00000
    330.00                 0                  0.00000
    360.00                 0                  0.00000
```

Figure 4.44 Sample output for the elevator example, using alternate strategy.

The primary advantage of special-purpose simulation languages is the reduction in programming time required by a simulation project. There are other reasons for choosing to use these languages, and often the choice is determined by past practice in an organization or by the desire to obtain a study which is readily comparable with other projects. Anyone involved with many simulation programming efforts will, in all probability, need to use several different special-purpose simulation languages.

The complete specifications and facilities of the PL/I language are contained in the appropriate manuals of various computer manufacturers. For the IBM System 360/370, the F-level version of the language, see references [4] and [5]. For additional information on programming techniques for processing lists, see reference [6]. Similarly, reference [7] discusses the preprocessor facilities of PL/I.

The computer routines presented in this chapter are only the skeleton of a simulation programming system. But they can be extended to provide a very useful aid in programming simulations. The best guides to desirable extensions are the various simulation languages which have had wide application.

REFERENCES

1. Consolidated Analysis Centers Inc.: "SIMSCRIPT II.5 Reference Handbook," Los Angeles, 1972.
2. IBM Corporation: "General Purpose Simulation System 1360 Introductory User's Manual," H20-0304, White Plains, N.Y., 1967.
3. IBM Corporation: "General Purpose Simulation System 1360 User's Manual," H20-0326, White Plains, N.Y., 1967.
4. IBM Corporation: "IBM System/360: PL/I Reference Manual," C28-8201, White Plains, N.Y.,
5. IBM Corporation: "IBM System/360 Operating System: PL/I(F) Programmer's Guide," C28-6594, White Plains, N.Y.,
6. IBM Corporation: "Introduction to the List Processing Facilities of PL/I," GF20-0015; "Techniques for Processing Data Lists in PL/I," GF20-0018; "Techniques for Processing Pointer Lists and Lists of Lists in PL/I," GF20-0019, White Plains, N.Y., 1971.
7. IBM Corporation: "An Introduction to the Compile-Time Facilities of PL/I," C20-1689, White Plains, N.Y., 1968.
8. Kiviat, P. J., R. Villanueva, and H. Markowitz: "The SIMSCRIPT II Programming Language," Prentice-Hall, Englewood Cliffs, N.J., 1969.
9. Marsaglia, G., and T. A. Bray: A Convenient Method for Generating Normal Variables, *SIAM Review*, vol. 6, no. 3, pp. 260–264, 1964.
10. Pritsker, A. A. B.: "The GASP IV Simulation Language," Wiley, New York, 1975.

EXERCISES

4.1 Write a PL/I procedure which will print out the contents of all elements in a list of the type used in the example of this chapter. The name of the procedure should be PRNTLST, and the only parameter should be the list NAME pointer. The elements should not be removed from the list.

4.2 Modify the CONTROL procedure text in the preprocessor library to provide the option of a trace feature which will print the contents of each SCHEDUL element immediately prior to the corresponding event routine execution.

4.3 Add a new member to the preprocessor library named OBTIV that can be used to record time-integrated data for a variable. It should be similar to library members OBSERV and PRTOBS.

4.4 Use the programming system of this chapter to simulate a single-server queuing system. Assume that the arrivals to this system are exponentially distributed with a mean interarrival time of 30 s and that the service time is exponentially distributed with a mean of 20 s. Compare your results with the theoretical values for this system.

4.5 Simulate the inventory simulation example for a range of stock control level values from 10 to 50 units. Make a plot of the average weekly profit versus the stock control level.

4.6 Modify the interactive computer system example to print out the average value and standard deviation of the computer response time and a histogram of these values. The computer response time is the period between the operator request event and the computer reply event.

4.7 Modify the elevator system example of Sec. 4.4 so that no more than 10 passengers can be in a car at one time.

4.8 Assume that in Fig. 4.35, the following statements are added to the procedure between present statements 42 and 43:

IF (RND(ELNUM) < .01) THEN S(ELNUM,*) = 1:

What physical event does this addition simulate?

4.9 Consider a gas station that has two service lanes. Each lane has room for two cars, but only one car can be serviced at any one time in a given lane. Assume that potential customers arrive at the station site with a mean interarrival time of 5 min, exponentially distributed. If no lane is empty, 25 percent of the potential customers will bypass the station; and if both lanes are filled, all potential customers bypass the station. The service times for all customers are approximately normally distributed, with a mean value of 6 min and a standard deviation of $1\frac{1}{2}$ min, but no service times of less than 3 min or more than 9 min occur. Simulate this system to determine what percentage of potential customers is lost and the percentage of time service is actually being provided in each lane.

4.10 Assume that there is a small concrete plant which can produce a batch of concrete, 25-yd³ in volume, in a period of 30 min. After the concrete is produced, it is placed in a 50-yd³-capacity hopper. The plant can start another batch after this operation but only when the hopper contains less than 25-yd³. Also assume there are 10 trucks of 5-yd³ capacity which are to be loaded from the hopper. The time to load each truck is 5 min. The trucks deliver the concrete to various sites, and the travel times correspond to the following frequency distribution:

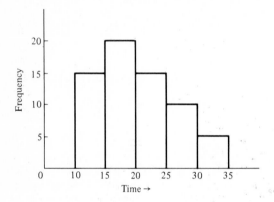

At the site the truck must wait to unload. This waiting time is exponentially distributed with a mean of 10 min. Unloading time is uniformly distributed in a range from 5 to 15 min. The return trip to the plant requires the same time as the outbound trip. Operation of this system starts each day at 8 A.M. with 50-yd³ of concrete in the hopper and all trucks at the plant, empty and ready to load. No new batch of concrete can be started after 2:30 P.M., and no truck can leave the plant after 3:20 P.M. Simulate this system to determine the average amount of concrete which can be delivered in a day and the amount of time after 4 P.M. trucks will require to complete the last trip. Include overtime of each truck in this last amount.

FIVE

SPECIAL-PURPOSE SIMULATION LANGUAGES

Simulation programs for three example systems were developed in Chap. 4. The objective of that presentation was to demonstrate a general approach to programming simulations and to indicate how common features of these programs could be generated using library-type routines and procedures. This library of simulation programming aids can be expanded to include a vast number of program segments and source code sets. Although enlarging these libraries can reduce the programming effort, this also tends to make the programming system less accessible because the library is constantly changing and growing in size.

Special-purpose simulation languages represent a further step toward reducing the programming effort required in simulations. These facilities incorporate many of the features which could be included in a library, into a programming language. This relieves the programmer of the task of linking to the library routines. It also fixes the library, which provides well-defined operations available to the users.

Many special-purpose simulation languages have been developed, and all that have remained in use do provide an effective programming method for certain types of simulation problems. Each of these languages, to some extent, emphasizes a particular type of system-modeling approach. This characteristic can be very helpful in developing simulation models, but it may also tend to restrict the type of models considered. This restriction is often not due to limitations of the language but rather due to the fact that some types of operations are more conveniently provided by that language.

Learning a new programming language is not an easy task. It requires a careful study of the language manuals and considerable practice in writing programs. Most people are reluctant to spend this effort unless they are convinced that it is necessary to achieve a useful purpose. In this case of special-purpose simulation languages, it is not only programming convenience that justifies such an effort. Often the most useful results from learning one of these languages are the new simulation concepts and techniques contained in the language and the ability to read programs written in the language. The use of programming languages as a means of communication between people is of great importance and can be made much easier by the use of specialized languages.

This chapter will introduce the basic programming procedures and illustrate some of the techniques of two special-purpose simulation languages, SIM-SCRIPT [10] and GPSS [6]. These are the most widely used languages of this type, at least in the United States, and are good examples of successful developments in this area. The approach used is to present the examples of Chap. 4, programmed in these languages, as a means of introducing a limited number of language features and concepts. The objective of this chapter is to give a brief overview of the languages that shows the potential advantages they offer and that provides enough details to guide the preparation of a few simple programs. This material is sufficient to begin a study of these languages, but their efficient use and a full appreciation of their capabilities require reference to the appropriate language manuals.

5.1 THE SIMSCRIPT LANGUAGE

SIMSCRIPT was originally developed at the Rand Corporation in the early 1960s as a tool to improve the discrete-event simulation capabilities of that organization's research personnel. Dr. H. M. Markowitz was the principal designer of the original version, SIMSCRIPT I, and the later, extended version, SIM-SCRIPT II. The language was modified and improved over a period of years and has become useful in other areas of applications programming as well. A version of the language denoted as SIMSCRIPT II.5 has been supported by Consolidated Analysis Center, Inc., since 1972. This corporation markets and maintains compiler programs, documentation, and instructional services for the general computing public. The availability of this type of support is a primary reason for the wide use of the language.

The event-scheduling programming approach used in Chap. 4 corresponds to the programming technique used in SIMSCRIPT. Simulation programs for the examples of Chap. 4, written in SIMSCRIPT, will result in executing operations very similar to the PL/I programs of that chapter. The major difference is that many of the necessary operations are built-in parts of the SIMSCRIPT language.

5.1.1 The Inventory System Example in SIMSCRIPT

Figure 5.1 is a listing of a SIMSCRIPT II.5 program for the inventory system example of Sec. 4.2. The program consists of a PREAMBLE section, a MAIN section, and several ROUTINE and EVENT sections. The format used in SIM-SCRIPT is free form, similar to that of PL/I, but the end of statements is not denoted by a semicolon; a period may be used, but this is optional. The line numbers shown in Fig. 5.1 are not included in the program but are added by the language processor for identification purposes.

The PREAMBLE section is used to declare or define characteristics of certain variables used in the simulation program. This section must be the first one so that these programs begin with the one-word statement PREAMBLE. The statement shown in line 2 of this section specifies that all numerical variables will have real values unless defined to be an integer. The statement of line 3 declares that the system, or process being modeled, has a list or a set of entities with the name ORDERS. Recall that in the program of Sec. 4.2 a list with the name ORDERS was created to store elements which included data regarding the number of items requisitioned by each order. A similar set is specified by the statement of line 3, and the elements of this set are defined by the statement of line 5. This statement assigns the name ORDER to denote an element of this set and the name NUMBER to denote a parameter of this element. Since any particular order will be in the system for only part of the simulation, it is declared within the TEMPORARY ENTITIES subsection of the PREAMBLE. Line 6 defines another subsection of the preamble which declares the names of the EVENT NOTICES. Note that the names given for the event notices, SALE, INVTORY, and RECEIVE, are the same as those used for the event routines in the program of Sec. 4.2. The names serve the same function in both programs. Lines 7 and 8 are used to define a number of global variables which are available for use throughout the program. These variables have the same names and are used for the same purposes as many of the external variables of the program of Sec. 4.2. Space allocation for global variables in SIMSCRIPT is similar to static allocation in PL/I.

Line 9 illustrates the manner in which arrays are declared in SIMSCRIPT. The variable STKLEV is used to store data needed to compute the average value of stock level, just as it was in the program of Sec. 4.2. Actually this part of the program is not necessary since SIMSCRIPT includes built-in facilities for collecting time-integrated values but is included to provide greater correspondence between the SIMSCRIPT and PL/I programs for this example.

The preamble section concludes with an END statement as do all sections of a SIMSCRIPT program.

The MAIN program section is where program executing begins. The statement in line 2 of this section allocates memory space and specifies the range for the one-dimensional array variable STKLEV. A RESERVE statement can appear in any section except the preamble of a SIMSCRIPT program. The statement of line 3 of the main program causes the subprogram routine INITIAL to be executed.

The routine INITIAL, as shown in Fig. 5.1, performs basically the same operations performed by the main procedure INVENEX shown in Fig. 4.18 and by the procedure INITIAL shown in Fig. 4.17. That is, it sets parameter values and schedules the first occurrence of the events SALE and INVTORY. The method used here for setting parameter values is similar to the form of assignment statements in PL/I and FORTRAN but requires the introductory keyword

```
1   PREAMBLE
2   NORMALLY MODE IS REAL
3   THE SYSTEM OWNS AN ORDERS
4   TEMPORARY ENTITIES
5   EVERY ORDER HAS A NUMBER AND MAY BELONG TO THE ORDERS
6   EVENT NOTICES INCLUDE SALE, INVTORY AND RECEIVE.
7   DEFINE STOCK, SALES, ONORDER, LOSTSLS, INVTPRD, INVTLEV, DELTIME,
8       NOORDERS, NOINVT AND ENDTIME AS VARIABLES.
9   DEFINE STKLEV AS A 1-DIM ARRAY
10  END


1   MAIN
2   RESERVE STKLEV(*) AS 3
3   CALL INITIAL
4   START SIMULATION
5   END


1   ROUTINE INITIAL
2   LET STOCK = 20.0
3   LET INVTPRD = 120.0
4   LET INVTLEV = 30.0
5   LET DELTIME = 60.0
6   LET ENDTIME = 1200.0
7   SCHEDULE A SALE IN 2 DAYS
8   SCHEDULE AN INVTORY IN 9 DAYS
9   RETURN   END


1   EVENT SALE SAVING THE EVENT NOTICE
2   DEFINE RNEXP TO MEAN EXPONENTIAL.F(5.0,1)
3   RESCHEDULE THIS SALE IN RNEXP DAYS
4   IF STOCK > 0.0
5       ADD 1 TO SALES
6       SUBTRACT 1 FROM STOCK
7   ALWAYS
8   IF STOCK = 0.0
9       ADD 1 TO LOSTSLS
10  ALWAYS   CALL STAT
11  RETURN   END


1   EVENT INVTORY SAVING THE EVENT NOTICE
2   RESCHEDULE THIS INVTORY IN INVTPRD DAYS
3   LET TOT = STOCK + ONORDER
4   IF TOT < INVTLEV
5       SCHEDULE A RECEIVE IN DELTIME DAYS
6       CREATE AN ORDER
7       LET NUMBER = INVTLEV - TOT
8       FILE ORDER IN ORDERS
9       LET ONORDER = ONORDER + NUMBER
10  ALWAYS   CALL STAT
11  RETURN   END


1   EVENT RECEIVE
2   REMOVE THE FIRST ORDER FROM ORDERS
3   LET STOCK = STOCK + NUMBER
4   LET ONORDER = ONORDER - NUMBER
5   CALL STAT
6   RETURN   END


1   ROUTINE STAT
2   IF EVENT.V = I.SALE
3       LET STKLEV(1) = STKLEV(2) * (TIME.V - STKLEV(3)) + STKLEV(1)
4       LET STKLEV(2) = STOCK
5       LET STKLEV(3) = TIME.V
6   ALWAYS
7   IF EVENT.V = I.INVTORY
8       ADD 1 TO NOINVT
9   ALWAYS
10  IF EVENT.V = I.RECEIVE
11      LET STKLEV(1) = STKLEV(2) * (TIME.V - STKLEV(3)) + STKLEV(1)
12      LET STKLEV(2) = STOCK
13      LET STKLEV(3) = TIME.V
14      ADD 1 TO NOORDERS
15  ALWAYS   IF TIME.V > ENDTIME
16          CALL OUTPUT
17  ALWAYS
18  RETURN   END


1   ROUTINE OUTPUT
2   LET PROFIT = SALES*20.0 - STKLEV(1)*.03 - LOSTSLS*10.0 - NOINVT*50.0   THUS
3   LET PROFIT = PROFIT - NOORDERS*15.0
4   LET AVSL = STKLEV(1)/TIME.V
5   LET AVWP = PROFIT*5.0/TIME.V
6   START NEW PAGE
7   PRINT 7 LINES WITH PROFIT, SALES, LOSTSLS, AVSL, TIME.V, AVWP
    RESULTS OF INVENTORY SYSTEM SIMULATION
        TOTAL PROFIT            = *******.**
        NUMBER OF SALES         = *****
        NUMBER OF LOST SALES    = *****
        AVERAGE STOCK LEVEL     = ****.**
        TIME PERIOD             = ****.**
        AVERAGE WEEKLY PROFIT   = ****.**
8   STOP
9   END
```

Figure 5.1 A SIMSCRIPT program for simulating an inventory system.

LET. As shown by the statements of lines 7 and 8, SIMSCRIPT provides a simple and straightforward statement for scheduling the occurrence of events. The RETURN statement of line 9 causes execution to proceed with the statement following the CALL INITIAL statement of the main program.

The START SIMULATION statement, line 4 of the main program, passes control to a built-in timing routine. This timing routine functions in a similar manner to the CONTROL procedures used in Chap. 4. The timing routine selects and removes the next scheduled event, executes the corresponding event routine, and then repeats the sequence. This continues until the execution of an event routine causes a STOP statement to be executed or until no events remain on the schedule, in which case control passes to the statement following START SIMULATION. Thus a test for ending the simulation is not included in the SIMSCRIPT timing routine. The SIMSCRIPT timing routine does contain a feature such that external events can be read in from input/output units.

The execution of the program in Fig. 5.1 proceeds by executing the various event routines in order as they are scheduled. The functions carried out in the event routines correspond very closely to the operations of the PL/I event routines of Sec. 4.2. The EVENT statement names an event routine and may include optional keywords. In the SALE event, the keyword phrase SAVING THE EVENT NOTICE is used to improve execution efficiency, since each SALE event gives rise to another SALE event. Note that in line 3 of this routine, RE-SCHEDULE is used because the event notice was saved. The statement of line 2 defines a variable named RNEXP to correspond to a built-in function EXPONENTIAL.F, which is an exponential random number generator. In this case, the mean value is 5 and the random number stream 1 is used. The variable RNEXP was not necessary but was included to emphasize the correspondence with the function of that name used in the procedure of Fig. 4.16.

The use of the IF statement in SIMSCRIPT is illustrated in the SALE event routine. When the statement of line 4 in this routine is executed, if the value of the variable STOCK is greater than 0, the statements in lines 5 and 6 will be executed. Otherwise, execution control passes to the ALWAYS statement of line 7. That is, if the logical condition is satisfied, the statements following the IF statement are executed; if the condition is not true, these statements are skipped. In either case, execution proceeds with the statement following ALWAYS. The keyword ALWAYS can be replaced by the equivalent keyword ELSE or OTHERWISE. SIMSCRIPT includes a number of optional choices for keywords, such as A or AN and THE or THIS, in order to make the intent of the program clearer to a reader. However, in the case of the IF clause, it is important to remember that ELSE and OTHERWISE mean the same as ALWAYS; in particular, remember ELSE does not have the same meaning here as it does in a PL/I IF clause.

Lines 5, 6 and 9 of the SALE event subprogram illustrate alternative forms of the arithmetic assignment statements available in SIMSCRIPT. These statements could have been written as:

```
LET SALES = SALES + 1
LET STOCK = STOCK − 1
LET LOSTSLS = LOSTSLS + 1
```

The event routines of Fig. 5.1 follow very closely the event procedures of Fig. 4.16. The statements required for adding an element to the ORDERS set are shown in lines 6, 7, and 8 of EVENT INVTORY. The element is first created; then a value is assigned to its attribute, the variable NUMBER; then the element is filled in the set. The operation of removing an element from the set is illustrated by the statement of line 2 in EVENT RECEIVE. When an element is removed, the variable NUMBER, as used in the statements of lines 3 and 4, is assigned the value associated with the removed element. In this example of set operations in SIMSCRIPT, default properties were used for the set. For this case, the FILE statement resulted in adding an element as the last one in the set, and in the REMOVE statement, the first element was specified. This resulted in a FIFO set discipline. In SIMSCRIPT II.5, sets can be defined with a variety of disciplines and elements may be added to and removed from sets in several different ways. These operations include all those available in the list-handling routines of Sec. 4.1.1. In addition to these features, SIMSCRIPT II.5 includes a number of more general capabilities. For example, sets may have elements which contain other sets and elements may be members of more than one set. The extensive set-handling facilities included in SIMSCRIPT II.5 represent very powerful modeling techniques and are well worth careful study.

The event routines in the program of Fig. 5.1 include a call statement to a routine named STAT just prior to their RETURN statement. In the PL/I program for this example, this operation was provided in the timing routine CONTROL. The ROUTINE STAT subprogram carries out the same operations as the procedure STAT of Fig. 4.19 and, in addition, tests for the condition of simulation time exceeding the value specified for the ENDTIME variable. This routine uses some of the automatically generated SIMSCRIPT variables. The variable EVENT.V is assigned a value corresponding to the type of event to be executed. This serves the same purpose as the TYPE variable used in the programs of Chap. 4. The variables I.SALE, I.INVTORY, and I.RECEIVE have the values assigned to those events. The variable TIME.V has a value equal to the current simulated time. There are a large number of automatically generated variables of this type which are available to the programmer using SIMSCRIPT.

If the simulation time exceeds the specified ENDTIME value, the OUTPUT subprogram, which prints out a report and stops the program execution, is called. This routine gives a simple example, in the statement of line 7, of the type of output formatting available in SIMSCRIPT. The program termination statement, STOP, is shown in line 8.

The output values produced by the program of Fig. 5.1 are not identical to the output shown in Fig. 4.21 because of the difference in random numbers used. The random number generators used with SIMSCRIPT vary with different computer implementations. The IBM System 360/370 uses a multiplicative congruential generator [12] similar to but not identical with the one given in Fig. 4.13. Ten different streams of random numbers are available. The automatically generated SIMSCRIPT array variable SEED.V serves the same purpose as the array SEED in Fig. 4.13 and is accessible to and may be modified by the programmer.

Comparing the SIMSCRIPT program of Fig. 5.1 with the program of Sec. 4.2 should convey the basic structure of simulation programming in this language and the nature of its built-in facilities. While there is a strong similarity with the programming approach used in Chap. 4, there are differences in the implementation of the SIMSCRIPT language, and the facilities provided are far more extensive than those covered in the previous chapter. However, the PL/I programs previously presented should provide a framework for understanding many of the concepts contained in the SIMSCRIPT language.

5.1.2 The Timeshared Computer System Example in SIMSCRIPT

Several additional features of SIMSCRIPT are illustrated in the program listed in Fig. 5.2. This is a simulation program for the timesharing computer system example of Sec. 4.3. Once again, most of the variable names are chosen to correspond to those used in the PL/I simulation program for this example. The execution logic of these two programs is also very similar.

As shown in the statements of lines 3, 7, and 8 of the preamble section, the set used to store the state of each terminal is given the name TERM, and the elements stored in this set are referred to as a TERMINAL. The five data items stored in these elements are the same as in the PL/I program but are identified by the names STATUS, INPUT.LENGTH, OUTPUT.LENGTH, EXECUTION.TIME, and ID.NUMBER. The elements of this set are created in the INITIAL subprogram in much the same way as in the INITIAL procedure of Fig. 4.29. The statement of line 3 in the INITIAL routine sets up a DO loop with a counter I having a range of integer values from 1 to 12. This loop includes all statements which follow until the LOOP statement of line 8 is encountered. Thus 12 elements are created and placed in the set TERM with ID.NUMBER values from 1 to 12. A call to the event routine REQUEST is used to assign the remaining parameter values for each element. The statement used to schedule these events, in line 7, includes the clause GIVEN I. The function of this clause may be understood by recalling that in the PL/I event procedure REQUEST, listed in Fig. 4.23, the identification number of the terminal making the request was included in the SCHEDULE list and used in the event procedure. Data items, in addition to the event time and type, may be included in the SIMSCRIPT built-in schedule of future events by defining the additional item as a variable in the event-notices subsection of the preamble and identifying the variable as GIVEN in the statement defining the event subprogram. This operation is illustrated for the REQUEST event by the statements in line 11 of the preamble and in line 1 of the REQUEST event subprogram of Fig. 5.2. Similarly, an additional data item is added to the schedule of future events for the EXECU and REPLY events.

The REQUEST event subprogram illustrates the use of two built-in SIM-SCRIPT functions, RANDOM.F and INT.F, which generate a uniformly distributed random value between 0 and 1 and which return a rounded integer value, respectively. These functions are used to produce the appropriately distributed random values for input message lengths. This event routine also uses two programmer-defined discrete random functions named FNCOTL and FNCEXL to specify values for the output message length and the CPU execution time requirement, respectively. The method for defining this type of variable is illustrated by the statements of lines 4, 5, 16, and 17 of the preamble. The values associated with these functions are input by the READ statements of lines 4 and 5 of the MAIN program segment of Fig. 5.2. The input data for function FNCOTL is

.2   10   .4   20   .6   30   .8   100   1.0   150*

Comparing this with the FNCOTL internal procedure shown in Fig. 4.23 indicates that this is the form used in SIMSCRIPT to define a discrete random distribution function.

The REQUEST event subprogram also illustrates the method of labeling statements in SIMSCRIPT. The statement of line 8 is given the label SET by placing this name, enclosed by single quote marks, prior to the statement. Control is transferred to this statement by the second statement in line 5. Use of comments in SIMSCRIPT is illustrated in line 7, where double quote marks indicate the beginning of a comment and its end. Comments may also be ended by the end of a line.

An example of the data-collection facilities in SIMSCRIPT is given by the statements included in lines 18 to 21 of the preamble section of the program listed in Fig. 5.2. These statements cause the mean value, standard deviation, and number of observations of the variables POLL.TIME and EXEC.TIME to be recorded each time that these variables are assigned a new value. This occurs in the statements of line 18 in the POLL event subprogram and of line 34 of the EXECU event subprogram. The values collected are printed out by the statements of lines 5 and 6 in the OUTPUT routine. The format of the output report produced by this routine is essentially the same as that produced by the procedure of Fig. 4.30, as illustrated in Fig. 4.31.

The two example programs presented in this section include only a limited subset of the statements and options available in the SIMSCRIPT programming language. But this should be sufficient to indicate some of the significant advantages and conveniences offered by this language for simulation programming. It should also be evident that the design and development of this language has emphasized an effort to make SIMSCRIPT programs easily readable.

5.2 THE GPSS LANGUAGE

The second simulation language we consider represents a significantly different approach to the problem of programming simulations. The General-Purpose Simulation System (GPSS) differs from SIMSCRIPT both in the timing algorithm and the model structure used and in the nature and goals of the language design.

The original version of GPSS was presented in 1961 [4] and has been developed and supported primarily by the IBM Corporation. The language has evolved through several versions, and at the present time, two versions, GPSS/360 [7] and GPSS V [5], are supported by IBM. GPSS/360 is a compatible subset of the more powerful and newer version, GPSS V. The language has been implemented on several other manufacturers' machines, and these implementations include variations in the language. However, most of these implementations are consistent with the GPSS/360 version which is used in this section.

The programming approach used in Chap. 4 and in the SIMSCRIPT examples of the previous section was based on event scheduling. GPSS uses what is called the *process interaction approach* for modeling and programming simulations. This approach includes the event-scheduling feature; that is, it generates a list of scheduled events to be executed in the future. But it also carries out, at each event time, an activity scan of another list of conditional events which may be able to occur because of the execution of the scheduled event.

To illustrate the concept of an activity-scan operation, we present the case of a simple single-server queuing system. There are two scheduled events required to model this system: a customer arrival event and a customer departure event. There is also a conditional event which corresponds to a customer starting the service operation and includes the scheduling of a departure event to occur in the future. This conditional event occurs at one of two possible times: at an arrival event if the server is not busy and the waiting line is empty or at a departure event if the waiting line is not empty. The event scheduling approach requires that both event routines, arrival and departure, test for the conditional event and provide for executing the required operations. The activity-scanning approach represents the beginning of service as a conditional event and attempts to carry out this event prior to each fetch of the next scheduled event. This scanning feature makes it possible to simplify the programming requirements for conditional events.

The process interaction approach to modeling stresses the interaction between processes in describing a system. Rather than modeling changes in the system state, this approach describes the progress of entities, referred to as *transactions*, through the system. The GPSS language includes a number of statements which represent the various processes or activities that may occur in a system. These statements are called block types, and GPSS utilizes a flowchart representation as an aid to writing programs. The concept used in programming is to represent the movement of transactions through the system in flowchart form.

```
 1  PREAMBLE
 2  NORMALLY MODE IS REAL
 3  THE SYSTEM OWNS A TERM
 4  THE SYSTEM HAS A FNCOTL RANDOM STEP VARIABLE
 5  THE SYSTEM HAS A FNCEXL RANDOM STEP VARIABLE
 6  TEMPORARY ENTITIES
 7  EVERY TERMINAL HAS A STATUS, AN INPUT.LENGTH, AN OUTPUT.LENGTH,
 8    AN EXECUTION.TIME, AN ID.NUMBER AND MAY BELONG TO THE TERM
 9  EVENT NOTICES INCLUDE POLL
10  EVERY EXECU HAS A PERIOD
11  EVERY REQUEST HAS A SENDER
12  EVERY REPLY HAS A RECIEVER
13  DEFINE ENDTIME, POLL.TIME, EXEC.TIME AS VARIABLES
14  DEFINE B AS A 1-DIM ARRAY
15  DEFINE WAIT AS A 2-DIM ARRAY
16  DEFINE FNCOTL AS A REAL, STREAM 4 VARIABLE
17  DEFINE FNCEXL AS A REAL, STREAM 8 VARIABLE
18  TALLY PTM AS THE MEAN, PTSD AS THE STD.DEV AND PTN AS THE NUMBER
19    OF POLL.TIME
20  TALLY ETM AS THE MEAN, ETSD AS THE STD.DEV AND ETN AS THE NUMBER
21    OF EXEC.TIME
22  END


 1  MAIN
 2  RESERVE WAIT(*,*) AS 12 BY 11
 3  RESERVE B(*) AS 12
 4  READ FNCOTL
 5  READ FNCEXL
 6  CALL INITIAL
 7  START SIMULATION
 8  END


 1  ROUTINE INITIAL
 2  LET ENDTIME = 150
 3  FOR I = 1 TO 12, DO
 4    CREATE A TERMINAL
 5    LET ID.NUMBER = I
 6    FILE TERMINAL IN TERM
 7    SCHEDULE A REQUEST GIVEN I NOW
 8  LOOP
 9  SCHEDULE A POLL AT 0.00
10  RETURN  END
```

```
 1  EVENT POLL SAVING THE EVENT NOTICE
 2  RESCHEDULE THIS POLL IN 1 UNITS
 3  LET X = TIME.V    LET Y = X + 1    LET Z = X
 4  REMOVE THE FIRST TERMINAL FROM TERM
 5  FOR I = 1 TO 12, DO
 6    IF (Y - X - 0.01) > (INPUT.LENGTH/300)
 7      IF STATUS IS NOT EQUAL TO 1 LET X = X + 0.01
 8      ALWAYS
 9      IF STATUS IS EQUAL TO 1
10        LET X = X + 0.01 + INPUT.LENGTH/300
11        LET STATUS = 2    LET INPUT.LENGTH = 0.00
12      ALWAYS    FILE TERMINAL IN TERM
13      REMOVE THE FIRST TERMINAL FROM TERM
14  LOOP
15    ALWAYS
16    FILE TERMINAL IN TERM
17    LET REMAINING.TIME = Y - X
18    LET POLL.TIME = X - Z
19  SCHEDULE AN EXECU GIVEN REMAINING.TIME AT X
20  CALL STAT GIVEN I
21  RETURN  END


 1  EVENT EXECU GIVEN PERIOD
 2  LET X = TIME.V    LET Z = X    LET Y = PERIOD + X
 3  LET XL = 0.0
 4  'REPEAT' IF XL IS EQUAL TO X GO TO OUT
 5    ALWAYS LET XL = X
 6  FOR I = 1 TO 12, DO
 7    IF (Y - X - 0.01) IS LESS THAN 0.0 GO TO OVER
 8    ALWAYS
 9    REMOVE FIRST TERMINAL FROM TERM
10    IF STATUS = 3
11      IF (Y - X - 0.01) > (OUTPUT.LENGTH/300)
12        LET X = X + 0.01 + OUTPUT.LENGTH/300
13        SCHEDULE A REPLY GIVEN ID.NUMBER AT X
14        LET STATUS = 4
15        GO TO SKIP
16      ALWAYS
17        LET W = (Y - X - 0.01)*300
18        SUBTRACT W FROM OUTPUT.LENGTH
19        LET X = Y
20        GO TO SKIP
21    ALWAYS
22    IF STATUS = 2
23      LET X = X + 0.01
24      SUBTRACT 1 FROM EXECUTION.TIME
25      IF EXECUTION.TIME = 0.0
26        LET STATUS = 3
27      ALWAYS
28    ALWAYS
29  'SKIP' FILE TERMINAL IN TERM
30  LOOP
31  'OVER'
32  GO TO REPEAT
33  'OUT'
34  LET EXEC.TIME = X - Z
35  CALL STAT GIVEN I
36  RETURN  END
```

Figure 5.2 Timesharing computer system example in SIMSCRIPT.

```
1    EVENT REPLY GIVEN RECIEVER
2    DEFINE RND TO MEAN RANDOM.F(1)
3    IF RND < 0.8
4    LET X = 5
5    GO TO SKIP
6    ALWAYS
7    LET X = 30.0
8    'SKIP' LET Y = EXPONENTIAL.F(X,2)
9    SCHEDULE A REQUEST GIVEN RECIEVER IN Y UNITS
10   CALL STAT GIVEN RECIEVER
11   RETURN   END
```

```
1    EVENT REQUEST GIVEN SENDER
2    DEFINE RND TO MEAN RANDOM.F(1)
3    FOR I = 1 TO 12, DO
4    REMOVE THE FIRST TERMINAL FROM TERM
5    IF IC.NUMBER = SENDER GC IC SET
6    ALWAYS FILE TERMINAL IN TERM
7    LOOP  ''THIS INDICATES THE END OF THE DO LOOP''
8    'SET'  LET STATUS = 1
9    LET X = FNC*75 + 5
10   LET INPUT.LENGTH = INT.F(X)
11   LET OUTPUT.LENGTH = FNCCTL
12   LET EXECUTION.TIME = FNCEXL
13   FILE TERMINAL IN TERM
14   CALL STAT GIVEN SENDER
15   RETURN  END
```

```
1    ROUTINE STAT GIVEN TNUMB
2    IF EVENT.V = 1,REPLY
3    LET X = TIME.V - B(TNUMB)
4    LET Y = 1.0
5    FOR I = 1 TO 11, DO
6    IF X IS LESS THAN Y GO TO SKIP
7    ALWAYS LET Y = Y + 1.0
8    LOOP
9    'SKIP'  ADD 1 TO WAIT(TNUMB,I)
10   ALWAYS
11   IF EVENT.V = 1,REQUEST
12   LET B(TNUMB) = TIME.V
13   ALWAYS
14   IF TIME.V > ENDTIME
15   CALL OUTPUT
16   ALWAYS
17   RETURN  END
```

```
1    ROUTINE OUTPUT
2    START NEW PAGE
3    PRINT 5 LINES THUS
INTERACTIVE SYSTEM PERFORMANCE

4    PRINT 2 LINES WITH TIME.V THUS
SIMULATION TIME PERIOD      ****.**

5    PRINT 2 LINES WITH PTM, PTSD, PTN  THUS
POLLING TIME    MEAN = *.******    STD DEV = *.*****    OBS = ***

6    PRINT 2 LINES WITH ETM, ETSD, ETN  THUS
EXECUTION TIME  MEAN = *.******    STD DEV = *.*****    OBS = ***

7    FOR I = 1 TO 12, DO
8    PRINT 3 LINES WITH I  THUS
TERMINAL   **

UPPER LIMIT    OBSERVATIONS    PERCENTAGE
9    LET SUM = 0.0
10   FOR J = 1 TO 11, DO
11   ADD WAIT(I,J) TO SUM
12   LOOP
13   FOR J = 1 TO 11, PRINT 1 LINE WITH J, WAIT(I,J), WAIT(I,J), WAIT(I,J)/SUM  THUS
**.**       ***                   0.******
14   PRINT 3 LINES  THUS

15   LOOP
16   STOP
17   END
```

Figure 5.2 (Continued)

143

5.2.1 A GPSS Single-Server Queue Model

To introduce the GPSS programming technique we will consider an example of programming a single-server queuing system. A flowchart for the customers, or transactions, is shown in Fig. 5.3. This flowchart represents processes encountered by the transaction as it moves through the system, and uses various block types available in GPSS. The first block generates transactions at some specified rate; that is, it schedules the arrival of customers at certain times during the simulation. Block 2 places the transaction in a FIFO queue. The transaction proceeds to the next block, which corresponds to seizing the server facility. However, if the server has already been seized by another transaction but not yet released by that transaction, then the transaction just generated will be blocked and cannot proceed. But the attempt to seize the server will become a conditional event. When the transaction is able to seize the server, it moves through block 4, which removes it from the waiting line, and enters block 5. This is an ADVANCE-type block where the transaction will remain for a specified interval of simulated time. After this period, the transaction moves through blocks 6, 7, and 8 and then leaves the system. At this time the activity scan will check the list of conditional events, and if any other transactions are in the waiting-line queue, another transaction will be moved to block 5.

An ADVANCE-type block is the only block type which requires elapsed simulated time for its transit. Thus, when a transaction enters an ADVANCE

Block

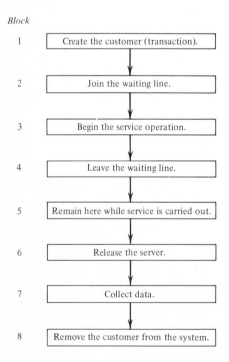

1   Create the customer (transaction).

2   Join the waiting line.

3   Begin the service operation.

4   Leave the waiting line.

5   Remain here while service is carried out.

6   Release the server.

7   Collect data.

8   Remove the customer from the system.

Figure 5.3 A flowchart for transactions in a single-server queuing system.

```
BLCCK                                                                        CARD
NUMBER   *LCC    CPERATICN  A,B,C,D,E,F,G              COMMENTS              NUMBEF
                                                                               1
                 SIMULATE                                                      2
         * A SINGLE SERVER QUEUEING SYSTEM IN GPSS                             3
         *                                                                     4
         1       FUNCTION   FN1,C24              EXPONENTIAL RANDCM NUMBER FUNCTION   5
         0.0,0.0/0.1,0.104/0.2,0.222/0.3,0.355/C.4,0.509/0.5,0.69             6
         0.6,0.915/0.7,1.2/0.75,1.38/0.8,1.6/0.E4,1.83/0.88,2.12              7
         0.9,2.3/0.92,2.52/0.94,2.81/0.95,2.99/0.96,3.2/0.97,3.5             8
         0.98,3.9/0.99,4.6/0.995,5.3/0.998,6.2/0.999,7./0.9997,8.             9
         *                                                                    10
1                GENERATE   30,FN1               CREATE CUSTOMERS             11
2                QUEUE      LINE                  ENTER WAITING LINE          12
3                SEIZE      SERVR                 BEGIN SERVICE               13
4                DEPART     LINE                  LEAVE WAITING LINE          14
5                ADVANCE    20,FN1                SERVICE CPERATION           15
6                RELEASE    SERVR                 FINISH SERVICE              16
7                TABULATE   CATA                  RECORD DATA                 17
8                TERMINATE  1                     REMOVE CUSTOMER FRCM SYSTEM 18
         *                                                                    19
         DATA    TABLE      M1,20,10,30           DEFINE TABLE FCR SYSTEM TRANSIT TIME  20
         *                                                                    21
                 START      3000                  RUN SIMULATION FCR 3000 CUSTCMERS  22
                 ENC                                                          23
```

Figure 5.4 A GPSS program for simulating a single-server queuing system.

block, it causes a future event to be scheduled which will cause the transaction to again start moving through the system represented by the flowchart. So the transactions move either until they are blocked by some system condition or until they enter an ADVANCE block.

The GPSS coding for this example is shown in Fig. 5.4, enclosed by the dashed lines. This program listing uses the standard formatting where the first position of an input line is used to indicate a comment by inserting a * symbol. A statement label, if used, is placed in positions 2 to 6. These labels and other symbolic names in GPSS must be from three to five characters in length, and the first three characters must be letters of the alphabet. The block-type name or other operation name specified by the statement begins in position 8. Beginning in position 19, a series of fields may be present, each separated by commas and having no embedded blanks. Anything following the first blank in the fields section is treated as a comment.

Coding can be input with a less rigid format which uses the first line position as the starting point for the statement label and separates the four possible sections by using a single blank. Thus, if the statement label is omitted, the block-type name would begin in position 2. This type of format is easier to use, particularly if input is prepared at a terminal, since it minimizes the number of keystrokes required. However, the standard format is much easier to read.

The block numbers indicated in Fig. 5.4 for the block-type statements correspond to the block numbers of Fig. 5.3. In GPSS, transactions are created by using the GENERATE-type statement. In this example, the first two fields of this statement are utilized. The first, field A, specifies the mean value of simulation time between each transaction, and the second, field B, specifies a modifier for varying the time between the generation of transactions. In this case, the mean time is specified as 30 time units, and the modifier is function 1, which is denoted as FN1. This function is defined by the statement of card 5. In this statement, the variable in field A, RN1, represents a uniform random number source and is the independent input for the function being defined. Field B specifies that the function is continuous and has 24 data points. The data-point values are given in cards 6 to 9 and correspond to the coordinates of points which lie on the cumulative probability curve of an exponentially distributed random variable with a mean of 1. Thus the result of the operation specified in block 1 is that transactions will be generated with exponentially distributed random interarrival times having a mean value of 30 time units.

A QUEUE-type block causes a transaction to enter a FIFO list which is named in field A of the statement. A SEIZE-type block causes a transaction to enter a facility which is named in field A of the statement. A facility in GPSS can contain at most one transaction. When a transaction is generated in block 1, it will proceed into block 2. This is always possible since there is no limit on the number of transactions which may be in a GPSS queue. The transaction will attempt to move into block 3, but if the facility named SERVR is occupied, it will be blocked from further progress through the system until it can enter the SERVR facility. When the transaction can enter block 3, it always proceeds to block 4, which removes it from the LINE queue, and then to block 5. The ADVANCE block causes the transaction to be delayed for some period of time. In this statement, fields A and B are used in the same manner as in the GENERATE statement. This results in the transaction being delayed for an exponentially distributed random period of time having a mean value of 20 time units.

When the transaction leaves the ADVANCE block, it proceeds through block 6, which removes it from the SERVR facility. Next it moves through block 7, which causes a value to be added to a table named DATA. This table is defined in the statement of card 20, where field A specifies the information collected in the table. In this case, M1 denotes the transit time of a transaction, i.e., the period of time elapsed since the transaction was generated. Thus, each time a transaction moves through block 7, it causes a value to be added into the table DATA equal to the time that the transaction spent in the ADVANCE block plus any time during which it may have been blocked while waiting to enter the SERVR facility. Fields B, C, and D of the TABLE statements are used to specify the upper limit of the first interval, the interval size, and the number of intervals, respectively, for a histogram.

The transaction then continues to block 8, where it is removed from the system and causes the terminate count to be incremented by 1.

As shown in Fig. 5.4, a SIMULATE control card is used to indicate the start of the program, and an END control card is used to denote the end of the program. The START control card is used to specify the length of a simulation run. In this case, the run continues until the terminate count reaches 3000.

GPSS automatically provides an output report which summarizes the results of each simulation run. A portion of this output for the program above is shown in Fig. 5.5. For each facility in the model, this data includes the percentage of total simulation time during which the facility was occupied, the number of transactions which occupied it, and the average period of time each transaction remained in the facility. In this example, the values for the SERVR facility are

FACILITY	AVERAGE UTILIZATION	NUMBER ENTRIES	AVERAGE TIME/TRAN	SEIZING TRANS. NO.	PREEMPTING TRANS. NO.
SERVR	.648	3000	19.327		

QUEUE	MAXIMUM CONTENTS	AVERAGE CONTENTS	TOTAL ENTRIES	ZERO ENTRIES	PERCENT ZEROS	AVERAGE TIME/TRANS	$AVERAGE TIME/TRANS	TABLE NUMBER	CURRENT CONTENTS
LINE	16	1.293	3000	1026	34.1	38.578	58.629		

$AVERAGE TIME/TRANS = AVERAGE TIME/TRANS EXCLUDING ZERO ENTRIES

TABLE DATA ENTRIES IN TABLE	MEAN ARGUMENT	STANDARD DEVIATION	SUM OF ARGUMENTS	
3000	57.905	56.125	173718.000	NON-WEIGHTED

UPPER LIMIT	OBSERVED FREQUENCY	PER CENT OF TOTAL	CUMULATIVE PERCENTAGE	CUMULATIVE REMAINDER	MULTIPLE OF MEAN	DEVIATION FROM MEAN
20	882	29.39	29.3	70.6	.345	-.675
30	365	12.16	41.5	58.4	.518	-.497
40	257	8.56	50.1	49.8	.690	-.319
50	241	8.03	58.1	41.8	.863	-.140
60	202	6.73	64.8	35.1	1.036	.037
70	146	4.86	69.7	30.2	1.208	.215
80	127	4.23	73.9	26.0	1.381	.393
90	141	4.69	78.6	21.3	1.554	.571
100	106	3.53	82.2	17.7	1.726	.750
110	78	2.59	84.8	15.1	1.899	.928
120	76	2.53	87.3	12.6	2.072	1.106
130	62	2.06	89.4	10.5	2.245	1.284
140	53	1.76	91.1	8.8	2.417	1.462
150	28	.93	92.1	7.8	2.590	1.640
160	33	1.09	93.2	6.7	2.763	1.819
170	27	.89	94.1	5.8	2.935	1.997
180	20	.66	94.7	5.2	3.108	2.175
190	27	.89	95.6	4.3	3.281	2.353
200	36	1.19	96.8	3.1	3.453	2.531
210	23	.76	97.6	2.3	3.626	2.709
220	14	.46	98.1	1.8	3.799	2.886
230	10	.33	98.4	1.5	3.971	3.066
240	13	.43	98.8	1.1	4.144	3.244
250	3	.09	98.9	1.0	4.317	3.422
260	6	.19	99.1	.8	4.490	3.600
270	3	.09	99.2	.7	4.662	3.778
280	5	.16	99.4	.5	4.835	3.957
290	3	.09	99.5	.4	5.008	4.135
300	5	.16	99.7	.2	5.180	4.313
OVERFLOW	8	.26	100.0	.0		

AVERAGE VALUE OF OVERFLOW   319.50

Figure 5.5 Portion of the GPSS output report.

reasonably close to the specified values of

$$\rho = 20/30 = .667$$

$$T_s = 20$$

Similarly, for each queue in the model, a number of observations are reported. For the LINE queue, which corresponds to the waiting line, the average time each transaction is in this queue is not far from the theoretical value

$$T_w = \frac{\rho T_s}{1 - \rho} = 40$$

Also the percentage of transactions which did not wait in LINE is approximately equal to the theoretical value

$$(1 - \rho)100 = 33.3$$

The output produced by the table DATA is also included in Fig. 5.5. The mean value 57.905 is only a little less than the theoretical value

$$T_q = \frac{T_s}{1 - \rho} = 60$$

and the cumulative percentage values differ only slightly from the theoretical values of $Q(t)$ for this example.

From Fig. 5.4, it is clear that GPSS provides a very concise method for programming simple queuing systems. One of the primary objectives in the design of the GPSS language has been to keep the number of programming statements and structures limited. By doing this, the language is more accessible to occasional users than it would be if a greater variety of programming options were available.

The time variable in GPSS is an integer-valued number, as are most other variables. In this example of Fig. 5.4, the function data points and random number input are floating-point values, but the value returned for FN1 is an integer. This characteristic causes certain scaling effects in GPSS programs. For example, if in the program of Fig. 5.4, the mean interarrival time-field value is changed to 300 and the mean service time-field value changed to 200, the output value for the mean system time is not 10 times 57.905 but instead is 665.996. This rather large change indicates the potential significance of the type of number representation used in various implementations.

5.2.2 The Inventory System Example in GPSS

There is a specialized block diagram notation for GPSS programs which can be directly converted to the coding representation. An example of this notation is given in Fig. 5.6, which presents a program for simulating the inventory system described in Sec. 4.2. Each block uses a special symbol to represent a GPSS block type with specific field-parameter specification. This example uses two types of transactions that follow separate flow paths to model the system. The block diagram for the processing of sales is shown on the left side of Fig. 5.6 and that for processing inventory counts is shown on the right side. The coded form of this program is shown in Fig. 5.7.

This example uses GPSS savevalue entities to store the various values needed in the model. The SAVEVALUE statement uses field A to specify a particular savevalue entity. If this number is followed by a + sign, then the value specified in field B is added to the entity. Similarly, a − sign indicates the field B value is to be subtracted from the entity. If neither sign is given, then the value specified in field B replaces the present value stored in the entity. Thus, the operation of block 3 is to subtract 1 from the value of savevalue 1 (denoted X1). Block 4 adds 1 to X2, and block 5 adds the value of variable 2 (denoted V2) to the seventh savevalue entity. The operation carried out in block 6 is to store the value of the present simulation time (denoted C1) in X8.

After a transaction representing a sale is generated, it moves to a TEST block where the value of X1 is compared with 0. If X1 is not equal to 0, the transaction

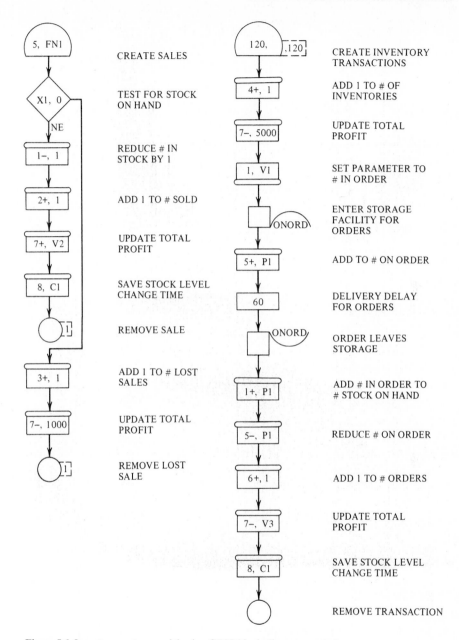

Figure 5.6 Inventory system model using GPSS block-diagram symbols.

moves on to block 3; but if X1 is equal to 0, the transaction is transferred to the block labeled AAA (8). X1 is used to retain the number of items in stock and is set to an initial value of 30 at the start of a simulation by the statement in card 37. X2 is used to retain the total number of sales, and X7 is the total profit

```
BLOCK                                                                            CARD
NUMBER  *LOC   OPERATION   A,B,C,D,E,F,G              COMMENTS                   NUMBER
               *                                                                   1
               SIMULATE                                                            2
        * AN INVENTORY SYSTEM IN GPSS                                              3
               *                                                                   4
        1      FUNCTION    RN1,C24          EXPONENTIAL RANDOM NUMBER FUNCTION     5
    0.,0.,0./0.1,0.104/0.2,0.222/0.3,0.355/0.4,0.509/0.5,0.69                      6
    0.6,0.915/0.7,1.2/0.75,1.38/0.8,1.6/0.84,1.83/0.88,2.12                        7
    0.9,2.3/0.92,2.52/0.94,2.81/0.95,2.99/0.96,3.2/0.97,3.5                        8
    0.98,3.9/0.99,4.6/0.995,5.3/0.998,6.2/0.999,7./0.9997,8.                       9
               *                                                                  10
1              GENERATE    5,FN1            CREATE SALES                          11
2              TEST NE     X1,0,AAA         TEST FOR STOCK ON HAND                12
3              SAVEVALUE   1-,1             REDUCE # IN STOCK BY 1                 13
4              SAVEVALUE   2+,1             ADD 1 TO # SOLD                        14
5              SAVEVALUE   7+,V2            UPDATE TOTAL PROFIT                    15
6              SAVEVALUE   8,C1             SAVE STOCK LEVEL CHANGE TIME           16
7              TERMINATE   1                REMOVE SALE                           17
8       AAA    SAVEVALUE   3+,1             ADD 1 TO # LOST SALES                  18
9              SAVEVALUE   7-,1000          UPDATE TOTAL PROFIT                    19
10             TERMINATE   1                REMOVE LOST SALE                      20
               *                                                                  21
11             GENERATE    120,,120         CREATE INVENTORY TRANSACTIONS         22
12             SAVEVALUE   4+,1             ADD 1 TO # OF INVENTORIES             23
13             SAVEVALUE   7-,5000          UPDATE TOTAL PROFIT                    24
14             ASSIGN      1,V1             SET PARAMETER TO # IN ORDER           25
15             ENTER       ONORD            ENTER STORAGE FACILITY FOR ORDERS     26
16             SAVEVALUE   5+,P1            ADD TO # ON ORDER                      27
17             ADVANCE     60               DELIVERY DELAY FOR ORDERS             28
18             LEAVE       ONORD            ORDER LEAVES STORAGE                   29
19             SAVEVALUE   1+,P1            ADD # IN ORDER TO # STOCK ON HAND     30
20             SAVEVALUE   5-,P1            REDUCE # ON ORDER                      31
21             SAVEVALUE   6+,1             ADD 1 TO # ORDERS                      32
22             SAVEVALUE   7-,V3            UPDATE TOTAL PROFIT                    33
23             SAVEVALUE   8,C1             SAVE STOCK LEVEL CHANGE TIME           34
24             TERMINATE                    REMOVE TRANSACTION                    35
               *                                                                  36
               INITIAL     X1,30            SET STARTING VALUE FOR STOCK LEVEL    37
        ONORD  STORAGE     3                STORAGE FOR OUTSTANDING ORDERS        38
        1      VARIABLE    30-X1-X5         # OF ITEMS IN AN ORDER                39
        2      VARIABLE    2000-3*(X1+1)*(C1-X8)                                   40
        3      VARIABLE    1500+3*(X1-P1)*(C1-X8)                                  41
               *                                                                  42
               START       240              RUN FOR 240 SALES OPPORTUNITIES       43
               END                                                                44
```

Figure 5.7 GPSS code for the inventory system model.

achieved in the simulation. In this program, the total profit is obtained by accumulating the effect of each transaction. Thus in block 5, X7 is increased by the profit from a sale (2000 representing \$20) minus the carrying charges which have occurred since the last change in stock value: $[3*(X1 + 1)*(C1 - X8)]$. Similarly, in block 9, the penalty value (1000) due to a lost sale is subtracted from the total profit.

After a transaction representing an inventory is generated, the number of inventories taken, X4, is incremented and the cost of the inventory count (5000) is subtracted from the total profit. Every transaction has at least 12 parameter values associated with it, and in block 14, parameter 1 of a transaction moving through this block has the value of V1 assigned to it. Note that the variable values are recomputed for each transaction and that V1 will equal the number of items requested in the order resulting from an inventory count. The transaction then enters a storage device named ONORD. A storage unit in GPSS is similar to a facility except that it may contain more than one transaction at the same time. The maximum number of transactions permitted in a storage device is specified in a statement such as that of card 38. X5 is used to store the number of items on order. The transaction is delayed 60 days in the advance block to represent the time required for delivery of the order. After leaving this block, operations are carried out which simulate the receipt of an order, and then the transaction is terminated. Note that in this block (24), no count is specified in field A, so these transactions do not increment the terminate count used with the START operation.

The contents of all savevalue entities are automatically printed out at the end of the simulation, so that data equivalent to that printed out in the program of Sec. 4.2 will be available from this GPSS program.

Comparing this program for simulating the inventory system example with the programs for simulating this system given in Secs. 4.2 and 5.1 shows how the program logic is simplified and the coding effort is reduced as more specialized features are provided. Of course, this specialization does tend to introduce restrictions in terms of the model varieties available for representing systems.

The two GPSS examples presented above illustrate the basic approach used for programming in this language. The logic of the programs should be easy to follow and does embody the fundamental concept of modeling in GPSS. There are a number of other block types and operations available in this language and many additional options which may be used with each block type. Some of these features are included in the next example.

5.2.3 The Elevator System Example in GPSS

The coding of a simulation program for the elevator system example of Sec. 4.4 is shown in Fig. 5.8. This example requires the use of more complex set-handling operations than are available with the QUEUE block, which only provides for a first in–first out discipline. In GPSS, this type of operation is provided by *user chains*. Transactions are placed in these sets by a LINK-type block and are removed from the sets by the action of an UNLINK-type block.

Examples of the use of the LINK operation are shown in blocks 11 and 17 of Fig. 5.8. These blocks are in the path followed by transactions representing passengers for the elevator system. When one of these transactions moves to block 11, it is placed on a user chain named WAITN and remains there until removed. The transactions are placed on the chain in the order of their arrival (FIFO) but are removed on the basis of their parameter values. Specifically, parameter 4 is assigned a unique value that is a function of its arrival floor and desired direction of travel. These transactions are removed by the UNLINK operation of block 46.

Block 46 is in the path followed by two transactions which represent the two elevator cars of the system. Thus, the passengers are removed from the WAITN chain as the result of actions of the cars. The fields in the UNLINK blocks of this example are used as follows: field A specifies the user chain from which transactions are to be removed; field B specifies the block to which the removed transactions are sent; field C specifies the number of transactions to be removed; field D specifies a parameter number; and field E specifies a value. The operation

```
BLOCK                                                                    CARD
NUMBER  *LOC   OPERATION  A.B.C.D.E.F.G              COMMENTS           NUMBER
               *                                                            1
               SIMULATE                                                     2
               * AN ELVEATOR SYSTEM IN GPSS                                 3
               *                                                            4
        1      FUNCTION   FN1.C24       EXPONENTIAL RANDOM NUMBER FUNCTION   5
  0.0.0.0/0.1.0.104/C.2.0.222/C.3.0.355/C.4.0.509/0.5.0.69                   6
  0.6.0.915/0.7.1.2/0.75.1.38/0.8.1.6/0.84.1.83/0.88.2.12                    7
  0.9.2.3/0.92.2.52/0.94.2.81/0.95.2.99/0.96.3.2/0.97.3.5                    8
  0.98.3.9/0.99.4.6/0.995.5.3/0.998.6.2/0.999.7.0.9997.8.                    9
        2      FUNCTION   RN2.D11       ARRIVAL FLOOR DISTRIBUTION          10
  0.11.1./0.42.2./0.47.3./0.57.4./0.64.5./0.71.6./0.78.7./0.85.8./0.91.9.   11
  0.96.10./1..11.                                                           12
        3      FUNCTION   RN3.D11       DESTINATION FLOOR DISTRIBUTION      13
  0.2.1./0.42.2./0.46.3./0.57.4./0.64.5./0.71.6./0.78.7./0.85.8./0.91.9.    14
  C.96.10./1..11.                                                           15
        4      FUNCTION   P2.L2         BRANCH CN TRAVEL CIRECTION          16
  1.EEA/2.EEB                                                               17
        5      FUNCTION   P2.L2         BRANCH CN TRAVEL DIRECTION          18
  1.HHC/2.HHD                                                               19
        6      FUNCTION   P2.D2         LAST FLOCR IN THIS DIRECTION        20
  1.11/2.1                                                                  21
        7      FUNCTION   P2.D2         CHANGE DIRECTION OF TRAVEL          22
  1.2/2.1                                                                   23
        8      FUNCTION   P2.D2         TEMPORARY FLOCR TRIAL VALUE         24
  1.0/2.12                                                                  25
               *                                                           26
               *                                                           27
  1            GENERATE   5.FN1.2       CREATE PASSENGERS, FIRST AT TIME=2  28
  2            ASSIGN     1.FN2         ARRIVAL FLOOR                       29
  3     AAA    ASSIGN     2.FN3         DESTINATICN FLOOR                   30
  4            TEST NE    P1.P2.AAA     IF EQUAL GO TO AAA                  31
  5            ASSIGN     3.V1          DIRECTION OF TRAVEL, 1=UP, 2=DOWN   32
  6            ASSIGN     4.V2          CODE VALLE FOR REMCVING FRCM WAITN  33
  7            MSAVEVALUE 2+.P3.P1.1    ADD 1 TO # WAITING MATRIX           34
  8            GATE LS    IDLE.AAB      CHECK FCR IDLE ELEVATCR             35
  9            SAVEVALUE  1.P1          PASS FLCOR NUMBER TO IDLE ELEVATOR  36
  10           LOGIC R    IDLE          START ELEVATOR                      37
  11    AAB    LINK       WAITN.FIFO    PUT PASSENGER ON WAITN CHAIN        38
               *                                                           39
  12    BBB    TABULATE   TIMEW         RECORD WAITING TIME                 40
  13           MSAVEVALUE 1.X2.P2.1     SET STOP BUTTON                     41
  14           MSAVEVALUE 3+.X2.P2.1    ADD 1 TC # ONBOARD MATRIX           42
  15           ASSIGN     4.X2          STORE CAR #                         43
  16           ASSIGN     5.V3          CODE VALUE FOR REMCVING FROM RICER  44
  17           LINK       RIDER.FIFO    PUT PASSENGER ON RIDER CHAIN        45
               *                                                           46
  18    CCC    TABULATE   TIMEQ         RECORD SYSTEM TIME                  47
  19           TERMINATE  1             REMOVE PASSENGER FRCM SYSTEM        48
               *                                                           49
               *                                                           50
  20           GENERATE   1...2         CREATE 2 ELEVATOR CARS              51
  21           SAVEVALUE  3+.1                                              52
  22           ASSIGN     1.X3          SET PARAMETER 1 TC CAR #            53
  23           ASSIGN     2..3          SET STATUS TO IDLE                  54
  24           ASSIGN     3..1          SET PRESENT POSITION TO FLOCR 1     55
  25    DDD    LOGIC S    IDLE          SET IDLE LOGIC SWITCH               56
  26           GATE LR    IDLE          WAIT FOR CALL                       57
  27           ASSIGN     4.X1          DESTINATION FLOOR                   58
  28    EEE    ASSIGN     2.V4          SET DIRECTION OF TRAVEL             59
  29           TRANSFER   FN.4          FIND TRAVEL TIME                    60
  30    EEA    ASSIGN     5.V5                                              61
  31           TRANSFER   .EEC                                             62
  32    EEB    ASSIGN     5.V6                                             63
```

Figure 5.8 The elevator system example in GPSS.

is to examine each transaction on the chain, in order, and to remove that transaction if the value stored in its parameter, specified in field D, is equal to the
value specified in field E. In the case of block 46, the values of the passenger
transaction's fourth parameter are compared with the value of variable 9. This
value is generated by the elevator transaction that entered block 46. For example,
if the elevator car has arrived at the fifth floor going up, then it has P3 equal to 5
and P2 equal to 1. So V9 will be set equal to 25. The transactions stored in
WAITN which have P4 equal to 25 are those which are waiting at floor 5 with
destination up.

```
33       EEC     ADVANCE       P5                        DELAY FCR TRAVEL TIME TO NEXT FLCCR      64
34       EED     ASSIGN        3,P4                      NEW FLOOR POSITICN                       65
35               MSAVEVALUE    1,P1,P3,0                 CLEAR STCP REQUEST                       66
36               UNLINK        FIDER,CCC,MX3(P1,P3),5,V7     UNLCAD PASSENGERS                    67
37               SAVEVALUE     4,MX3(P1,P3)              STORE # CF PASSENGERS UNLOADED           68
38               MSAVEVALUE    3,P1,P3,0                 CLEAR # CNBOARD MATRIX                   69
39               TEST E        P3,1,GGA                  IF NOT FLOOR 1, GO TC GGA                70
4C               ASSIGN        2,1                       CHANGE CIRECTION TC UP                   71
41               TRANSFER      ,GGB                                                               72
42       GGA     TEST E        P3,11,GGB                 IF NOT FLOOR 11, GC TO GGB               73
43               ASSIGN        2,2                       CHANGE DIRECTION TO DCWN                 74
44       GGB     ADVANCE       V8                        DELAY FCR STOP AT FLCCR                  75
45               SAVEVALUE     2,P1                      PASS CAR # TO PASSENGERS                 76
46               UNLINK        WAITN,BBB,MX2(P2,P3),4,V9     LCAD PASSENGERS                      77
47               MSAVEVALUE    2,P2,P3,0                 CLEAR # WAITING MATRIX                   78
48               ADVANCE       1                         WAIT FOR PASSENGERS TO BE LOACED         79
49               SAVEVALUE     5,1                       COUNTER FCR # CF TRIES                   80
5C               SAVEVALUE     3,P3                      TRIAL VALUE FCR NEXT FLOOR               81
51       HHA     ASSIGN        6,10                      USE P6 FCR LOCP COUNTER                  82
52       HHB     TRANSFER      FN,5                      INCREMENT NEXT FLCCR #                   83
53       HHC     SAVEVALUE     3+,1                      ADC 1                                    84
54               TRANSFER      ,HHE                                                               85
55       HHD     SAVEVALUE     3-,1                      SUBTRACT 1                               86
56       HHE     TEST NE       MX1(P1,X3),1,III          GO TC III IF STOP REQUESTEC              87
57               TEST E        MX2(P2,X3),0,III          GO TO III IF PASSENGER WAITING           88
58               TEST NE       X3,FN6,HHF                TEST FOR TOP OR BCTTCM FLOOR             89
59               SAVEVALUE     5+,1                      INCREMENT TRIES CCUNTER                  90
60               TEST L        X5,21,HHG                 TEST FOR COMPLETICN                      91
61               LOOP          6,HHB                     REPEAT LCCP                              92
62       HHF     ASSIGN        2,FN7                     CHANGE CIRECTION OF TRAVEL               93
63               SAVEVALUE     3,FN8                     NEXT FLOCR TRIAL VALUE (+ OR -1)         94
64               TRANSFER      ,HHA                                                               95
65       HHG     ASSIGN        2,3                       SET ELEVATOR IDLE                        96
66               TRANSFER      ,CDD                                                               97
67       III     ASSIGN        4,X3                      SET DESTINATICN FLCOR VALUE              98
68               TEST NE       P3,P4,EED                 IF SAME FLOOR, SKIP CELAY                99
69               TRANSFER      ,EEE                                                              100
         *                                                                                      101
         *                                                                                      102
         1       VARIABLE      EV1+1                     PASSENGER DIRECTION CF TRAVEL           103
         1       BVARIABLE     P1'G'P2                   0 IF GOING UP, 1 IF DCWN                104
         2       VARIABLE      P3*20+P1                  CCDE FOR WAITN CHAIN                    105
         3       VARIABLE      P4*100+P3*20+P2           CCDE FOR RIDER CHAIN                    106
         4       VARIABLE      EV2+1                     ELEVATOR DIRECTICN CF TRAVEL            107
         2       BVARIABLE     P3'G'P4                   0 IF UP, 1 IF DCWN                      108
         5       VARIABLE      P4-P3+5                   TRAVEL TIME (UP)                        109
         6       VARIABLE      P3-P4+5                   TRAVEL TIME (DOWN)                      110
         7       VARIABLE      P1*100+P2*20+P3           CCDE FOR WAITN CHAIN                    111
         8       VARIABLE      X4+MX2(P2,P3)+4           TIME RECLIRED FOR STCP (LESS 1)         112

    9    VARIABLE      P2*20+P3                 CCDE FOR RIDER CHAIN                            113
    *                                                                                          114
    1    MATRIX        X,2,11                   STCRES STOP REQUESTS(CAR #, FLCCR #)           115
    2    MATRIX        X,2,11                   STCRES # PASSENGERS WAITING(DIREC-             116
    *                                                     TICN, FLCCR #)                       117
    3    MATRIX        X,2,11                   STCRES # PASSENGERS CNBOARD(CAR #,             118
    *                                                     FLCCR #)                             119
    *                                                                                          120
 TIMEW  TABLE         M1,10,10,25              WAITING TIME TABLE                             121
 TIMEG  TABLE         M1,10,10,30              SYSTEM TIME TABLE                              122
    *                                                                                          123
         START         150                      RUN FOR 150 PASSENGER TRIPS                   124
         START         100                                                                    125
         START         100                                                                    126
         ENC                                                                                  127
```

Figure 5.8 (Continued)

User chains provide all the list-handling facilities needed for GPSS trans-actions which are blocked and not moving through the system model. Similar capabilities for lists containing transactions which continue to move through the system are also available in GPSS.

The program of Fig. 5.8 uses a more general version of savevalues, known as *matrix savevalues*. These are simply two-dimensional arrays of savevalue entities. Three of these arrays are defined in the statements of cards 115 to 119. Each has 2 rows and 11 columns. The matrix savevalue 1 is used to store the stop requests for passengers on board the elevator cars. The row number corresponds to the car number and the column number corresponds to the floor number. Thus, when a passenger transaction moves through block 13, a 1 is placed in row X2 (the car number) and column P2 (the destination floor) or matrix savevalue 1. The values stored in these arrays may be specified as in block 56; that is, MX1 (P1,X3) equals the value stored in the matrix savevalue 1 position with the row number specified by parameter 1 and column number specified by savevalue 3.

Two uses of the TRANSFER-type block are illustrated in Fig. 5.8. Block 31 results in an unconditional transfer of any entering transaction to the block with the label EEC. Note that field A in block 31 has been left blank. In block 29, field A of the TRANSFER block contained FN, which indicates a transfer conditioned on a FUNCTION. In this case the function number, as specified in field B, is 4. This function, defined in cards 16 and 17, causes an entering transaction to be transferred to statements labeled EEA or EEB depending on the value of its second parameter. This parameter will have the value 1 if the car is going up, or the value 2 if going down.

The program of Fig. 5.8 uses a logic switch named IDLE to control the flow of transactions. This switch is set by the action of block 25 and is reset by the action of block 10. The GATE block, 8, tests if this switch is set. If IDLE is set, a transaction moves from block 8 to block 9, but if it is reset the transaction is transferred to block 11. The GATE block, 26, tests IDLE for the reset condition. If it is reset, the transaction moves on to block 27, but if not, the transaction remains in block 26 until IDLE is reset.

The logic used in the GPSS elevator system simulation program is somewhat different than that used in the program of Sec. 4.4. But it should be possible to follow the operations using the program listing, including the comments, and the aspects of GPSS discussed in this section.

Although only a limited number of the features available in GPSS are included, these examples should indicate to the reader the relative ease with which many types of models can be programmed and simulated using this language.

5.3 SELECTION OF PROGRAMMING METHODS

Some of the advantages of special-purpose simulation languages should be evident from the examples that have been presented in this chapter. The reduction in the amount of code required does reduce the time needed for programming and can result in more readable programs. Both SIMSCRIPT and GPSS also have error-checking features and tracing routines which are particularly helpful in debugging simulation programs. Other conveniences, such as those for data input, model modification, and repetition of runs, were not used in the examples but are available in these languages.

These advantages may suggest that the logical approach to programming simulations is to select the best special-purpose simulation language and then use it exclusively. As a practical matter, this is usually not possible and in terms of developing knowledge of the field, it is not desirable.

One of the primary goals of any computer language is to provide the programmer with a convenient method of specifying certain important computer operations. Languages differ with respect to what operations are considered important, and these are chosen on the basis of the type of application the language is directed toward. Normally it is true that the wider the area of application, the more complex the language.

These characteristics carry over to the simulation languages. There are many of these languages, and each offers some unique advantages. In almost every case, there is some application for which a specific language may be considered superior to any other language. In view of this, all these languages should be recognized as useful and appropriate for certain purposes.

However, the choice of a language for a specific simulation task is often determined by other considerations. A major factor is the knowledge and experience of the programmer. If the task is not large and must be completed in a short period of time, it is best to use a language familiar to the programmer. Also, the availability of languages to the programmer is often a major limitation. Restrictions of this type are critical primarily when the simulation projects are only occasional activities of the programmer.

In many cases simulation programming becomes a major activity requiring appreciable labor hours over an extended period of time. This occurs in two types of situations. One situation is where a particular class of problem must be solved for many different systems. The other situation is where the simulation of a single system is undertaken as a long-term project.

In the first of these two situations, where a similar problem is solved for many different systems, special-purpose simulation languages offer their greatest advantages. In these cases, the similarities in the various problem formulations can be used to develop language features which greatly reduce the programming task. It is interesting to note that some of these languages appear to have very little relationship to any general-purpose programming language. For example, general programming experience is not very helpful in understanding the logic of GPSS programs. The reason for this is that GPSS was designed to be conveniently used by analysts without previous programming experience. This is a quite feasible goal for special-purpose languages. Of course, since GPSS can be applied to a very wide range of problems, it does contain features which do require techniques associated with general-purpose programming.

In the second situation, where a single simulation program is being extended and maintained over a period of many months, a special-purpose language may not be preferable to a general-purpose language. Programs of this type tend to become quite large, and thus, efficient execution becomes more critical. In this case the added effort to develop the specialized routines, such as those in Chap. 4, may be justified in order to gain added flexibility in programming.

An example of the possible advantages offered by using a general-purpose language is in selecting the algorithm and data structure for the event-scheduling operation. Both SIMSCRIPT and GPSS use a list structure similar to that described in Chap. 4, which is quite effective for small lists. However, as the number of events in the list grows, significant performance improvements can be achieved using indexed lists and specialized algorithms [3, 15, 16].

There will, no doubt, be many future improvements in special-purpose simulation languages. New languages will be developed and old ones will be improved. These developments will provide both added convenience and new concepts for simulation programming.

5.4 BACKGROUND AND REFERENCES

The development and general characteristics of simulation programming languages have been reviewed in articles by Tocher [14] and Kiviat [11]. A survey of a number of these languages is given by Kay [9]. Shannon [13] discusses simulation programming languages and presents a procedure for selecting the proper special-purpose language based on the nature of the simulation problem.

The basic simulation algorithms for both SIMSCRIPT and GPSS are described by Gordon [6]. The process-interaction approach is discussed in detail by Franta [2].

The language manuals [1, 8] are revised periodically and different versions are used with different machine implementations. Current versions of the SIMSCRIPT manuals may be obtained from CACI, Inc., 12011 San Vicente Boulevard, Los Angeles, CA 90049. Manuals for GPSS may be ordered from any local Data Processing Sales office of the IBM Corporation.

REFERENCES

1. Consolidated Analysis Centers, Inc.: "SIMSCRIPT II.5 Reference Handbook," Los Angeles, 1972.
2. Franta, W. R.: "A Process View of Simulation," American Elsevier, New York, 1977.
3. Franta, W. R., and K. Maly: "An Efficient Data Structure for the Simulation Event Set," *Communications of the ACM*, vol. 20, no. 8, pp. 596–602, August 1977.
4. Gordon, G.: "A General Purpose System Simulation Program," *Proceedings EJCC*, Washington, D.C., pp. 87–104, Macmillan, New York, 1961.
5. Gordon, G.: "The Application of GPSS V to Discrete System Simulation," Prentice-Hall, Englewood Cliffs, N.J., 1975.
6. Gordon, G.: "System Simulation," 2d ed., Prentice-Hall, Englewood Cliffs, N.J., 1978.
7. Gould, R. L.: "GPSS/360—An Improved General Purpose Simulation," *IBM Systems Journal*, vol. VIII, no. 3, pp. 16–27, 1969.
8. IBM Corporation: "General Purpose Simulation System V, User's Manual," Form SH 20-0851, White Plains, N.Y.
9. Kay, I. M.: "Digital Discrete Simulation Languages: A Discussion and an Inventory," Fifth Annual Simulation Symposium, Annual Simulation Symposium, Tampa, Fla., 1972.
10. Kiviat, P. J., R. Villanueva, and H. Markowitz: "The SIMSCRIPT II Programming Language," Prentice-Hall, Englewood Cliffs, N.J., 1969.
11. Kiviat, P. J.: Simulation Languages, in T. H. Naylor (ed.), "Computer Simulation Experiments with Models of Economic Systems," pp. 406–489, Wiley, New York, 1971.
12. Payne, W. H., J. R. Rabung, and T. P. Bogyo: "Coding the Lehmer Pseudorandom Number Generator," *Communications of the ACM*, vol. 12, no. 2, pp. 85–86, February 1969.
13. Shannon, R. E.: "System Simulation: The Art and Science," Prentice-Hall, Englewood Cliffs, N.J., 1975.
14. Tocher, K. D.: Simulation: Languages, in J. A. Aromofsky (ed.), "Progress in Operations Research," vol. III, pp. 71–133, Wiley, New York, 1969.

15. Vaucher, J. G., and P. Duval: "A Comparison of Simulation Event List Algorithms," *Communications of the ACM*, vol. 18, no. 4, pp. 223–230, April 1975.
16. Wyman, F. P.: "Improved Event-Scanning Mechanisms for Discrete Event Simulations," *Communications of the ACM*, vol. 18, no. 6, pp. 350–353, June 1975.

EXERCISES

5.1 Do the initial conditions for the program of Fig. 5.1 differ from those of the program of Sec. 4.2?

5.2 If line 3 of ROUTINE INITIAL, Fig. 5.2, is changed to

FOR I = 1 TO 10, DO

what changes will this cause in the program's execution?

5.3 Simulate a single-server queuing system using SIMSCRIPT. Assume that the arrivals to this system are exponentially distributed with a mean interarrival time of 40 s and that the service time is exponentially distributed with a mean of 30 s. Compare your results with the theoretical values for this system.

5.4 Repeat Exercise 4.9 using SIMSCRIPT.

5.5 Repeat Exercise 4.10 using SIMSCRIPT.

5.6 In Fig. 5.5, what is the theoretical value for the percentage of observations which should occur in the OVERFLOW interval of the TABLE for DATA?

5.7 In Fig. 5.7, eight savevalue entities, numbered 1 through 8, are used to store certain values. What variable names, used in the PL/I program of Sec. 4.2 and the SIMSCRIPT program of Fig. 5.1, correspond to the savevalue numbers?

5.8 Modify the elevator simulation program of Fig. 5.8 so that no more than 12 passengers can be in a car at one time.

5.9 Repeat Exercise 4.9 using GPSS.

5.10 Repeat Exercise 4.10 using GPSS.

SIX

SIMULATION EXPERIMENTS

Simulation is essentially an experimental approach to solving problems. A model is developed, in the form of a computer program, using known or assumed relationships among certain variables. The simulation experiment is conducted by assigning particular values to the model's constants and initial conditions for the variables, and then executing the program using these values in order to determine the behavior of all the system variables. Since the simulated system is completely determined by the assumed model, it may appear that this type of experiment will not lead to any new information about the system. However, the model specifies only certain relationships among variables, and even though these properties determine all other relationships, some effects are not, in general, readily obtainable except by observing model behavior over a period of time and under various conditions. Thus, it is usually necessary to conduct a series of simulation runs, or experiments, in order to establish the interactions among certain variables.

Simulation experiments are often used in developing the model of a system. But in this chapter we assume that an adequate model of the system and its environment has been developed and that it includes random elements. This presumes that the model was developed in order to answer certain specific questions which caused the study to be undertaken. So we are interested here in determining the properties of a random output variable.

In this chapter, we will consider techniques relating to procedures for conducting simulation experiments. The basic objective of these methods is to improve the efficiency of the experimental procedure. The methods covered are not given a rigorous mathematical development but rather are intended to provide an intuitive introduction to this important aspect of simulation.

6.1 VARIANCE-REDUCTION TECHNIQUES

We have interpreted the values resulting from simulations as being samples selected from an underlying probability distribution. Thus, when we consider the results for a particular variable, we make use of statistical procedures to provide an evaluation. Typically, we calculate the mean value $\bar{x}$ for a variable and establish a confidence interval or perform some hypothesis test relative to this value. The efficiency of these procedures is dependent on the variance associated with the estimator. That is, the larger the variance, the more samples that are required to achieve a specified level of confidence, and this corresponds to longer simulation runs and increased cost for computer resources. Several methods have been developed for improving the efficiency of the sampling procedure in simulations, and they are usually referred to as *variance-reduction techniques.*

The techniques we consider reduce the variance of the estimator by replacing the original sampling procedure by a new procedure that yields the same expected value but with a smaller variance. In discussing these techniques, we assume that the purpose of the simulation is to estimate the mean value of a variable. Although the purpose of a simulation may be to estimate some other property of a variable, for example, how often it exceeds some value, this case may be reduced to that of estimating the mean of a new variable which has a mean equal to the probability that the original variable exceeded the specified value.

6.1.1 Stratified Sampling

To introduce the idea of stratified sampling, consider the probability density function of Fig. 6.1. Assume that a uniform random number generator is used in conjunction with the cumulative distribution function to generate 30 random numbers $x_1, x_2, \ldots, x_{30}$ which have the specified distribution. We wish to use these values to estimate the mean value of the distribution.

Given the theoretical distribution function, we can determine the variance of

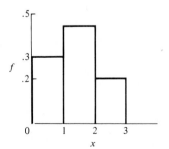 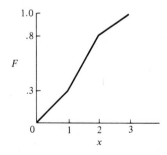

Figure 6.1 Example density and distribution function.

the estimate. The expected value for the samples, x_i, is

$$\mu = E(x) = \int_0^3 xf(x)\, dx = 1.4$$

and their variance is

$$\sigma^2 = E[(x-\mu)^2] = \int_0^3 (x-\mu)^2 f(x)\, dx$$

$$= \frac{(.3)(x-1.4)^3}{3}\bigg|_0^2 + \frac{(.5)(x-1.4)^3}{3}\bigg|_1^2 + \frac{(.2)(x-1.4)^3}{3}\bigg|_2^3$$

$$= .55813$$

The variance of the mean value of the 30 observations is then

$$\text{var}\,(\bar{x}) = \sigma^2/30 = .018644 \ldots$$

Next we consider an alternate method for sampling the distribution of Fig. 6.1. We again generate 30 random numbers, but this time we generate 10 values for x which lie in the range (or *strata*) of 0 to 1, 10 more in the range 1 to 2, and 10 in the range 2 to 3. If we denote the variables in each range as x_1, x_2, and x_3, respectively, the random values may be generated using the cumulative density functions shown in Fig. 6.2. The average values for the 10 samples in each range are denoted as $\bar{x}_1$, $\bar{x}_2$, and $\bar{x}_3$. We may then estimate the mean value of the original distribution by using the probabilities that x lies in the various ranges:

$$\bar{x}_{st} = \sum_{j=1}^{3} p_j \bar{x}_j = (.3)\bar{x}_1 + (.5)\bar{x}_2 + (.2)\bar{x}_3$$

where the subscript st indicates the stratified estimate. The variance of this estimator is

$$\text{var}\,(\bar{x}_{st}) = \sum_{j=1}^{3} p_j^2 \, \text{var}\,(\bar{x}_j)$$

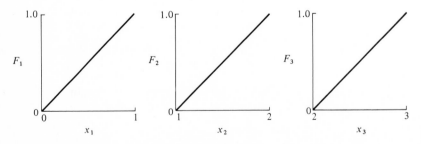

Figure 6.2 Distribution functions of stratified variables.

The variances for the stratified variables x_1, x_2, x_3 are

$$\sigma_1^2 = \int_0^1 (x - .5)^2 \, dx = \frac{1}{12} = .08333 \ldots$$

$$\sigma_2^2 = \int_1^2 (x - 1.5)^2 \, dx = \frac{1}{12}$$

$$\sigma_3^2 = \int_2^3 (x - 2.5)^2 \, dx = \frac{1}{12}$$

and

$$\text{var} \, (\bar{x}_i) = \sigma_i^2 / 10$$

so

$$\text{var} \, (\bar{x}_{st}) = (.3)^2 \left(\frac{1/12}{10}\right) + (.5)^2 \left(\frac{1/12}{10}\right) + (.2)^2 \left(\frac{1/12}{10}\right) = \frac{.38}{120} = .0031666 \ldots$$

Thus, the variance of the mean value found by this alternate procedure is just slightly greater than one-sixth the variance of the mean obtained in the first procedure.

This result shows that to achieve the same value of variance in the straight-forward sampling procedure will require almost 6 times as many samples (i.e., 177 versus 30) as with the alternate procedure. Or interpreted another way, the confidence interval for the alternate procedure is only about 40 percent of the size of that obtained with the first procedure.

An intuitive explanation of this procedure is that we have imposed an additional constraint on the random variables used in this example. That is, we have reduced the randomness or variation of these variables. The uniformly distributed values in the first case were in the range 0 to 1; whereas the second case was equivalent to using uniform distributions in the ranges 0 to .3, .3 to .8, and .8 to 1.0. While the expected results are the same, the variance was significantly reduced. It should be clear that the minimum variance would have been obtained if 30 percent of the samples were used to estimate x_1, 50 percent for x_2, and 20 percent for x_3.

Variance-reduction techniques have been extensively developed for use in a type of simulation often referred to as *Monte Carlo studies*. These studies are primarily concerned with types of problems such as evaluating an integral, for example,

$$I = \int_a^b g(x) \, dx \tag{1}$$

by using random numbers. Note that I is equal to the expected value of $g(x)$ in the interval $a \leq x \leq b$ times the width of the interval $(b - a)$. Random sampling can be used to estimate the expected value of $g(x)$, although this problem is deterministic since it has no random events included in its definition. The term "Monte Carlo methods" is sometimes used to denote *variance-reduction tech-*

niques. However, many of the procedures applied in these problems are not readily applicable to the type of simulations we have considered in this book. There are two primary reasons for this: first, the system response to a stochastic input variable, e.g., $g(x)$ in (1), is not explicitly known in most simulation studies but is rather the result of a computer program. The second reason is that in Monte Carlo studies, the observations are independent; whereas in many types of simulations, such as the examples of Chap. 4, these observations are often correlated.

The example of stratified sampling considered above was an example of distribution sampling and is closely related to the Monte Carlo technique, where stratification can be used very effectively. For the simulation of complex systems, there is no general procedure available that assures obtaining the considerable benefits which can be achieved by stratification. In these cases it is usually necessary to develop variance-reduction techniques specific to the problem. Despite this difficulty, it should be clear that the concept of stratification is of great potential value in improving the efficiency of simulation studies.

To illustrate the use of stratified sampling in a simulation program, we will modify the checkout counter example of Chap. 2. In this problem, random numbers were used to select the time between customer arrivals and the time required to be checked at the counter. One approach for obtaining stratified samples of interarrival times is to modify the GENARIV procedure as shown in Fig. 6.3.

This modification ensures that, for every 100 samples of the uniform distribution in the range 0 to 1, we will have 10 samples in each of the ranges 0 to .1, .1 to .2, etc. This is accomplished by rejecting those values which would cause the frequency of samples in the subintervals to exceed 10 per 100. A similar modification is used with procedure GENCOT.

```
         GENARIV: PROCEDURE;    /*SCHEDULE NEXT CUSTOMER ARRIVAL*/

STMT LEVEL NEST
  1                     GENARIV: PROCEDURE;    /*SCHEDULE NEXT CUSTOMER ARRIVAL*/
  2    1                DCL(TIME) FIXED BINARY(31) EXTERNAL;
  3    1                DCL(SA,SB) FIXED BINARY(31);
  4    1                DCL FNC(16) FLOAT INITIAL(.18,.33,.45,.56,.64,.71,.77,.82,.86,.89,
                                                   .92,.94,.96,.98,.99,1.00) STATIC;
  5    1                DCL N FIXED BINARY(31) INITIAL(0) STATIC;
  6    1                DCL F(10) FIXED BINARY(31) STATIC;
  7    1                J = 0;   DO WHILE(J < 2);
  9    1    1           CALL GENRND(X);  /*GENERATE UNIFORMILY DISTRIBUTED NUMBER X*/
 10    1    1           J = 0;        DO I = 1 TO 10 WHILE(J < 1);    Y = I;    Y = Y/10.;
 14    1    2                          IF(X < Y)    THEN DO;    F(I) = F(I) + 1;
 17    1    3                                                  IF(F(I)<=10)
 18    1    3                                                  THEN J = 2;
 19    1    3                                                  ELSE J = 1;
 20    1    3                                                  END;
 21    1    2                          END;
 22    1    1           END;    N = N + 1;    IF(N=100) THEN DO;    N = 0;    F = 0;
 28    1    1                                                      END;
 29    1                DO I = 1 TO 16;   IF X<FNC(I)
 31    1    1                             THEN DO;
 32    1    2                                        SA = TIME + 2*I;    SB = 1;
 34    1    2                                        CALL SCHED(SA,SB);
 35    1    2                                        RETURN;
 36    1    2                                        END;
 37    1    1           END;   END GENARIV;
```

Figure 6.3 A GENARIV procedure modified for stratified sampling.

Table 6.1 Nonstratified and stratified results from ten 1-h simulated time runs

Run	Initial SEED value	Average waiting time	
		Original	Stratified
1	1956987325	96.56	94.66
2	1156987325	101.03	106.01
3	1908986825	104.97	117.59
4	1508586121	96.50	83.08
5	1468582113	106.15	99.60
6	1472622913	78.18	137.10
7	1480662953	153.23	89.77
8	1521070957	99.63	97.75
9	1448546925	86.21	106.18
10	1721082113	159.60	84.65
$\bar{x}$		108.206	101.639
s^2		646.629	239.357
s		25.429	15.471

The checkout counter simulation program was run using 10 different initial values for the random variate SEED. The results for average waiting time, from the original program and from the modified program, are shown in Table 6.1. In this specific case, the use of stratified sampling reduces the variance of average customer waiting time to 37 percent of its original value.

6.1.2 Antithetic Sampling

Assume that we have made K runs of a simulation and calculated an unbiased estimate X_j of some variable on each run. The final estimate, then, is

$$\bar{X} = \frac{1}{K} \sum_{j=1}^{K} X_j$$

which has variance

$$\text{var}(\bar{X}) = \frac{1}{K}\left[\sum_{j=1}^{K} \text{var}(X_j) + 2\sum_{i=1}^{K}\sum_{j=i+1}^{K} \text{cov}(X_i, X_j) \right]$$

If the runs are independent, then the covariance terms are 0. However, if the sum of the covariance terms is negative, then a smaller variance will be obtained than with independent replications. This is the idea behind the use of *antithetic variates*.

Consider the generation of a sequence of uniformly distributed random numbers in the range (0,1). Assume we obtain a sequence

$$\mu_1, \mu_2, \ldots, \mu_n$$

Next we generate another sequence μ_i' by using the previously obtained values and the relation

$$\mu_i' = 1 - \mu_i$$

then the expected value for both μ_i and its antithetic variate μ_i' is $\frac{1}{2}$ and

$$\text{var} (\mu_i) = \text{var} (\mu_i') = 1/12$$

In addition,

$$\text{cov} (\mu_i, \mu_i') = E\{[\mu_i - E(\mu_i)][\mu_i' - E(\mu_i')]\}$$
$$= E[(\mu_i - 1/2)(1/2 - \mu_i)] = -E[(\mu_i - 1/2)^2]$$
$$= -\text{var} (\mu_i) = -1/12$$

Thus, the variance of the mean value obtained from combining two runs is zero. This, of course, should be true since every value used in the averaging process has a corresponding value on the opposite side of and equidistant from the mean.

Although we can use this technique to assure the proper mean value for uniformly distributed variates, the effect changes as we transform these numbers to other variables. To illustrate this, consider generating a sequence of exponentially distributed numbers using

$$x_i = -a \log (\mu_i)$$

and then a second sequence using

$$x_i' = -a \log (1 - \mu_i)$$

In this case,

$$E(x_i) = E(x_i') = a$$
$$\text{var} (x_i) = \text{var} (x_i') = a^2$$

and

$$\text{cov} (x_i, x_i') = E[(x_i - a)(x_i' - a)]$$
$$= a^2 E\{[\log \mu_i - 1][\log (1 - \mu_i) - 1]\}$$
$$= a^2 \left[\int_0^1 \log \mu \log (1 - \mu) \, d\mu - 1\right] = a^2(1 - \pi^2/6)$$
$$\simeq -.645 \, a^2$$

Thus, if we found the mean values of the sequences x_i and x_i' and then used the average of these two values as our estimate of the mean value a, the variance of this estimate would be less than the variances of the mean value of either sequence x_i or sequence x_i', but it would not be zero.

In most simulations, input variables are transformed in a variety of ways. These transformations, as in the exponential transformation above, tend to reduce the negative correlation of their input. Nevertheless, there is always the possibility that some of the negative correlation will occur in the output and produce a smaller variance.

We will again modify the checkout counter program to illustrate the use of our variance-reduction technique. The program could be modified so that every other run would use $(1 - \mu_i)$ as the uniform random number rather than μ_i. Then the average values from two successive runs could be used. A more convenient method to obtain the antithetic values is based on the fact that if μ_i is from a multiplicative generator,

$$\mu_i = \rho\mu_{i-1} \qquad \text{mod } m$$

then, if a new seed μ_0' is used to obtain a second sequence, and

$$\mu_0' = m - \mu_0$$

then the second sequence μ_i' will have the property

$$\mu_i' = 1 - \mu_i$$

Thus, if we change the initial value of SEED to

$$2^{31} - 1956987325 = 190{,}496{,}323$$

the uniform variates used in the simulation will be antithetic to those of the original run.

To use antithetic sampling with the checkout counter example, both the interarrival times and the checkout periods in the second run should be generated by antithetic variates. This means that two different sequences of uniform random numbers should be used in generating these random variables. The original program was modified to use two different random number streams. The results from 10 runs using the modified program, and the results from the corresponding runs using antithetic uniform variates, are shown in Table 6.2. In this case, the variances of the 20 values for the average waiting time is equal to 239.91, and the variance of the means of pairs of these values would be expected to be

$$\frac{239.91}{2} = 119.95$$

which is less than the variance of the means of antithetic pairs. Thus, in this case, the use of antithetic sampling increased the variance in average waiting time.

This result may be surprising or even seem unreasonable. It is true that for queuing systems of the type discussed in Sec. 3.4, antithetic variates are usually quite effective in reducing variance. The reason for this is that if one run had a heavy workload for the server, because of relatively short interarrival times and long service times, the antithetic run would be expected to have a light workload. This would result in a pair of values for average waiting times, one relatively large and one relatively small in the antithetic runs. However, in the checkout counter example, the timing of the opening and closing of counters is a very

Table 6.2 Results from antithetic sampling simulations

Run	Average waiting time		Mean value
---	Original variates	Antithetic variates	
1	104.30	103.58	103.94
2	95.81	72.09	83.95
3	86.11	106.86	96.485
4	89.04	85.67	87.355
5	81.35	76.41	78.88
6	86.59	76.04	81.315
7	77.04	96.21	86.625
8	75.03	95.94	85.485
9	130.15	110.81	120.48
10	71.56	104.50	88.03
$\bar{x}$	89.70	92.81	91.25
s^2	298.22	202.88	158.67

significant factor. Thus, in this case a heavy (or light) workload for the checkers does not necessarily result in a long (or short) average waiting time during a simulation period.

6.1.3 Common Random Numbers

In the previous sections, we have considered the use of techniques to reduce the variance in estimates of mean values. The use of these techniques was illustrated by applying them to the checkout counter simulation. The primary objective in that example was to determine the change in mean waiting time as a function of the change in counter closing delay. Thus, we were more interested in the accuracy of the difference in average waiting times due to differences in delay, than in the accuracy of the individual values of average waiting times.

If our objective is to determine differences in system response due to a change in some system parameter, it is intuitively reasonable to compare the system responses under the same circumstances. For the checkout counter example, this suggests that the same arrival pattern and the same checkout time distributions should be used to obtain samples of the differences. Moreover, the same initial conditions should be used for both the simulations from which the difference is obtained.

This implies that the same, or common, random numbers should be used to generate the arrivals and the checkout times for the comparison runs. If we let $\bar{x}_1$ be the average waiting time obtained from a simulation with delay value 1 and let $\bar{x}_2$ be the corresponding value for delay value 2, then the variance of the difference will be

$$\text{var}\,(\bar{x}_1 - \bar{x}_2) = \text{var}\,(\bar{x}_1) + \text{var}\,(\bar{x}_2) - 2\,\text{cov}\,(\bar{x}_1, \bar{x}_2)$$

If common random variables are used, there will be correlation between the two responses $\bar{x}_1$ and $\bar{x}_2$ and the variance of their difference will be reduced if the covariance term can be made positive.

Some results from the checkout counter example are given in Table 6.3. Separate random number streams were used for generating data in groups a and b. The differences using common random numbers are shown in Table 6.3. If the differences had been computed using the 5-s delay results from part a and the 45-s delay results from part b and vice versa, the average of all the differences would remain the same, but the variance would be much greater. Specifically, the variance would increase from approximately 16 to 64.

The technique of using common random conditions to determine differences is usually very effective in simulation studies.

Table 6.3 Checkout counter results using common random numbers

a. SEED initial value 1,956,987,325			
Hour	5-s delay waiting time	45-s delay waiting time	Difference
1	85.66	53.67	31.99
2	99.03	64.23	34.80
3	99.32	66.19	33.13
4	89.34	57.27	32.07
5	78.09	48.56	29.53
6	74.61	48.36	26.25
7	87.62	50.86	36.76
8	87.78	52.58	35.20
9	94.02	67.06	26.94
10	88.19	48.86	39.33
$\bar{x}$	88.36	55.76	32.60

b. SEED initial value 736,481,529			
Hour	5-s delay waiting time	45-s delay waiting time	Difference
1	83.98	51.45	32.53
2	83.92	59.79	24.13
3	97.42	63.82	33.60
4	85.12	51.01	34.11
5	87.68	57.86	29.82
6	92.09	61.08	31.01
7	95.24	58.10	37.14
8	84.00	54.60	29.40
9	99.91	62.46	37.45
10	91.83	58.92	32.91
$\bar{x}$	91.12	57.91	33.21

6.2 OPTIMIZATION PROCEDURES

In many simulation studies, one objective is to determine the best values for certain parameters of the model. For the inventory control problem, the objective is to determine values for the stock control level, the time between inventory, and the reorder point, which result in the maximum profit (or minimum cost). The process of determining the maximum or minimum value of some criterion function is called an *optimization procedure.*

In this discussion of optimization procedures, we will denote the quantity to be optimized, i.e., the criterion function, as

$$J(x)$$

to emphasize that it is a function of x, where x may be a single independent variable, a vector of such variables, a function of some other independent variable, or even a vector of functions of several independent variables. We assume that $J(x)$ is a scalar-valued function of x.

To introduce some of the basic ideas of optimization procedures, we will initially consider the case where $J(x)$ is a continuous function of a single variable x which is restricted to values in the range $a < x < b$. Figure 6.4 illustrates some possible shapes for various criterion functions. For J_1, there is no unique value for x which gives a maximum value for the criterion function. For J_2 and J_3, maximum value occurs for x at the boundary value b. For J_3 and J_4, the value $x = c$ gives a locally maximum value for J but not the true maximum value. For J_5, the value $x = c$ does give the true maximum.

If a criterion function has only one maximum value in a given range for x, it is called a *unimodal function.* In Fig. 6.4, J_5 and J_2 are unimodal. Note that for all the criterion functions shown, except for the constant J_1, in a region about the true optimum, $J(x)$ is unimodal.

The purpose of optimization procedures is to find the value of x which gives the maximum (or minimum) value of $J(x)$ in an efficient manner. This means that it is necessary to restrict the range of x about the true optimum in order to assure the validity of this assumption. There is no general method to do this, it usually requires an investigation of the shape of the function $J(x)$.

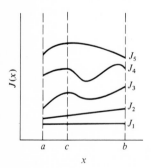

Figure 6.4 Criterion function shapes.

In many models which represent physical processes, the unimodel assumption is a reasonable one, but any optimization procedure should begin with an exploratory study of J as a function of x. The objective of this initial stage is to locate the regions in which the criterion function is unimodal. If there is more than one such region, a local optimum should be found for each, then the local optimum should be compared in order to determine the true optimum.

In simulation studies, the usual situation is that the properties of $J(x)$ are not known analytically, but for specified values of x, the corresponding value of J can be calculated. In these circumstances, the method for determining the optimum must be some type of search procedure. That is, we must choose specific values of x at which to look for the optimum value of $J(x)$. The objective of our optimization procedure is to guide the choice of these x values so that the optimum will be found in an efficient manner.

6.2.1 Search Methods—Single-Variable, Deterministic Case

Assume that for a specified value x_i, we can find the value of $J(x_i)$ with known accuracy, and that $J(x)$ is unimodal for the range $a < x < b$. Further, assume that we wish to run a fixed number n of simulations to determine the optimum of $J(x)$. That is, we wish to choose n values of x: $x_1, x_2, \ldots, x_n$, then find $J(x_1)$, $J(X_2), \ldots, J(x_n)$, and on the basis of these results, estimate the value of x which yields the optimum value of $J(x)$. The placing of the trial points x_i will be called a *search plan*. We wish to find the best search plan.

Consider the case in which only two trial values, x_1 and x_2, are used where $x_1 < x_2$ and let the unimodal range be $0 < x < 1$. There are three possible results in this case:

$$(a)\ J(x_1) > J(x_2)$$
$$(b)\ J(x_1) < J(x_2)$$
$$(c)\ J(x_1) = J(x_2)$$

After obtaining these results, the only thing we can say about the location of the value of x, which we will denote as x_*, that yields the maximum value of J is, in each case:

$$(a)\ 0 \leq x_* \leq x_2$$
$$(b)\ x_1 \leq x_* \leq 1$$
$$(c)\ x_1 \leq x_* \leq x_2$$

These statements are based on the unimodal nature of $J(x)$. The three cases are illustrated in Fig. 6.5, with the interval of uncertainty which contains x_* denoted by l_a, l_b, l_c.

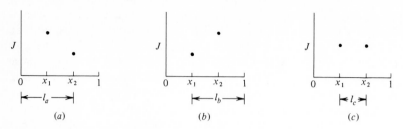

Figure 6.5 The three possible results of two trials.

Now consider what is the best location for the two trial values of x in this example. Intuitively the best locations for x_1 and x_2 would be the locations which minimize the interval of uncertainty. But the size of this interval depends upon the resulting values for J. One way to define the best locations is to choose those values which will give the minimum interval of uncertainty for the worst possible results. That is, choose x_1 and x_2, so that the largest of the possible intervals, l_a, l_b, and l_c will be a minimum. Let ε represent the smallest separation between x values for which a difference between $J(x)$ values can be accurately detected. Then the values for x_1 and x_2 which are the best locations using this definition are

$$x_1 = .5 - \varepsilon/2$$
$$x_2 = .5 + \varepsilon/2$$

and the maximum possible region of uncertainty is

$$l_2 = .5 + \varepsilon/2$$

To generalize the above approach to the case of n trial points, let

$$0 < x_1 < x_2 < \ldots < x_n < 1$$

then the interval of uncertainty after n trials will be

$$l_n = (x_{k+1} - x_{k-1})$$

for some value of k from 1 to n. Our approach to finding the best search plan is to choose the location of the trial points x_i such that l_n is minimized. Thus the interval of uncertainty after n trials for the best search plan is given by

$$l_n = \min_{\{x_i\}} \max_{1 \le k \le n} (x_{k+1} - x_{k-1})$$

where $x_o = 0$ and $x_{n+1} = 1$.

Using the above approach, the search plan, assuming that n is an even number, is to place the trial points at locations given by

$$x_k = \frac{(1 + \varepsilon)[(k + 1)/2]}{(n/2) + 1} - \left[\left(\frac{k + 1}{2} \right) - \left(\frac{k}{2} \right) \right] \varepsilon \qquad k = 1, 2, \ldots, n$$

where the terms in square brackets are replaced by the largest integer which is less than or equal to the term in the bracket. The maximum interval of uncertainty corresponding to this search plan is

$$l_n = \frac{1 + \varepsilon}{(n/2) + 1}$$

As a general rule, using an odd number of trial points with this approach is inefficient.

As an illustration of this method, for the case of $n = 6$, the trial points would be located as follows:

$$x_1 = \tfrac{1}{4}(1 + \varepsilon) - \varepsilon$$

$$x_2 = \tfrac{1}{4}(1 + \varepsilon)$$

$$x_3 = \tfrac{1}{2}(1 + \varepsilon) - \varepsilon$$

$$x_4 = \tfrac{1}{2}(1 + \varepsilon)$$

$$x_5 = \tfrac{3}{4}(1 + \varepsilon) - \varepsilon$$

$$x_6 = \tfrac{3}{4}(1 + \varepsilon)$$

A possible result of these trials is shown in Fig. 6.6. These results indicate that the value of x which maximizes J lies in the region between x_2 and x_4, and contains the value of x_i which resulted in the largest value for J.

The previous figure also suggests an approach to improve the search plan. The trial points x_3 and x_4 are at the same locations which would have been chosen if only two trials were to be conducted. If the criterion function had been evaluated at points x_3 and x_4 first, the results would have indicated that the maximum of $J(x)$ occurred for $x < x_4$. Thus, the determination of $J(x_5)$ and $J(x_6)$ was not necessary. In fact, using two trials enables us to reduce the interval of uncertainty to one-half (neglecting ε), and this is true at any point in the search.

Procedures which choose the locations of all trial points before evaluating the criterion function are called *simultaneous search plans*. Those which use results found at previous trial points to guide the selection of the next trial point are called *sequential search plans*. It should be clear that sequential search plans can be far more efficient.

The sequential search plan of placing the next two trial points about the center of the remaining interval of uncertainty is often called the dichotomous search procedure. It is an effective method but is not the best sequential search

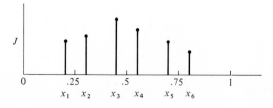

Figure 6.6 Example results—simultaneous search plan.

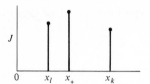

Figure 6.7 Interval of uncertainty—Fibonacci search.

plan in the sense that it minimizes the maximum remaining interval of uncertainty. The best method in this case is known as the *Fibonacci search procedure*.

The Fibonacci search method gives a maximum remaining interval of uncertainty, after n experiments, of:

$$l_n = \frac{l_1 + F_{n-2}\varepsilon}{F_n}$$

where l_1 is the original unimodal region, and F_n and F_{n-2} are the nth and $n - 2$ Fibonacci numbers. The Fibonacci numbers are defined by the sequence

$$F_0 = F_1 = 1$$

$$F_k = F_{k-1} + F_{k-2} \qquad k = 2, 3, \ldots$$

A general property of this method is that if we denote the interval of uncertainty after j trials as l_j, then

$$l_{j-1} = l_j + l_{j+1} \qquad j = 2, 3, \ldots, (n-1)$$

That is, the region of uncertainty after $j - 1$ trials is the sum of the regions of uncertainty that will result after the next two points. So, after $j - 1$ experiments, we have the situation shown in Fig. 6.7, where x_+ denotes the value of x which gave the largest value of J so far, and the interval l_{j-1} is bounded by some trial points x_l and x_k. After the next experiment, either the trial point x_j or the trial point x_+ will correspond to the largest value of J, and in either case the remaining interval of uncertainty will be l_j. Therefore, both x_+ and x_j must be at a distance l_j from an endpoint of the interval l_{j-1}. Thus, we have the situation shown in Fig. 6.8, and in general, at each step of the procedure, the next trial point is placed in the remaining interval of uncertainty at a position which is symmetric to the midpoint of the interval with the value of x_+. Thus if we can place the first trial point correctly, the remaining points can be found using this symmetry principle.

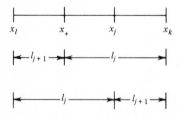

Figure 6.8 Location of next trial point—Fibonacci search.

To locate the first trial point, it can be shown that

$$l_2 = \frac{F_{n-1}l_1 + (-1)^n\varepsilon}{F_n}$$

Thus, given the initial interval of the search, l_1, and the number of experiments n, we know where to place x_1.

As an illustration of Fibonacci search, consider the case where the initial interval is from 0 to 1, the minimum separation between trial points is $\varepsilon = .05$, and five experiments are to be carried out. Then

$$l_2 = \frac{F_4(1) + (-1)^5(.05)}{F_5} = .61875$$

so

$$x_1 = .61875$$

and by symmetry

$$x_2 = 1 - x_1 = .38125$$

If we assume that

$$J(x_2) > J(x_1)$$

then l_2 is the interval from 0 to .61875, and

$$x_+ = .38125$$

Thus the next trial point is

$$x_3 = .61875 - .38125 = .2375$$

Assuming that

$$J(x_2) > J(x_3)$$

then l_3 is the interval from .2375 to .61875, and

$$x_4 = .61875 - (.38125 - .2375) = .475$$

Now if

$$J(x_2) > J(x_4)$$

then l_4 is (.2375, .475), and

$$x_5 = .475 - (.38125 - .2375) = .33125$$

Finally, if

$$J(x_5) > J(x_2)$$

then $l_5 = (.2375, .38125)$. This example is illustrated by Fig. 6.9.

In some cases, it may not be desirable to specify n before starting the experiments. For these problems, the same procedure as a Fibonacci search can be

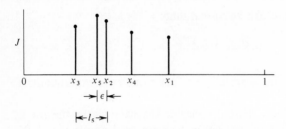

Figure 6.9 Example results of Fibonacci search.

used, but with the first trial point determined by

$$l_2 = l_1/\tau$$

where

$$\tau = \frac{1 + \sqrt{5}}{2} = 1.618 \ldots$$

This method is historically known as the "golden section." For large values of n, (F_{n-1}/F_n) is very close to $1/\tau$, so the two methods are very nearly the same.

In some problems, x cannot vary continuously but only over a finite number of points. For example, in the inventory problem, the stock control level can only have integer values. In this case, the permitted values of x may be called *lattice points*, and the procedure to find an optimum over these points is called a *lattice search*.

The Fibonacci method can be readily adapted to lattice search. This is done by numbering the lattice points in order from 1 to j. If $j + 1$ is equal to F_n for some value of n, then the Fibonacci method is applied to the lattice points with n trials and $\varepsilon = 0$. For example, assume that x can take on seven values, 21, 24, 29, 33, 35, 40, 43. Then $j = 7$ and $j + 1 = 8 = F_5$. For five experiments, the initial trial point is

$$l_2 = \frac{F_4 l_1}{F_5} = \frac{5 \times 8}{8} = 5$$

using l_1 as $j + 1$. Thus, the first trial point is the fifth lattice point ($x = 35$), and

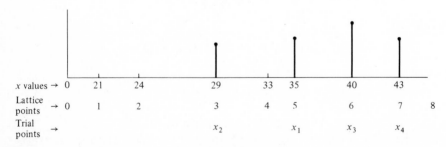

Figure 6.10 Example of Fibonacci search over lattice points.

the second trial point is the third lattice point ($x = 29$). The third trial point will be either the second or the sixth lattice point depending on whether $J(29)$ or $J(35)$ is the larger. A possible result for this example is illustrated in Fig. 6.10. Note that lattice points 0 and 8 are considered to be the outer boundaries and that only $n - 1$ trials are required to find the optimum x value.

If the number of lattice points j is not such that $j + 1 = F_n$ for some n, then the smallest n such that $j + 1 < F_n$ is used. In this case, a sufficient number k of fictitious lattice points are added so that $j + k + 1 = F_n$. The Fibonacci search is carried out over the $j + k$ points, although experiments are not performed at the fictitious points. The number of experiments required in this case will be either $n - 1$ or $n - 2$.

6.2.2 Search Methods—Single-Variable, Nondeterministic Case

For most simulations in which search procedures are applied, the results used to determine the value of $J(x)$ are only estimates of its true value. While it is possible to reduce the error in the estimate of $J(x)$ by obtaining additional replications, this requires increased computer usage.

Note that in the case of the Fibonacci search, a certain portion of the region of uncertainty was eliminated by comparing two values, $J(x_i)$ and $J(x_k)$. Now, if two estimated values of $J(x)$ were in error by a sufficient amount, the decision as to which of the two values was larger could be wrong. If this happened, the region which contained the true optimum of J would be eliminated from further consideration, and the search results would be wrong.

This means that in order to use the Fibonacci search, the accuracy in determining $J(x)$ and the size of the separation between trial points, ε, must be sufficient to preclude an error in comparing two values of the criterion function. In some cases, these restrictions may be reasonable and Fibonacci search can be an efficient method for finding an optimum. In other cases, it may be more efficient to use less accurate estimates of $J(x)$ and a different type of search method.

In order to introduce this other type of search method, we will first consider the problem of finding the root of a function before considering the problem of searching for an optimum point. That is, we assume that $R(x)$ is a function of a single variable x, and that within some region a to b, $(a < b)$, it has a single root x_*; i.e.,

$$R(x_*) = 0$$

and that

$$R(x) < 0 \quad \text{for } a < x < x_*$$

$$R(x) > 0 \quad \text{for } x_* < x < b$$

It is also assumed that the estimates for $R(x_i)$, denoted by $r(x_i)$, contain random errors denoted by δ_i; that is,

$$r(x_i) = R(x_i) - \delta_i$$

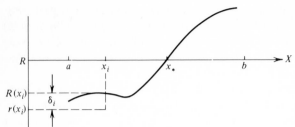

Figure 6.11 Illustration of measurement error.

Figure 6.11 illustrates an example of this situation.

A search method known as the *Robbins-Monro procedure* can be used to find the root in this case. This procedure places the next trial point $j + 1$ according to the outcome of the immediately preceding experiment using the relation

$$x_{j+1} = x_j - a_j r(x_j)$$

In this equation, a_j is one of a sequence of positive numbers which approach 0 as the search progresses; i.e.,

$$\lim_{j \to \infty} a_j = 0$$

This sequence must also have the properties:

$$\sum_{j=1}^{\infty} a_j = \infty \qquad \sum_{j=1}^{\infty} a_j^2 < \infty$$

These conditions are satisfied by the harmonic series

$$a_j = 1/j \qquad j = 1, 2, \ldots$$

which are the largest values possible for a_j.

For this search method, the size of the distance between successive trial points depends on the estimated value $r(x_j)$ and on the number a_j. Thus, the differences between trial points decrease as the search proceeds. It is possible that the estimated value $r(x_j)$ may differ in sign from the true value $R(x_j)$, so that the trial point moves farther away from the root in some instances. But, if certain conditions on the function $R(x)$ and the error estimate are met, the process will eventually converge to the root.

The conditions which guarantee convergence are: (1) the value of R must not go to infinity within the interval of x considered; (2) the estimated values $r(x)$ for any fixed x must be unbiased, i.e., if enough trial points are taken at a particular point x_j, the average value of the $r(x_j)$ approaches the true value $R(x_j)$; and (3) the estimation errors δ_i are of finite variation. This last condition may be interpreted to mean that the estimates are not very much in error very often. They can be very much in error occasionally. In most simulations, it is reasonable to assume that these conditions are met.

The *Kiefer-Wolfowitz procedure* is a method used in searching for the maximum of a unimodal function $J(x)$. It is similar to the Robbins-Monro procedure. The Kiefer-Wolfowitz procedure uses a pair of experiments or trial points at each stage in order to estimate the derivative of the criterion function. Specifically at the jth stage, the trial points for the experiments are $x_j - c_j$ and $x_j + c_j$, and the derivative at x_j is estimated by

$$\frac{r(x_j + c_j) - r(x_j - c_j)}{2c_j}$$

where, as before, r denotes the estimated value for the function, in this case J. This is illustrated in Fig. 6.12. The center of the next pair of trial points, x_{j+1}, is given by

$$x_{j+1} = x_j + \frac{a_j}{c_j}[r(x_j + c_j) - r(x_j - c_j)]$$

The sequence of numbers, a_j and c_j, satisfies the following conditions:

$$\lim_{j\to\infty} a_j = 0 \qquad \lim_{j\to\infty} c_j = 0$$

$$\sum_{j=1}^{\infty} a_j = \infty \qquad \sum_{j=1}^{\infty} (a_j/c_j)^2 < \infty$$

The additional conditions required to guarantee convergence of the Kiefer-Wolfowitz procedure are that the derivative of J with respect to x be bounded (not infinite) within the region of interest and that the measurement errors satisfy the same conditions as required for convergence of the Robbins-Monro procedure.

Even though the convergence of the procedure may be guaranteed, there are situations where the convergence may be very slow. Such cases may occur if the function $J(x)$ has inflection points. In this circumstance, a normalized version of the Kiefer-Wolfowitz method can be used; i.e.,

$$x_{j+1} = x_j + a_j \operatorname{sgn}[r(x_j + c_j) - r(x_j - c_j)]$$

where sgn $\{u\}$ denotes the sign of u, i.e., equals $+1$ if $u > 0$ or -1 if $u < 0$.

Another modification which usually accelerates the convergence of the Kiefer-Wolfowitz method is based on the following reasoning. In general, the

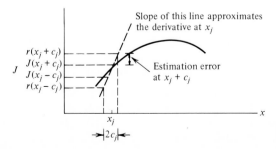

Figure 6.12 Example of step in the Kiefer-Wolfowitz procedure.

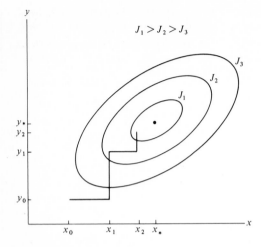

Figure 6.13 Two-dimensional search—one variable at a time.

procedure takes large steps in x when far away from the peak value of J and shortens the steps when approaching the goal. When far away from the peak, the estimation errors will probably not cause an error in step direction, but near the peak, this is much more likely. This suggests that in order to speed the convergence, the step size should not be shortened until the direction of search changes. Thus, the iteration equation becomes

$$x_{j+1} = x_j + \frac{a_k}{c_k} \left[r(x_j + c_k) - r(x_j - c_k) \right]$$

where the index j increases at each step, but the index k increases only if the sign of the term in the brackets differs from its sign at the previous step.

Both the Robbins-Monro method and the Kiefer-Wolfowitz method are examples of what are known as *stochastic approximation procedures.* They both use first-order approximations in their iteration formulas. Methods which use higher-order approximations are available and are discussed in reference [11].

6.2.3 Multidimensional Search

Often search problems involve more than one independent variable. For example, the criterion function may be a function of two variables, x and y. It is possible to approach these problems by applying a single-variable search to each independent variable in succession.

This approach is illustrated in Fig. 6.13, where the value of the criterion function $J(x, y)$ is represented by contour lines. If the search is initiated at the point (x_0, y_0), then the first search would reach the point (x_1, y_0); the second, point (x_1, y_1); and so on. This procedure would approach the optimum and can be extended to criterion functions of many independent variables. However, it is a lengthy procedure and can be very slow and may not approach the optimum if the criterion function contour lines have certain types of shapes.

This approach can be improved upon by carrying out the search operation along a line which is the direction of maximum increase in J from a given point. This direction can be determined approximately at the point (x_0, y_0) by evaluating J at three points

$$J(x_0, y_0)$$

$$J(x_0 + \Delta x, y_0)$$

$$J(x_0, y_0 + \Delta y)$$

The derivative of J in the x and y directions is then estimated by

$$m_x = \frac{J(x_0 + \Delta x, y_0) - J(x_0, y_0)}{\Delta x}$$

$$m_y = \frac{J(x_0, y_0 + \Delta y) - J(x_0, y_0)}{\Delta y}$$

The direction of steepest ascent, also called the *gradient direction*, can be represented parametrically as

$$x = x_0 + m_x \lambda \qquad y = y_0 + m_y \lambda$$

The single-variable search procedure can then be carried out by using λ as the independent variable. An example of this method is shown in Fig. 6.14, where the criterion function is the same as in Fig. 6.13.

Using the gradient direction with single-variable search is effective in some cases but may fail to approach an optimum if the criterion function contour lines are irregular. If it happens that the contour lines in the two independent variable cases are circles, then the gradient direction would go through the optimum point, and this could be reached with one single-variable search operation. This would occur regardless of where the search originated. It is very unusual for the

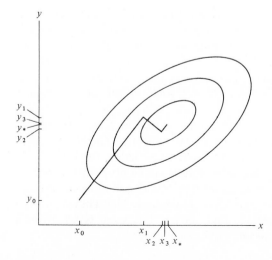

Figure 6.14 Two-dimensional search in the gradient direction.

criterion function contour lines to be circular, but in some neighborhood about the optimum point, the contours will be elliptical. This is due to the fact that if the criterion function is expressed as a Taylor series expansion in terms of the independent variables, at the optimum the first-order terms are 0 and the second-order terms dominate, at least in some small region.

If the criterion function contour lines are assumed to be elliptical, then there exist certain relationships which can be used to improve the search procedure. In Figs. 6.13 and 6.14, the contour lines are (approximately) elliptical. If this is the case, and the gradient directions at (x_0, y_0) and (x_1, y_1) in Fig. 6.14 are correct, then a line from the point (x_0, y_0) through the point (x_2, y_2) would pass through the optimum point. Thus, the optimum could be found after three single-variable search operations.

This type of relationship exists in the multivariable case and is the basis for a set of general optimum-seeking procedures referred to as *partan methods* [11]. These methods will converge to the optimum in a finite number of steps if the contours are ellipsoidal or if the contours are radially similar. For other contour shapes, it is not possible to guarantee convergence; but partan methods can be applied, and experience has shown that they are often highly effective.

There are many difficulties possible in applying a multidimensional search, and many different approaches may be needed in searching for an optimum. There is no reliable way to compare various methods in advance, so, often a problem of this type requires a trial-and-error approach.

The stochastic approximation procedures can also be generalized to the multidimensional case [11]. It often turns out that because of their more conservative nature, these methods do not encounter as many difficulties in converging as do the more efficient deterministic procedures.

6.3 EXPLORATORY EXPERIMENTATION

The methods discussed in the preceding section assume that the questions to be considered in the simulation have been defined in terms of the behavior of one or more particular measurements of system performance. It was also assumed that these measurements are continuous functions of a reasonably small number of continuous control parameters. These control parameters may be limited to a finite number of values, but their effect on the performance measures is assumed to be continuous.

In many systems, there are factors which may change in a discrete manner that cannot be associated with any range of real numbers. These qualitative factors are often policy-type specifications in the system model. For example, in the inventory control problem, the delay between placing an order and its receipt could be assumed to be a constant, to be a normally distributed random variable, or to have some empirical random distribution. These three different cases could be considered as different values for a single factor, but there is no obvious method with which to place these cases in a numerical order.

For highly complex systems, in addition to qualitative factors, there may be a large number of potential quantitative control parameters, too many to investigate in detail.

In the initial stage of experimentation with a simulation model, we are often interested in identifying the significant control parameters and factors. In this section, a technique is presented which can be used to test the significance of both qualitative factors and continuous control parameters as to their effect on a performance measure. The objective of this technique is to reduce the number of parameters and conditions which must be considered in the later stages of experimentation.

In the following discussion, the term *factor* will be used to denote an input variable of the simulation which may be qualitative or quantitative. The term *level* will denote either a particular policy specified for a qualitative factor or a value given to a quantitative parameter. This is consistent with the literature in this subject area.

We first consider the problem of choosing specific levels for the factors to be used in the experiments. The method to be discussed is called *factorial design*. The primary advantage of the factorial design approach is that it can produce the maximum degree of averaging-out of experimental error. Another important feature of these designs is the ability to measure interactions between factors.

Consider the case where we are interested in examining the effects of two input factors, x and y, on the simulation output variable Z. Assume that we specify two levels for each, x_1 and x_2, and y_1 and y_2. The factorial design in this case would specify four experiments using the following conditions:

Experiment number	x level	y level	Output result
1	x_1	y_1	Z_1
2	x_2	y_1	Z_2
3	x_1	y_2	Z_3
4	x_2	y_2	Z_4

Using the four results, we can estimate the effect that x has on Z by the differences $Z_2 - Z_1$ and $Z_4 - Z_3$. The average of these differences is called the *main effect* of x:

$$\text{Main effect } x = \tfrac{1}{2}(Z_2 - Z_1) + \tfrac{1}{2}(Z_4 - Z_3)$$

Similarly,

$$\text{Main effect } y = \tfrac{1}{2}(Z_3 - Z_1) + \tfrac{1}{2}(Z_4 - Z_2)$$

Generally, the two differences used in calculating the main effect of x and y will not be equal. This may be due to experimental error and also may be due to the change made in the other control factor. This interaction between the factors is estimated by one-half of the change in the simple effects of each variable:

$$\text{Interaction } xy = \tfrac{1}{2}[(Z_4 - Z_3) - (Z_2 - Z_1)] = \tfrac{1}{2}[(Z_4 - Z_2) - (Z_3 - Z_1)]$$

This approach can be extended to the case of several factors, each having several levels. The basic idea is to conduct experiments at all possible combinations of conditions.

To consider the effects of random experimental error, a straightforward approach would be to repeat each experiment Z_i several times and use the average values $\bar{Z}_i$ and their sample variances to test whether any of the computed differences are significant. However, it would be more efficient if we could combine results at different experimental conditions to estimate the variance due to each factor. It is possible to use the observations obtained in a factorial experiment to test the significance of the main effects and interactions by the method of *analysis of variance* (ANOVA).

To introduce the ANOVA method, we will consider the case where experiments are carried out when one factor, x, is changed. The factor x takes on J different levels, and K replications of the experiment are run at each level. The observations of the results of these experiments will be denoted by

$$Z_{j,k} \qquad j = 1, 2, \ldots, J \qquad k = 1, 2, \ldots, K$$

If we denote the average of the observations at one level as

$$\bar{Z}_{j,.} = \sum_{k=1}^{K} \frac{Z_{j,k}}{K} \qquad j = 1, 2, \ldots, J$$

and the overall average as

$$\bar{Z}_{..} = \sum_{j=1}^{J} \frac{\bar{Z}_{j,.}}{J}$$

then it can be shown that

$$\sum_{j=1}^{J} \sum_{k=1}^{K} (Z_{j,k} - \bar{Z}_{..})^2 = \sum_{j=1}^{J} \sum_{k=1}^{K} (\bar{Z}_{j,.} - \bar{Z}_{..})^2 + \sum_{j=1}^{J} \sum_{k=1}^{K} (Z_{j,k} - \bar{Z}_{j,.})^2 \qquad (1)$$

Now if we assume (or hypothesize) that the change in level of x has no effect, then all the observations come from a single population. The variance of this population can be estimated by

$$\hat{\sigma}^2 = \frac{1}{JK - 1} \sum_{j=1}^{J} \sum_{k=1}^{K} (Z_{j,k} - \bar{Z}_{..})^2 \qquad (2)$$

Under this hypothesis, the variance of the observation averages is estimated by

$$\text{var}\,(\bar{Z}_{j,.}) = \frac{1}{J-1} \sum_{j=1}^{J} (\bar{Z}_{j,.} - \bar{Z}_{..})^2$$

But since the variance for an average is related to the variance of the observations; i.e.,

$$\text{var}\,(\bar{Z}_{j,.}) = \text{var}\, \frac{Z_{j,k}}{K} = \frac{\sigma^2}{K}$$

we can estimate σ^2 by

$$\hat{\sigma}^2 = \frac{1}{J-1} \sum_{j=1}^{J} \sum_{k=1}^{K} (\bar{Z}_{j,.} - \bar{Z}_{..})^2 \tag{3}$$

Independent of any hypothesis on the effect of factor x, the variance of the observations can be estimated by

$$\text{var}(Z_{j,k}) = \frac{1}{K-1} \sum_{k=1}^{K} (Z_{j,k} - \bar{Z}_{j,.})^2$$

and this is equivalent to

$$\hat{\sigma}^2 = \frac{1}{J(K-1)} \sum_{j=1}^{J} \sum_{k=1}^{K} (Z_{j,k} - \bar{Z}_{j,.})^2 \tag{4}$$

What has been shown is that the two terms on the right-hand side of Eq. (1) are estimators for the variance of the experimental results if the hypothesis of no factor effect holds. It can be shown that the estimators in (3) and (4) are independent under this assumption.

The estimate given by (3) is the sum of squares between levels of the factor and is said to have $J-1$ degrees of freedom. The estimate from (4) is the sum of squares within levels and is said to have $J(K-1)$ degrees of freedom.

If the factor x does influence the experimental results, then the expected value of the estimate from Eq. (4) will still be equal to σ^2, but the "between levels" estimate from (3) will have a different expected value.

The statistic

$$S = \frac{\hat{\sigma}^2 \quad \text{from (3)}}{\hat{\sigma}^2 \quad \text{from (4)}}$$

under the hypothesis of no factor influence is the ratio of two independent estimators of σ^2. Thus S is the ratio of two independent, χ^2-distributed random variables with degrees of freedom $J-1$ and $J(K-1)$, and this ratio has the $F_{J-1, J(K-1)}$-distribution. The estimate of (3) increases if there is factor effect so that high values of S lead to rejection of the hypothesis of no factor influence.

ANOVA can be used with experimental results involving more than one factor. If there were I factors, $x_1, x_2, \ldots, x_I$, and we let

$$Z_{i,j,k} \qquad i = 1, \ldots, I \qquad j = 1, \ldots, J \qquad k = 1, \ldots, K$$

represent the experimental results for factor i at level j and replication k, then the total sums of squares

$$\sum_{i=1}^{I} \sum_{j=1}^{J} \sum_{k=1}^{K} (Z_{i,j,k} - \bar{Z}_{.,.,.})^2$$

can be partitioned into several independent sums of squares, as in Eq. (1) above. These sums can then be used to test for the significance of main effects and interaction in a manner similar to the one-factor case. Computer programs are available for carrying out ANOVA of factorial experiments [9].

To illustrate the nature of the results produced by the ANOVA method, we will consider an example with hypothetical results. Assume that the inventory control example of Sec. 3.2 was run using three different models for the length of time which elapses between the placing of an order and receipt of the items ordered. The three models correspond to (1) a constant value, (2) an exponentially distributed random variable, and (3) a normally distributed random variable. Also assume that the values obtained for average weekly profit, from five different runs of each case, were

1. 10, 11, 12, 13, 14
2. 8, 9, 10, 11, 12
3. 6, 7, 8, 9, 10

These hypothetical values clearly indicate that the average weekly profit varied with the form of the model for delivery time delay.

Applying the ANOVA procedure to the assumed data gives

$$\bar{z}_{1,.} = \frac{10 + 11 + 12 + 13 + 14}{5} = 12$$

$$\bar{z}_{2,.} = 10$$

$$\bar{z}_{3,.} = 8$$

$$\bar{z}_{..} = \frac{12 + 10 + 8}{3} = 10$$

and from Eq. (3),

$$\hat{\sigma}^2 = \frac{1}{3-1} \sum_{j=1}^{3} \sum_{k=1}^{5} (\bar{z}_{j,.} - \bar{z}_{..})^2 = 20$$

and from Eq. (4)

$$\hat{\sigma}^2 = \frac{1}{(3)(4)} \left| \sum_{j=1}^{3} \sum_{k=1}^{5} (z_{j,k} - \bar{z}_{j,.})^2 \right| = 2.5$$

Thus,

$$S = 20/2.5 = 8$$

which is a relatively large value of S and, using the value of $F_{.9,2,12}$, would permit the rejection of the hypothesis of no factor influence at a 90 percent confidence level.

The hypothetical data values used above can be assigned to the different factor levels in a random manner. Two such arrangements, and the corresponding ANOVA calculations, are as follows:

1. (a) 9, 8, 8, 11, 12
   (b) 10, 9, 12, 13, 10
   (c) 7, 11, 6, 10, 14

$$\bar{z}_{1,.} = 9.6 \qquad \bar{z}_{2,.} = 10.8 \qquad \bar{z}_{3,.} = 9.6 \qquad \bar{z}_{..} = 10$$
$$\hat{\sigma}_3^2 = 2.4$$
$$\hat{\sigma}_4^2 = 5.433$$
$$S = .442$$

2. (a) 8, 6, 12, 9, 10
   (b) 7, 10, 9, 11, 12
   (c) 10, 13, 11, 8, 14

$$\bar{z}_{1,.} = 9 \qquad \bar{z}_{2,.} = 9.8 \qquad \bar{z}_{3,.} = 11.2 \qquad \bar{z}_{..} = 10$$
$$\hat{\sigma}_3^2 = 6.2$$
$$\hat{\sigma}_4^2 = 4.8$$
$$S = 1.292$$

The total variance of the 15 data values is 5; and with the random orderings, both Eqs. (3) and (4) gave reasonably close estimates of this variance. But when the data was ordered to correspond to different average values for each factor with the same variance within each factor, the estimate from Eq. (3) was high. That is, with factor effects, the variance estimate obtained from differences between the overall average and the level averages increased.

This example illustrates the type of question which can be investigated by single-factor ANOVA. It should be noted that if the results of an actual study similar to this example do indicate that the nature of delivery times has an effect on the net profit, it could still be true that this effect is independent of changes in values for stock control levels and inventory period. If this were the case, the inventory control problem could be studied using the simplified model. The more general, multiple-factor form of ANOVA can be used to investigate interactions between factors.

6.4 DETERMINATION OF SAMPLE SIZE AND STOPPING RULES

The determination of the number of runs made before stopping an experiment is probably the decision that most affects the efficiency of a simulation exercise. Clearly the number of runs, or the sample size, is ultimately determined by the level of confidence required of the output measurement. Specifying a value for the level of confidence requires some knowledge of the behavior of the output variable and is dependent on how the result of the simulation is to be used. Just as an initial exploration is needed in an optimization procedure, a preliminary study of the results of a few runs is needed to judge the behavior of an output variable before setting a confidence level.

If the output variable values can be considered to be independent and normally distributed, the confidence-interval approach can be used to determine the sample size required to estimate the mean value to a given precision at a given confidence level. For example, if we wish to determine the mean value of the output variable $\bar{x}$ to within δ units at a confidence level α, we have

$$\text{Prob}\,[\,|\bar{x} - \mu| < \delta\,] = 1 - \alpha$$

where

$$\delta = t_{1-\alpha/2,n-1}\,\frac{S}{n} \tag{1}$$

and

$$n = (t_{1-\alpha/2,n-1})^2\,\frac{S^2}{\delta^2} \tag{2}$$

Since both the variance estimate S^2 and the t value will vary with n, this last relationship can give only an estimate for the sample size n. However, if the value of δ is calculated at the end of each run, this value can be used as a stopping rule for the simulation. In some cases, it is more practical to estimate values of n at some point in the repetitions and test the value of δ only when the estimated value of n is reached.

A general scheme for implementing this stopping rule and estimating the number of runs required, in an iterative manner, is shown in Fig. 6.15. In this figure, n_0 is a value selected to provide a reasonable first estimate for S^2, and ∇ represents the calculated value of the confidence interval.

Stopping rules can also be developed using the nonparametric estimates of Sec. 3.2.5. Similarly, if the purpose of the simulation is to determine if two variables have different mean values, the hypothesis test of Sec. 3.2.4(ii) can be used to derive a stopping rule. In this case, of course, if no difference exists, the stopping rule may never be satisfied.

If the output variable has autocorrelated values, the type of procedure indicated in Fig. 6.15 may be used for the stopping rule. However, in this case, the estimation of the variance S^2 is a considerably more complex computation and often is surprisingly far from the true value of the variance. Procedures for estimating the variance of autocorrelated variables are given by Fishman [3]. The recommended method is to obtain an autoregressive model representation for the variable and from this model derive a variance estimator. A technique for constructing autoregressive models for time series data is presented in Chap. 7.

The fact that the variance estimates for autocorrelated variables cannot be adequately checked for accuracy, even in a statistical sense, requires that stopping rules be overly conservative. That is, the Type I error value, α, must be reduced to compensate for possible error in the variance estimate. Moreover, how much this reduction should be cannot be estimated, so it is left to the judgment of the experimentor. This situation makes the regenerative-states approach particularly attractive for determining stopping rules.

In Sec. 3.6, the regenerative-states method was discussed and several

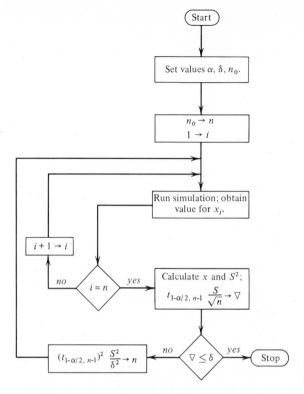

Figure 6.15 Flowchart for stopping rule.

measurements were defined which are made in each epoch between the occurrence of the regenerative state. These measurements are not the only ones which can be made. In fact, enough different measurements of this type can be made to completely reconstruct the entire behavior of a system. We may represent any number of these measurements as components of a vector $\underline{x}$. For example, the measurements discussed in Sec. 3.6, made in epoch j, may be represented as

$$\underline{x}_j = (p_j, b_j, l_j, w_j, n_j)^T \tag{3}$$

where T denotes the transpose of the vector. If we represent the vector of mean values as $\underline{\mu}$ and the covariance matrix as $\underline{\Sigma}$, then we may use as estimates for these quantities:

$$\bar{\underline{x}} = \frac{1}{n} \sum_{j=1}^{J} \underline{x}_j$$

$$\underline{S} = \frac{1}{n-1} \sum_{j=1}^{J} (\underline{x}_j - \bar{\underline{x}})(\underline{x}_j - \bar{\underline{x}})^T$$

Suppose that we wish to estimate some ratio of these measurements,

$$h = \frac{a\underline{\mu}}{b\underline{\mu}}$$

where $\underline{a}$ and $\underline{b}$ are arbitrary row vectors with constant components. For example, using the representation of $\underline{x}$ given in Eq. (3) and the values

$$\underline{a} = 0, 0, 0, 1, 0$$

$$\underline{b} = 0, 0, 0, 0, 1$$

then h would be the mean waiting time.
  We use

$$\hat{h} = \frac{\underline{a}\bar{\underline{x}}}{\underline{b}\bar{\underline{x}}}$$

as a first estimate for h. An improved estimate is provided by

$$\tilde{h} = \hat{h}\{1 + [\underline{A}(\underline{a}, \underline{b}, \underline{S}, \bar{\underline{x}}) - \underline{A}(\underline{b}, \underline{b}, \underline{S}, \bar{\underline{x}})]/J\} \tag{4}$$

where

$$\underline{A}(\underline{\theta}, \underline{\phi}, \Gamma, \underline{\gamma}) = \frac{\underline{\theta} \, \Gamma \, \underline{\phi}^T}{\underline{\theta}\underline{\gamma}\underline{\phi}\underline{\gamma}} \qquad \underline{\theta}\underline{\gamma} \neq 0, \ \underline{\phi}\underline{\gamma} \neq 0$$

The variance of $\hat{h}$ may be estimated by

$$\text{vâr } \hat{h} = \hat{h}^2[\underline{A}(\underline{a}, \underline{a}, \underline{S}, \bar{\underline{x}}) - 2\underline{A}(\underline{a}, \underline{b}, \underline{S}, \bar{\underline{x}}) + \underline{A}(\underline{b}, \underline{b}, \underline{S}, \bar{\underline{x}})]/J \tag{5}$$

In addition, a confidence interval for h is given by

$$\text{Prob } \{\hat{h}[\underline{B}(\underline{\Sigma}) - \underline{C}(\underline{\Sigma})] < h < \hat{h}[\underline{B}(\underline{\Sigma}) + \underline{C}(\underline{\Sigma})]\} = 1 - \alpha \tag{6}$$

$$B(\underline{\Sigma}) = \frac{[J - Q^2\underline{A}(\underline{a}, \underline{b}, \underline{\Sigma}, \bar{\underline{x}})]}{[J - Q^2\underline{A}(\underline{b}, \underline{b}, \underline{\Sigma}, \bar{\underline{x}})]} \qquad \underline{A}(\underline{b}, \underline{b}, \underline{\Sigma}, \bar{\underline{x}}) < J/Q^2$$

$$C^2(\underline{\Sigma}) = B^2(\underline{\Sigma}) - \frac{[J - Q^2\underline{A}(\underline{a}, \underline{a}, \underline{\Sigma}, \bar{\underline{x}})]}{[J - Q^2\underline{A}(\underline{b}, \underline{b}, \underline{\Sigma}, \bar{\underline{x}})]} \qquad \underline{C}^2(\underline{\Sigma}) \geq 0$$

and Q is the $(1 - \alpha/2)$ fractile point of the standard normal distribution. The covariance matrix $\underline{\Sigma}$ may be replaced by its estimate $\underline{S}$ if J is large (≥ 100). The results of using the above example values of $\underline{a}$ and $\underline{b}$ in these formulas are given in Sec. 3.6.

  Although Eqs. (5) and (6) can be used to supply the calculations required in a procedure similar to that of Fig. 4.8, this is not the recommended method for achieving specified accuracy in estimating h [4]. The preferred method is to specify the number of epochs, J, to be used in each simulation run. Then after the first run, use Eq. (4) to provide an estimate of h, denoted as $\tilde{h}_1$. An independent replication of the simulation run is used to produce $\tilde{h}_2$. Similarly, $\tilde{h}_3, \tilde{h}_4, \ldots, \tilde{h}_k$ are generated sequentially.

After every other run, i.e., when k is odd, calculate

$$\bar{Y}_k = \frac{1}{k} \sum_{l=1}^{k} \tilde{h}_l$$

$$s_k^2 = \frac{1}{k-1} \sum_{l=1}^{k} (\tilde{h}_l - \bar{Y}_l)^2$$

Then the simulation procedure is stopped when

$$s_k^2 < k \frac{\delta^2}{(t_{1-\alpha/2,k-1})^2}$$

At this point, the value of h will lie within $\pm\delta$ of $\bar{Y}_k$ with probability $1 - \alpha$. There may be some erosion of the confidence level in this procedure, but it has been shown that if $1 - \alpha$ is specified as .95, then its true value is at least .929, even in the worst case. Similarly, with $1 - \alpha$ specified as .99, then it is at least .984.

Experience with this sequential estimation procedure has indicated that the use of the most frequently occurring regenerative state in any particular run is an effective method to reduce run time. Also, the antithetic-variates method has been very effective in these applications.

6.5 BACKGROUND AND REFERENCES

The general problem of designing statistical experiments is discussed in references [1] and [2]. A number of papers which discuss special aspects of simulation experiments are included in the book edited by Naylor [8].

The two volumes by Kleijnen [5] give extensive coverage of statistical design and analysis techniques oriented toward digital simulation. This work requires only a basic knowledge of statistics as a prerequisite and gives detailed illustrations of many methods. Variance-reduction methods are covered thoroughly, and the bibliography includes most of the significant references in this area published prior to 1973.

Reference [11] by Wilde is an excellent introduction to the concepts of search methods. A more theoretical presentation of these methods is given by Stone [10]. The book by Kuester and Mize [6] includes programs to implement the major optimization procedures.

Analysis of variance as applied to simulation is discussed by Mihram [7]. Chapter 22 of reference [9] includes instructions for using the programming system SPSS for analysis of variance computations. This package is available at most university computer centers.

The discussion in Sec. 6.4 on using the regenerative-states approach to achieve specified accuracy follows that of Fishman [4]. His paper describes the simulation procedure and results for a multiserver queuing system that represents an airline reservations office. It also provides additional references for this technique.

REFERENCES

1. Bartee, E. M.: "Statistical Methods in Engineering Experiments," Merrill, Columbus, Ohio, 1966.
2. Davis, O. L. (ed.): "The Design and Analysis of Industrial Experiments," Hafner, New York, 1963.
3. Fishman, G. S.: "Concepts and Methods in Discrete Event Digital Simulation," Wiley, New York, 1973.
4. Fishman, G. S.: "Achieving Specific Accuracy in Simulation Output Analysis," *Communications of the ACM*, vol. 20, no. 5, pp. 310–315, May 1977.
5. Kleijnen, J. P. C.: "Statistical Techniques in Simulation," vols. 1 and 2, Marcel Dekker, Inc., New York, 1974.
6. Kuester, J. L., and J. H. Mize: "Optimization Techniques with FORTRAN," McGraw-Hill, New York, 1973.
7. Mihram, G. A.: "Simulation: Statistical Foundations and Methodology," Academic, New York, 1972.
8. Naylor, T. H. (ed.): "The Design of Computer Simulation Experiments," Duke University Press, Durham, N.C., 1969.
9. Nie, N. H., et al.: "Statistical Package for the Social Sciences," 2d ed., McGraw-Hill, New York, 1975.
10. Stone, L. D.: "Theory of Optimal Search," Academic, New York, 1975.
11. Wilde, D. J.: "Optimum Seeking Methods," Prentice-Hall, Englewood Cliffs, N.J., 1964.

EXERCISES

6.1 In the example of Sec. 6.1.1, what would the variance of the estimate of the mean be if 30 percent of the samples were used to estimate x_1, 50 percent for x_2, and 20 percent for x_3?

6.2 Modify the GENCOT procedure of the checkout counter example such that for each 100 samples of checkout time generated, the frequency distribution will be identical to that of Fig. 2.9. Using this procedure, and the GENARIV procedure of Fig. 6.3, run the simulation program and compare the results with those of Table 6.1.

6.3 Discuss how (*a*) stratified sampling, (*b*) antithetic sampling, and (*c*) common random numbers could be used to reduce the variance of the results obtained with the inventory example of Sec. 4.2.

6.4 Assume that in a simulation model, we wish to find the largest value for an output variable Z as a function of an input variable X. If the Fibonacci method is used to search in the range of X from 60 to 150, what values of X should be used in the first two trials? Assume a total of 10 trials are to be made and that any two trial values of X should be separated by at least .5.

6.5 How many trial evaluations of $J(x)$ are needed to reduce the interval of uncertainty to 1 percent of its original value if the minimum separation between trials is .25 percent of the original interval of uncertainty?

6.6 Assume that a criterion function $J(v,w)$ is a unimodal function of both v and w in the ranges $0 < v < 100$ and $0 < w < 40$. Further assume that three experiments have been made with the results:

$$J(50, 20) = 14.1$$

$$J(51, 20) = 14.5$$

$$J(50, 21) = 14.9$$

What is the best location for the next experiment, assuming that Fibonacci search is to be used in the gradient direction? The search is to be over the specified ranges and have a total of five experiments, none of which are closer than a distance of 1.

6.7 Consider the inventory system problem of Sec. 4.2. Assume that the optimum value for INVT-LEV is in the range from 10 to 60 and for INVTPRD is from 60 to 180. Further, assume the following results have been obtained from runs of the simulation program:

INVTLEV	INVTPRD	Average weekly profit
30	120	$10.97
30	130	$10.30
35	120	$11.82

If a Fibonacci search is to be used to find the optimum values for these two parameters, what should the values of these parameters be for the next two simulation experiments?

6.8 Assume that a criterion function is given by

$$J = 7 + .5x - .5x^2$$

and that we wish to search in the region $0 \le x \le 20$ for the maximum of J using the Kiefer-Wolfowitz procedure. Write a program to simulate this situation. Assume that the measured values of J differ from the actual values by δ, where δ is normally distributed with a mean of 0 and a variance of 1.

6.9 For the search procedure described in Exercise 6.7, it is necessary to compare the values obtained for average weekly profit from simulation runs with two different sets of parameter values. It is necessary that the runs be long enough that we can determine which of the two sets of parameter values yielded the higher value of average weekly profit with a confidence level of 95 percent. Show, by means of a flowchart, how we can stop the simulation runs when this level of confidence has been reached.

6.10 Determine the optimum values for the stock control level and period between inventories for the inventory control example of Sec. 4.2. Use a gradient approach to guide the selection of succeeding trial points.

6.11 Assume that Z is a simulation output variable and that X is a parameter of the associated simulation model. If the following results were obtained from 15 simulation runs, does the value of X have a significant effect on the value of Z?

X	Z
10	4.7, 5.2, 5.5, 4.9, 5.1
15	5.7, 5.1, 6.2, 5.3, 5.9
20	6.3, 5.2, 5.4, 6.7, 5.8

6.12 Run the inventory control example using three different models for the length of time between the placing of an order and receipt of the items ordered. The models for this variable are

(a) A constant equal to 60 days
(b) An exponentially distributed random variable with $\mu = 60$ days
(c) A normally distributed random variable with $\mu = 60$ and $\sigma^2 = 5$

Do the resulting values indicate that the different models influence the value of the average weekly profit?

SEVEN

MODELING TECHNIQUES FOR SYSTEM INPUTS

Building a model for a system is the first step in developing a simulation study. Usually this is the most difficult and the most critical step in the project. The model must be sufficiently detailed to represent the aspects of the system behavior being studied and must approximate the behavior of the real system. But the success of a simulation effort often depends upon keeping the model simple enough that it can be understood and manipulated by those who would use it. Obtaining good models for complex systems, in many cases, depends more on the intuition and ingenuity of the model builder than on the use of formal methods.

Although there are certain principles that apply to model development, this is a subject which is very dependent on the type of process being modeled. In most processes, a theoretical basis exists which should properly be included in the model. Aspects of the general modeling problem are discussed in the final chapter of this book. In this chapter, the discussion is limited to techniques which are useful in developing models from data which appears to be random and where very little knowledge is available as to the underlying process which produced that data. This situation often arises in defining input variables for a simulation, although these techniques are also used in other aspects of model development.

In this chapter, we first consider the problem of specifying a probability distribution for random variables. For this case it is assumed that the observations are not correlated. Next we consider models which can be used to represent correlated random variables. Specifically, we consider how to construct time series models which have the minimum number of parameters but which adequately represent the dependence between elements of an observed sequence. One use of these models is to provide independent input data for simulation programs, and this type of application is illustrated by an example.

The time series models may also be used to estimate the variance of correlated sequences for use in the stopping rule described in Sec. 6.4. This procedure is discussed in Sec. 7.4.

The topics covered in this chapter are only an introduction to an extensive body of work related to modeling stochastic variables. However, they should provide an understanding of basic concepts used for this purpose.

7.1 PROBABILITY DISTRIBUTION MODELS

In this section, we consider the problem of modeling a set of data as a probability distribution function. We assume that a set of observations $x_1, x_2, \ldots, x_n$ of a variable is available. The procedure is to assume that these observations are independent and came from a particular specified distribution. This assumption is then statistically tested, and if the observed data does not indicate this assumption should be rejected, the parameters of the assumed distribution are estimated using the observed data.

It is important to realize that we are not trying to find a distribution which gives the best fit to the data. That is, we do not search through a long list of distributions and choose the one which cannot be rejected at the highest confidence level. The selection of the assumed distribution model should be based on the properties of the physical processes which generated the data whenever possible.

The advantage of using a theoretical distribution function is that it provides more information about the underlying population than is available from the observations. But if there is no reason to assume that a given theoretical distribution is appropriate, then an empirical distribution obtained directly from the observations is all the information that is available.

7.1.1 The Chi-Squared Goodness-of-Fit Test

The most commonly used and most versatile procedure for evaluating distributional assumptions is the *chi-squared goodness-of-fit test*. A particular form of this test was used in Sec. 3.3 to test the assumption that a set of numbers obtained from a random number generator had a uniform distribution. In that example, we grouped the data into k intervals and counted the number of samples f_j in each interval. Using these frequency values, a particular statistic was calculated which had the chi-square distribution with $(k-1)$ degrees of freedom. This test is valid for any distribution with arbitrary density function $p(x)$. If the intervals are defined by $(y_0, y_1), \ldots, (y_{k-1}, y_k)$, the test statistic is

$$U = \sum_{j=1}^{k} \frac{(f_j - nz_j)^2}{nz_j} \tag{1}$$

where

$$z_j = \int_{y_{j-1}}^{y_j} p(x)\, dx \tag{2}$$

As the number of sample values n and the number of intervals k increase, the statistic given by (1) tends to have the chi-squared distribution with $k - 1$ degrees of freedom.

To illustrate this test, we consider the set of numbers given in Table 7.1. These 50 values were obtained from the RNNORM procedure shown in Fig. 4.15, using an initial seed value of 1468582113, a mean value of 9, and a standard deviation of 3. We will test the hypothesis that these values are samples from a normal distribution with these parameters.

In order to calculate the statistic given by (1), we must specify the intervals using Eq. (2). As a general rule, there should be at least five observations in each group. One approach could be to take the five smallest observations as a group; then using the assumed distribution and estimated parameters, determine the probability for that group of data. For example,

$$z_1 = \int_{x_1}^{x_5} \frac{1}{\sqrt{2\pi} \; \hat{\sigma}} \rho^{-(x-\mu)^2/2\hat{\sigma}^2} \; dx$$

where x_i are the ordered observations; i.e., x_1 is the smallest observation and x_5 is the fifth smallest observation. An alternate approach is to determine intervals of equal probability and use these to group the data. For the normal distribution, if we wish to define five equally probable intervals, we may use a table of the cumulative normal distribution (with $\mu = 0$ and $\sigma = 1$) to find that

$$\text{Prob}\,[- \infty < x < -.842] = .2$$

$$\text{Prob}\,[- \infty < x < -.253] = .4$$

$$\text{Prob}\,[- \infty < x < +.253] = .6$$

$$\text{Prob}\,[- \infty < x < +.842] = .8$$

Thus, the intervals defined by

$[-\infty,(\mu - .842\sigma)], [(\mu - .842\sigma), (\mu - .253\sigma)], [(\mu - .253\sigma), (\mu + .253\sigma)],$

$[(\mu + .253\sigma), (\mu + .842\sigma)], [(\mu + .842\sigma),\infty]$

Table 7.1 Fifty random numbers generated using RNNORM

9.107	12.787	6.221	7.968	9.830
10.002	4.320	8.679	8.711	7.800
10.646	2.972	7.273	12.281	6.979
7.627	11.423	6.413	8.350	3.715
11.962	7.060	7.328	8.438	14.420
5.695	6.480	8.168	3.994	6.359
12.758	8.285	7.555	10.123	7.861
5.561	4.731	6.964	6.936	6.991
12.137	7.258	10.257	10.543	14.317
6.343	13.378	5.297	9.995	11.223

are equally probable. For the example data of Table 7.1, this gives the intervals and frequency counts shown below:

j	Interval	f_j	z_j
1	$(-\infty, +6.47)$	12	.2
2	$(6.47, 8.24)$	15	.2
3	$(8.24, 9.76)$	6	.2
4	$(9.76, 11.53)$	9	.2
5	$(11.53, +\infty)$	8	.2

We may now calculate the test statistic and compare it with values of the chi-squared distribution. From Eq. (1), the test statistic is

$$U = \frac{[(12-10)^2 + (15-10)^2 + (6-10)^2 + (9-10)^2 + (8-10)^2]}{(50 \times .2)} = 5$$

Now for the chi-square cumulative distribution with 4 degrees of freedom, the 95 percent point has a value of 9.49.

If the computed value for the statistic U had exceeded 9.49, the chances that it came from a normal distribution would have been less than 1 in 20. Since it is less, we cannot reject the hypothesis with a confidence level of 95 percent.

In this example, the mean and variance for the assumed normal distribution were known. A more common problem is when these parameter values are estimated using the samples. For this case, these estimates are

$$\hat{\mu} = \frac{1}{n} \sum_{i=1}^{n} x_i \qquad\qquad = 8.430 \qquad\qquad (3)$$

$$\hat{\sigma}^2 = \frac{1}{n-1} \sum_{i=1}^{n} (x_i - \hat{\mu})^2 \qquad\qquad = 7.593 \qquad\qquad (4)$$

Using these estimates and the five equally probable intervals for a normal distribution gives the following data:

j	Interval	f_j	z_j
1	$(-\infty, 6.11)$	8	.2
2	$(6.11, 7.74)$	15	.2
3	$(7.74, 9.12)$	10	.2
4	$(9.12, 10.75)$	7	.2
5	$(10.75, +\infty)$	10	.2

Now Eq. (1) gives

$$U = 3.8$$

As is to be expected, the use of sample estimates reduces the value of the test statistic. But this also reduces the number of degrees of freedom for the distribution that the statistic tends toward. Since two additional conditions on the data are imposed by Eqs. (3) and (4), the statistic U defined by Eq. (1) may tend to have the chi-squared distribution with $k - 3$ degrees of freedom. However, this is not necessarily true; the number of degrees of freedom will be somewhere between $k - 1$ and $k - 3$.

For this example, the value of U obtained using the sample estimate 3.8 is less than $\chi^2_{2,.95}$, which is 5.99. So there is no indication that the hypothesis that the samples came from a normal distribution can be rejected at the 5 percent significance level. If the sample estimates did yield a value for U that was between $\chi^2_{2,.95}$ and $\chi^2_{4,.95}$, then the conservative approach would be to obtain more sample data in order to make a decision on the hypothesis at the 5 percent significance level.

The chi-squared goodness-of-fit test is best suited to those cases where there are a relatively large number of data values.

7.1.2 Kolmogorov-Smirnov Test

The *Kolmogorov-Smirnov test* is an alternate procedure for evaluating the hypothesis that a sample of data was drawn from a particular continuous distribution. This test may be more effective in the case of a small number of samples than the chi-squared test. Although, as with other nonparametric tests, the probability of Type II error may be greater.

The basic technique of this test is to determine the difference between the cumulative distribution $F_n(x)$ of the sample data and the cumulative distribution $F(x)$ assumed for the population from which the samples were taken. The empirical function is defined as

$$F_j(x) = \begin{cases} 0 & x < x_1 & j = 0 \\ j/n & x_j < x < j + 1 & j = 1, 2, \ldots, n - 1 \\ 1 & x_n < x & j = n \end{cases}$$

where, in this case, the samples have been reordered into a nondecreasing sequence, i.e,

$$x_1 \leq x_2 \leq x_3 \leq \cdots \leq x_n$$

The test uses the following quantities:

$$D_j = \max_{x_j < x < x_{j+1}} \left| F(x) - F_j(x) \right| \qquad j = 0, 1, \ldots, n$$

$$D = \max_{0 \leq j \leq n} D_j \qquad x_0 = 0 \qquad x_{n+1} = \infty$$

Test statistic D has a distribution which does not depend on the function $F(x)$. As n increases, the quantity $\sqrt{n}\,D$ approaches a known cumulative limiting distribution which gives the probability of this value occurring with the assumed underlying population distribution. Alternately, tables are available that give critical values for D at various significance levels and for given sample size n [5]. A short table of these values is given in App. C.

To illustrate the steps of this procedure, we may use the 10 values shown in the first column of Table 7.1. These points after reordering, and the values and ranges for $F_n(x)$ are shown below:

$x_1 = 5.561$	$F_0(x) = 0$	$x < 5.561$
$x_2 = 5.695$	$F_1(x) = .1$	$5.561 < x < 5.695$
$x_3 = 6.343$	$F_2(x) = .2$	$5.695 < x < 6.343$
$x_4 = 7.627$	$F_3(x) = .3$	$6.343 < x < 7.627$
$x_5 = 9.107$	$F_4(x) = .4$	$7.627 < x < 9.107$
$x_6 = 10.002$	$F_5(x) = .5$	$9.107 < x < 10.002$
$x_7 = 10.646$	$F_6(x) = .6$	$10.002 < x < 10.646$
$x_8 = 11.962$	$F_7(x) = .7$	$10.646 < x < 11.962$
$x_9 = 12.137$	$F_8(x) = .8$	$11.962 < x < 12.137$
$x_{10} = 12.758$	$F_9(x) = .9$	$12.137 < x < 12.758$
	$F_{10}(x) = 1.0$	$12.758 < x$

If we now assume that the underlying distribution for these sample values is normal with a mean of 9 and a standard deviation of 3, the computation of D is carried out as follows:

$$D_0 = \max_{0 < x < x_1} \left| F(x) - F_0(x) \right| = \max_{0 < x < 5.561} \left| F(x) - 0 \right|$$

The value of $F(5.561)$ is the value of the cumulative distribution of a normal distribution with $\mu = 9$ and $\sigma = 3$. Using

$$y_1 = \frac{x_1 - 9}{3} = -1.146$$

and the table of the cumulative standard normal distribution, we find

$$F(5.561) = .126$$

and this is the largest value for $F(x)$ in the range from 0 to 5.561.

Thus,

$$D_0 = .126$$

Now,

$$D_1 = \max_{5.561 < x < 5.695} \left| F(x) - .1 \right|$$

$$= \max\left(|.126 - .1|, |.135 - .1| \right) = .035$$

Similarly,

$$D_2 = .065$$
$$D_3 = .112$$
$$D_4 = .086$$
$$D_5 = .131$$
$$D_6 = .108$$
$$D_7 = .138$$
$$D_8 = .052$$
$$D_9 = .048$$
$$D_{10} = .105$$

Therefore,

$$D = D_7 = .138$$

The interpretation of the D_j values as deviations between the sample cumulative distribution and the assumed cumulative distribution is illustrated for this example in Fig. 7.1.

As may be verified using the data from Table A.6, the value of D in this example is much less than the critical value, even at the 20 percent significance level. That is, we cannot reject the hypothesis that the samples came from the

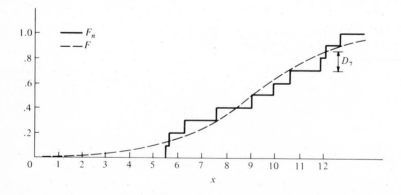

Figure 7.1 Comparison between the sample and assumed cumulative distributions.

assumed distribution even if we are willing to take a 20 percent chance of being wrong.

In this example, additional information, other than the 10 sample values, was used to specify the mean and variance of the assumed distribution. If we had used the mean value and variance of the 10 samples to estimate these parameters, this would have reduced the calculated value of D and would reduce the accuracy of the test. For the case of normal or exponential distributions, the test can be modified to compensate for the use of parameters based on the sample data [2].

The Kolmogorov-Smirnov test can be extended to evaluate the hypothesis that two different sets of samples came from the same underlying distributions [3].

7.2 TIME SERIES MODELS

In our previous examples of simulations, we have assumed that the external effects on the system, which were stochastic in nature, were due to independent random effects. Based on observations or because of physical reasons, a particular theoretical distribution was often chosen and used in the simulation. At other times, a strictly empirical distribution is used. Procedures for specifying these distributions have been discussed in the previous section.

The assumption of independence of the random effects in many cases masks important aspects of the external disturbances which influence a system. Very often data which represents naturally occurring processes is in the form of a time series where observations are dependent. Just as this type of phenomenon occurred in the simulation models we have considered, it also occurs in the external processes of the environment which provide input to the systems we wish to study.

If the random effects which influence a system are dependent, it is necessary that a simulation of the system include this in order to achieve a valid representation of the actual system environment. For this reason, we consider here procedures for specifying a time series model based on empirical data.

The approach used in developing time series models will be to present certain model types which are sufficient to represent particular classes of time series. Then techniques for selecting the type of model appropriate to specific data are presented. After that, methods are considered for estimating the parameters of the selected model based on the data. Note that this process is similar to that used in specifying distributions for independent observations. The difference is in the models used.

The models that we consider are based on the idea that a time series of dependent observations can be regarded as being generated from a series of independent disturbances. Specifically, as represented in Fig. 7.2, we assume that the input at time t, a_t, to the process L is a sequence of independent random variables having a normal distribution with mean of 0 and variance σ_a^2.

The process L transforms this input series to the output series z_t in which the

Figure 7.2 Process L input and output.

successive values are dependent. The process L is a linear operation so that the output is simply a weighted sum of previous inputs:

$$z_t = a_t + \theta_1\, a_{t-1} + \theta_2\, a_{t-2} + \cdots \qquad (1)$$

A more general model could include some nonzero mean value for the output; i.e.,

$$z_t' = z_t + \mu$$

but if this is the case, we can still use Eq. (1) and consider z_t to be deviations of the real output from its mean value.

The model of Eq. (1) is for a general linear process where the system output is represented by a weighted sum of past and present values of the input. Alternatively, the system output can be represented as the weighted sum of past output values and the present input:

$$z_t = a_t + \phi_1 z_{t-1} + \phi_2\, z_{t-2} + \cdots \qquad (2)$$

The relationship between the θ_i and ϕ_i weighting factors can be expressed in terms of a backward-shift operator B, defined by

$$Bz_t = z_{t-1} \qquad B^j z_t = z_{t-j}$$

Defining the functions

$$\Theta(B) = 1 + \sum_{j=1}^{\infty} \theta_j B^j$$

$$\Phi(B) = 1 + \sum_{j=1}^{\infty} \phi_j B^j$$

We then have, from (1) and (2),

$$z_t = \Theta(B)a_t$$

$$\Phi(B)z_t = a_t$$

thus
$$\Phi(B) = \Theta^{-1}(B) \qquad (3)$$

Equation (3) may be used to find the ϕ_i's if the θ_i's are known and vice versa.

The general linear process represented by (1) or (2) is not very useful if an infinite number of parameters are needed to give an adequate representation of the data. Fortunately, models of this type which contain only a few parameters are often adequate in practical applications. We will next consider some special cases of the general model and their properties.

(i) Autoregressive model Consider the case of a model of the form given by Eq. (2) in which only the first p values of ϕ_j are nonzero. This model would have the equation:

$$z_t = a_t + \phi_1 z_{t-1} + \phi_2 z_{t-2} + \cdots + \phi_p z_{t-p} \qquad (4)$$

The model represents what is called an *autoregressive process of order p.*

The first-order autoregressive process model is

$$z_t = \phi_1 z_{t-1} + a_t \qquad (5)$$

For this case, the function

$$\Phi(B) = 1 - \phi_1 B$$

and by using Eq. (3), we find that

$$\Theta(B) = \Phi(B)^{-1} = \frac{1}{1 - \phi_1 B} = 1 + \phi_1 B + \phi_1^2 B^2 + \phi_1^3 B^3 + \cdots$$

So that the model of Eq. (5) could also be represented as

$$z_t = a_t + \phi_1 a_{t-1} + \phi_1^2 a_{t-2} + \phi_1^3 a_{t-3} + \cdots + \phi_1^j a_{t-j} + \cdots \qquad (6)$$

The finiteness of Eq. (5) makes it much more convenient than Eq. (6).

(ii) Moving average model The model of Eq. (1) with a finite number of weighting terms is

$$z_t = a_t - \theta_1 a_{t-1} - \theta_2 a_{t-2} - \cdots - \theta_q a_{t-q} \qquad (7)$$

This represents what is called a *moving average process of order q.*

The general first-order moving average model,

$$z_t = a_t - \theta_1 a_{t-1}$$

can be represented as an autoregressive model but would require an infinite number of parameters, just as the first-order autoregressive model leads to an infinite-order moving average model.

Thus, it is clear that the choice of model form makes a great deal of difference in the size of the model required to represent a particular process. A process that is truly of the autoregressive type cannot be well represented by a moving average model and vice versa.

(iii) Mixed autoregressive–moving average models In some cases a process will be neither strictly of the autoregressive nor moving average type. In these instances, in order to obtain a model with a small number of parameters, we will use the representation:

$$z_t = \phi_1 z_{t-1} + \cdots + \phi_p z_{t-p} + a_t - \theta_1 a_{t-1} - \cdots - \theta_q a_{t-q} \qquad (8)$$

Models of this type have an order specified by values for both p and q.

In order to give a physical interpretation to these models, we may refer back to Sec. 3.5. The models defined by Eqs. (1) and (2) of that section are first-order moving average models. They include one term, e_{i-1}, which denotes how the present value is influenced by the past value. A moving average model of order q is one where the last q values of the sequence influence the present value and thus represents a system where a disturbance at one point in time will affect the state of the system q time periods in the future.

In Sec. 3.5.4, a third time series model was introduced [Eq. (15)] which included a periodic component. This model can be represented by an autoregressive model of order 5. An autoregressive model of order p has periodic repetitions of length p time units. Thus, autoregressive models may be used to represent systems which exhibit cyclic behavior.

The autocorrelation and spectral density functions for these three models are shown in Fig. 3.14. Note that the first-order moving average model has one nonzero autocorrelation value and the autoregressive-type model has an oscillating autocorrelation function. This characteristic is useful in identifying the nature of a model which may be appropriate to represent a given set of time series data.

The mixed autoregressive–moving average models can represent both inertialike and cyclic behavior. Of course, these models are not adequate to represent all time series data.

The assumption that the time series is generated by a linear transformation of a sequence of independent samples from a normal distribution is not always reasonable. This and restrictions on permissible values for the parameters, such as Eq. (12), limit the effectiveness of these models in representing some time series. However, these models have proved to be appropriate for many real time series and are a convenient means for generating random values with prescribed autocorrelation functions.

7.2.1 Autocorrelations

The basic analysis tool for selecting a model to fit time series data is the autocorrelation function. For this reason, we next develop relations for the autocorrelation functions of the three model types.

(i) Autoregressive model If we multiply Eq. (4) by z_{t-k}, we obtain

$$z_t z_{t-k} = \phi_1 z_{t-1} z_{t-k} + \phi_2 z_{t-2} z_{t-k} + \cdots + \phi_p z_{t-p} z_{t-k} + a_t z_{t-k}$$

Then, taking expected values and noting that a_t and z_{t-k} are uncorrelated if $k > 0$, we have

$$R_k = \phi_1 R_{k-1} + \phi_2 R_{k-2} + \cdots + \phi_p R_{k-p} \qquad k > 0 \qquad (9)$$

also, dividing all terms by R_0 gives

$$r_k = \phi_1 r_{k-1} + \phi_2 r_{k-2} + \cdots + \phi_p r_{k-p} \qquad k > 0 \qquad (10)$$

These difference equations satisfied by the autocovariances and autocorrelations are similar to the difference equation, (4), satisfied by the variable z_t, except that the present disturbance term a_t is deleted.

The general solution of the linear difference equation, (10), is

$$r_k = \alpha_1 S_1^{-k} + \alpha_2 S_2^{-k} + \cdots + \alpha_p S_p^{-k} \tag{11}$$

where the α_i's are constants and the S_i's are the p roots of the characteristic equation:

$$1 - \phi_1 S - \phi_2 S^2 - \ldots - \phi_p S^p = 0$$

For real values of ϕ_i, each root will be either real or one of a complex conjugate pair. In order to have a bounded solution, the roots must satisfy the relation

$$|S_i| > 1 \tag{12}$$

Thus, the real roots contribute a damped exponential to the autocorrelation function given by (11). A complex pair of roots contribute a damped sine wave to this function. So the autocorrelation function of a stationary autoregressive process will consist of damped exponentials and damped sine waves.

Yule-Walker equations If we substitute into Eq. (10) the values

$$k = 1, 2, \ldots, p$$

we obtain a set of linear equations for the ϕ_i's in terms of the r_i's:

$$r_1 = \phi_1 + r_1 \phi_2 + \cdots + r_{1-p} \phi_p$$
$$r_2 = r_1 \phi_1 + \phi_2 + \cdots + r_{2-p} \phi_p$$
$$\vdots \tag{13}$$
$$r_p = r_{p-1} \phi_1 + r_{p-2} \phi_2 + \cdots + \phi_p$$

Since

$$r_j = r_{-j}$$

Eq. (13) is a system of p linear algebraic equations. If the autocorrelations are known, the coefficients $\phi_1, \ldots, \phi_p$ can be found. If we replace the theoretical autocorrelations r_k by the estimated autocorrelations $\hat{r}_k$, this gives the *Yule-Walker estimates* of the parameters ϕ_i.

The first step in specifying an autoregressive model is to choose the order p. The basic idea is that the autoregressive parameters ϕ_j should be zero for j greater than p. The procedure then is to compute ϕ_i, starting with $i = 1$, and successively test the hypothesis that the autoregression order is i against the alternate hypothesis that the order is greater than i. A method for doing this is presented in Sec. 7.4.

(ii) Moving average model Multiplying Eq. (7) by z_{t-k} and taking expected values give the following expression for the autocovariances of the moving average model:

$$R_k = E[(a_t - \theta_1 a_{t-1} - \cdots - \theta_q a_{t-q})(a_{t-k} - \theta_1 a_{t-k-1} - \cdots - \theta_q a_{t-k-q})]$$

$$= \begin{cases} (-\theta_k + \theta_1\theta_{k+1} + \theta_2\theta_{k+2} + \cdots + \theta_{q-k}\theta_q)\sigma_a^2 & k = 1, 2, \ldots, q \\ 0 & k > q \end{cases}$$

Since

$$R_0 = (1 + \theta_1^2 + \theta_2^2 + \cdots + \theta_q^2)\sigma_a^2$$

The autocorrelation function is

$$r_k = \begin{cases} \dfrac{-\theta_k + \theta_1\theta_{k+1} + \cdots + \theta_{q-k}\theta_q}{1 + \theta_1^2 + \theta_2^2 + \cdots + \theta_q^2} & k = 1, 2, \ldots, q \\ 0 & k > q \end{cases} \tag{14}$$

If estimated values for the autocorrelations, $\hat{r}_1, \hat{r}_2, \ldots, \hat{r}_q$, are used with Eq. (14), the moving average parameters θ_i can be estimated. However, (14) is a set of nonlinear equations which require some type of iterative procedure for solution. The results are only estimates but are useful in identifying the order required in the model.

(iii) Mixed autoregressive–moving average model Multiplying Eq. (8) by z_{t-k} and taking expected values give the following relation for the autocovariances of mixed models:

$$R_k = \phi_1 R_{k-1} + \cdots + \phi_p R_{k-p} + V_k - \theta_1 V_{k-1} - \cdots - \theta_q V_{k-q} \tag{15}$$

where

$$V_j = E(z_{t-j} a_t)$$

represents the cross covariances between z and a. Since the output z_{t-k} at time $t - k$ depends only on inputs that have occurred up to that time,

$$V_j = 0 \qquad \text{for} \qquad j > 0$$

Therefore,

$$R_k = \phi_1 R_{k-1} + \cdots + \phi_p R_{k-p}$$

when $\qquad k \geq q + 1$

and $\qquad r_k = \phi_1 r_{k-1} + \phi_2 r_{k-2} + \cdots + \phi_p r_{k-p} \qquad k \geq q + 1 \tag{16}$

Thus a mixed model will have q autocorrelations that depend on both parameters ϕ_i and θ_i, and a total of $p + q$ values, as determined by Eq. (15), divided by R_0. These values can then be used as starting values in Eq. (16) to determine the remaining autocorrelations.

To illustrate this operation, consider the example:

$$z_t = \phi_1 z_{t-1} + a_t - \theta_1 a_{t-1}$$

The equivalent of Eq. (15) in this case is

$$R_k = \phi_1 R_{k-1} + V_k - \theta_1 V_{k-1}$$

Thus,

$$R_0 = \phi_1 R_{-1} + V_0 - \theta_1 V_{-1} \qquad = \phi_1 R_1 + V_0 - \theta_1 V_{-1}$$
$$R_1 = \phi_1 R_0 + V_1 - \theta_1 V_0 \qquad = \phi_1 R_0 - \theta_1 V_0$$

Now,

$$V_0 = E(z_t a_t) \qquad = E(\phi_1 z_{t-1} a_t + a_t^2 - \theta_1 a_{t-1} a_t)$$
$$= E(a_t^2) \qquad = \sigma_a^2$$
$$V_{-1} = E(z_{t+1} a_t) \qquad = E(\phi_1 z_t a_t + a_{t+1} a_t - \theta_1 a_t^2)$$
$$= \phi_1 \sigma_a^2 - \theta_1 \sigma_a^2$$

So we have,

$$R_0 = \phi_1 R_1 + \sigma_a^2 - \theta_1 (\phi_1 - \theta_1)\sigma_a^2$$
$$R_1 = \phi_1 R_0 - \theta_1 \sigma_a^2$$

These two equations may be solved to give

$$R_0 = (1 - 2\phi_1\theta_1 + \theta_1^2) \frac{\sigma_a^2}{1 - \phi_1^2}$$

The remaining autocovariances are given by

$$R_j = \phi_1 R_{j-1} \qquad j = 2, 3, \ldots$$

7.2.2 Nonstationary Linear Models

For the models considered previously in this section, it was assumed that the processes being modeled were stationary. This is equivalent to assuming that the distribution of observations is independent of the time of observation; i.e., auto-correlation functions are dependent only on the difference in time between ob-servations.

Stationarity can be interpreted as meaning that a process remains in equilibrium about a constant mean. But often empirical time series do not behave as if they had a constant mean. There are two types of deviations from equilibrium which we will consider: trend and seasonal. Trend effects refer to relatively smooth changes in the mean value of the observations. An example of this could be in the size of the population served by a store, which exhibits a fairly slow, smooth increase or decrease. Seasonal effects represent periodic changes in the mean value of the observations. For a retail operation, this could be variations in average number of customers each hour, which varies with a period of 1 day, or possibly with a period of 1 week.

The general model we have considered is

$$\Phi(B)z_t = \Theta(B)a_t \tag{17}$$

If all the roots of $\Phi(B)$ are greater than 1 in magnitude, this model represents a stationary process. If one or more of these roots has a magnitude less than 1, then the model represents an unstable process. That is, the autocorrelation function will contain exponential terms that increase without bounds. There are processes that contain unstable components, but for the type of time series data we are interested in fitting, the data will not exhibit unlimited growth in the region we are trying to represent. So, if we use this model for nonstationary processes, the only possibility is to let one or more roots have a magnitude equal to 1.

A model with d roots equal to 1 would have the form

$$\Phi(B)(1 - B)^d z_t = \Theta(B)a_t \tag{18}$$

or, equivalently,

$$\Phi(B)w_t = \Theta(B)a_t$$
$$w_t = \nabla^d z_t \tag{19}$$

where ∇ is called the *difference operator*. Note that in this case the time series z_t can be obtained by integrating the stationary series w_t, d times. So this model, (18), is called the autoregressive-integrated moving average (ARIMA) model. ARIMA models can be used to account for trend effects in time series data.

The method used to fit an ARIMA model is to difference the time series values z_t as many times as needed to produce the stationary process w_t. If the estimated autocorrelation function does not decrease rapidly for increasing lag K, this is considered evidence that the process is not stationary.

If a time series contains seasonal effects with some period s, then there are similarities between observations which are s intervals apart. For example, if the data values correspond to monthly measurements, and if the seasonal effects have a period of 1 yr, then the measurements for any particular month are related to the measurement for that month in the preceding year.

To introduce the method for including seasonal effects in time series models, we consider a specific example. Assume that the year-to-year effects between monthly data in a given time series with yearly seasonal effects can be represented by one difference operation and a first-order moving average model:

$$(1 - B^{12})z_t = \alpha_t - \theta_{1,s}\alpha_{t-12} = (1 - \theta_{1,s}B^{12})\,\alpha_t$$

The components α_t in this model are not assumed to be independent random values. In fact, it is likely that these components will contain correlation between successive monthly measurements. Now assume that the month-to-month relationship may be represented by the model:

$$\alpha_t = a_t - \theta_1 a_{t-1} = (1 - \theta_1 B)a_t$$

Then, the multiplicative model

$$(1 - B^{12})z_t = (1 - \theta_1 B)(1 - \theta_{1,s} B^{12})a_t$$

$$z_t - z_{t-12} = a_t - \theta_1 a_{t-1} - \theta_{1,s} a_{t-12} + \theta_1 \theta_{1,s} a_{t-13}$$

could be used as the model to represent this time series.

The general approach for developing models for time series which include seasonal effects is to use a model of the form

$$\Phi_s(B^s) \, (1 - B^s)^D z_t = \theta_s(B^s)\alpha_t \tag{20}$$

to represent the correlations due to seasonal effects of period s. Then a second general ARIMA model:

$$\Phi(B) \, (1 - B)^d \alpha_t = \theta(B)a_t \tag{21}$$

is used to represent the relationship between successive values of α_t. The product of these two models may then provide an adequate representation of the time series data.

In developing models with seasonal effects, the period s is determined from inspection of the general shape of the data, and the determination of the specific forms of the models given by (20) and (21) can be carried out independently.

7.2.3 Model Identification and Estimation

In order to specify a model for representing a particular set of time series data, it is necessary to identify the class of the model and to estimate the parameters of that model. The model class is determined by the order of the various functions included in the model. That is, the class is determined by,

1. The number p of autoregressive parameters $\phi_1, \phi_2, \cdots, \phi_p$
2. The number q of moving average parameters $\theta_1, \theta_2, \cdots, \theta_q$
3. The number d of difference operations

The basic information used for identification is the autocorrelation functions. We now consider how these functions are used in this process.

The first-order term to be identified is d, the number of difference operations. The basic idea used here is that if the autocorrelation function does not die out rapidly, a difference operation is needed. To illustrate, typical autocorrelation functions for stationary mixed autoregressive–moving average models are as shown in Fig. 7.3a. All these functions exhibit a dominantly exponential damping. A nonstationary process would have an autocorrelation function which does not exhibit this type of damping, as, for example, in Fig. 7.3b. If time series of this type are differenced, the tendency is for the autocorrelation function of the differenced data to have the exponentially damped shape. For models of this type, one

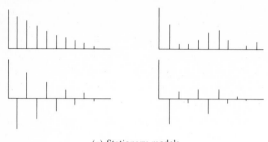

(a) Stationary models

(b) Nonstationary models

Figure 7.3 Typical autocorrelation functions.

or two differencing operations are usually sufficient and this corresponds to d equal to 1 or 2.

After the d value is determined, the resulting time series can be used to identify the order of p and q. This is accomplished by examining the general appearance of the autocorrelation function and a function of the auto-correlations.

To illustrate this latter function, consider a second-order autoregressive process:

$$z_t = \phi_1 z_{t-1} + \phi_2 z_{t-2} + a_t$$

The Yule-Walker Eqs. (13) show that the autocorrelations for this process are

$$r_1 = \phi_1 + r_1\phi_2$$
$$r_2 = r_1\phi_1 + \phi_2$$
$$r_3 = r_2\phi_1 + r_1\phi_2 \tag{22}$$
$$\vdots$$
$$r_j = r_{j-1}\phi_1 + r_{j-2}\phi_2$$

These autocorrelations may decrease rapidly, but there will be an infinite number of them. Now consider the situation where an alternate autoregressive model is used to represent this process, for example, a process of order k with $k > 2$:

$$z_t = \phi_{1k} z_{t-1} + \phi_{2k} z_{t-2} + \cdots + \phi_{kk} z_{t-k} + a_t$$

The ϕ_{ij} terms will satisfy the Yule-Walker equations also. For example, if $k = 3$, these equations will be

$$r_1 = \phi_{13} + r_1\phi_{23} + r_2\phi_{33}$$

$$r_2 = r_1\phi_{13} + \phi_{23} + r_1\phi_{33} \tag{23}$$

$$r_3 = r_2\phi_{13} + r_1\phi_{23} + \phi_{33}$$

$$\vdots$$

The first three of these equations can be solved for the parameters ϕ_{13}, ϕ_{23}, and ϕ_{33}. However, using the actual values of r_i given in (22) will result in the solutions:

$$\phi_{13} = \phi_1$$

$$\phi_{23} = \phi_2$$

$$\phi_{33} = 0$$

A similar result will hold any time an assumed model has larger order than the actual process. Thus, the ϕ_{ij} terms, called *partial autocorrelations*, will all be 0 for i and j greater than p.

This example illustrates that for an autoregressive process, the number of nonzero partial autocorrelation values is equal to the order of the process. Moreover, the partial autocorrelations are equal to the parameters of the process.

For a moving average process, we have seen that the autocorrelations are 0 beyond the qth value. Partial autocorrelations for these processes will trail off in the manner that autocorrelations trail off for autoregressive processes.

Thus, the procedure for identifying a process as being autoregressive of order p is to calculate the partial autocorrelations for a relatively large (10 to 20) value of k. The autocorrelation function should trail off exponentially, and the partial autocorrelation function should cut off sharply after p terms. Since estimates are used for the autocorrelations, the functions will not be precisely of this form but should have this general shape.

Similarly, a moving average process of order q should have an autocorrelation function which cuts off after q terms and a partial autocorrelation function which trails off exponentially.

If both the autocorrelation function and the partial autocorrelation functions trail off, this suggests that a mixed autoregressive–moving average model is needed.

Models of the type discussed in this section are primarily useful for representing low-order processes. Specifically, most experience with these models is limited to the case where p, q, and d are 0, 1, or 2. This means that the processes being represented exhibit very pronounced random behavior.

After the model class has been identified, the parameters are estimated. For autoregressive models, the estimated partial autocorrelations obtained from the Yule-Walker equations give a reasonable approximation for the model parameters. This is not true for the moving average models. Efficient maximum-likelihood estimates for all the model parameters are given in chapter 7 of the text by Bos and Jenkins [1].

7.3 A MODEL FOR THE WORKLOAD OF A REMOTE JOB INPUT STATION

This section presents an example which is used to illustrate the modeling approach discussed in the previous section. The physical system considered is that of a computer job input station. The specific case is a station where computer users submit jobs to a central computer through a card reader, receive output from a line printer and prepare jobs on a group of keypunch machines. The station is open from 8 A.M. until midnight.

Assume that we wish to have the number of jobs submitted at this station as one of the inputs to a simulation program used to study the central computer system. In particular, we wish to generate these job arrivals in a random manner but with statistical characteristics which reflect the real-life operation.

Table 7.2 gives the number of jobs submitted in each 1-h period during 3 weeks operation of a station of this type on a college campus. It is reasonable to assume that within any 1-h period, the job input interarrival times can be adequately represented as having an exponential distribution. However, it is obvious from the data of Table 7.2 that the average interarrival time varies from hour to hour and that there are periodic effects in the day-to-day sequence of these values. This type of relationship should be expected, as should weekly variations in average interarrival times. In the actual data, there are significant weekly variations, but by omitting data for Saturdays and Sundays, most of this variation is avoided.

The first 48 estimated autocorrelations, $\hat{r}_i$, of the time series given in Table 7.2 are shown in Fig. 7.4, which also shows the estimated partial autocorrelations,

Table 7.2 Number of jobs submitted each hour at an RJE station

HOUR OF DAY		8AM	9AM	10AM	11AM	12AM	1PM	2PM	3PM	4PM	5PM	6PM	7PM	8PM	9PM	10PM	11PM
WEEK	DAY																
1	MON	19	45	59	71	59	49	93	80	69	76	59	66	85	80	57	30
1	TUES	15	41	79	80	62	68	92	92	84	72	42	35	50	61	86	45
1	WED	9	33	54	71	54	54	61	51	69	56	45	48	55	55	74	29
1	THUR	15	38	60	80	46	76	81	66	70	50	26	48	55	60	73	41
1	FRI	21	52	55	66	92	60	72	85	81	52	38	41	36	55	39	32
2	MON	11	22	48	45	56	82	77	68	51	40	38	61	98	76	62	20
2	TUES	23	66	93	86	78	33	59	58	40	46	46	51	42	48	50	27
2	WED	8	28	44	50	79	47	55	65	71	55	24	62	77	49	40	24
2	THUR	0	49	87	69	61	67	51	55	83	44	45	69	67	57	50	33
2	FRI	4	72	97	74	62	50	70	73	37	71	24	26	26	48	51	46
3	MON	6	59	75	79	91	101	82	53	85	64	45	67	106	75	75	76
3	TUES	1	66	105	69	79	68	97	78	99	73	35	53	71	55	85	32
3	WED	3	32	52	83	72	55	64	86	77	77	38	63	67	61	71	29
3	THUR	18	66	55	91	83	30	102	92	107	23	33	84	54	52	60	26
3	FRI	6	50	75	73	83	74	76	64	55	58	36	49	39	44	52	31

$\hat{\phi}_{ii}$. The presence of the daily periodic variations are indicated by the auto-correlation values for lags of 16, 32, and 48. These values are large and do not appear to be decreasing as the lag value increases. This suggests that a difference operation is needed in the seasonal model. So a new series, $\{w_t\}$, is formed from the original series of Table 7.2, which will be denoted by $\{z_t\}$, using the operation

$$w_t = (1 - B^{16})z_t = z_t - z_{t-16} \qquad (1)$$

The series $\{w_t\}$ will consist of 16 less data points than does $\{z_t\}$.

Figure 7.5 gives the estimated correlation functions for the series $\{w_t\}$ using the same format as that of Fig. 7.4. As shown in Fig. 7.5, the difference operation has changed the autocorrelation value at lag 16 to a large negative value, but this type of value does not recur at lag values of 32 or 48. Thus, we may assume that one difference operation is adequate to produce a stationary series $\{w_t\}$. However, the data of Fig. 7.5 indicates that additional operations are needed to adequately model the relationships between day-to-day values.

The following values are from Fig. 7.5:

k	$\hat{r}_k$	$\hat{\phi}_{kk}$
16	$-.55$	$-.489$
32	$.09$	$-.338$
48	$.12$	$-.045$

This data suggests that for a lag period of 16, there is one nonzero auto-correlation term and the partial autocorrelations trail off exponentially. This corresponds to the behavior of a first-order moving average process (with period 16). Thus a model of the form

$$w_t = (1 - \theta_1 B^{16})\alpha_t$$

is considered. For this model, from Eq. (14) of Sec. 7.2, we have

$$r_1 = \frac{-\theta_1}{1 + \theta_1^2}$$

but if $\hat{r}_{16} = -.55$ is used to approximate r_1 in this equation, there is no solution for θ_1. However, values for θ_1 in the range from .5 to 1.0 give values for r_1 in a range from $-.4$ to $-.5$ which is reasonable close to the r_{16} value. By exploring results with various values of θ_1, the model

$$w_t = (1 - .75B^{16})\alpha_t \qquad (2)$$

was found to give the $\{\alpha_t\}$ sequence with estimated autocorrelations as shown in Fig. 7.6. This series does not appear to include any significant effects of period 16, so we conclude that (1) and (2) give a reasonable model for what we have referred to as seasonable effects.

AUTOCORRELATIONS

LAG	A_VAR	VALUE
0	456.30	1.00
1	210.31	0.42
2	23.27	0.05
3	-19.23	-0.04
4	-55.09	-0.11
5	22.51	0.05
6	34.51	0.07
7	-39.32	-0.08
8	-117.31	-0.24
9	-81.34	-0.16
10	5.04	0.01
11	-14.77	-0.03
12	-44.74	-0.09
13	-32.69	-0.07
14	-8.23	-0.02
15	149.33	0.30
16	242.75	0.49
17	118.30	0.24
18	-25.13	-0.05
19	-67.56	-0.14
20	-84.08	-0.17
21	-20.56	-0.04
22	-19.04	-0.04
23	-82.70	-0.17
24	-95.44	-0.19
25	-74.99	-0.15
26	15.10	0.03
27	-2.13	-0.00
28	-54.57	-0.11
29	-18.15	-0.04
30	0.29	0.00
31	161.65	0.33
32	250.77	0.51
33	104.88	0.21
34	-9.84	-0.02
35	-65.96	-0.13
36	-58.66	-0.12
37	6.38	0.01
38	21.13	0.04
39	-30.47	-0.06
40	-106.95	-0.22
41	-38.27	-0.08
42	21.75	0.04
43	-13.20	-0.03
44	-12.96	-0.03
45	-16.36	-0.03
46	-7.78	-0.02
47	133.17	0.27
48	228.14	0.46

Figure 7.4 Correlation functions for the original data series $\{z_t\}$.

The data of Fig. 7.6 shows that, except for $\hat{r}_1$ and $\hat{\phi}_{11}$, all autocorrelations and partial autocorrelations for $\{\alpha_t\}$ are less than .20 in magnitude. Since these values appear to vary in a somewhat random manner within this range of magnitude, we conclude that this reflects the level of irreducible random variation in the data.

The values for $\hat{r}_1$ and $\hat{\phi}_{11}$ of the $\{\alpha_t\}$ sequence can be readily reduced by assuming a first-order autoregressive model, or a first-order moving average model, for this data. Using the autoregressive model

$$(1 - .3B)\alpha_t = a_t \tag{3}$$

gives the sequence $\{a_t\}$ with properties as shown in Fig. 7.7. Very similar results would have been obtained using

$$\alpha_t = (1 + .3B)a_t$$

PARTIAL AUTOCORRELATIONS

```
PHI(  1,  1) =   0.425     -----------------------
PHI(  2,  2) =  -0.163       ----------
PHI(  3,  3) =   0.009          -
PHI(  4,  4) =  -0.110         -------
PHI(  5,  5) =   0.174          ---------
PHI(  6,  6) =  -0.048          ----
PHI(  7,  7) =  -0.121         --------
PHI(  8,  8) =  -0.200       ------------
PHI(  9,  9) =   0.066          ----
PHI(10,10) =   0.066          ----
PHI(11,11) =  -0.149        ---------
PHI(12,12) =  -0.097         ------
PHI(13,13) =   0.058          ---
PHI(14,14) =   0.072          ----
PHI(15,15) =   0.325          ------------------
PHI(16,16) =   0.220          -----------
PHI(17,17) =  -0.075         -----
PHI(18,18) =  -0.144        ---------
PHI(19,19) =  -0.009          --
PHI(20,20) =  -0.156        ---------
PHI(21,21) =  -0.020          --
PHI(22,22) =  -0.161        ----------
PHI(23,23) =  -0.029          ---
PHI(24,24) =   0.073          ----
PHI(25,25) =  -0.010          --
PHI(26,26) =   0.107          ------
PHI(27,27) =  -0.060         ----
PHI(28,28) =  -0.074         -----
PHI(29,29) =   0.075          ----
PHI(30,30) =  -0.063         -----
PHI(31,31) =   0.211          -----------
PHI(32,32) =   0.151          --------
PHI(33,33) =  -0.051         ----
PHI(34,34) =  -0.017          --
PHI(35,35) =   0.025          --
PHI(36,36) =  -0.034          ---
PHI(37,37) =   0.030          --
PHI(38,38) =   0.033          --
PHI(39,39) =   0.005          -
PHI(40,40) =  -0.080         -----
PHI(41,41) =   0.125          -------
PHI(42,42) =  -0.052         ----
PHI(43,43) =  -0.026          ---
PHI(44,44) =   0.019          -
PHI(45,45) =   0.004          -
PHI(46,46) =  -0.060         -----
PHI(47,47) =   0.080          ----
PHI(48,48) =   0.136          -------
```

Figure 7.4 (Continued)

The series $\{a_t\}$ appears to be reasonably close to a sequence of independent random events, so we may assume that the model given by Eqs. (1), (2), and (3) is a reasonable representation of the interdependence between the observations of the original sequence of data $\{z_t\}$. This result indicates that the number of jobs submitted per hour basically follows a daily pattern with some positive correlation between successive hours. This does seem to be an intuitively reasonable result.

The steps outlined above are an example of identifying a potential time series model. This procedure, as indicated in the example, is often somewhat arbitrary. After this identification stage, more precise estimates of the model parameters should be made. Also, an effort should be made to verify the model in some manner and, if indicated, revise the model class. We will not consider these parameter estimation techniques which are given by Box and Jenkins [1]. We will consider certain aspects of the verification of this model later, in Chap. 8.

AUTOCORRELATIONS

LAG	A_VAR	VALUE
0	486.79	1.00
1	141.17	0.29
2	80.46	0.17
3	67.46	0.14
4	25.77	0.05
5	91.60	0.19
6	97.90	0.20
7	95.60	0.18
8	-6.59	-0.01
9	-44.30	-0.09
10	-47.08	-0.10
11	-56.85	-0.12
12	9.97	0.02
13	-29.36	-0.06
14	-55.22	-0.11
15	-82.31	-0.17
16	-269.12	-0.55
17	-86.96	-0.18
18	-60.07	-0.12
19	-48.79	-0.10
20	-39.23	-0.08
21	-67.93	-0.14
22	-98.35	-0.20
23	-79.29	-0.16
24	25.11	0.05
25	-20.38	-0.04
26	3.80	0.01
27	18.94	0.04
28	-47.57	-0.10
29	17.54	0.04
30	40.24	0.08
31	52.48	0.11
32	43.54	0.09
33	22.11	0.05
34	29.25	0.06
35	17.59	0.04
36	35.34	0.07
37	56.29	0.12
38	80.83	0.17
39	89.10	0.18
40	2.86	0.01
41	87.08	0.18
42	67.11	0.14
43	18.85	0.04
44	98.42	0.20
45	19.33	0.04
46	0.53	0.00
47	6.21	0.01
48	60.39	0.12

Figure 7.5 Correlation functions for the series $\{w_t\}$.

Assuming that the model defined by Eqs. (1), (2), and (3) is adequate, we next consider the question of how to use it. This model may be written as

$$(1 - .3B)(1 - B^{16})z_t = (1 - .75B^{16})a_t$$

or

$$z_t = a_t - .75a_{t-16} + .3z_{t-1} + z_{t-16} - .3z_{t-17} \qquad (4)$$

Equation (4) is the most convenient form of model representation for forecasting future values for the data points z_t.

Using Eq. (4) to generate values for z_t requires that a number of starting values be available. In particular, it is necessary to store 17 sequential values of the number of jobs per hour. These values are used, together with random values for a_t which are normally distributed with a mean of 0 and a variance of 261.31, as indicated in Fig. 7.7. The value of a_{t-16} is assumed to be 0 for the first 16 iterations of Eq. (4). The starting values can be any sub-sequence of the original

PARTIAL AUTOCORRELATIONS

```
PHI(  1,  1) =   0.290      -----------------
PHI(  2,  2) =   0.089      -----
PHI(  3,  3) =   0.076      ----
PHI(  4,  4) =  -0.018      --
PHI(  5,  5) =   0.173      ---------
PHI(  6,  6) =   0.113      ------
PHI(  7,  7) =   0.075      ----
PHI(  8,  8) =  -0.152      ---------
PHI(  9,  9) =  -0.116      -------
PHI(10,10) =  -0.089      ------
PHI(11,11) =  -0.094      ------
PHI(12,12) =   0.049      ---
PHI(13,13) =  -0.067      -----
PHI(14,14) =  -0.046      ----
PHI(15,15) =  -0.072      -----
PHI(16,16) =  -0.489      ------------------------
PHI(17,17) =   0.119      ------
PHI(18,18) =  -0.006      --
PHI(19,19) =   0.028      --
PHI(20,20) =  -0.033      ---
PHI(21,21) =   0.068      ----
PHI(22,22) =  -0.056      ----
PHI(23,23) =   0.034      --
PHI(24,24) =   0.058      ---
PHI(25,25) =  -0.150      ---------
PHI(26,26) =   0.006      -
PHI(27,27) =  -0.016      -
PHI(28,28) =  -0.046      ----
PHI(29,29) =   0.063      ----
PHI(30,30) =   0.018      -
PHI(31,31) =   0.019      -
PHI(32,32) =  -0.338      ------------------
PHI(33,33) =   0.090      -----
PHI(34,34) =  -0.007      --
PHI(35,35) =   0.041      ---
PHI(36,36) =  -0.066      -----
PHI(37,37) =   0.137      --------
PHI(38,38) =   0.058      ---
PHI(39,39) =   0.149      --------
PHI(40,40) =  -0.004      --
PHI(41,41) =   0.115      ------
PHI(42,42) =   0.066      ----
PHI(43,43) =  -0.075      -----
PHI(44,44) =   0.087      -----
PHI(45,45) =  -0.021      ---
PHI(46,46) =   0.015      -
PHI(47,47) =   0.051      ---
PHI(48,48) =  -0.045      ----
```

Figure 7.5 (Continued)

values. These values are, of course, related to specific hours of the day.

Generating the autocorrelated sequence $\{z_t\}$ by this method will occasionally result in negative values and very large values. Since negative values are not possible, and the original data points had a maximum value of 107, any result from Eq. (4) that has a value less than 0 or greater than 107 should be rejected and another value (using another random a_t value) obtained.

The results of using this technique with the first 17 values of the original data are shown in Table 7.3. These values do exhibit daily variations somewhat similar to those of the original data, and they have the same primary autocorrelation effects. This similarity decreases as the distance from the initial values increases. Also, the most obvious differences are in the predicted values for the first hour of each day. This suggests the following procedure if a large number of values are needed as input data for simulations. The starting values should consist of the 16 data points of one day from the original data plus the first hour of the following day. The model represented by Eq. (4) is then used to generate data for the remaining 15 hours of a simulated day.

```
AUTOCORRELATIONS

LAG     A_VAR    VALUE
 0     288.18    1.00     ----------------------------------------------------
 1      89.87    0.31     -------------------
 2      45.48    0.16     --------
 3      50.83    0.18     ---------
 4      13.31    0.05     ---
 5      45.04    0.16     --------
 6      54.58    0.19     ----------
 7      44.31    0.15     --------
 8      -0.04   -0.00     --
 9     -12.77   -0.04     ----
10       0.57    0.00     -
11     -15.68   -0.05     ----
12       8.96    0.03     --
13      21.37    0.07     ----
14      -3.13   -0.01     --
15       7.64    0.03     --
16     -27.96   -0.10     ------
17     -11.64   -0.04     ----
18     -11.09   -0.04     ---
19      -6.19   -0.02     ---
20     -17.32   -0.06     -----
21     -14.02   -0.05     ----
22     -18.20   -0.06     -----
23     -10.78   -0.04     ---
24       9.55    0.03     --
25     -11.17   -0.04     ---
26       9.55    0.03     --
27       3.10    0.01     -
28      -7.19   -0.02     ---
29      35.79    0.12     -------
30      21.58    0.07     ----
31      33.68    0.12     ------
32      26.12    0.09     -----
33       5.96    0.02     --
34      16.30    0.06     ---
35       3.82    0.01     -
36       6.55    0.02     --
37      20.93    0.07     ----
38      41.37    0.14     --------
39      45.39    0.16     --------
40      -9.90   -0.03     ---
41      17.69    0.06     ----
42      17.92    0.06     ----
43      -3.85   -0.01     --
44      43.25    0.15     --------
45      30.93    0.10     ------
46      -0.59   -0.00     --
47       3.11    0.01     -
48      21.12    0.07     ----
```

Figure 7.6 Correlation functions for the series $\{\alpha_t\}$.

By using all the different days of the original data and various sequences of random numbers, an unlimited amount of test data may be generated. This test data should provide a close approximation to the type of daily workload which may be expected at the remote job entry station. It should be intuitively obvious that the test data generated by this method gives a better approximation to the expected daily behavior than could be obtained using independent samples from any single distribution.

7.4 ESTIMATING THE ORDER OF AUTOREGRESSIVE MODELS

Our previous example shows that for real data the order and form of an appropriate time series model is not necessarily obvious. Specifically, Fig. 7.6 indicates that the autocorrelations for the data series $\{z_t\}$ do not converge to 0 as the lag

PARTIAL AUTOCORRELATIONS

```
PHI(  1,  1) =   0.312      ------------------
PHI(  2,  2) =   0.067      ----
PHI(  3,  3) =   0.122      -------
PHI(  4,  4) =  -0.053      ----
PHI(  5,  5) =   0.149      --------
PHI(  6,  6) =   0.102      ------
PHI(  7,  7) =   0.068      ----
PHI(  8,  8) =  -0.135      --------
PHI(  9,  9) =  -0.062      -----
PHI(10,10) =   0.009        -
PHI(11,11) =  -0.062        ------
PHI(12,12) =   0.034        --
PHI(13,13) =   0.054        ---
PHI(14,14) =  -0.011        --
PHI(15,15) =   0.050        ---
PHI(16,16) =  -0.126        --------
PHI(17,17) =   0.028        --
PHI(18,18) =  -0.054        ----
PHI(19,19) =   0.013        -
PHI(20,20) =  -0.103        -------
PHI(21,21) =   0.041        ---
PHI(22,22) =  -0.038        ---
PHI(23,23) =   0.063        ----
PHI(24,24) =   0.050        ---
PHI(25,25) =  -0.057        ----
PHI(26,26) =   0.082        -----
PHI(27,27) =  -0.024        ---
PHI(28,28) =  -0.017        --
PHI(29,29) =   0.141        ---------
PHI(30,30) =  -0.010        --
PHI(31,31) =   0.109        ------
PHI(32,32) =  -0.028        ---
PHI(33,33) =   0.000        -
PHI(34,34) =  -0.009        --
PHI(35,35) =  -0.008        --
PHI(36,36) =  -0.084        ------
PHI(37,37) =   0.073        ----
PHI(38,38) =   0.133        --------
PHI(39,39) =   0.088        -----
PHI(40,40) =  -0.116        -------
PHI(41,41) =   0.066        ----
PHI(42,42) =   0.012        -
PHI(43,43) =  -0.046        ----
PHI(44,44) =   0.038        --
PHI(45,45) =   0.046        ---
PHI(46,46) =  -0.041        ----
PHI(47,47) =   0.044        ---
PHI(48,48) =   0.075        ----
```

Figure 7.6 (Continued)

value increases. This effect may be due to the fact that the process which produced the series cannot be accurately represented by an autoregressive model, or it may be due to the particular values which appear in the given limited range of the sequence. In either case, the time series can be approximated by an autoregressive model of some order. In this section, we consider a statistical test which may be used to specify the order for an approximate autoregressive model.

The primary reason for considering only the autoregressive model is that this form can be estimated with a considerably less complicated procedure than that required by the more general time series models. And too, the autoregressive model provides a convenient method for generating autocorrelated random variables and for estimating the variance of a time series. These are probably the most useful results of time series analysis for simulation studies.

Section 7.2.3 indicates that for an autoregressive model of order p, the partial autocorrelations, determined by the solutions of the Yule-Walker equations, are equal to the parameters of the autoregressive model. If the assumed order of the

AUTOCORRELATIONS

LAG	A_VAR	VALUE
0	261.31	1.00
1	-2.17	-0.01
2	7.72	0.13
3	38.01	0.15
4	-14.21	-0.05
5	29.16	0.11
6	32.75	0.13
7	32.21	0.12
8	-9.28	-0.04
9	-14.23	-0.05
10	9.01	0.03
11	-20.40	-0.08
12	7.72	0.03
13	21.56	0.08
14	-11.73	-0.04
15	17.83	0.07
16	-29.59	-0.11
17	-1.04	-0.00
18	-6.84	-0.03
19	1.81	0.01
20	-12.84	-0.05
21	-4.73	-0.02
22	-12.91	-0.05
23	-9.29	-0.04
24	17.00	0.07
25	-18.15	-0.07
26	12.73	0.05
27	2.54	0.01
28	-19.86	-0.08
29	34.57	0.13
30	3.01	0.01
31	22.35	0.09
32	16.60	0.06
33	-6.24	-0.02
34	14.37	0.06
35	-2.61	-0.01
36	-0.47	-0.00
37	8.80	0.03
38	25.19	0.10
39	40.05	0.15
40	-29.82	-0.11
41	16.60	0.06
42	15.21	0.06
43	-22.58	-0.09
44	39.30	0.15
45	19.86	0.08
46	-10.41	-0.04
47	-2.60	-0.01
48	23.08	0.09

Figure 7.7 Correlation functions for the series $\{a_t\}$.

autoregressive model is greater than the true value p, only the first p values of the corresponding partial autocorrelations will be nonzero. Thus, by fitting successively autoregressive models of orders 1, 2, 3, ... and calculating the partial autocorrelations, the order of the appropriate autoregressive model can be determined. Of course, the estimated values of the partial autocorrelations will not exactly equal 0, but by means of statistical tests the appropriate order can be estimated. Such a procedure is presented in this section.

The Yule-Walker equations are a system of linear equations and may require lengthy computational sequences if large values of the autoregressive order p are considered. The partial autocorrelations can be estimated more conveniently by using the following recursive technique. For a given sequence of time series data $\{x_t\}$, the mean, autocovariances, and autocorrelations are estimated by

$$\bar{x} = \frac{1}{n} \sum_{t=1}^{n} x_t \tag{1}$$

PARTIAL AUTOCORRELATIONS

```
PHI(  1,  1) = -0.008        --
PHI(  2,  2) =  0.029        --
PHI(  3,  3) =  0.146        --------
PHI(  4,  4) = -0.053        ----
PHI(  5,  5) =  0.105        ------
PHI(  6,  6) =  0.112        ------
PHI(  7,  7) =  0.141        --------
PHI(  8,  8) = -0.074        -----
PHI(  9,  9) = -0.088        ------
PHI(10,10) =  0.000          -
PHI(11,11) = -0.074          -----
PHI(12,12) = -0.035          --
PHI(13,13) =  0.057          ---
PHI(14,14) = -0.007          --
PHI(15,15) =  0.086          -----
PHI(16,16) = -0.109          -------
PHI(17,17) =  0.011          -
PHI(18,18) = -0.054          ----
PHI(19,19) =  0.028          --
PHI(20,20) = -0.108          -------
PHI(21,21) =  0.018          -
PHI(22,22) = -0.052          ----
PHI(23,23) =  0.033          --
PHI(24,24) =  0.078          ----
PHI(25,25) = -0.058          ----
PHI(26,26) =  0.071          ----
PHI(27,27) =  0.002          -
PHI(28,28) = -0.059          ----
PHI(29,29) =  0.126          -------
PHI(30,30) = -0.002          --
PHI(31,31) =  0.115          ------
PHI(32,32) =  0.007          -
PHI(33,33) =  0.004          -
PHI(34,34) = -0.005          --
PHI(35,35) =  0.017          -
PHI(36,36) = -0.102          -------
PHI(37,37) =  0.004          -
PHI(38,38) =  0.107          ------
PHI(39,39) =  0.154          --------
PHI(40,40) = -0.090          ------
PHI(41,41) =  0.035          --
PHI(42,42) =  0.036          --
PHI(43,43) = -0.047          ----
PHI(44,44) =  0.009          -
PHI(45,45) =  0.060          ---
PHI(46,46) = -0.034          ---
PHI(47,47) =  0.011          -
PHI(48,48) =  0.088          -----
```

Figure 7.7 (Continued)

$$\hat{R}_k = \frac{1}{n} \sum_{t=1}^{n-k} (x_t - \bar{x})(x_{t+k} - \bar{x}) \qquad k = 0, 1, 2, \ldots \tag{2}$$

$$\hat{r}_k = \frac{\hat{R}_k}{\hat{R}_0} \tag{3}$$

Then the partial autocorrelations may be estimated recursively using the equations:

$$\hat{\phi}_{11} = \hat{r}_1 \tag{4}$$

$$\hat{\phi}_{ll} = \frac{\hat{r}_l - \sum_{j=1}^{l-1} \hat{\phi}_{l-1,j}\hat{r}_{l-j}}{1 - \sum_{j=1}^{l-1} \hat{\phi}_{l-1,j}\hat{r}_j} \qquad l = 2, 3, \ldots \tag{5}$$

$$\hat{\phi}_{lj} = \hat{\phi}_{l-1,j} - \hat{\phi}_{ll}\hat{\phi}_{l-1,l-j} \qquad j = 1, 2, \ldots, l-1 \tag{6}$$

Table 7.3 Values forecasted by the model, Eq. (4)

HOUR OF DAY		8AM	9AM	10AM	11AM	12AM	1PM	2PM	3PM	4PM	5PM	6PM	7PM	8PM	9PM	10PM	11PM
WEEK	DAY																
1	MON	19	45	59	71	59	49	93	80	69	76	59	66	85	80	57	30
1	TUES	15	33	54	81	93	58	102	59	64	84	67	77	106	63	70	50
1	WED	24	22	36	69	89	50	84	24	36	74	75	102	98	30	85	45
1	THUR	32	41	33	97	102	12	78	32	59	55	66	100	96	49	101	75
1	FRI	52	22	9	94	98	29	65	17	70	65	93	101	96	45	97	46
2	MON	45	29	39	95	94	26	34	12	73	68	66	81	72	28	100	60
2	TUES	40	26	61	103	70	18	1	21	74	91	82	78	94	14	75	34
2	WED	13	23	73	101	85	33	16	64	94	107	89	100	96	45	95	22
2	THUR	28	33	91	105	80	36	21	77	64	59	30	54	85	37	78	25
2	FRI	6	22	58	73	46	18	41	86	78	60	41	63	104	44	59	34
3	MON	14	9	55	87	40	23	51	77	87	54	45	81	97	34	52	43
3	TUES	14	19	81	83	48	7	23	39	32	40	8	102	81	27	83	46
3	WED	46	51	93	100	78	7	18	47	86	50	8	102	51	7	80	28
3	THUR	33	66	75	82	42	6	34	25	103	80	18	81	45	37	72	35
3	FRI	32	81	56	79	14	20	11	23	98	93	17	63	31	10	56	30

Equation (5) is first used to calculate $\hat{\phi}_{22}$; then Eq. (6) is used to find $\hat{\phi}_{21}$. Next, $\hat{\phi}_{33}$ is found using (5); then $\hat{\phi}_{31}$ and $\hat{\phi}_{32}$ are calculated using (6). In a similar manner, the partial autocorrelations are found for successively larger values of l.

For each successive value of l, the following approximate autoregressive model is assumed:

$$x_t = \hat{\phi}_{11}x_{t-1} + \hat{\phi}_{21}x_{t-2} + \cdots + \hat{\phi}_{ll}x_{t-l} + a_t \tag{7}$$

For this model, the residual variance can be estimated by

$$\hat{\sigma}_l^2 = \hat{R}_0\left(1 - \sum_{i=1}^{l} \hat{\phi}_{il}\hat{r}_i\right) \tag{8}$$

In order to test the hypothesis that the order of the sequence $\{x_t\}$ is equal to some value l, we use the fact that the distribution of the statistic

$$F_{nql} = \left(\frac{\hat{\sigma}_l^2}{\hat{\sigma}_q^2} - 1\right)\left(\frac{n-q}{q-l}\right) \tag{9}$$

for q greater than the true order has been shown [4] to converge to that of the F distribution with $(n - q)$ and $(q - l)$ degrees of freedom as n increases. This means that if n and q are sufficiently large and l is, in fact, the true autoregressive order, then

$$\text{Prob}\ [F_{nql} < F_{1-a,\,n-q,\,q-l}] \sim 1 - \alpha \tag{10}$$

where $F_{1-\alpha,\,n-q,\,q-l}$ is the $(1 - \alpha)$ fractile point of the cumulative F distribution for $(n - q)$ degrees of freedom in the numerator and $(q - l)$ degrees of freedom in the denominator.

By choosing a relatively large value of q; that is, $q > l$, the statistic from (9) may be calculated for various values of l and compared with the appropriate values from the F distribution. If the inequality of expression (10) holds, we may accept the hypothesis that l is the true value of the autoregressive order, at the specified significance level.

To illustrate this procedure, we will consider the final step in the model-fitting procedure used in the previous section. In that example, after selecting the seasonal model, the sequence $\{\alpha_t\}$ was produced, which had correlations as shown in Fig. 7.6. From observation of Fig. 7.6, it was concluded that a first-order autoregressive model appeared to be appropriate to represent this series. This conclusion may be examined by applying the test presented in this section.

Table 7.4 shows the values calculated for the series $\{\alpha_t\}$. For this case, the value of n was 224 and the value selected for q was 48. The residual variances were calculated using Eq. (8) and the test statistic was calculated by Eq. (9). The values from the F distribution were calculated using the MDFI subroutine of the IMSL library [6]. These results show that we may reject the hypothesis that the sequence is of autoregressive order 0 if we are willing to accept a 5 percent chance of error. However, we cannot reject this hypothesis with a 99 percent confidence level. Rejecting the hypothesis that the autoregressive order is 1 would require accepting a relatively large chance of error. Thus, we conclude that the sequence $\{\alpha_t\}$ can probably be represented by an autoregressive model of order 1.

As a further illustration of this estimation method, Table 7.5 gives some of the test values for the sequence $\{w_t\}$ from the example of Sec. 7.3. In this case, the method indicates that the proper autoregressive model is probably of order 32.

An autoregressive model for a sequence of values may also be used to provide an estimate for the variance of the mean value of the variable. The relationship used for this purpose is

$$n \text{ var } (\bar{x}) \approx \frac{\hat{\sigma}_l^2}{(1 - \sum_{i=1}^{l} \hat{\phi}_{il})^2} \tag{11}$$

where l is the autoregressive order determined by the test presented above. Equation (11) provides an estimate for n times the variance of the mean value of x taken over n observations. If n is sufficiently large, then the quantity $n \text{ var } (\bar{x})$

Table 7.4 Values for testing the autoregressive order of $\{\alpha_t\}$

Autoregressive order l	Residual variance	Test statistic	Values for F_α, $n - q$, $q - l$		
			$\alpha = .90$	$\alpha = .95$	$\alpha = .99$
0	288.18	1.538	1.371	1.501	1.786
1	260.15	1.054	1.375	1.507	1.796
2	258.98	1.055	1.380	1.513	1.807
3	255.13	1.004	1.384	1.519	1.818
4	254.42	1.013	1.394	1.526	1.830
5	248.74	0.922	1.399	1.533	1.842

Table 7.5 Values for testing the autoregressive order of $\{w_t\}$

Autoregressive order	Residual variance	Test statistic	Values for $F_\alpha, n - q, q - l$		
			$\alpha = .90$	$\alpha = .95$	$\alpha = .99$
0	486.79	4.236	1.371	1.501	1.786
1	445.85	3.648	1.375	1.507	1.796
2	442.35	3.668	1.380	1.513	1.807
⋮	⋮	⋮	⋮	⋮	⋮
14	393.09	3.833	1.450	1.614	1.986
15	391.08	3.902	1.459	1.625	2.007
16	297.40	1.742	1.467	1.638	2.029
17	293.21	1.693	1.476	1.651	2.053
18	293.20	1.749	1.486	1.665	2.078
⋮	⋮	⋮	⋮	⋮	⋮
30	280.67	2.373	1.681	1.952	2.631
31	280.56	2.508	1.709	1.995	2.716
32	248.42	1.099	1.741	2.043	2.816
33	246.41	1.068	1.777	2.099	2.931

should approximate a value for the variance of x which may be used in statistical tests that assume that the observed values of x are independent.

Thus, given a correlated time series $\{x_i\}$, an approximate autoregressive model may be constructed and, using (11), the value of n var $(\bar{x})$ estimated. Then, for example, a confidence interval for the mean value $\bar{x}$ may be computed using

$$\text{Prob}\left[\bar{x} - (t_{1-\alpha/2, v})\left(\frac{n \text{ var }(\bar{x})}{n}\right)^{1/2} < \mu < \bar{x} + (t_{1-\alpha/2, v})\left(\frac{n \text{ var }(\bar{x})}{n}\right)^{1/2}\right] = 1 - \alpha$$

In this equation, the value of n is the number of observations in the series $\{x_i\}$ less the autoregressive model order l. The degrees of freedom, v, will be less than $n - l - 1$, but for large values of n, the student's t distribution approaches a normal distribution, so this is not usually a critical point.

Similarly, this approach may be used in other analysis procedures, such as the stopping rule of Sec. 6.5, which require estimates for this type of variance. It should be noted that this method provides only an approximation to the desired variance and should be used conservatively.

7.5 BACKGROUND AND REFERENCES

Statistical tests for distributional assumptions for independent random samples are discussed in references [3] and [7]. Many tests of this type have been developed and evaluated. The most widely applicable of these tests are available in many of the statistical programs libraries, as in, for example, the IMSL described in [6].

The time series modeling approach presented in this chapter is a brief introduction to the methods developed by Box and Jenkins [1]. In that reference, the methods are carefully developed in detail and are extended to, among other things, transfer function models. Transfer function models may be used to represent the relationship between two random sequences where one sequence is assumed to generate the second. Thus these methods are potentially of great use in developing and simplifying system models in simulations as well as in developing models for exogenous input-variable representations.

The IMSL library [6] contains computer programs for carrying out model development using the Box and Jenkins approach. While this technique requires a certain amount of judgment in its use, programs of this type reduce the effort required to investigate the various possibilities.

The technique of Sec. 7.4 for estimating autoregressive model order and the use of sample autoregressive parameters in estimation are derived and illustrated in the text by Fishman [2]. This reference also includes a computer program listing for a routine to carry out the required computations.

REFERENCES

1. Box, G. E. P., and G. M. Jenkins: "Time Series Analysis: Forecasting and Control," rev. ed., Holden-Day, Inc., Publisher, San Francisco, 1976.
2. Fishman, G. S.: "Concepts and Methods in Discrete Event Digital Simulation," Wiley, New York, 1973.
3. Ghedenko, B. V.: "The Theory of Probability," Chelsea Publishing Company, New York, 1962.
4. Hannan, E.: "Multiple Time Series," Wiley, New York, 1970.
5. Hogg, R. V., and E. A. Tanis: "Probability and Statistical Inference," Macmillan, New York, 1977.
6. International Mathematical and Statistical Libraries, Inc.: "Reference manual," IMSL LIB2-0006, Houston, Tex., 1977.
7. Kendall, M. G., and A. Stuart: "The Advanced Theory of Statistics," vol. 2, Hafner, New York, 1963.

EXERCISES

7.1 Generate 100 random numbers x_i using the subroutine RNNORM with a mean of 10 and a standard deviation of 5. Generate 100 random numbers y_i using the subroutine RNEXP with a mean of 10. Use the chi-squared test to evaluate the hypothesis that

    (a) The x_i came from a normal distribution with $\mu = 10$, $\sigma = 5$
    (b) The y_i came from a normal distribution with $\mu = 10$, $\sigma = 5$
    (c) The x_i came from an exponential distribution with $\mu = 10$
    (d) The y_i came from an exponential distribution with $\mu = 10$

7.2 Repeat Exercise 7.1 using 25 samples each of x_i and y_i.

7.3 Repeat the hypothesis tests of Exercise 7.1 but use the Kolmogorov-Smirnov test. Use sample sizes of 25, as in Exercise 7.2.

7.4 Assume that a process can be represented by the autoregressive model

$$z_t = .75z_{t-1} - .5z_{t-2} + a_t$$

where a_t is a normally distributed random variable with a mean of 0 and standard deviation of 1. What is the autocorrelation function for this model?

7.5 Repeat Exercise 7.4 for the moving average model

$$z_t = a_t - .6a_{t-1} - .3a_{t-2}$$

7.6 Repeat Exercise 7.4 for the mixed model

$$z_t = .7z_{t-1} + a_t - .4a_{t-1} - .1a_{t-2}$$

7.7 Model (3) of Fig. 3.14 may be represented, neglecting the average value of 100, by a fifth-order autoregressive model

$$z_t = a_t + \phi_1 z_{t-1} + \phi_2 z_{t-2} + \phi_3 z_{t-3} + \phi_4 z_{t-4} + \phi_5 z_{t-5}$$

What are the appropriate values for the parameters $\phi_1, \ldots, \phi_5$?

7.8 Determine an appropriate second-order autoregressive model for the time series having the following values for the first and second autocorrelations:

(a) $r_1 = +.5$ $r_2 = +.3$
(b) $r_1 = +.5$ $r_2 = -.3$
(c) $r_1 = -.5$ $r_2 = +.3$
(d) $r_1 = -.5$ $r_2 = -.3$

7.9 Determine an appropriate second-order moving average model for the time series of Exercise 7.8a and c.

7.10 For a second-order moving average model, it is necessary that the roots of the characteristic equation:

$$1 - \theta_1 S - \theta_2 S^2 = 0$$

be such that

$$|S| < 1$$

Verify that this condition is met if

$$\theta_2 + \theta_1 < 1$$

$$\theta_2 - \theta_1 < 1$$

$$-1 < \theta_2 < 1$$

7.11 Consider a single-server queuing system with exponentially distributed service times with a mean of 20 s. Assume that the interarrival times may be represented by the model

$$x_i = 30 + .75x_{i-1} - .50x_{i-2} + a_i$$

where i corresponds to the ith customer to arrive and a_i are normally distributed random values with 0 mean and a standard deviation of 3 s. Simulate this system and compare the results with that of Exercise 4.4.

CHAPTER
EIGHT

VERIFICATION AND VALIDATION PROCEDURES

The previous chapters of this book have emphasized techniques for the programming and analysis of simulation experiments. This chapter is concerned with the stage of a simulation study which would logically occur between the programming stage and the experiment stage. The objective of the validation stage is to ensure that the simulation program is a proper representation of the system being studied, so that the results to be obtained from the experiments will be the results which would be obtained from the real system. This is a very important part of simulation studies and should be a major part of this type of project. However, it must be recognized that this objective of proving the simulation correct can only be approached, not achieved.

The primary limitation in validating a simulation is the problem of relating the model to the real system. The model is never a complete representation of the real system, and the real system is never completely known. Because of this, there are difficult questions even as to what is meant by the validation of a model. In simulation the goal is to have a model which represents the real system adequately for the purposes of the study for which it is used. This leads to the viewpoint that a model is valid if the results obtained from its simulation are valid. This, then, implies that the proper validation procedure is to compare results obtained from a simulation study with the real system. While this is a reasonable attitude to hold in evaluating the final results of a study, it tends to overlook the fact that validation procedures should be a part of the development process for a simulation. In any simulation, there are many opportunities for making errors, and efforts should certainly be made to find possible errors before trying to apply the final results.

Validation procedures depend very heavily upon the conditions under which the study is performed and upon the knowledge, experience, and judgment of those conducting the study. The criterion for accepting or rejecting a model is a function primarily of how the model is to be used, and it also depends upon the available alternatives. In this chapter, some techniques which may be useful for validation are presented. The examples illustrate the purposes of this process.

The first section of this chapter discusses certain concepts related to developing models. These topics are primarily related to evaluating models, not to the more general question of building models. Some aspects of building models are discussed later, in Chap. 10.

The second section presents techniques which are useful in checking the simulation program. These checks are intended to verify that the algorithms of the program reproduce the logical structure of the model as intended.

Sections 8.3 and 8.4 cover two approaches for evaluating the effectiveness of the model. Their aim is to provide a means of testing the agreement between the behavior of the model and that of the real system. Even though these procedures cannot provide the final validation of the model, they can either increase confidence in the model or indicate the need for changes in the model.

8.1 THE MEANING OF MODEL VALIDITY

The model is intended to produce behavior which is similar to that of the real system. It is based on the modeler's knowledge and understanding of the real system. There are no precise rules for specifying the entities, attributes, and activities that should be included in the model. But the more that is known about the system, in terms of appropriate theory, data, and experience, the more exact the model can be. However, a primary goal of modeling is to achieve a simplified model which does not include all the details known about the real system and yet has sufficiently similar behavior. This simplification is often critical in achieving a successful simulation study.

The need for model simplification has been illustrated [1, 6] by the curves shown in Fig. 8.1. The curve labeled "cost of model" is intended to indicate that in order for the model to match the behavior of the real system, its cost increases and approaches infinity as some measure of validity approaches 1. This cost would include, for example, the effort to develop the model, expenses of gathering data on the system, and execution time for the simulation runs. The curve labeled "value of the model" indicates that there is a limit to the usefulness of a model regardless of how accurate it may be. This curve is based on an assumption that the model has less value as its accuracy decreases but does not lose all its value until it loses all its validity. The third curve is the ratio of the "value of model" curve and the "cost of model" curve, and thus, it indicates the benefits to be gained from the model per unit cost.

Figure 8.1 is a conceptual representation only. There is no significance in the fact that the benefit/cost curve peaks near the point where validity = .5. Nor is there any meaning in the measure validity = .5. What is illustrated is the idea

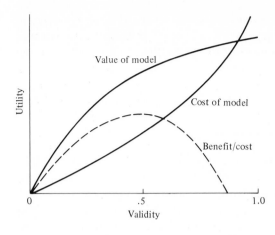

Figure 8.1 Conceptual value of model accuracy.

that increasing the accuracy of the model beyond some point is not practical in terms of benefits to be gained. The validity of this idea rests upon the assumption that the usefulness of the model decreases only slightly with slightly increased inaccuracies. This is not true beyond some limited range, since for any model, as it becomes less representative of the true system, there is a point at which it becomes useless. Nevertheless, the concept illustrated by Fig. 8.1 is usually appropriate for simulation studies.

The value of a model can only be established in relation to its use. This may be illustrated in a simplified manner by considering the inventory problem introduced in Sec. 4.2. For that example, the ultimate use of the model was to determine the values of stock control level and inventory period which would result in the largest expected average weekly profit. In this case, the potential benefits from an improved choice of these control values can be estimated in dollars. This figure could serve to establish guidelines as to how much money should be spent in studying the problem.

For the inventory system example, a reduction of accuracy in the model does not necessarily eliminate all its value. The model is used to choose between alternate values for the control parameters, and as long as it is sufficiently accurate to correctly indicate which of two possible control values is more likely to produce greater profits, it is adequate.

As we have noted previously, a simulation involving random variables cannot yield definite answers; it is only possible to establish statistical confidence in the answers. In any simulation, possible errors in the model should be considered in evaluating the confidence level of any particular result. As an illustration, consider using the inventory example simulation program to compare the results of using stock control levels of 30 and 40. In this problem, the most critical model parameter is the average demand rate for the product. The uncertainty in this value will contribute to the uncertainty in the choice between the two stock control values and should be included in the simulations used to make this choice.

The case of comparing different stock control levels in an inventory system is one where much greater effort in establishing an accurate model and conducting the experiments is required as the separation between the two levels is decreased. Also, the benefits to be gained, as measured by expected profits, from obtaining accurate results decrease. This is an example where the concept illustrated by Fig. 8.1 is appropriate.

8.2 VERIFYING THE PROGRAM

The purpose of verifying the program is to determine whether or not the model is properly programmed; that is, does the program behave as the model is intended to behave? Thus verification of a simulation program is simply part of what is commonly known as the program-debugging process. There are aspects of simulations which afford somewhat different techniques for this purpose than those available for general computer software. Although here we consider only special methods for simulation programs, any program verification procedure may be helpful.

The presence of randomness in a stochastic model presents difficulties in detecting errors in a simulation program. The inexactness of statistical testing can mask errors in program logic. The most direct and effective technique for overcoming this problem is to simply remove the random variations during a part of the program verification procedure.

When separate procedures are used to generate random variables in a program, to remove the random effects it is only necessary to temporarily replace these procedures with routines which always return some constant value or some specified sequence of values. For example, in the program of Sec. 4.3, all random values were obtained by calls to the procedures RND and RNEXP. For purposes of testing the program, these procedures could be replaced by alternate versions which upon execution would always result in

$$RND(I) = .5$$

$$RNEXP(I, X) = X$$

With the random component removed from the program, it is possible to determine precisely what the model behavior should be. To illustrate this, we consider the effect of using the above constant values in the time-sharing computer system simulation program of Sec. 4.3. For this example, the calls to RND and RNEXP all occur in the REPLY procedure shown in Fig. 4.23. From this procedure, we see that with the RND and RNEXP procedures modified as above, all requests to the computer from the terminals will occur 5 time units after a reply is received by that terminal. Moreover, for each request the input command message length will be 42, the output message length will be 30, and the execution time required will be .09.

Since the system is initialized (see Fig. 4.29) by scheduling a polling event at TIME = 0 and placing input commands at each terminal, we can determine what the simulation should do by following the logic of the specified model. The model gives priority to the computer operation of polling the terminals and reading input commands. Thus, for this nonstochastic version, each terminal will require

$$\text{Polling time} + \text{message input time} = .01 + \frac{42}{300} = .15$$

seconds for service. Thus, the first 1.8 s of the simulation should be devoted entirely to the reading in of the 12 input commands. After that period, the program for each message will be executed in order, using time slices of .01 s, which will require a total of 1.08 s. Since an additional polling operation of .12-s duration will be required during the third second of the simulation, the first reply message for a terminal should be available at TIME = 3. Each output message will require

$$.01 + 30/300 = .11$$

seconds. Therefore, during the fourth second of the simulation, the computer should have time to poll all terminals and send out eight reply messages. The first reply should be completed at

$$\text{TIME} = 3 + .12 + .11 = 3.23$$

so the next input message should be scheduled to arrive at TIME = 8.23. The other terminal reply messages should be sent out during the fifth second of the simulation, and after that, the computer should remain idle, except for polling, until TIME = 9.

The events just described are what should happen if the program behaves as does the logical description of the model. By checking the events that do occur in the program and comparing these with the events that should occur in the model, a check on program accuracy is provided. This procedure does not check for all possible errors in programming the model, but it is a very effective technique for detecting discrepancies between the model and the program.

In order to observe the action and effect of simulation events, it is necessary to add output statements at the proper points in the simulation program. There are many ways in which this can be done, and one approach is illustrated in Fig. 8.2. This listing shows a CONTROL procedure for the timesharing system simulation example, which includes some basic features which are useful in tracing the effects of event execution. This version of the CONTROL procedure includes two new parameters: TRACEON, which is used to activate and deactivate the trace feature, and TRACEI, which is used to select options within the trace feature. Two special event types have been added for use in specifying the periods of simulation time during which the trace output is to be printed. By scheduling an event with TYPE = 98 at some desired time, the trace output will be initiated at that point in the simulation. Similarly, a TYPE = 99 event can be used to end a period during which this output is generated.

In general, a trace routine should print out all state variables that may be changed by an event routine each time that event routine is executed. But often, all this data is not needed or desired. In the example-trace feature, shown in Fig.

```
                    CONTROL: PROCEDURE; /*TIMING ROUTINE*/


STMT LEVEL NEST
  1                         CONTROL: PROCEDURE; /*TIMING ROUTINE*/
  2     1                   DCL (TIME,ENDTIME,TYPE) FLOAT EXTERNAL, STOP FIXED BIN(31) EXTERNAL;
  3     1                   DCL (TRACEI,TRACEON) FIXED BIN(31) EXTERNAL;
  4     1                   DCL SCHEDUL POINTER EXTERNAL;
  5     1                   DCL INFO(5) FLOAT EXTERNAL;
  6     1                     CALL INITIAL;    /*INITIALIZE THE SYSTEM*/
  7     1                     DO WHILE (TIME < ENDTIME & STOP = 0);
  8     1    1                CALL GETTOP(SCHEDUL,INFO);
  9     1    1                A = 0;    DO I = 1 TO 5;
 11     1    2                          A = A + ABS(INFO(I));    END;
 13     1    1                IF A = 0 THEN STOP = 1;
 15     1    1                ELSE DO;    TIME = INFO(1);    TYPE = INFO(2);
 18     1    2                  IF TRACEON = 1 THEN
 19     1    2                    IF (TRACEI > 0) THEN
 20     1    2                      DO;   PUT EDIT('TIME = ',TIME,'  TYPE = ',TYPE,'  INFO3 = ',
                                          INFO(3),'   INFO4 = ',INFO(4),'   INFO5 = ',INFO(5))
 22     1    3                          (SKIP(2), 5 (A,F(5,2)));   END;
 23     1    2                  IF TYPE = 1 THEN CALL   POLL ;
 25     1    2                  ELSE;
 26     1    2                  IF TYPE = 2 THEN CALL   EXECU ;
 28     1    2                  ELSE;
 29     1    2                  IF TYPE = 3 THEN CALL   REPLY ;
 31     1    2                  ELSE;
 32     1    2                  IF TYPE = 4 THEN CALL   REQUEST ;
 34     1    2                  ELSE;   IF TYPE = 98 THEN TRACEON = 1;
 37     1    2                  ELSE;   IF TYPE = 99 THEN TRACEON = 0;
 40     1    2                  END;
 41     1    1                CALL STAT;    /*COLLECT STATISTICS*/
 42     1    1                IF TRACEON = 1 THEN
 43     1    1                  IF TRACEI > 1 THEN CALL TRACE;
 45     1    1                END;
 46     1                    CALL OUTPUT;    /*PRINT REPORT*/
 47     1                    RETURN;
 48     1                 END CONTROL;
```

Figure 8.2 A control procedure, trace feature included.

8.2, the parameter TRACEI is used to select the level of output data generated. If TRACEI is set equal to 1, then only the information from the event scheduler is printed out. If this parameter is set to a value greater than 1, then additional output is generated by calling a procedure named TRACE. One version of this procedure, for use with the timesharing system simulation example, is shown in Fig. 8.3. This procedure, TRACE, prints out sufficient information to determine the effect of each event-routine execution. For the polling and executing events, this information consists of the system state as contained in the list named

```
                    TRACE: PROCEDURE;


STMT LEVEL NEST
  1                         TRACE: PROCEDURE;
  2     1                   DCL (TIME,ENDTIME,TYPE) FLOAT EXTERNAL, STOP FIXED BIN(31) EXTERNAL;
  3     1                   DCL (TRACEI,TRACEON) FIXED BIN(31) EXTERNAL;
  4     1                   DCL (SCHEDUL,TERM) POINTER EXTERNAL;
  5     1                   DCL INFO(5) FLOAT EXTERNAL;
  6     1                     IF TYPE = 1 THEN
  7     1                       DO;   PUT EDIT('AFTER POLLING EVENT, TERMINAL DATA IS:')
  9     1    1                        (SKIP,A);    CALL PRNTLST(TERM);    END;
 11     1                     ELSE;    IF TYPE = 2 THEN
 13     1                       DO;   PUT EDIT('AFTER EXECUTION EVENT, TERMINAL DATA IS:')
 15     1    1                        (SKIP,A);    CALL PRNTLST(TERM);    END;
 17     1                     ELSE;    IF TYPE = 3 THEN
 19     1                       PUT EDIT('REPLY TO TERMINAL',INFO(5)) (SKIP,A,F(3));
 20     1                     ELSE; IF TYPE = 4 THEN
 22     1                       PUT EDIT('REQUEST FROM TERMINAL',INFO(5))  (SKIP,A,F(3));
 23     1                     RETURN;
 24     1                 END TRACE;
```

Figure 8.3 A procedure for generating trace output for each event type.

TERM. To print out the contents of this list, the procedure PRNTLST, shown in Fig. 8.4, is used.

Portions of the example-trace-feature output are shown in Fig. 8.5. These results are for the case where the random values in the simulation program have been replaced by constants as suggested above. The values for message lengths and execution times are as expected. Also, as expected, the first reply to a terminal occurs at TIME = 3.23, and the next request from this terminal occurs at TIME = 8.23. However, as seen from the results for the first polling and execution events, the computer model does not read all input messages prior to beginning program execution. This is due to the assumption in the model that if a polling event does not have enough time, before the next polling event is due to occur, to read in a complete input command message, then the polling event is terminated and the remaining time is devoted to an execution event. This may or may not be the manner in which the real timesharing computer system operates and requires more information about the system than was given in Sec. 4.3. Thus, this debugging technique serves to probe the assumptions contained in the programmed model.

This particular example and results are not sufficient to verify the timeshared computer system simulation. But it should be evident that this approach can be used for extensive comparisons between the model logic and the program behavior. Additional special cases should be analyzed and executed to test other features of the program. These other cases should include situations in which the behavior of the random variables is checked. Of course, it is usually not possible to check all steps and options in a program, but the verification process should be adequate to give a very high level of confidence in the simulation program.

In addition to its value in program debugging, a trace routine is often essential to the analysis of simulation experiments. All widely used special-purpose simulation languages have a feature of this type, and one should be included in any simulation program. However, for efficiency, this feature may be omitted in the version of the program used for lengthy production runs.

The trace features shown in Fig. 8.2 are included in a version of the preprocessor library control procedure. The name of this member is CONTROLT,

```
        PRNTLST: PROCEDURE(NAME);


STMT LEVEL NEST
  1                    PRNTLST: PROCEDURE(NAME);
  2     1              DCL  1 FOR_EACH_LIST   BASED(PN),
                              2 FIRST         POINTER,
                              2 LAST          POINTER,
                              2 ACCESS        CHARACTER(4),
                              2 PRIO_INDEX    FIXED BINARY(15);
  3     1              DCL  1 LIST_CONTENTS   BASED(PD),
                              2 ITEM(5)       FLOAT,
                              2 NEXT_ELEMENT  POINTER;
  4     1              DCL (NAME,PT) POINTER;
  5     1                PT = NAME->FIRST;
  6     1                DO WHILE (PT ¬= NULL);
  7     1    1              PUT EDIT(PT->ITEM) (SKIP, 5 F(10,3));
  8     1    1              PT = PT->NEXT_ELEMENT;    END;
 10     1                RETURN;
 11     1              END PRNTLST;
```

Figure 8.4 A procedure to print the contents of a list.

```
TIME =   0.00   TYPE =   1.00 INFO3 =   0.00   INFO4 =   0.00   INFO5 =   0.00
AFTER POLLING EVENT, TERMINAL DATA IS:
        1.000      42.000     30.000      9.000      8.000
        1.000      42.000     30.000      9.000      9.000
        1.000      42.000     30.000      9.000     10.000
        1.000      42.000     30.000      9.000     11.000
        1.000      42.000     30.000      9.000     12.000
        2.000       0.000     30.000      9.000      1.000
        2.000       0.000     30.000      9.000      2.000
        2.000       0.000     30.000      9.000      3.000
        2.000       0.000     30.000      9.000      4.000
        2.000       0.000     30.000      9.000      5.000
        2.000       0.000     30.000      9.000      6.000
        1.000      42.000     30.000      9.000      7.000

TIME =   0.90   TYPE =   2.00 INFO3 =   0.10   INFO4 =   0.90   INFO5 =   7.00
AFTER EXECUTION EVENT, TERMINAL DATA IS:
        2.000       0.000     30.000      8.000      5.000
        2.000       0.000     30.000      8.000      6.000
        1.000      42.000     30.000      9.000      7.000
        1.000      42.000     30.000      9.000      8.000
        1.000      42.000     30.000      9.000      9.000
        1.000      42.000     30.000      9.000     10.000
        1.000      42.000     30.000      9.000     11.000
        1.000      42.000     30.000      9.000     12.000
        2.000       0.000     30.000      7.000      1.000
        2.000       0.000     30.000      7.000      2.000
        2.000       0.000     30.000      7.000      3.000
        2.000       0.000     30.000      7.000      4.000

TIME =   1.00   TYPE =   1.00 INFO3 =   0.00   INFO4 =   0.00   INFO5 =   0.00
AFTER POLLING EVENT, TERMINAL DATA IS:
        2.000       0.000     30.000      8.000      6.000
        2.000       0.000     30.000      9.000      7.000
        2.000       0.000     30.000      9.000      8.000
        2.000       0.000     30.000      9.000      9.000
        2.000       0.000     30.000      9.000     10.000

                        |
                        |
                        |
                        |

TIME =   3.23   TYPE =   3.00 INFO3 =  30.00   INFO4 =   0.00   INFO5 =   3.00
REPLY TO TERMINAL   3

TIME =   3.34   TYPE =   3.00 INFO3 =  30.00   INFO4 =   0.00   INFO5 =   4.00
REPLY TO TERMINAL   4

TIME =   3.46   TYPE =   3.00 INFO3 =  30.00   INFO4 =   0.00   INFO5 =   6.00
REPLY TO TERMINAL   6

                        |
                        |
                        |
                        |

TIME =   8.23   TYPE =   4.00 INFO3 =  30.00   INFO4 =   0.00   INFO5 =   3.00
REQUEST FROM TERMINAL   3

TIME =   8.34   TYPE =   4.00 INFO3 =  30.00   INFO4 =   0.00   INFO5 =   4.00
REQUEST FROM TERMINAL   4

TIME =   8.46   TYPE =   4.00 INFO3 =  30.00   INFO4 =   0.00   INFO5 =   6.00
REQUEST FROM TERMINAL   6
```

Figure 8.5 Portions of the trace output for the computer system example, random effects removed.

although the procedure produced by this text is named CONTROL. Thus, to include this trace feature in the programming examples of Chap. 4, it is only necessary to replace the preprocessor statement

%INCLUDE CONTROL;

with the statement

%INCLUDE CONTROLT;

in the cards used to generate the CONTROL procedure and to add the statement

DCL (TRACEON,TRACEI) FIXED BIN(31) EXTERNAL;

in the main procedure. An additional procedure named TRACE is also required in this case.

8.3 COMPARING MODEL DATA WITH REAL SYSTEM DATA

One of the primary approaches used in the model-validation process is to compare data generated by the model with corresponding data obtained from observation of the real system. In the first cycle of model development, this usually requires that the data which is gathered on the real system be divided into two parts. One part is used to develop the model, and the other part is used to test the model validity.

The usual condition for this type of testing is that both the test data from the real system and the model-generated data will be stochastic variables. Thus, the problem of comparing this data corresponds to two-sample statistical testing. That is, we have the case of two sets of samples from two distinct underlying population distributions, and we wish to establish statistical inference regarding these distributions. Specifically, we are interested in testing the hypothesis that these distributions, or their parameters, are the same.

Two tests of the two-sample type were discussed in Sec. 3.2.4, on comparing the means and variances of two normal populations. Those tests require the assumption that the data values be independent samples from a normal distribution. The assumption of a normal distribution can be relaxed by using a nonparametric test; one example being the two-sample version of the Kolmogorov-Smirnov test mentioned in Sec. 7.1. For nonindependent samples, the comparison will depend upon tests of the correlation functions and spectrum of the data sequence.

In order to demonstrate the nature of this approach to validation, we will consider the particular case of testing the time series model developed in Sec. 7.3. For this model, a set of forecasted data was given in Table 7.3, and this data will be considered to be the predicted values for the number of jobs submitted each hour. The predicted values will be assumed to be for a period following the period for which the original system data, as given in Table 7.2 and used to develop the model, was observed. The actual system data for this second 3-week period is given in Table 8.1. The objective in this example is to test for differences between the data of Table 7.3 and Table 8.1. The procedure used is to show how several different tests can be used for comparisons of this type. This is not meant to imply that these specific tests are necessary or adequate for model validation but rather to show that tests of this type can be used to explore the level of confidence we may hold for the predictive capability of a model.

Table 8.1 Test values for number of jobs submitted each hour, a continuation of the data in Table 5.1

HOUR OF DAY		8AM	9AM	10AM	11AM	12AM	1PM	2PM	3PM	4PM	5PM	6PM	7PM	8PM	9PM	10PM	11PM
WEEK	DAY																
4	MON	9	28	40	43	47	90	86	90	100	58	45	29	64	75	62	20
4	TUES	33	41	63	61	50	57	47	34	39	55	52	46	35	32	60	13
4	WED	20	53	51	59	69	75	72	90	67	51	35	29	55	84	74	19
4	THUR	19	56	78	46	51	53	65	60	74	65	55	32	57	65	60	25
4	FRI	6	43	76	107	82	68	55	69	61	71	43	57	59	52	53	24
5	MON	47	53	76	82	67	84	76	86	78	67	71	86	60	102	86	36
5	TUES	32	66	47	54	76	53	89	54	57	56	37	62	57	71	35	24
5	WED	15	28	58	79	78	70	89	63	60	79	86	103	99	84	83	37
5	THUR	30	67	70	81	64	79	84	85	77	92	70	57	67	70	65	36
5	FRI	20	63	62	43	87	97	72	76	57	45	42	55	58	42	47	28
6	MON	10	27	61	57	38	63	70	106	70	47	39	50	48	93	66	43
6	TUES	47	67	71	62	66	53	69	76	68	44	33	89	74	82	85	36
6	WED	21	58	69	76	50	58	85	79	56	81	37	30	43	64	45	32
6	THUR	23	42	47	77	64	33	90	76	55	59	77	52	51	55	74	32
6	FRI	14	33	43	47	44	58	103	72	97	55	54	35	54	56	71	25

The time series model was developed to provide data representing a computer-input job stream. Since the processing of jobs each day is completed with no carryover to the next day, the total daily number of jobs is a significant measure and the model should predict this quantity reliably. Table 8.2 gives the total number of jobs submitted daily, as predicted by the model and as observed in the real system. If we assume that the values in Table 8.2 are independent samples from two normal distributions, we may use the tests of Sec. 3.2.4 to compare the means and variances of these two distributions.

Specifically, we may test the hypothesis that the mean of the predicted values, μ_x, is equal to the mean of the real values, μ_y, assuming equal variances. Using the procedure of Sec. 3.2.4, we calculate the statistics

$$S_{ii}^2 = \frac{[(15-1)(11,136) + (15-1)(13,250)]}{15 + 15 - 2} = 12,194$$

$$t_{ii} = \frac{911 - 932}{[110(30/225)^{1/2}]} = -.51$$

Since $t_{.95, 28} = 1.697$, the hypothesis of equal means cannot be rejected at a 10 percent significance level. Similarly, the hypothesis of equal variances can be tested by comparing the statistic

$$F = \frac{S_y^2}{S_x^2} = 1.19$$

with the value $F_{.95, 14, 14} = 2.42$. Thus the hypothesis of equal variances cannot be rejected.

Table 8.2 Total number of jobs submitted daily, predicted and actual

	Predicted by the model			Results from the real system	
Day	Number of jobs	Rank	Day	Number of jobs	Rank
1	997	22	1	892	14
2	1081	27	2	718	2
3	940	21	3	903	16.5
4	1029	25	4	861	8.5
5	999	23	5	926	20
6	922	19	6	1157	30
7	882	11	7	870	10
8	1054	26	8	1111	29
9	903	16.5	9	1094	28
10	833	5	10	894	15
11	848	6	11	888	13
12	783	3	12	1022	24
13	852	7	13	884	12
14	832	4	14	907	18
15	713	1	15	861	8.5

$\bar{x} = 911$ estimated means $\bar{y} = 932$

$S_x^2 = 11{,}136$ estimated variances $S_y^2 = 13{,}250$

There are a number of nonparametric tests for studying differences between independent samples. Several of these tests are presented and illustrated in chapter 6 of the text by Siegel [7]. We will employ one of these with our example, the Mann-Whitney U Test. This test is particularly sensitive to differences in the mean value of the two distributions. Thus we have an alternate evaluation of the comparison carried out with the t test above.

The Mann-Whitney U Test uses ranking values to compute a test statistic. The rank of 1 is given to the smallest value in the combined group of samples, rank 2 is assigned to the next lowest, etc. Table 8.2 includes this type of ranking for the daily job total values. The rank values are summed for the two groups; for example, using the data of Table 8.2,

$$R_1 = 22 + 27 + \cdots + 4 + 1 = 216.5$$

$$R_2 = 14 + 2 + \cdots + 18 + 8.5 = 248.5$$

The test statistic U is the smaller of the two values obtained from

$$U_1 = n_1 n_2 + \tfrac{1}{2}n_1(n_1 + 1) - R_1$$

$$U_2 = n_1 n_2 + \tfrac{1}{2}n_2(n_2 + 1) - R_2$$

where n_1 and n_2 are the number of samples in the two groups. The relation

$$U_2 = n_1 n_2 - U_1$$

can be used to reduce the number of calculations in this procedure or to check their accuracy. For our example,

$$U_1 = (15)(15) + \tfrac{1}{2}(15)(16) - 216.5 = 128.5$$

$$U_2 = (15)(15) + \tfrac{1}{2}(15)(16) - 248.5 = 96.5$$

So the value of U used as the test statistic is 96.5.

This test is based on the concept that if the two groups of samples came from the same or equivalent distributions, then any particular sequence of ordered samples is equally likely. Thus, by evaluating the number of sequences which give a value of U less than some value U', and comparing this result with the number of sequences possible, the probability of obtaining a value of U less than U' can be obtained. Critical values of this type, for sample sizes of up to 20 in each group, have been calculated and are available in references [7] and [9]. For example, with $n_1 = n_2 = 15$, the probability of U being less than 72 is 10 percent. So the hypothesis that the data of Table 8.2 came from the same distribution cannot be rejected with a significance level of 10 percent.

For larger sample sizes, the distribution of U rapidly approaches the normal distribution with

$$\text{Mean } \mu_U = \tfrac{1}{2}n_1 n_2$$

$$\text{Variance } \sigma_U^2 = \frac{1}{12}\, n_1 n_2(n_1 + n_2 + 1)$$

That is, with either group size larger than 20, the significance of an observed value of U may be determined by using

$$z = \frac{U - \mu_U}{\sigma_U}$$

which is practically normally distributed with 0 mean and unit variance. Thus, the probability associated with the occurrence of values as low as an observed z, under the hypothesis of one underlying distribution, may be determined from a table of the cumulative standard normal distribution.

The results of applying the Mann-Whitney U Test to our example tend to support the contention that the time series model produces adequate values for the daily total number of jobs. However, it is interesting to note that in the ranking values, shown in Table 8.2, the last six values predicted by the model had ranks in the range from 1 to 7. This suggests again that as the model predictions are projected farther from the starting values, they become less accurate.

Up to this point in our example, we have tested only the model results summed over a 1-day period. This is an important aspect of the model performance and serves to illustrate methods for evaluating results of model behavior over a period of simulation time. In many cases, the model behavior over a period of simulation is its most significant effect. In other cases, the model behavior at each point in simulation time is important. For these cases, it is necessary to compare a sequence of model data with a sequence of real data.

Many procedures have been developed for comparing the output of dynamic stochastic models with empirical data. Several examples may be found in the book by Kashyap and Rao [3]. These procedures are rather lengthy and will not be considered here. Instead, we will show how some of the procedures which have been presented previously in this book may be used for testing certain aspects of this type of model performance. These procedures are related to the more general testing methods which have been developed.

In specifying time series models, we assumed that the data sequences could be generated by a linear process operating on a sequence of independent, normally distributed random variables having a mean of 0. Thus, if the model developed in Sec. 7.3 is adequate to represent the test data sequence of Table 8.1, the residuals obtained from applying that model should have such a distribution. That is, if we calculate

$$a_t = z_t - .3z_{t-1} - z_{t-16} + .3z_{t-17} - .75a_{t-16}$$

using z values taken from Table 8.1 (and $a_t = 0$ for $t \le 17$), the sequence of values for a_t ($18 \le t \le 240$) should be independent samples from a normally distributed population with a mean of 0. This result can be statistically tested.

Specifically, we can test for a mean of 0 using the t test; we can test for the normal distribution shape by using the chi-squared test or the Kolmogorov-Smirnov test; and we can test for independence by testing the autocorrelation function.

Calculating the series $\{a_t\}$ as indicated above results in data with an estimated mean and variance of

$$\bar{x} = -.090$$

$$s^2 = 278.81$$

These values lead to a 90 percent confidence interval for the true mean of

$$-1.93 < \mu < +1.75$$

Since $\mu = 0$ is well within this range, we cannot reject the hypothesis that the mean value of a_t is 0.

The values of this series $\{a_t\}$ can also be grouped as shown in Table 8.3 in order to apply the chi-squared goodness-of-fit test to the hypothesis that a_t is normally distributed. The calculated test statistic value, 6.01, is less than the 50 percent point of the cumulative χ^2 distribution with 9 degrees of freedom (or with 7). This indicates that if a_t is normally distributed, a larger test statistic value than that observed would be expected at least half of the time. Thus, we certainly cannot reject the hypothesis that a_t is normally distributed.

In order to test the independence of the residuals, we may use the autocorrelation function of the series $\{a_t\}$. These values are shown in Fig. 8.6 and appear to have a random pattern with no coefficients having a significant magnitude. The procedure of Sec. 7.4 can be used to test the significance of the autocorrelation values. For the hypothesis that the sequence $\{a_t\}$ is of autoregressive order greater than 0, the test statistic is .781. Since $F_{.9, 174, 48} = 1.371$, we may reject this hypothesis without accepting any appreciable chance of error.

These tests do not prove that the model developed in Sec. 7.3 is capable of predicting the future hourly job-rate input from the terminal. But they do indi-

Table 8.3 Calculation of χ^2 test statistic for the residuals $\{a_t\}$

j	Interval	Frequency, f_j	Probability, z_j
1	$a_t < -21.40$	20	.1
2	$-21.40 < a_t < -14.06$	23	.1
3	$-14.06 < a_t < -8.75$	23	.1
4	$-8.75 < a_t < -4.23$	23	.1
5	$-4.23 < a_t < 0$	31	.1
6	$0 < a_t < 4.23$	19	.1
7	$4.23 < a_t < 8.75$	23	.1
8	$8.75 < a_t < 14.06$	16	.1
9	$14.06 < a_t < 21.40$	23	.1
10	$21.40 < a_t$	22	.1

$$n = 223$$

$$U = [(20 - 22.3)^2 + (23 - 22.3)^2 + \cdots + (22 - 22.3)^2]/22.3 = 6.01$$

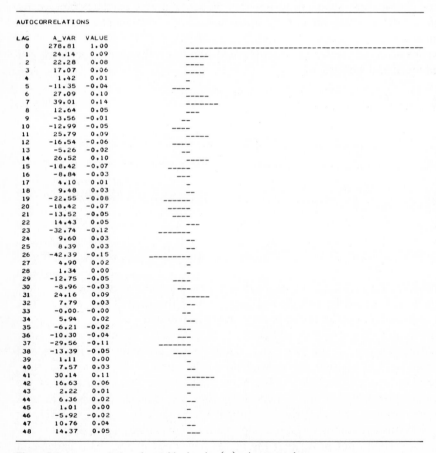

AUTOCORRELATIONS

LAG	A_VAR	VALUE
0	278.81	1.00
1	24.14	0.09
2	22.28	0.08
3	17.07	0.06
4	1.42	0.01
5	-11.35	-0.04
6	27.09	0.10
7	39.01	0.14
8	12.64	0.05
9	-3.56	-0.01
10	-12.99	-0.05
11	25.79	0.09
12	-16.54	-0.06
13	-5.26	-0.02
14	26.52	0.10
15	-18.42	-0.07
16	-8.84	-0.03
17	4.10	0.01
18	9.48	0.03
19	-22.55	-0.08
20	-18.42	-0.07
21	-13.52	-0.05
22	14.43	0.05
23	-32.74	-0.12
24	9.60	0.03
25	8.39	0.03
26	-42.39	-0.15
27	4.90	0.02
28	1.34	0.00
29	-12.75	-0.05
30	-8.96	-0.03
31	24.16	0.09
32	7.79	0.03
33	-0.00	-0.00
34	5.94	0.02
35	-6.21	-0.02
36	-10.30	-0.04
37	-29.56	-0.11
38	-13.39	-0.05
39	1.11	0.00
40	7.57	0.03
41	30.14	0.11
42	16.63	0.06
43	2.22	0.01
44	6.36	0.02
45	1.01	0.00
46	-5.92	-0.02
47	10.76	0.04
48	14.37	0.05

Figure 8.6 Autocorrelations for residual series $\{a_t\}$ using test values.

cate that certain basic patterns in this variable that existed during the first 3 weeks of observations were repeated during the next 3 weeks of operation. This should provide some degree of confidence in the validity of this model.

8.4 SENSITIVITY ANALYSIS

In most simulation models, some of the data used to develop the model is subject to error, and often the model is used to explore situations where the operating conditions differ from those for which data was observed. Therefore, in order to establish confidence in model validity, it is necessary to determine that reasonable changes in model parameters or operating conditions do not lead to unreasonable changes in model performance. One approach to testing this aspect of model behavior is by the use of sensitivity analysis.

Sensitivity analysis views the model as an input-output process. The basic technique is to vary an input to the model, by using incremental changes, and observe the incremental changes in an output variable. The ratio of these changes is referred to as the *sensitivity of the output to the specified input*. If this ratio is constant over a range of values of input changes, then the relationship between the specified input and output variables is linear. In this case, the effect of changes in the input variable is readily predicted, and the relationship between these input and output variables is easily understood. It is reasonable for the sensitivity of a model to be approximately constant for small changes in the input variable, but the sensitivity is not usually constant over a large range of values. When the magnitude of the input changes leads to significant changes in the sensitivity, the effectiveness of the model deteriorates.

To give a concrete example of model sensitivity, we will again consider the inventory system example. As mentioned in Sec. 8.1, the most critical parameter in this model is the average demand rate for the product. Clearly, the net profit and best choice of control parameters are very dependent on the rate at which the items are sold. We may determine the sensitivity of the average weekly profit to the average demand rate by executing the simulation program with various values for this rate. Figure 8.7a shows the values obtained for average weekly profit for various values of average periods between sales. These results were obtained with fixed values for the control factors, stock control level, and period between inventory, specifically those values shown in Fig. 4.18. This curve reaches a peak at an average demand rate of about one sale every 5 days which is the nominal values used previously with this example. This condition is not typical and does not correspond to optimal control values in this case. The sensitivity coefficients for average weekly profit to average time between sales correspond to the derivative of this curve and are shown in Fig. 8.7b. Although this sensitivity is not constant over this range, its value does not change drastically until the demand rate increases to an average greater than a sale every 2 days. This suggests that the form of the model used in these calculations may be of questionable value at higher demand rates.

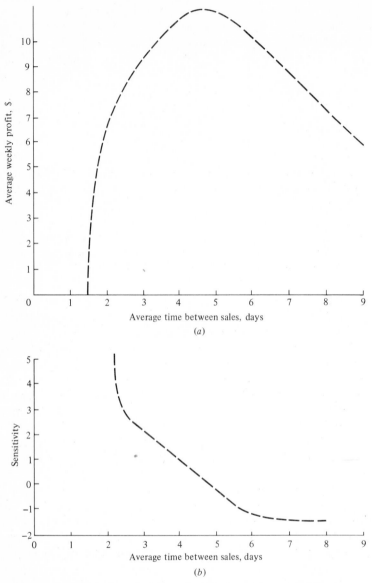

Figure 8.7 Sensitivity function of average weekly profit to average time between sales for the inventory system model.

It is easy to see why this model exhibits a large change in sensitivity for these conditions. As the demand rate increases, the number of sales increases, but with a fixed stock control level, the number of lost sales increases even faster. Since this model assumes a loss of $10 for each lost sale, presumably due to customer dissatisfaction, at higher demand rates the calculated profit decreases and even becomes negative. A much higher than expected demand rate would probably occur because of shortages of the item at other retailers, and the lost sales may then be to individuals looking for this one item and who would not be regular customers of the modeled store. In this case, the $10 penalty for not having the item in stock may not be appropriate.

The basic idea of using sensitivity analysis for model validation is to search for regions of input-parameter changes for which the sensitivity changes drastically. It is particularly important that such changes do not occur for relatively small changes in the nominal parameter value. The use of sensitivity analysis to validate discrete-event models has not been formalized and is at present primarily used to explore the nature of these models. This technique has been much more thoroughly developed for use with continuous models [8]. Despite the limited theoretical bases available, this method can be very helpful in establishing confidence in a discrete-event model.

Sensitivity analysis is also a valuable tool for the analysis of simulation results. It was stated in Sec. 8.1 that any uncertainty in the model should be included in the simulation studies used to decide between values for control parameters. An example of this situation would be where uncertainty in the demand rate is included in the inventory system simulation. This would arise if some probability distribution were available for the estimated future average time between sales. With this distribution, simulations could be carried out using an additional random factor to represent the uncertainty in this parameter. An alternate method to carry out this type of analysis would be to use the sensitivity function in conjunction with the demand rate distribution. For example, assume that the best estimate for average time between sales was that any value between 4 and 6 days was equally likely. Then, the average weekly profit could be estimated by obtaining data as given in Fig. 8.7, then adjusting the value obtained at 5 days by adding the average value of the sensitivity in the range of 4 to 6. This use of the sensitivity function would be computationally more efficient and would provide additional information as to the effect of uncertainty in predicting the time between sales.

8.5 BACKGROUND AND REFERENCES

An introduction to the general question of model validation and the basic approaches to this problem are provided by the papers of Hermann [2] and Mihram [4]. These articles contain a concise summary of the philosophical arguments related to this topic. This subject is also discussed in chapter 6 of the text by Shannon [6]. Each of these references emphasizes the importance of one validation technique, not considered here, which is to make use of expert opinion. That is, the model should appear to be reasonable to those individuals having the most knowledge and experience with the system under study. Such a condition is, of course, almost equivalent to model validation.

A procedure for the use of sensitivity analysis in model validation has been described by Miller [5]. The particular model used in that study was of the continuous type, but the procedure could be applied to a discrete-event model.

Model validation is an extremely important phase of simulation but very dependent on the nature of the problem being studied. Case studies of successful modeling and simulation projects will probably prove to be the best source for useful ideas in this area.

REFERENCES

1. Anshoff, H. E., and R. L. Hayes: "Role of Models in Corporate Decision Making," *Proceedings of IFORS Sixth International Conference*, Dublin, Ireland, August 1972.
2. Hermann, C. H.: "Validation Problems in Games and Simulation," *Behavioral Science*, vol. 12, pp. 216–231, 1967.
3. Kashyap, R. L., and A. R. Rao: "Dynamic Stochastic Models from Empirical Data," Academic, New York, 1976.
4. Mihram, G. A.: "Some Practical Aspects of the Verification and Validation of Simulation Models," *Operations Research Quarterly*, vol. 23, no. 1, pp. 17–29, 1973.
5. Miller, D. R.: "Sensitivity Analysis and Validation of Simulation Models," *Journal of Theoretical Biology*, vol. 48, pp. 345–360, 1974.
6. Shannon, R. E.: "System Simulation: The Art and Science," Prentice-Hall, Englewood Cliffs, N.J., 1975.
7. Siegel, S.: "Nonparametric Statistics for the Behavioral Sciences," McGraw-Hill, New York, 1956.
8. Tomovic, R., and M. Vukobratovic: "General Sensitivity Theory," American-Elsevier, New York, 1972.
9. Walsh, J. E.: "Handbook of Nonparametric Statistics I," Van Nostrand, Princeton, N.J., 1962.

EXERCISES

8.1 Modify the TRACE procedure of Fig. 8.3 such that when the parameter TRACEI is equal to 2, only the event type and time of occurrence are printed out.

8.2 Write a TRACE procedure, similar to that of Fig. 8.3, that will provide options for printing out all the state variables which are changed by a particular event execution following the execution of that event in the elevator system example.

8.3 Using the data of Fig. 4.31, test the hypothesis that the mean wait time for terminal 1 and for terminal 2 are equal. Assume that the wait time for each observation in an interval is the same. For example, assume that the wait time for observations with upper limit 3.00 is 2.50.

8.4 Test the assumption that the following data series:

t	z	t	z	t	z
1	−.2	6	−.1	11	−.3
2	+.3	7	0	12	−.2
3	+.4	8	−.1	13	−.3
4	+.7	9	0	14	−.6
5	−.2	10	−.4	15	−.5

can be represented by the model:

$$z_t = .9z_{t-1} + a_t - .5a_{t-1}$$

8.5 The following table gives corresponding values for an input variable x and an output variable z:

$$z = 105, 115, 125, 134, 140, 143$$

$$x = 10, 12, 14, 16, 18, 20$$

Sketch an estimated function that gives the sensitivity of z to x.

8.6 For the timesharing computer system example of Sec. 4.3, determine the sensitivity of the average polling time to the average reply message length.

NINE

CONTINUOUS SUBSYSTEMS IN DISCRETE-EVENT MODELS

We have viewed simulation as a method for studying the behavior of systems as they change over a period of time. The dynamics of processes, particularly continuous physical devices, are usually represented mathematically by means of differential equations. Often such devices are included in systems which are most appropriately represented by discrete-event models. This chapter presents a method for including subsystems described by ordinary differential equations in the simulation programming procedure of Chap. 4.

The material in this chapter covers some basic concepts of ordinary differential equations and their numerical solution. No attempt is made to cover the very broad field of computing solutions to differential equations. Here the emphasis is on illustrating the problems involved in combining equations of this type into discrete-event simulations.

9.1 A DIFFERENTIAL EQUATION MODEL

Often the application of physical principles leads to describing processes by differential equations. A familiar example is the motion of a free body, for which Newton's second law states that the mass of the body times its acceleration is equal to the sum of the forces acting on the body. Applying this principle to an elevator car results in the following equation:

$$M \frac{d^2x}{dt^2} = F_c - W$$

or

$$M\ddot{x} = F_c - W$$

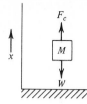

Figure 9.1 Force diagram for an elevator car.

where M is the mass of the car, W is the weight of the car ($W = Mg$) and is the force acting to move the car down, F_c is the force exerted on the car by the cable, and acceleration is the second derivative with respect to time of the car's vertical position x.

If the force F_c is supplied by a two-phase induction motor, the application of other physical laws gives the following approximate relation between this force, the motor control voltage e_c, and the motor shaft rotational speed ω:

$$F_c = K_1 e_c - K_2 \omega \qquad |e_c| \le E$$

where K_1, K_2, and E are constants determined by the motor characteristics. The elevator car position x is directly related to the motor shaft position θ,

$$x = K_3 \theta$$

and

$$\frac{d\theta}{dt} = \dot{\theta} = \omega$$

Combining these equations gives the following relationship between the car position x and the motor control voltage e_c:

$$M\ddot{x} + (K_2/K_3)\dot{x} + W = K_1 e_c$$

One possible method for controlling the elevator position is to use a reference voltage x_r for each floor and the difference between this value and the actual value of x to generate the motor control voltage. That is, let

$$e_c = f(x_r - x)$$

with the functional relationship as shown in Fig. 9.2. The complete system is represented schematically in Fig. 9.3. Within the linear range of the functional

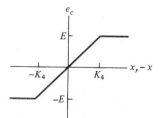

Figure 9.2 Relation between control voltage e_c and position error $(x_r - x)$.

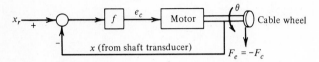

Figure 9.3 Block diagram of the elevator-position control system.

relationship between e_c and $(x_r - x)$, the overall equation for the elevator motion is

$$M\ddot{x} + (K_2/K_3)\dot{x} + (EK_1/K_4)x = (EK_1/K_4)x_r - W \tag{1}$$

Equation (1) is a second-order, linear, ordinary differential equation of the form

$$a\ddot{x} + b\dot{x} + cx = d \tag{2}$$

The solution to this equation can be obtained as a closed-form expression by standard techniques. The nature of this solution varies with the relationship between the constants b and c. If we consider the case where

$$b^2 - 4ac > 0$$

we have the overdamped form of the solution to Eq. (2), which is

$$x(t) = \frac{d}{c} + \left[\frac{d}{c} - x(0)\right](p_2 e^{p_1 t} - p_1 e^{p_2 t})(b^2 - 4ac)^{-1/2}$$

$$- (\dot{x}(0))(e^{p_1 t} - e^{p_2 t})(b^2 - 4ac)^{-1/2} \tag{3}$$

where

$$p_1 = \frac{-b + \sqrt{b^2 - 4ac}}{2a} \qquad p_2 = \frac{-b - \sqrt{b^2 - 4ac}}{2a}$$

assuming the following parameter values for the elevator system:

$$W = 3200 \text{ lb } (\therefore M = 3200/32 = 100 \text{ slugs})$$

$$E = 200 \text{ V}$$

$$K_1 = 100 \text{ lb/V}$$

$$K_2 = 2000 \text{ lb/rad/s}$$

$$K_3 = 1 \text{ ft/rad}$$

$$K_4 = 20 \text{ ft}$$

Then, Eq. (1) becomes

$$100\ddot{x} + 2000\dot{x} + 1000x = 1000x_r - 3200$$

The solution to this equation, for initial conditions $x(0) = 0$ and $\dot{x}(0) = 0$, and reference input $x_r = 10$ ft, is shown in Fig. 9.4. In this case, the value of e_c always remains less than E, so Eq. (1) is valid. Note that the final value of $x(t)$, i.e., the steady state value, differs from the reference value by the amount WK_4/EK_1. In

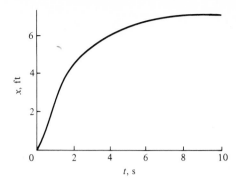

Figure 9.4 Elevator position response to $x_r = 10$.

an elevator system, the weight of the car can be balanced by a counterweight. However, weight variations due to passengers will cause the simplified control system used here to have position errors. We may assume that the final car positioning is accomplished by another control system, not included in this model, which takes over when the car reaches a point sufficiently near a floor and with sufficiently small velocity.

Equation (3) may be used to determine the elevator motion as long as $|x_r - x| \leq 20$, which corresponds to a trip with a distance of one or two floors. Although it is possible to find closed-form solutions for $(x_r - x)$ beyond this range, it is usually more convenient to use numerical integration to solve the differential equations directly. Also, if a more accurate representation of the relation between F_c, e_c, and ω were used, it would not be possible to obtain closed-form solutions to the resulting nonlinear differential equations. Thus, numerical solutions for differential equations are necessary.

9.2 NUMERICAL INTEGRATION

The basic idea of numerical integration can be illustrated by a technique known as *Euler's method*. In this procedure, the solution to a first-order, ordinary differential equation:

$$\dot{x}(t) = f(x, t) \qquad x(0) = a$$

is approximated by using the iterative formula:

$$x[h \cdot (i + 1)] = x(h \cdot i) + h \cdot f[x(h \cdot i), h \cdot i] \qquad i = 0, 1, 2, \ldots$$

This method is illustrated in Fig. 9.5. As shown in this figure, the method introduces a small amount of error at each step, and this error can lead to increased error at the next step because the derivative will be evaluated with a value of x that differs from the true value of x.

It is easy to see that the accuracy of Euler's method could be improved by taking one step, as above, then evaluating the derivative at the end of that step, and using the average of the derivatives at the two end points to reevaluate the step. This "improved" Euler's method has the following iterative formula, using

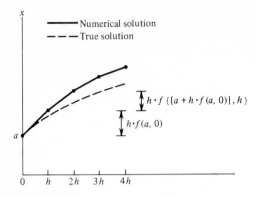

Figure 9.5 Numerical integration using Euler's method.

the notation $x_i = x(h \cdot i)$ and $t_i = h \cdot i$:

$$x'_{i+1} = x_i + h \cdot f(x_i, t_i)$$

$$x_{i+1} = x_i + (h/2)[f(x_i, t_i) + f(x'_{i+1}, t_{i+1})]$$

This equation is one example of a family of formulas that are called *Runge-Kutta methods*. These methods are classified by order, where the order is equal to the number of times the derivative is evaluated at each step.

A very common fourth-order Runge-Kutta method for numerical integration is represented by the following formulas:

$$K_1 = f(x_i, t_i)$$

$$K_2 = f\left(x_i + \frac{K_1 h}{2}, t_i + \frac{h}{2}\right)$$

$$K_3 = f\left(x_i + \frac{K_2 h}{2}, t_i + \frac{h}{2}\right)$$

$$K_4 = f(x_i + K_3 h, t_i + h) \tag{4}$$

$$x_{i+1} = x_i + \left(\frac{h}{6}\right)(K_1 + 2K_2 + 2K_3 + K_4)$$

The order of the method is also equal to the highest exponent of h in the Taylor series expansion of $f(x, t)$ that is matched by using the formula. Thus, the error at each step is approximately

$$e_T = Kh^5$$

where K is some constant.

We can use this error estimate to devise a procedure which can automatically adjust to achieve some specified limit on this error. Assume that we use Eq. (4) to calculate a value for x_1 using a particular value of h. Then the true value of x at $t = h$ is

$$x_1 + Kh^5$$

Now if we use $h/2$ to calculate x_1' by using Eq. (4) twice, and then if the fifth derivative of x is reasonably constant in this interval, the true value of x at $t = h$ would be

$$x_1' + 2K\left(\frac{h}{2}\right)^5$$

But this means that

$$x_1 + Kh^5 = x_1' + \frac{Kh^5}{16}$$

$$x_1' - x_1 = \frac{15Kh^5}{16}$$

and the error between the true value of x at $t = h$ and the computed value x_1' is

$$\frac{(x_1' - x_1)}{15}$$

Thus, we may use this value to compare to a specified permissible error, and if it is less, use

$$x_1' + \frac{(x_1' - x_1)}{15}$$

as the estimate for the true value. If the error exceeds that permitted, the value of h can be reduced, for example, to one-half its original value, and the process repeated.

It should be noted that the estimate is only for the error due to inaccuracies in the integration formula. It does not include the error due to errors which may have occurred at previous steps. However, reducing the step size does reduce both the error due to truncation in the formulas and that due to propagation from step to step. Thus, the basic technique for improving the accuracy of solutions obtained by Runge-Kutta methods is to reduce the size of the step change in the independent variable.

Runge-Kutta methods are not the most efficient procedures for the numerical integration of differential equations. However, they are less complex to program than the more efficient techniques and are less sensitive to certain stability problems which arise in numerical integration.

Although the Runge-Kutta formulas given above are for the integration of a single first-order differential equation, they are readily extended to a system of first-order differential equations. That is, for the system of equations

$$\underline{\dot{x}} = \underline{f}(\underline{x}, t)$$

where $\underline{x}$ and $\underline{f}$ are n-dimensional vectors, we may use Eq. (4) with x_i, f, and the Ks interpreted as vectors. Moreover, an ordinary differential equation of any order can be transformed to a system of first-order equations. For example, the second-order equation, Eq. (2) can be transformed by letting

$$x_1 = x$$
$$x_2 = \dot{x}$$

then we have the system of two first-order equations:

$$\dot{x}_1 = x_2$$
$$\dot{x}_2 = \frac{-bx_2 - cx_1 + d}{a}$$

A procedure for carrying out numerical integration is shown in Fig. 9.6. The vector form of Eq. (4) is implemented in the internal procedure named ONE-STEP. The value of the derivative vector f is obtained from an external procedure named DERIV. The integration procedure uses the error-checking method described above. Integration is performed over an internal using a step size HA and

```
          INTEGRA: PROCEDURE(Y,N,H,T); /*INTEGRATE Y(T) TO Y(T+H)*/

STMT LEVEL NEST
 1                     INTEGRA: PROCEDURE(Y,N,H,T); /*INTEGRATE Y(T) TO Y(T+H)*/
 2     1               DCL STOP FIXED BIN(31) EXTERNAL;
 3     1               DCL (ABSERR(4),RELERR(4)) FLOAT EXTERNAL;
 4     1               DCL (Y(1),H,T,XA(4),XB(4),XC(4),XD(4)) FLOAT;
 5     1               DCL N FIXED BINARY(15);
 6     1               HA = H;   DO I = 1 TO N;   XA(I) = Y(I);   END;   TS = T;
11     1               DO M = 1 TO 8 WHILE((H > 0 & TS < (T + 0.99*H))
                                          |(H < 0 & TS > (T + 0.99*H)));
12     1   1               CALL ONE_STEP(XA,XB,TS,HA);    HB = HA/2.;
14     1   1               CALL ONE_STEP(XA,XC,TS,HB);    TS = TS + HB;
16     1   1               CALL ONE_STEP(XC,XD,TS,HB);
17     1   1               IE = 0;    DO I = 1 TO N;   /*TEST ERROR LIMITS*/
19     1   2                   ERR = ABS(XD(I) - XB(I))/15.;
20     1   2                   IF (ERR    > (ABSERR(I) + RELERR(I)*ABS(XD(I))))
21     1   2                       THEN IE = 1;
22     1   2                   END;
23     1   1               IF IE = 0 THEN    /*ERROR WITHIN LIMITS*/
24     1   1                   DO;   DO I = 1 TO N;
26     1   3                       XA(I) = XD(I) + (XD(I) - XB(I))/15.;
27     1   3                       END;
28     1   2                   TS = TS + HB;    END;
30     1   1               ELSE DO;    TS = TS - HB;    HA = HB;    END;    /*REDUCE STEP SIZE*/
34     1   1               END;
35     1               IF IE = 0 THEN DO;
37     1   1               DO I = 1 TO N;    Y(I) = XA(I);    END;   T = TS;
41     1   1               END;
42     1               ELSE DO;    PUT EDIT('DID NOT MEET ERROR CRITERION')(SKIP,A);
44     1   1               PUT EDIT(XD,XB,HA,TS,H,T) (SKIP, 4 F(16,6));
45     1   1               STOP = 1;    END;
47     1               ONE_STEP: PROCEDURE(X,XX,TT,D);    /*INTEGRATE ONE STEP*/
48     2               DCL (K(4,4),F(4)) FLOAT;
49     2               DCL (X(1),XX(1),TT,D,T,DL) FLOAT;
50     2               DO I = 1 TO N;    XX(I) = X(I);    END;   T = TT;
54     2               DO J = 1 TO 4;
55     2   1               CALL DERIV(XX,F,T);
56     2   1               DO I = 1 TO N;    K(I,J) = F(I);    END;
59     2   1               IF J < 3 THEN DL = D/2.;
61     2   1               IF J = 3 THEN DL = D;
63     2   1               T = TT + DL;
64     2   1               DO L = 1 TO N;    XX(L) = X(L) + K(L,J)*DL;    END;
67     2   1               END;
68     2               DO I = 1 TO N;
69     2   1               XX(I) = X(I) + (D/6.)*(K(I,1)+2.*K(I,2)+2.*K(I,3)+K(I,4));
70     2   1               END;
71     2               END ONE_STEP;
72     1               END INTEGRA;
```

Figure 9.6 A one-step integration procedure with error checking.

a step size HB that is one-half HA. This integration is accomplished by the calls to ONE-STEP in statements 12 to 16. The estimation error in each operation is compared with a specified error in statements 18 to 22. The specified error is the sum of an absolute component and a relative value component and may be different for each equation of the system of first-order differential equations.

The parameters of the INTEGRA procedure are the state-variable array, denoted by Y, the number of equations N, the step size H, and the value of the independent variable T. The version of this procedure as shown in Fig. 9.6 is limited to, at most, four simultaneous differential equations. But it can be modified to handle a larger number by changing the declaration statements 2, 3, and 48. This version is also intended to carry out one integration step at each call. That is, the value of H is assumed to be sufficiently small so that usually the error criterion is met. This restriction can be relaxed by increasing the upper limit on M in statement 11.

An example of the DERIV procedure is shown in Fig. 9.7. The particular routine will supply the appropriate derivatives for the differential equations describing the elevator system of Fig. 9.3. The equations here have been modified to include the effects of using a counterbalance weight with the elevator. It has been assumed that the counterbalance is equal to the weight of the car with no passengers. Thus, in these equations, WT refers to only the weight of the passengers, and M is only the mass of the empty car.

The results of integrating the equations defined by this DERIV procedure, for a few different reference inputs and passenger weight values, are shown in Fig. 9.8. In these cases, the time required to reach the reference value does not change appreciably, but the passenger weight does affect the final value of the elevator position. The trajectories in Fig. 9.8 are all cases where differences between the elevator position and the reference value, $x_r - x$, are always less than K_4 in magnitude. This corresponds to the linear portion of the functional relationship shown in Fig. 9.2. The nature of the elevator motion for the case of $|x_r - x| > K_4$ is illustrated by the results shown in Fig. 9.9.

9.3 COMBINING DISCRETE-EVENT AND CONTINUOUS MODELS

System models may contain subsystems which are represented by differential equations and other interrelated processes which are represented by discrete-event models. In this section, we consider some problems which arise in the simulation of these combined models.

The differential equation part of the model could be simulated as a discrete-event process and be included in the simulation programming procedure discussed in Chap. 4. For example, Euler's method could be used for the numerical integration, and each step of this procedure would correspond to a specific event. In this case, the integration formulas would be part of an event routine, and this event routine would schedule the next occurrence of the integration event. If there

```
          DERIV: PROCEDURE(X,F,T);

STMT LEVEL NEST
  1                        DERIV: PROCEDURE(X,F,T);
  2      1                  DCL (X(1),F(1),T) FLOAT;
  3      1                  DCL (K1,K2,K3,K4,E,G,M,REF,WT) FLOAT EXTERNAL;
  4      1                  EC = (E/K4)*(REF - X(1));
  5      1                  IF (ABS(EC) > E) THEN
  6      1                                   IF EC > 0 THEN EC = E;    ELSE EC = -E;
  9      1                  F(1) = X(2);
 10      1                  F(2) = (-(K2/K3)*X(2) + K1*EC - WT)/(M + WT/G);
 11      1                  RETURN;
 12      1                END DERIV;
```

Figure 9.7 A DERIV procedure for the elevator-position control system.

is interaction between the various parts of the model, then it would be necessary to include these effects in some of the nonintegration event routine programs. If Euler's method is used for the integration, this coordination between event routines would not be particularly difficult. However, if more efficient and more complex integration procedures are used, this coordination becomes complex. For this reason, it is desirable to separate the numerical integration procedures from the discrete-event procedures in a simulation programming system.

There are two types of events that may cause interaction between the discrete-event and continuous portions of a model. One of these is an event that occurs independent of the subsystem modeled by the differential equations, and

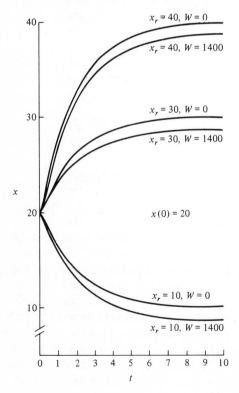

Figure 9.8 Solutions of the elevator-position control equation.

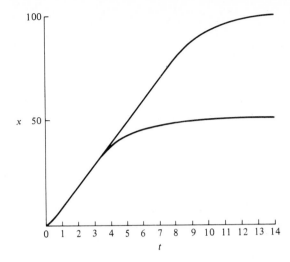

Figure 9.9 Solutions of the elevator-position control equation with nonlinear effect.

the other is an event that occurs because of some function of the dependent variables of the differential equations. As an illustration of these event types, consider the simulation of an elevator system where the passenger arrivals and trip demands are represented by a discrete-event model, and the motion of the elevator is represented by differential equations. In this case, a passenger arrival occurs independently, but the event of an elevator arriving at a particular floor occurs as the result of the elevator-position variable reaching a certain value. Both of these events cause an interruption in the integration procedure. Although it may appear that a passenger arrival would not necessarily require interrupting the integration, it would if there were two elevators and one was moving and one was idle.

A modified version of the simulation control flowchart of Fig. 4.7, which includes the capability for integrating differential equations, is shown in Fig. 9.10. In this procedure, the integration proceeds independently of the discrete events until either the next scheduled discrete event occurs or until a dependent event is triggered by the dependent variables of the differential equation. For an independent discrete event, the integration step size is adjusted so that the integration time will correspond to the next event time. For a dependent event, integration is adjusted in order to assure that the value of the variable which initiates the event is within a required tolerance.

To illustrate the procedures required to program the simulation of a combined model, we modify the elevator example given in Chap. 4. The modification is to include the differential equations developed in Sec. 9.1 to describe the motion of each of the two elevator cars. The CONTROL procedure used for this example is shown in Fig. 9.11. This procedure implements the flowchart of Fig. 9.10. The integration steps are carried out by calls to the INTEGRA procedure of Fig. 9.6. The test for occurrence of a dependent event is carried out by an external procedure named CHECK, and for this example, the only type of dependent

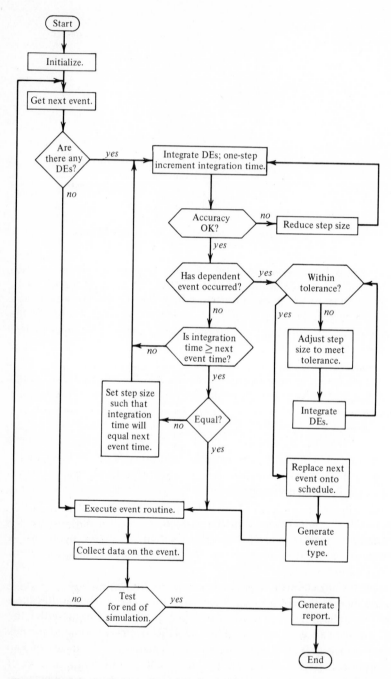

Figure 9.10 A block diagram of the CONTROL procedure for combined discrete-event and differential equation models.

```
STMT LEVEL NEST
  1                  CONTROL: PROCEDURE; /*TIMING ROUTINE*/
  2     1              DCL (TIME,ENDTIME,TYPE) FLOAT EXTERNAL, STOP FIXED BIN(31) EXTERNAL;
  3     1              DCL SCHEDUL POINTER EXTERNAL;
  4     1              DCL INFO(5) FLOAT EXTERNAL;
  5     1              DCL (X(4),H,DETIME) FLOAT EXTERNAL, N FIXED BIN(15) EXTERNAL;
  6     1              DCL DEON FIXED BIN(15) EXTERNAL;
  7     1              CALL INITIAL;   /*INITIALIZE THE SYSTEM*/
  8     1              DO WHILE (TIME < ENDTIME & STOP = 0);
  9     1    1           CALL GETTOP(SCHEDUL,INFO);
 10     1    1           IF SUM(INFO) = 0 THEN STOP = 1;
 12     1    1           ELSE DO;   DETIME = TIME;
 14     1    2                 TIME = INFO(1);   TYPE = INFO(2);
                              /*INTEGRATE STATE EQUATIONS*/
 16     1    2             IP = 0;   IC = 0;   HA = H;
 19     1    2             DO WHILE(IP = 0 & DEON = 1);
 20     1    3               CALL INTEGRA(X,N,HA,DETIME);
 21     1    3               IF STOP = 1 THEN RETURN;
 23     1    3               CALL CHECK(X,N,DETIME,IC);   /*TEST FOR STATE EVENT OCCURS*/
 24     1    3               IF IC = 0 THEN   /*CONTINUE INTEGRATION*/
 25     1    3                  DO;   IF (DETIME + HA) >= TIME THEN
 27     1    4                         DO;   /*ADJUST STEP TO DISCREET EVENT TIME*/
 28     1    5                           HA = TIME - DETIME;
 29     1    5                           CALL INTEGRA(X,N,HA,DETIME);
 30     1    5                           IP = 1;   END;
 32     1    4                  END;
 33     1    3               ELSE DO;   /*GENERATE STATE EVENT*/
 34     1    4                 IT = 0;   /*TEST FOR TOLERANCE OF STATE VARIABLES*/
 35     1    4                 DO K = 1 TO 4 WHILE(IT = 0);
 36     1    5                   CALL TOLER(X,N,DETIME,IC,HB);
 37     1    5                     IF HB > 0 THEN IT = 1;
 39     1    5                     ELSE CALL INTEGRA(X,N,HB,DETIME);
 40     1    5                 END;
 41     1    4                 CALL ADDTO(SCHEDUL,INFO);   /*REPLACE NEXT EVENT*/
 42     1    4                 TIME = DETIME;   TYPE = 2;   IP = 1;   INFO(3) = IC;
 46     1    4               END;
 47     1    3             END;
                              /*EXECUTE DISCREET EVENT*/
 48     1    2             IF TYPE = 1 THEN CALL CALL;
 50     1    2             ELSE
 50     1    2             IF TYPE = 2 THEN CALL ARRIVE;
 52     1    2             ELSE
 52     1    2             IF TYPE = 3 THEN CALL LEAVE;
 54     1    2             END;
 55     1    1           CALL STAT;   /*COLLECT STATISTICS*/
 56     1    1         END;
 57     1            CALL OUTPUT;   /*PRINT REPORT*/
 58     1            RETURN;
 59     1          END CONTROL;
```

Figure 9.11 The CONTROL procedure for combined models.

event is the arrival of a car at a destination floor. This is the Type 2 event represented by routine ARRIVE.

The DERIV procedure for this example is listed in Fig. 9.12. The equations are the example of Sec. 9.2, except that there are two sets of equations, so that two elevators can be represented. The position variable P is used to determine when the cars are moving and, thus, when the corresponding derivative values are to be evaluated or set to 0.

In this example, it is assumed that the elevator stops when the car gets within 2 ft of the destination floor and either the velocity of the car is less than .25 ft per second or the car is not still traveling in the direction of the destination floor. This action is implemented in the CHECK procedure shown in Fig. 9.13. This procedure includes the TOLER procedure, which is intended to adjust the final car position but is only a dummy operation in this version of the example.

This modification required some changes in the ARRIVE and LEAVE event routines, the new versions of which are given in Figs. 9.14 and 9.15, respectively.

```
                 DERIV: PROCEDURE(X,F,T);

STMT LEVEL NEST
  1                        DERIV: PROCEDURE(X,F,T);
  2      1                    DCL  (X(1),F(1),T) FLOAT;
  3      1                    DCL  (FLOOR(2,11),D(2),S(2,11),P(2)) FIXED BIN(15) EXTERNAL;
  4      1                    DCL  (M,K1,K2,K3,K4,E,W(2),REF(2)) FLOAT EXTERNAL;
  5      1                    IF P(1) = 0 THEN DO;
  7      1    1                  F(1) = X(2);
  8      1    1                  EC = (E/K4)*(REF(1) - K3*X(1));
  9      1    1                  IF (ABS(EC) > E) THEN IF EC > 0 THEN EC = E;   ELSE EC = -E;
 13      1    1                  F(2) = (-K2*X(2)/K3 + K1*EC - W(1))/(M + W(1)/32.);
 14      1    1               END;
 15      1                    ELSE DO;   F(1) = 0;   F(2) = 0;   END;
 19      1                    IF P(2) = 0 THEN DO;
 21      1    1                  F(3) = X(4);
 22      1    1                  EC = (E/K4)*(REF(2) - K3*X(3));
 23      1    1                  IF (ABS(EC) > E) THEN IF EC > 0 THEN EC = E;   ELSE EC = -E;
 27      1    1                  F(4) = (-K2*X(4)/K3 + K1*EC - W(2))/(M + W(2)/32.);
 28      1    1               END;
 29      1                    ELSE DO;   F(3) = 0;   F(4) = 0;   END;
 33      1                    RETURN;
 34      1                 END DERIV;
```

Figure 9.12 The DERIV procedure for the modified elevator system example.

The only changes to the ARRIVE procedure are the method of determining the arrival floor number, statement 10, and the capability of turning off the integration routine if both cars are stopped, statements 54 and 55. In the LEAVE procedure, the next arrival event is no longer scheduled, but new features are added in statements 68 to 84. These features include setting the destination floor by assigning values to REF and determining the weight of the passengers. The number of passengers permitted on a car is limited to 14. This feature requires a new procedure named KOUNT, shown in Fig. 9.16, to count the number of elements on the cars lists.

The other subprocedures for this example are the same as those given in Sec. 4.4. The main procedure for executing this example is shown in Fig. 9.17 and the corresponding output is that of Fig. 9.18. These results are fairly close to those obtained with the discrete-event model of Sec. 4.4.

A continuous model for elevator motion, as added to the system model here,

```
                 CHECK: PROCEDURE(Y,N,T,I);

STMT LEVEL NEST
  1                        CHECK: PROCEDURE(Y,N,T,I);
  2      1                    DCL  (FLOOR(2,11),D(2),S(2,11),P(2)) FIXED BIN(15) EXTERNAL;
  3      1                    DCL  (Y(1),T) FLOAT,(N,I) FIXED BIN(15);
  4      1                    DCL  REF(2) FLOAT EXTERNAL;
  5      1                    I = 0;
  6      1                    IF P(1) = 0 THEN
  7      1                       DO;   IF ABS(Y(1) - REF(1)) < 2. THEN
  9      1    1                     IF(ABS(Y(1) - REF(1) + Y(2)) ¬< ABS(Y(1) - REF(1))
 10      1    1                        | ABS(Y(2)) < .25 ) THEN I = 1;
 11      1    1                  END;
 12      1                    IF P(2) = 0 THEN
 13      1                       DO;   IF ABS(Y(3) - REF(2)) < 2. THEN
 15      1    1                     IF(ABS(Y(3) - REF(2) + Y(4)) ¬< ABS(Y(3) - REF(2))
 16      1    1                        | ABS(Y(4)) < .25 ) THEN I = 2;
 17      1    1                  END;
 18      1                    RETURN;
 19      1                    TOLER: ENTRY(Y,N,T,I,H);
 20      1                    H = 3;
 21      1                    RETURN;
 22      1                 END CHECK;
```

Figure 9.13 The CHECK procedure for the modified elevator system example.

ARRIVE: PROCEDURE;   /*ELEVATOR ARRIVES AT A FLOOR*/

```
STMT LEVEL NEST
  1                    ARRIVE: PROCEDURE;   /*ELEVATOR ARRIVES AT A FLOOR*/
  2     1                DCL (TIME,ENDTIME,TYPE) FLOAT EXTERNAL, STOP FIXED BIN(31) EXTERNAL;
  3     1                DCL (FLOOR(2,11),D(2),S(2,11),P(2)) FIXED BIN(15) EXTERNAL;
  4     1                DCL (SCHEDUL,CAR1,CAR2,WAITING,OUT) POINTER EXTERNAL;
  5     1                DCL INFO(5) FLOAT EXTERNAL;
  6     1                DCL DEON FIXED BIN(15) EXTERNAL;
  7     1                DCL (X(4),REF(2)) FLOAT EXTERNAL;
  8     1                DCL (CAR,PNTR) POINTER;
  9     1                  ELNUM = INFO(3);   FLNUM = REF(ELNUM)/10.;
 11     1                  IF ELNUM = 1 THEN CAR = CAR1;   ELSE CAR = CAR2;
 14     1                  I = 3;   NUMEX = 0;
 16     1                  CALL FINDELE(CAR,I,'EQU',FLNUM,PNTR);
 17     1                  IF (PNTR ¬= NULL) THEN   /*UNLOAD PASSENGERS*/
 18     1                    DO;
 19     1   1              DO WHILE(PNTR ¬= NULL);
 20     1   2                CALL GETELE(CAR,INFO,PNTR);   NUMEX = NUMEX + 1;
 22     1   2                CALL ADDTO(OUT,INFO);   /*PUT DEPARTING PASSENGERS INTO OUT*/
 23     1   2                CALL FINDELE(CAR,I,'EQU',FLNUM,PNTR);   END;
 25     1   1              END;
 26     1                  IF FLNUM = 1 THEN D(ELNUM) = 1;
 28     1                  IF FLNUM = 11 THEN D(ELNUM) = 2;
 30     1                  NUMWT = FLOOR(D(ELNUM),FLNUM);   J = 2;
 32     1                  IF (NUMWT ¬= 0) THEN   /*LOAD WAITING PASSENGERS*/
 33     1                    DO;   I = 1;   K = 1;
 36     1   1              DO WHILE(I ¬> NUMWT & K ¬> 20);
 37     1   2                CALL FINDELE(WAITING,J,'EQU',FLNUM,PNTR);
 38     1   2                CALL GETELE(WAITING,INFO,PNTR);   /*GET PASSENGER AT THIS FLOOR*/
 39     1   2                IF INFO(2) < INFO(3) THEN DIREC = 1;   ELSE DIREC = 2;
 42     1   2                IF D(ELNUM) = DIREC THEN   /*MOVE PASSENGER TO CAR*/
 43     1   2                  DO;   INFO(4) = TIME;   CALL ADDTO(CAR,INFO);
 46     1   3                  S(ELNUM,INFO(3)) = 1;   I = I + 1;   END;
 49     1   2                ELSE CALL ADDTO(WAITING,INFO);   /*NOT RIGHT DIRECTION*/
 50     1   2                K = K + 1;   END;
 52     1   1              END;
 53     1                  P(ELNUM) = FLNUM;   /*CLEAR ARRAYS FOR THIS FLOOR*/
 54     1                  IF (P(1) ¬= 0 & P(2) ¬=0) THEN DEON = 0;
 56     1                  FLOOR(D(ELNUM),FLNUM) = 0;   S(ELNUM,FLNUM) = 0;
 58     1                  INFO(1) = TIME + 5 + NUMEX + NUMWT;
 59     1                  INFO(2) = 3;   INFO(3) = ELNUM;
 61     1                  CALL ADDTO(SCHEDUL,INFO);   /*SCHEDULE DEPARTURE*/
 62     1                  RETURN;
 63     1                END ARRIVE;
```

Figure 9.14 The ARRIVE procedure for the modified elevator system example.

would probably be required only if the simulation study included modifications in this motion. If, for example, the effect of changes in the elevator motor were to be considered, the differential equations of motion are needed. Otherwise, the period of time required to move from floor to floor can be adequately represented by delays in a totally discrete model. However, these delays should be more complex functions than the constants used in the earlier version of this example.

9.4 A NATURAL RESOURCE MANAGEMENT EXAMPLE

In this section, a model is developed for a hypothetical example of the growth pattern of two species of fish. The model is used to illustrate how simulation can be applied to manage, for the purpose of achieving increased productivity, a system occurring in nature. The example includes aspects of competitive behavior which do occur in the natural environment, although real biological systems require far more complex models in order to include all the significant interactive variables and parameters. The purpose of the example is to show that the study of such systems requires combined discrete and continuous simulations and to demonstrate certain techniques useful in programming these simulations.

```
                LEAVE: PROCEDURE;

STMT LEVEL NEST
  1                       LEAVE: PROCEDURE;
  2      1                   DCL (TIME,ENDTIME,TYPE) FLOAT EXTERNAL, STOP FIXED BIN(31) EXTERNAL;
  3      1                   DCL (SCHEDUL,CAR1,CAR2,WAITING,OUT) POINTER EXTERNAL;
  4      1                   DCL (FLOOR(2,11),D(2),S(2,11),P(2),ALT) FIXED BIN(15) EXTERNAL;
  5      1                   DCL (INFO(5),W(2),REF(2)) FLOAT EXTERNAL, CAR POINTER;
  6      1                   DCL DEON FIXED BIN(15) EXTERNAL;
  7      1                       ELNUM = INFO(3);     FLNUM = P(ELNUM);
  9      1                       IF D(ELNUM) = 3 THEN    /*SEND TO CALLER*/
 10      1                           DO;   NXFL = INFO(4);    D(ELNUM) = INFO(5);     END;
 14      1                       ELSE   /*FIND NEXT STOP*/
 14      1                           DO;   IF ALT = 1 THEN CALL ALTSTG(ELNUM,FLNUM);
 17      1      1                       OVR = 0;    NXFL = FLNUM;
 19      1      1                       IF D(ELNUM) = 1 THEN M = 1;    ELSE M = -1;
 22      1      1                       IF D(ELNUM) = 1 THEN N = 1;    ELSE N = 2;
 25      1      1                       DO WHILE((NXFL + M) < 12 & (NXFL + M) > 0 & OVR = 0);
 26      1      2                           NXFL = NXFL + M;    IF FLOOR(N,NXFL) ¬= 0 THEN OVR = 1;
 29      1      2                           IF (S(ELNUM,NXFL) = 1) THEN OVR = 1;     END;
 32      1      1                       IF OVR = 0 THEN    /*NO MORE SCHEDULED STOPS*/
 33      1      1                           DO;   IF D(ELNUM) = 1 THEN    /*CHECK FOR DOWN CALLS*/
 35      1      2                               DO;    L = 2;    I = 11;    K = -1;    J = 1;    END;
 41      1      2                           ELSE   /*CHECK FOR UP CALLS*/
 41      1      2                               DO; L = 1;    I = 1;    K = 1;    J = 11;    END;
 47      1      2                           DO WHILE(FLOOR(L,I) = 0 & I ¬= J);
 48      1      3                               I = I + K;    END;
 50      1      2                           IF I ¬= J THEN    /*CHANGE DIRECTION OF TRAVEL*/
 51      1      2                               DO;    D(ELNUM) = L;    NXFL = I;    END;
 55      1      2                           ELSE /*CHECK FOR PASSENGERS BELOW GOING UP OR ABOVE GOING DOWN*/
 55      1      2                               DO;    /*I IS NOW 1 OR 11*/
 56      1      3                                   DO WHILE(FLOOR(N,I) = 0 & I ¬= FLNUM);
 57      1      4                                       I = I + M;    END;
 59      1      3                                   IF I = FLNUM  THEN    /*SET ELEVATOR IDLE*/
 60      1      3                                       DO;   D(ELNUM) = 3;    RETURN;    END;
 64      1      3                                   NXFL = I;    END;
 66      1      2                           END;
 67      1      1                       END;
 68      1                       IF ELNUM = 1 THEN CAR = CAR1;    ELSE CAR = CAR2;
 71      1                       CALL KOUNT(CAR,NUMPASS);
 72      1                       IF NUMPASS > 14 THEN    /*CAR OVERLOADED*/
 73      1                           DO;    I = NUMPASS - 14;    NUMPASS = 14;
 76      1      1                           DO J = 1 TO I;    CALL GETBOT(CAR,INFO);
 78      1      2                               CALL ADDTO(WAITING,INFO);    END;
 80      1      1                           FLOOR(D(ELNUM),FLNUM) = FLOOR(D(ELNUM),FLNUM) + I;    END;
 82      1                       REF(ELNUM) = 10.*NXFL;    W(ELNUM) = 140.*NUMPASS;
 84      1                       DEON = 1;    P(ELNUM) = 0;
 86      1                       RETURN;
 87      1                   END LEAVE;
```

Figure 9.15 The LEAVE procedure for the modified elevator system example.

Assume that there is a species of small fish living in a lake. If x denotes the number of these fish, then the rate of increase of these fish, in the absence of any limiting factors, is approximately described by the equation:

$$\frac{dx}{dt} = ax \tag{1}$$

where a is some constant relating to their natural growth rate. Equation (1) indicates that x will increase exponentially without any limit. In any natural system, there will be a limited amount of resources, such as food or space, to support any species. If we assume that the maximum number of this species which could exist in the lake is equal to a constant b, then a more reasonable growth-rate equation would be

$$\frac{dx}{dt} = ax\left(1 - \frac{x}{b}\right) \tag{2}$$

where the $(1 - x/b)$ term reflects the competition between members of the species

```
        KOUNT: PROCEDURE(NAME,NUM);

STMT LEVEL NEST
  1                      KOUNT: PROCEDURE(NAME,NUM);
  2      1              DCL  1 FOR_EACH_LIST  BASED(PN),
                              2 FIRST         POINTER,
                              2 LAST          POINTER,
                              2 ACCESS        CHARACTER(4),
                              2 PRIO_INDEX    FIXED BINARY(15);
  3      1              DCL  1 LIST_CONTENTS  BASED(PD),
                              2 ITEM(5)       FLOAT,
                              2 NEXT_ELEMENT POINTER;
  4      1              DCL (NAME,IS) POINTER, NUM FIXED BIN(15);
  5      1              NUM = 0;
  6      1              IS = NAME->FIRST;
  7      1              DO WHILE(IS ¬= NULL);
  8      1    1            NUM = NUM + 1;   IS = IS->NEXT_ELEMENT;   END;
 11      1              RETURN;
 12      1          END KOUNT;
```

Figure 9.16 A KOUNT procedure for determining the number of elements in a list.

for resources. For fixed values of a and b, Eq. (2) would result in growth patterns of the type shown in Fig. 9.19.

Next we assume that in this same lake there is a species of large fish whose primary food is the species of small fish. The number of large fish, y, would have a growth-rate equation similar to (2), but the maximum number of this species is limited by the availability of food which is directly related to x, the number of the other species. Thus a reasonable growth-rate equation for the species of large fish is

$$\frac{dy}{dt} = cy\left(\frac{x}{d} - \frac{y}{e}\right) \tag{3}$$

Of course, if the small fish are being eaten by the large fish, the growth rate for x

```
        LIFT: PROCEDURE OPTIONS(MAIN);

STMT LEVEL NEST
  1                   LIFT: PROCEDURE OPTIONS(MAIN);
  2      1            DCL (TIME,ENDTIME,TYPE) FLOAT EXTERNAL, STOP FIXED BIN(31) EXTERNAL;
  3      1            DCL INFO(5) FLOAT EXTERNAL;
  4      1            DCL (SCHEDUL,CAR1,CAR2,WAITING,OUT) POINTER EXTERNAL;
  5      1            DCL (FLOOR(2,11),O(2),S(2,11),P(2),ALT) FIXED BIN(15) EXTERNAL;
  6      1            DCL OEON FIXED BIN(15) EXTERNAL;
  7      1            DCL SEED(8) FIXED BINARY(31) EXTERNAL INITIAL(1956987325,1156987325,
                      1908986925,1508586121,1468582113,1472622913,1480662953,1521070957);
  8      1            DCL OBSVDAT(2,3) FLOAT EXTERNAL;
  9      1            DCL (HISTPAR(13,3),HISTDAT(13,11)) FLOAT EXTERNAL;
 10      1            DCL (AVIAT,B(11,2),C(11,2)) FLOAT EXTERNAL;
 11      1            DCL (X(4),H,DETIME) FLOAT EXTERNAL, N FIXED BIN(15) EXTERNAL;
 12      1            DCL (ABSERR(4),RELERR(4)) FLOAT EXTERNAL;
 13      1            DCL (M,K1,K2,K3,K4,E,W(2),REF(2)) FLOAT EXTERNAL;
 14      1              HISTPAR(*,1) = 1.;   HISTPAR(*,2) = 1.;    HISTPAR(*,3) = 10.;
 17      1              HISTPAR(12,1) = 60.;   HISTPAR(12,2) = 3);   HISTPAR(12,3) = 10.;
 20      1              HISTPAR(13,1) = 60.;   HISTPAR(13,2) = 30.;   HISTPAR(13,3) = 10.;
 23      1              DO I = 1 TO 4;    ABSERR(I) = .001;   RELERR(I) = .002;   END;
 27      1              M = 100.;    K1 = 100.;   K2 = 1900.;   K3 = 1.;   K4 = 20.;
 32      1              E = 200.;   W = 0.;   X = 0.;
 35      1              T = 0.;   H = .1;   N = 4;
 38      1              ALT = 0;   DETIME = 0.;
 40      1              GET LIST(NO_RUNS);
 41      1              DO I = 1 TO NO_RUNS;   CALL CONTROL;   END;
 44      1          END LIFT;
```

Figure 9.17 The main procedure for the modified elevator system example.

```
ELEVATOR  SYSTEM  PERFORMANCE
```

```
SIMULATION  TIME  PERIOD        1801.41

TOTAL  TIME  IN  SYSTEM                MEAN = 137.75987    STD DEV =  69.00040    OBSERVATIONS =    345


DISTRIBUTION

UPPER LIMIT            OBSERVATIONS              PERCENTAGE
   60.00                   56                    0.16232
   90.00                   44                    0.12754
  120.00                   47                    0.13623
  150.00                   44                    0.12754
  180.00                   46                    0.13333
  210.00                   41                    0.11884
  240.00                   42                    0.12174
  270.00                   21                    0.06087
  300.00                    4                    0.01159
  330.00                    0                    0.00000
  360.00                    0                    0.00000

WAITING  TIME                         MEAN =  92.36749    STD DEV =  63.75458    OBSERVATIONS =    345


DISTRIBUTION

UPPER LIMIT            OBSERVATIONS              PERCENTAGE
   60.00                  130                    0.37681
   90.00                   41                    0.11884
  120.00                   42                    0.12174
  150.00                   57                    0.16522
  180.00                   37                    0.10725
  210.00                   30                    0.08696
  240.00                    8                    0.02319
  270.00                    0                    0.00000
  300.00                    0                    0.00000
  330.00                    0                    0.00000
  360.00                    0                    0.00000
```

Figure 9.18 Output for the modified elevator system example.

should be modified to include this effect. So Eq. (2) becomes

$$\frac{dx}{dt} = ax\left(1 - \frac{x}{b}\right) - fy \qquad (4)$$

The system of equations, (3) and (4), describes the primary interaction between the two species of fish. These are nonlinear equations and cannot be solved analytically.

In order to demonstrate certain characteristics of these equations, assume that the constant coefficients have the following values:

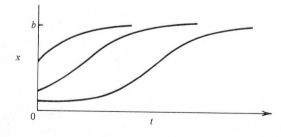

Figure 9.19 S-shaped growth patterns.

$$a = \frac{2}{30} = .667 \quad \text{day}^{-1}$$

$$b = 10,000,000$$

$$c = \frac{2}{90} = .222 \text{ day}^{-1}$$

$$d = 10,000,000$$

$$e = 36,000$$

$$f = 10 \quad \text{day}^{-1}$$

These values imply that the number of small fish x grows at a rate 3 times that of the number of large fish y. If there were no y fish, the maximum number of x fish would be 10,000,000.

With these coefficient values, the two species, if not disturbed by other effects, would reach a stable equilibrium point where

$$x = 4,600,000$$

$$y = 16,560$$

That is, at equilibrium there would be 16,560 predator fish and 4,600,000 of their prey. Now assume that the predator fish have commercial value and, at some point in time, 50 percent of these fish are caught and harvested. Then, the response of the system, i.e., the solution of Eqs. (3) and (4), is as shown in Fig. 9.20.

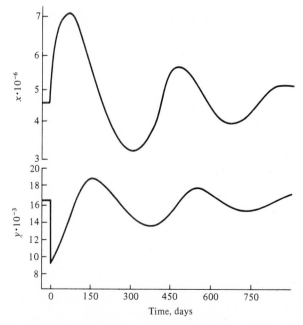

Figure 9.20 Response from equilibrium to a 50 percent harvest of predator.

The figure shows that both populations x and y respond to this disturbance, i.e., the harvesting, with oscillations about their equilibrium values. These oscillations are damped and, if no further disturbances occur, the system will return to the equilibrium state. Note that these oscillations do not have a fixed period and are not in phase.

The behavior of these equations can be better understood by constructing the boundaries between regions in the x and y plane for which the derivatives have positive and negative values. These boundaries are indicated by the solid lines in Fig. 9.21. The trajectory of the solution shown in Fig. 9.20 is indicated in Fig. 9.21 by a dashed line. Note that the direction of this trajectory lies in a different quadrant for each of the four regions determined by the derivative boundaries and that the trajectory becomes horizontal or vertical as it crosses these boundaries.

If we assume that the objective of managing this lake is to maximize the number of predator fish that can be caught per unit of time, then we are interested in determining the pattern for fishing which will yield this result. If the fishing operation is carried out by seining, then two parameters can be used to specify the fishing pattern: the period between the catches and the amount of predator fish taken each time. Using a simulation of this system and a search over a restricted range of these two parameters leads to an approximate optimal fishing pattern, which is to carry out the seining operation every 90 days and take 65 percent of the predators, or about 10,000 fish at each harvest. The system trajectory for this procedure is also shown in Fig. 9.21.

This optimal harvest policy keeps the system in a region where the growth rate of y is always relatively large, so that the average production of this species is increased. The optimization criterion assumed a small cost for the harvesting, and this solution is only an example of the type of optimal system operation for this process. The important point is that it is possible to operate the system in a

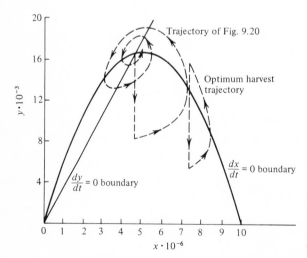

Figure 9.21 Trajectory characteristics for Eqs. (3) and (4).

region far from its equilibrium point in order to take advantage of its dynamic characteristics.

This is a hypothetical example and is not based on any real system. However, the predator-prey equations, (3) and (4), are typical of a class of equations which do approximate certain processes that occur in nature. The constants used with this example were selected in order to illustrate a particular type of behavior which is important in resource management. The purpose of this example is to introduce these properties of some natural systems, but the equations are much simpler than those for real systems.

There are several types of modifications that may be made to the system equations to approximate a more realistic model. One type of modification that is particularly important in simulation studies is the inclusion of random effects. Many random effects occur in environmental systems, but for this example, we will only consider one: the effect of weather on the growth rates of the two species of fish.

We shall assume that the major variations in growth rate are due to changes in average daily temperature and that the average yearly variations in this quantity can be approximated by a sinusoidal function. That is, we assume the average daily temperature, T, is approximated by

$$T = T_M + T_v \sin(\omega t + \psi) \tag{5}$$

where t = measure of time in days

ω = a constant such that 365ω equals 2π radians

ψ = a phase angle which is dependent on the choice of origin for t

The constant T_M is the mean annual temperature and T_v is an appropriate constant related to the change between average daily temperature in summer and winter. The random variations in T due to weather changes will be included by adding two random components, D_d and D_w, to this function as follows:

$$T = T_M + T_v \sin(\omega t + \psi + D_w) + D_d$$

The variable D_d represents daily weather variations and D_w represents longer-term weather patterns. The variable D_w is assumed to be a correlated time series represented by

$$D_w(\tau) = \phi_1 D_w(\tau - 1) + \phi_2 D_w(\tau - 2) + a_\tau$$

where a_τ is an independent, normally distributed random variable. The period of this series, τ, is assumed to be 1 week. The variable D_d will be assumed to be an independent random variable having some specified distribution and which changes each day.

The specific model used for average daily temperature will be

$$T = 60 + 20 \sin(.0172t + 4.96 + D_w) - (D_d - 5) \tag{6}$$

with D_d exponentially distributed with a mean of 5. The variable D_w will be assigned a new value each week using the autoregressive model:

$$D_w(\tau) = .8D_w(\tau - 1) - .2D_w(\tau - 2) + a_\tau \qquad (7)$$

with a_τ normally distributed with a mean of 0 and a standard deviation of .05. Equation (6) assumes the time variable has units of days and that the origin ($t = 0$) corresponds to January 1.

The model specified by Eqs. (6) and (7) is not a standard form for representing temperature variations. More commonly, extensive historical data is used to specify statistical descriptions for this quantity. However, this type of model is capable of representing average daily temperature variations, and its structure is typical of many models of random variations that are used with simulation studies.

The effect of average daily temperature on growth rates is

1. If T is greater than 60, growth rates are normal.
2. If T is less than 30, there is no growth.
3. For T between 30 and 60, the growth rate varies linearly with T; e.g., at $T = 45$, the growth rate is 50 percent of its normal value

Even though the random variables in Eq. (6) are functions of time, they cannot be generated conveniently in the DERIV procedure. Recall that the integration procedure evaluates the derivative several times during each step when integrating the differential equations. In order to achieve accurate integration, the random value must remain constant during each integration step. A convenient method for generating the random values is to use a discrete event for this purpose.

This approach to integrating the system equations is illustrated by the procedures listed in Figs. 9.22 to 9.24. The random values are generated by event routines contained in the procedure of Fig. 9.22. This procedure also contains the event routine HARVEST, which corresponds to the fishing operation where a

```
        DTMPVAR: PROCEDURE;

STMT LEVEL NEST
   1              DTMPVAR: PROCEDURE;
   2       1        DCL (TIME,ENDTIME,TYPE) FLOAT EXTERNAL, STOP FIXED BIN(31) EXTERNAL;
   3       1        DCL SCHEDUL POINTER EXTERNAL;
   4       1        DCL INFO(5) FLOAT EXTERNAL;
   5       1        DCL (X(2),PC) FLOAT EXTERNAL;
   6       1        DCL (DD,DW) FLOAT EXTERNAL;
   7       1        DCL (DWM1,DWM2) FLOAT STATIC;
   8       1        I = 1;   U = 5.;   DD = RNEXP(I,U);
  11       1        INFO(1) = TIME + 1.;   INFO(2) = 1;
  13       1        CALL ADDTO(SCHEDUL,INFO);
  14       1        RETURN;
  15       1        WTMPVAR: ENTRY;
  16       1        I = 1;   U = 0;   S = .05;   A = RNNORM(I,U,S);
  20       1        DW = 0.8*DWM1 - 0.2*DWM2 + A;
  21       1        DWM2 = DWM1;   DWM1 = DW;
  23       1        INFO(1) = TIME + 7.;   INFO(2) = 2;
  25       1        CALL ADDTO(SCHEDUL,INFO);
  26       1        RETURN;
  27       1        HARVEST: ENTRY;
  28       1        X(1) = X(1)*PC;
  29       1        RETURN;
  30       1      END DTMPVAR;
```

Figure 9.22 Event routines for the natural resource management example.

```
                DERIV: PROCEDURE(X,F,T);


STMT LEVEL NEST
  1                  DERIV: PROCEDURE(X,F,T);
  2     1             DCL (A,B,C,D,L,K) FLOAT EXTERNAL;
  3     1             DCL (X(2),F(2),T) FLOAT;
  4     1             DCL (DD,DW) FLOAT EXTERNAL;
  5     1             E = X(2)/K;
  6     1             F(1) = B*X(1)*(E - X(1)/L);
  7     1             F(2) = A*X(2)*(1. - E) - D*X(1);
  8     1             TEMP = 60. + 20.*SIN(.0172*T    + 4.96 + DW) - (DD - 5.);
  9     1             IF TEMP > 60. THEN ACTFAC = 1.;
 11     1                ELSE IF TEMP < 30. THEN ACTFAC = 0.;
 13     1                        ELSE ACTFAC = (TEMP - 30.)/30.;
 14     1             F(1) = F(1) *ACTFAC;
 15     1             F(2) = F(2) *ACTFAC;
 16     1             RETURN;
 17     1           END DERIV;
```

Figure 9.23 Procedure for evaluating derivatives of the predator-prey equations.

certain percentage of the predator fish is removed from the system. The average daily temperature is computed in the DERIV procedure of Fig. 9.23 and will vary slightly within any single integration step because of the time variable, but the random values will remain constant. The CONTROL procedure, Fig. 9.24, for

```
       CONTROL: PROCEDURE; /*TIMING ROUTINE*/


STMT LEVEL NEST
  1                 CONTROL: PROCEDURE; /*TIMING ROUTINE*/
  2     1            DCL (TIME,ENDTIME,TYPE) FLOAT EXTERNAL, STOP FIXED BIN(31) EXTERNAL;
  3     1            DCL SCHEDUL POINTER EXTERNAL ;
  4     1            DCL INFO(5) FLOAT EXTERNAL;
  5     1            DCL (X(2),H,DETIME) FLOAT EXTERNAL, N FIXED BIN(15) EXTERNAL;
  6     1            DCL DEON FIXED BIN(15) EXTERNAL;
  7     1            CALL INITIAL;   /*INITIALIZE THE SYSTEM*/
  8     1            DO WHILE (TIME < ENDTIME & STOP = 0);
  9     1   1         CALL GETTOP(SCHEDUL,INFO);
 10     1   1         IF SUM(INFO) = 0 THEN STOP = 1;
 12     1   1         ELSE DO;    DETIME = TIME;
 14     1   2          TIME = INFO(1);    TYPE = INFO(2);
                      /*INTEGRATE STATE EQUATIONS*/
 16     1   2          IP = 0;   IC = 0;   HA = H;
 19     1   2          DO WHILE(IP = 0 & DEON = 1);
 20     1   3           CALL INTEGRA(X,N,HA,DETIME);
 21     1   3           IF STOP = 1 THEN RETURN;
 23     1   3           CALL CHECK(IC);   /*TEST FOR STATE EVENT OCCURANCE*/
 24     1   3           IF IC = 0 THEN    /*CONTINUE INTEGRATION*/
 25     1   3            DO;   IF (DETIME + HA) >= TIME THEN
 27     1   4                   DO;   /*ADJUST STEP TO DISCREET EVENT TIME*/
 28     1   5                    HA = TIME - DETIME;
 29     1   5                    CALL INTEGRA(X,N,HA,DETIME);
 30     1   5                    IP = 1;   END;
 32     1   4                END;
 33     1   3           ELSE DO;  /*GENERATE STATE EVENT*/
 34     1   4             CALL ADDTO(SCHEDUL,INFO);   /*REPLACE NEXT EVENT*/
 35     1   4             TIME = DETIME;    TYPE = 3;   IP = 1;
 38     1   4           END;
 39     1   3          END;
                      /*EXECUTE DISCREET EVENT*/
 40     1   2          IF TYPE = 1 THEN CALL DTMPVAR;
 42     1   2          ELSE
 42     1   2          IF TYPE = 2 THEN CALL WTMPVAR;
 44     1   2          ELSE
 44     1   2          IF TYPE = 3 THEN CALL HARVEST;
 46     1   2          END;
 47     1   1         CALL STAT;   /*COLLECT STATISTICS*/
 48     1   1         END;
 49     1            CALL OUTPUT;   /*PRINT REPORT*/
 50     1            RETURN;
 51                 END CONTROL;
```

Figure 9.24 The CONTROL procedure for the natural resource management example.

this example is similar to the version shown in Fig. 9.11 and uses the same integration procedure shown in Fig. 9.6.

For this version of the simulation program, it is assumed that the fishing operation is a dependent event which occurs because of some condition detected by the CHECK procedure. In systems of this type, more productive management can usually be achieved by adjusting operations to system conditions. That is, in this example, more fish can be caught by harvesting when the system variables x and y meet certain conditions rather than by harvesting at fixed intervals or at fixed dates. This, of course, assumes that there is some method available to obtain physical measurements which can be used to estimate these variables.

The CHECK procedure is internal to the STAT procedure, shown in Fig. 9.25. This STAT procedure includes output statements for the random variables and stores selected values of the fish populations for use in the OUTPUT procedure. This OUTPUT procedure is internal to the INITIAL procedure as shown in Fig. 9.26.

The main procedure for this example is shown in Fig. 9.27. This version of the simulation program uses equilibrium conditions for the initial population values and a rule for harvesting which closely corresponds to that for the optimum harvest trajectory shown in Fig. 9.21. The plot produced by the OUTPUT procedure for these conditions is shown in Fig. 9.28. The primary effect on the system trajectory due to the addition of the average daily temperature influence on growth rate is to modify the time scale.

Even with the simplified equations of this example, the inclusion of random effects and a more comprehensive optimization criterion causes the search for an optimum harvesting policy to become a fairly lengthy process. Thus, problems of this type with more realistic models for natural systems usually result in large computational tasks. The solution of these problems can be very useful and does require combined discrete-event and continuous model simulations.

```
          STAT: PROCEDURE;

STMT LEVEL NEST
  1                     STAT: PROCEDURE;
  2      1              CCL (TIME,ENCTIME,TYPE) FLCAT EXTERNAL;
  3      1              CCL (DD,DW) FLCAT EXTERNAL;
  4      1              CCL (X(2),XP(52,2)) FLOAT EXTERNAL;
  5      1              CCL TOTC FLOAT STATIC INITIAL(0);
  6      1              IF TYPE = 1 THEN
  7      1                DO;
  8      1   1            PUT EDIT('DD = ',DD,'  AT TIME',TIME)(SKIP,A,F(4,1),A,F(5,0));
  9      1   1            TEMP = 60. + 20.*SIN(.0172*TIME + 4.96 + DW) - (DD - 5.);
 10      1   1            PUT EDIT(' TEMPERATURE = ',TEMP,', PCP ',X)(A,F(6,2),A,
 11      1   1              2 F(10,0));   END;
 12      1              ELSE IF TYPE = 2 THEN DC;  L = TIME/7.;   XP(L,*) = X;
 16      1   1            PUT EDIT('DW = ',DW,'  AT TIME',TIME)(SKIP,A,F(6,3),A,F(5,0));
 17      1   1            END;
 18      1              ELSE IF TYPE = 3 THEN DO;   TOTC = TCTC + (X(1)/.35)*.65;
 21      1   1            PUT EDIT('TOTAL CATCH =',TCTC) (SKIP,A,F(7,0));
 22      1   1              END;
 23      1              RETURN;
 24      1            CHECK: ENTRY(IC);
 25      1              IF X(1) > 1E600. THEN IC = 3;
 27      1                ELSE IC = 0;
 28      1              RETURN;
 29      1            ENC STAT;
```

Figure 9.25 The STAT procedure for the natural resource management example.

```
        INITIAL: PROCEDURE;

STMT LEVEL NEST
  1                    INITIAL: PROCEDURE;
  2      1               CCL SCHEDUL PCINTER EXTERNAL ;
  3      1                 I = 1;    CALL INITLST(SCHEDUL,'PRIO',I);
  5      1                 CALL DTMPVAR;    CALL WTMPVAR;
  7      1                 RETURN;
  8      1               OUTPUT: ENTRY;
  9      1                 CCL XP(52,2) FLOAT EXTERNAL;
 10      1                 CCL LINE(90) CHARACTER(1);
 11      1                 PUT EDIT('TIME','PREDATOR','PREY')(PAGE,A,X(2),A,X(4),A);
 12      1                 LINE = ' ';
 13      1                 DO I = 1 TC 52;    J = 90.*XF(I,1)/16000.;    K = 90.*(XP(I,2) -
 16      1      1                                    4000000)/6000000;    L = I*7;
 17      1      1               LINE(J) = '*';    LINE(K) = '.';
 19      1      1               PUT EDIT(L,XP(I,*),LINE)(SKIP,F(4,0), 2 F(10,0), 90 A);
 20      1      1               LINE(J) = ' ';    LINE(K) = ' ';
 22      1      1               END;
 23      1                 RETURN;
 24      1               END INITIAL;
```

Figure 9.26 The INITIAL procedure for the natural resource management example.

9.5 BACKGROUND AND REFERENCES

The numerical solution of differential equations is a major topic of many books devoted to numerical analysis and methods. References [2], [6], and [11] are widely used textbooks in this area. The more efficient techniques for the integration of ordinary differential equations make use of the fact that the solutions are continuous. For combined discrete-continuous systems, the solution, in general, is not continuous at the points where discrete events occur. Because of this, these techniques may not give improvement over one-step Runge-Kutta methods in this application. However, this condition depends upon the specific problem.

An improved version of the fourth-order Runge-Kutta integration method is given in Appendix One of Pritsker [9]. Integration routines from mathematical packages, such as DVERK from the IMSL [7], can be substituted for the INTE-GRA procedure given in this chapter by changing the parameter arguments passed to the procedure.

```
        FISHEX: PROCEDURE OPTIONS(MAIN);

STMT LEVEL NEST
  1                    FISHEX: PROCEDURE OPTIONS(MAIN);
  2      1               CCL (TIME,ENDTIME,TYPE) FLOAT EXTERNAL, STOP FIXED BIN(31) EXTERNAL;
  3      1               CCL SCHEDUL POINTER EXTERNAL;
  4      1               CCL INFO(5) FLOAT EXTERNAL;
  5      1               CCL XP(52,2) FLOAT EXTERNAL;
  6      1               CCL SEED(8) FIXED BINARY(31) EXTERNAL INITIAL(1956987325,1156987325,
                           1908986925,1508586121,1468582113,1472622913,1480662953,1521070957);
  7      1               CCL (X(2),H,DETIME) FLOAT EXTERNAL, N FIXED BIN(15) EXTERNAL;
  8      1               CCL DEON FIXED BIN(15) EXTERNAL;
  9      1               DCL(A,B,C,D,L,K) FLOAT EXTERNAL;
 10      1               CCL (ABSERR(4),RELERR(4)) FLOAT EXTERNAL;
 11      1               CCL PC FLOAT EXTERNAL;
 12      1                 PC = .35;
 13      1                 ABSERR(1) = 1.;    ABSERR(2) = 100.;    RELERR = .0001;
 16      1                 A = 2./30.;    B = 2./90.;    C = 1.0E-7;    K = 1.0E+7;    L = 36000.;
 21      1                 D = 10.;    N = 2;    H = .5;
 24      1                 TIME = 0.;    ENDTIME = 365.;    DEON = 1;
 27      1                 X(1) = 16560.;    X(2) = 4600000.;
 29      1                 CALL CONTROL;
 30      1               END FISHEX;
```

Figure 9.27 The main procedure for the natural resource management example.

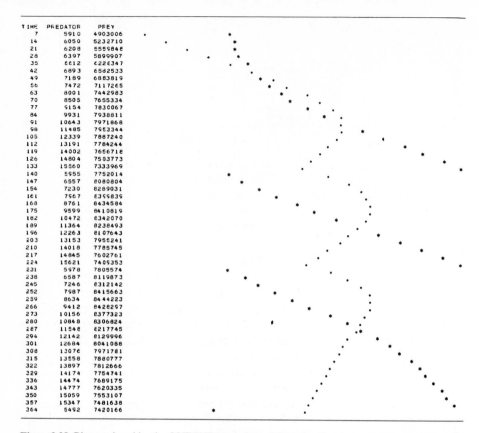

TIME	PREDATOR	PREY
7	5910	4903006
14	6050	5232710
21	6208	5559846
28	6397	5899907
35	6612	6226347
42	6893	6582533
49	7189	6883819
56	7472	7117265
63	8001	7442983
70	8505	7655334
77	9154	7830067
84	9931	7938811
91	10643	7971868
98	11485	7953344
105	12339	7887240
112	13191	7784244
119	14002	7656718
126	14804	7503773
133	15560	7333969
140	5955	7752014
147	6557	8080804
154	7230	8289031
161	7967	8359839
168	8761	8434584
175	9599	8410819
182	10472	8342070
189	11364	8238493
196	12263	8107643
203	13153	7955241
210	14018	7785745
217	14845	7602761
224	15621	7409353
231	5978	7805574
238	6587	8119873
245	7246	8312142
252	7987	8415663
259	8634	8444223
266	9412	8428297
273	10156	8377323
280	10848	8306824
287	11548	8217745
294	12142	8129996
301	12684	8041088
308	13076	7971781
315	13558	7880777
322	13897	7812666
329	14174	7754741
336	14474	7689175
343	14777	7620335
350	15059	7553107
357	15347	7481638
364	5492	7420166

Figure 9.28 Plot produced by the OUTPUT procedure of the natural resource management example.

The GASP simulation language [9, 10] includes features for handling combined discrete-continuous models, and SIMSCRIPT can be readily extended to these models [4].

The model used to represent the elevator car dynamics is a simplified but typical example of an engineering control system. An extensive theory has been developed for the analysis and design of these systems, and simulation is also widely used in their development [3, 8, 12]. In fact, simulation of continuous models is used in many areas of engineering design and probably represents the area of most successful practical application of computer simulation.

An introduction to the modeling approach used for the competition between two species is given in Section 9.2 of the book by Bender [1]. A more extensive discussion of this type of model may be found in reference [5].

REFERENCES

1. Bender, E. A.: "An Introduction to Mathematical Modeling," Wiley, New York, 1978.
2. Carnahan, B., H. A. Luther, and J. O. Wilkes: "Applied Numerical Methods," Wiley, New York, 1969.

3. D'Azzo, J. J., and C. H. Houpis: "Linear Control System Analysis and Design," McGraw-Hill, New York, 1975.
4. Delfosse, C. M.: "Continuous and Combined Simulation in SIMSCRIPT II.5," C.A.C.I., Inc., Arlington, Va., 1976.
5. Goel, N. S., S. C. Maitra, and E. W. Montroll: "On the Volterra and Other Nonlinear Models of Interacting Populations," *Review of Modern Physics*, vol. 43, pp. 231–276, 1971.
6. Hornbeck, R. W.: "Numerical Methods," Quantum Publishers, New York, 1975.
7. International Mathematical and Statistical Libraries, Inc.: "Reference Manual," IMSL LIB2-0006, Houston, Tex., 1977.
8. Kuo, B. C.: "Automatic Control Systems," 3d ed., Prentice-Hall, Englewood Cliffs, N.J., 1975.
9. Pritsker, A. A. B: "The GASP IV Simulation Language," Wiley, New York, 1974.
10. Pritsker, A. A. B., and R. E. Young: "Simulation with GASP-PL/1," Wiley, New York, 1975.
11. Ralston, A.: "A First Course in Numerical Analysis," McGraw-Hill, New York, 1965.
12. Shinners, S. M.: "Modern Control System Theory and Application," 2d ed., Addison-Wesley, Reading, Mass., 1978.

EXERCISES

9.1 Consider the elevator-position control described in Sec. 9.1. If the constant K_4 was reduced in value from 20 ft to 5 ft, what would be the effect on the motion of the elevator car?

9.2 The following coupled differential equations describe a servo-control system:

$$\ddot{x} + 18\dot{x} + 40x = y$$

$$\dot{y} + 7.2y = f(t) - x$$

where the variable $f(t)$ is an input to the system. Assume that these equations are to be integrated using the INTEGRA procedure of Fig. 9.6. Write an appropriate DERIV procedure for this program.

9.3 An alternate elevator-position control system could be used which has proportional plus integral compensation. That is, the motor-control voltage e_c could be generated by the function:

$$e_c = \frac{E}{K_4}(x_r - x) + K_5 \int_{t_r}^{t} (x_r - x)\, dt$$

where t_r is the time of departure for x_r. Modify the elevator example program of this chapter to simulate this type of control with $K_5 = 5$. *Hint*:

$$e_c(t_r) = \frac{E}{K_4}[x_r - x(t_r)]$$

$$\frac{de_c}{dt} = \frac{E}{K_4}\left(\frac{-dx}{dt}\right) + K_5(x_r - x)$$

9.4 What is the expected average temperature on the first day of spring (March 21) when using the model of Sec. 9.4?

9.5 For certain initial conditions, the predator-prey equations of Sec. 9.4 become unstable. Use the program of this section to find the nature of this instability.

TEN

A CRITIQUE OF THE SIMULATION APPROACH

The previous chapters have presented some of the techniques used in computer-based simulation studies. The emphasis has been on illustrating the details of procedures required for the programming and analysis of simulation models. Now that you have studied how to carry out simulations, the question as to when this approach should be used has no doubt occurred to you. That is, what problems should be solved with simulation techniques, and what conditions are necessary to achieve successful results?

These questions as to the proper use of simulation do not have well-defined answers. There have been many subjective discussions of the appropriate use of simulations, but these opinions have changed over a period of time and are the subject of considerable controversy. However, these questions are important and should be examined.

Our approach in this chapter will be to consider some problems that lead to simulation studies, to review a bit of the history of simulation, and to speculate of the direction of future developments. The objective is not to thoroughly cover these topics but to introduce the subjects and to indicate the nature of some basic ideas in these areas. Much of the literature on simulation emphasizes that this method is very much an intuitive process where success or failure depends heavily on the judgment and experience of those applying this tool. As an aid to intuition, it is important to form a perspective of the subject. The material in this chapter is intended to provide both encouragement and a starting point for further studies that will help you form a personal framework for relating the varied ideas and achievements of this field.

10.1 COMPUTING FOR INSIGHT

In the 1960s and 1970s, digital computer systems changed from specialized equipment understood and utilized by a small number of people to a basic component used in almost all areas of manufacturing, commerce, and government. The primary motivation for using these systems is to achieve economy. This has been achieved most readily and most widely in clerical-type work, that is, in maintaining records and generating printed material based on the information contained in those records. In applications of this type, the computer has been used to do what had previously been done by people, but faster, more accurately, and cheaper. Over a period of time, the manner in which these functions are carried out by computers has changed, but the basic functions are the same as were developed before the availability of these machines.

A second type of application is to do jobs which would not be feasible without computers. The computer characteristics that make it possible to do these new operations are speed, accuracy, and reliability. Systems of this type usually involve the computer functioning interactively with other machines or with humans. Applications of this kind have developed more slowly than those of the clerical type because they require greater change. This change is not just the introduction of computer equipment to facilitate present procedures but is also the introduction of new procedures, which usually means more people involved in greater adjustments.

A third category of computer applications has been described by the phrase "computing for insight." A major application of this kind is the use of computers to solve mathematical problems in the area of science and engineering. An early book on methods for these problems, by Hamming [5], used as a motto: "The purpose of computing is insight, not numbers." This may be interpreted in several ways, and one point of view is that the purpose of science is to achieve insight and that the computer can be used as a tool for science.

Simulations fall within the category of computing for insight. The goal of these projects is to increase understanding of the system studied and to be able to predict how the system will behave in the future and under altered conditions. This is, in essence, the same goal as that of science. So, from a philosophical standpoint, we may assume that the reason for using simulation is to extend scientific knowledge.

The basic procedure of the scientific method may be described as consisting of the following four steps:

1. Obtain observations or measurements of a physical system.
2. Formulate a hypothesis that attempts to explain the observations of the system.
3. On the basis of the hypothesis, by mathematical or logical deduction, predict future system behavior under altered conditions.
4. Test the hypothesis by performing experiments on the system such that predicted behavior can be compared with observations.

In simulation studies, step 2, the formulation of a hypothesis, corresponds to the construction of a programmed model; and step 3, the deduction process, is done by executing the program and experimenting with this model. It is important to recognize that building a computer model is not step 1 and performing simulation experiments is not step 4.

Most of the early development of computers was oriented toward obtaining a machine for solving mathematical problems of a type required in step 3 of the scientific procedure. The need for and the potential value of a device to automatically carry out computations was well recognized by physical scientists. The computer has proved to be a powerful tool in these types of applications and is useful in all phases of scientific investigation. In many areas the computer is necessary for continued progress. It is, of course, by no means sufficient to assure progress.

The new opportunities for scientific studies offered by simulation are provided by the new types of hypothesis available with computer models and the solution procedure available for making deductions. It has long been recognized that the behavior of many physical systems could be logically explained by discrete interactions between entities, but the mathematical methods were not available to represent these relations in a formulation from which general deductions could be made. Queuing systems are an example of this type of situation. Although some simple and idealized queuing problems had been solved prior to the availability of computer facilities, these solutions were not extended to more realistic problems nor were they recognized as having wide practical value. With simulation, it was easy to formulate a computer model for systems such as the checkout counter operation described in Chap. 2. There are many systems involving widely different physical entities which include a queuing-type operation. As experience with the simulation of these systems accumulated, it became evident that in many cases the idealized models solved by queuing theory were adequate to give reasonably good approximate solutions. Also, the insights gained through these simulations contributed to the development of many new results in queuing theory. In this manner, simulation has helped to develop scientific theory.

Simulation has been effectively used not only in what may be considered scientific studies but also in the application of knowledge. These applications of previously established results correspond to adapting studies and procedures which have been validated in real systems to slightly different situations. These can be described as design procedures as contrasted with scientific inquiry. The difference is primarily in the degree to which the application differs from previous work. Most practical applications of simulation are in designing because these studies are much more likely to be economically justified.

There are many examples of practical applications of simulation. The extent of its use and the value of the results appear to be increasing. However, there are also many examples where the use of simulation has not been effective. In fact, this situation occurs too frequently to be considered as due to a lack of basic skills or resources by those carrying out such studies. There is little doubt that a major portion of the efforts devoted to simulation studies must be considered wasted in terms of practical utility. Evidently there is some misunderstanding of the proper use of this technique.

The computer was recognized early as a new type of tool and as one which would have a major impact on human activities. As with most new tools, there were those who became overly optimistic as to what was possible with this technology. Many of the anticipated uses of computers have not yet occurred, and many attempts to apply computers have failed. The most common response in these cases has been that all that is needed to overcome the difficulties is cheaper equipment, better programmers, and more time. It is hard to imagine what the ultimate limits of humanity's use of computers will be, but it is necessary to recognize that at any time and for any real conditions there are practical limits as to what can be done. In the application of computers to simulation, this is a particularly significant consideration.

The ease with which simulation can be applied and the type of representations possible with computerized models have provided an impulse to a field of study known as *systems theory*. The rationale for systems theory can be introduced by Aristotle's statement: "The whole is more than the sum of its parts." This is interpreted to mean that when parts are combined and interaction occurs, the whole system contains characteristics or exhibits behavior which is not contained in any of its parts. Systems theory had its origin in biological science, where the methods which have had such great success in physical science seem to be of more limited value. That is, the characteristics of inanimate objects are evidently explained by applying the laws of physics to all the parts, but for living systems it seems that there are characteristics which cannot be explained by more detailed study of component parts. Even with inanimate components, interconnection of well-understood parts can lead to surprising behavior in the resulting system. Examples of this occur in engineering control systems where feedback-type interconnections are used, and there are similarities between the behavior of these systems and that of living systems. The systems theory approach emphasizes research into the organization of systems rather than the more detailed study of their parts.

The goal of systems theory is to establish unifying principles which are applicable to all types of organizations, including biological, behavioral, and social systems. The fact that systems theory is ready to consider, as reasonable subjects of scientific study, such things as large ecological systems, urban development, and the national economy, has given it a certain beguiling appeal.

Systems theory in the widest sense includes a number of distinct fields of study. These include general systems theory [12], cybernetics [15], information theory [10], theory of games [13], and operations research [2]. There are significant differences in the scope and methods of these fields, but they have the common goal of seeking to extend scientific knowledge to systems which exhibit organized complexity. Simulation is an important tool in all these fields and is primarily used for this same goal.

With this viewpoint as to the reason for using simulation, we will next consider the primary limitation to the practical use of simulation. But before moving on, it should be emphasized that at the present time most computer usage is for productive work of the type described in the first two paragraphs of this section. Computing for insight is still a relatively minor part of the total use of computers. Thus, despite the great potential of the computer to extend our understanding of the world, this is not the primary reason for the development of computer technology.

10.2 SIMULATION MODELING

The most critical component of any simulation is the model. A useful model must provide a reasonable approximation of the real system and include the major effects that occur in the system. It must also be simple enough to understand and manipulate and, most importantly, it must be sufficiently simple that the modeling and simulation is economically feasible. Economic feasibility means that the total costs of the project should be justified by the expected gain from its completion. Even if the expected gain is considered priceless, there is still a limitation on the model complexity because of the amount of resources available.

We may consider the development of a model as a scientific study and as such it should proceed by the scientific method. The first step, observation of the system, does not require any specific set of measurements. All that is necessary is sufficient data to formulate an hypothesis. The hypothesis, or in this case the proposed model, can be based not only on measurements of the system but also on the insights and experience of the modeler. In many cases a useful model is more the product of intuition than a logical deduction from observations. The third step of the scientific method applied to developing a simulation model consists of experimenting with the model and uses techniques of the type covered in this book. The fourth step, comparing system behavior with the behavior predicted by the model, is the primary limiting factor in extending the simulation approach.

To understand this limitation, it is helpful to briefly review the major trends in the development of simulation. The first applications of computer-based simulations as a practical, widely based activity with shared technology were in engineering design work for the aircraft and chemical processing industries. This technology was based on the analog computer, which was primarily suited to the solution of ordinary differential equations. In these fields, there was sufficient scientific theory to guide the formulation of continuous-type models for representing complex systems. The computer was needed to solve the models, mainly due to the presence of nonlinear effects. This field developed during the 1950s and was the dominant use of simulation in this period. The value of simulations in these areas is well established and remains an essential element in work of this type. The digital computer, with its additional features, has supplanted the analog computer in most of this work, although analog machines continue to be used for certain functions.

The use of digital computers for simulation opened up the possibility of considering discrete models. Thus, it became much more convenient to study certain types of models which had been developed to describe economic activity and management procedures. This led to the development of simulation as a tool for the management of business enterprises. During the 1960s, an extensive literature appeared describing methods for solving management problems through simulation. These problems included queuing situations, inventory systems, transportation systems, and materials-handling systems. Generally agreed-upon models have evolved for use in these problem areas [8].

While business management applications represent the major new developments in simulation during the 1960s, this decade also included the most notable project in which simulation was a dominant factor. The Apollo project for the manned moon mission is the number one success story of computer-based simulation. This project was dependent on simulation for the design of both the physical equipment and the operational procedures used with the mission. The extensive use of simulation in this project and the successful completion of the project contributed heavily to the confidence held in this technique.

During the 1970s, there was a major effort to extend the application of simulation to governmental policy questions. The motivation for this effort was the desire to address problems of economic development, social relationships, and environmental concerns. The importance of these problems and dissatisfaction with the effectiveness of government policy in these areas became significant political questions in the 1960s. As one element of the response to this situation, government funds were used to support many efforts directed toward developing simulation models for some very large and complex systems. These projects had the ultimate goal of providing methods to evaluate and recommend government policy decisions of far-reaching consequence. It is encouraging to note that there is very little evidence that any of these studies has yet been used to determine any government policy decisions. This is encouraging because it is obvious that none of these models is adequate to predict the major effects that will occur in any real economic system, social organization, or environmental process.

The fundamental problem in developing models for complex biological, economic, or social systems is the impossibility of performing controlled experiments on large, animated systems. Controlled experiments are those in which the environment and conditions of the system are under the complete control of the experimentor. In these situations, the effect of changes in any one system parameter can be determined by holding all other parameters at specified values. Although absolutely complete control over a real system is not possible, in many physical systems, under laboratory conditions, all the significant system parameters can be controlled. This capability of using controlled laboratory experiments to test hypotheses has contributed greatly to the success of the physical sciences.

Controlled experiments are not possible in the study of, for example, economic systems. Consider using changes in tax rates to experimentally determine their effect. If one such rate were lowered for 1 year and raised for the next, the changes observed in some measure, such as unemployment rate during these 2 years, could not be assumed to be caused by the tax rate changes. There are many factors which influence the unemployment rate, and all these factors will not be the same in different years. This is an oversimplified illustration, but it does emphasize the fact that in some systems it is not possible to control the system during experiments intended to test a hypothesis or model.

10.2.1 The Urban Dynamics Model

As an example of the type of problems considered and the approaches used in applying simulation to governmental policy questions, we will consider the Urban Dynamics study by Forrester [3]. This is not really a typical example of studies in this area; in fact, it probably represents the extreme nonempirical approach to developing a model. But it is an easily understood example which illustrates both the problems and the potential of work in this area.

The urban dynamics model is intended to represent the life cycle of a "city" with fixed land boundaries. The primary interest is to show how the population, economic activities, and housing facilities within a city grow and reach an equilibrium over a period of time. The major variables used in the model are represented as the x_i's in Fig. 10.1. Three variables are used to represent each of the three sectors which correspond to business activity, housing supply, and popu-

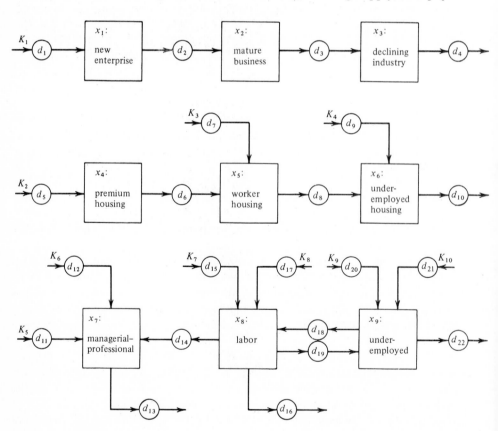

Figure 10.1 Urban dynamics model flowchart.

lation. Businesses are classified as one of three types: a new enterprise (x_1), a mature business (x_2), or a declining industry (x_3). The distinction among these types is that new enterprises are assumed to be more profitable than the average business and to provide employment opportunities with higher-than-average skill level and compensation. Mature businesses correspond to average conditions, and declining industries have lower profits and less desirable employment conditions. The value of x_1 represents the total number of new enterprises, measured in units related to number of employees, at any one point in time. Similarly, x_2 and x_3 represent the total number of mature businesses and declining industries, respectively.

It is assumed that additions to the group of new enterprises occur because of the formation of new companies and that, over a period of time, a typical company will go from a new enterprise to a mature business. Then, later it becomes a declining industry and finally dies and leaves the system. The model does not consider individual companies, only the aggregate groups x_1, x_2, and x_3, so that only average behavior is represented. The equations used in the model, for the business sector, are of the form:

$$\frac{dx_1}{dt} = d_1 K_1 - d_2 x_1$$

$$\frac{dx_2}{dt} = d_2 x_1 - d_3 x_2$$

$$\frac{dx_3}{dt} = d_3 x_2 - d_4 x_3$$

The parameter K_1 is an external input related to the rate at which new enterprises are formed. The variables d_i determine the rate at which, on the average, businesses are started, mature, decline, and die. The origin of these equations is indicated by the flow diagram of Fig. 10.1. The equations for the other two sectors can be easily derived from this figure. Thus, the basic form is a continuous model using nine state variables to characterize the city.

In the urban dynamics model, the rate variables d_i are very complex functions of the conditions within the system and include numerous relationships involving other variables in addition to the state variables. For example, the rate of new enterprise construction d_1 is a function of the relative availability of labor and land, the tax rate within the city, and the ratio of managerial-professional population to the number of managerial jobs, as well as the state variables x_1, x_2, and x_3. The equations used to compute the d_i variables include nonlinear functional relationships and exponential approximations to time delays, and often separate effects enter into the equations as multiplicative factors.

The specific rate equations used in the urban dynamics model were not derived from any data. They were formulated by including the factors which Forrester believed to be important, and values were assumed which were believed to be in an appropriate range.

The actual model used was intended to represent only a hypothetical urban area. The general nature of the results is illustrated by Fig. 10.2, which shows the simulation results for the three variables representing the business sector. During the first 100 years in this figure, the city is in a growth stage with rapid growth of new enterprises (x_1) and mature businesses (x_2) and with a relatively low number of declining industries. In the maturity stage, from 100 to 200 years, each of the variables peak and decline, with the ratios of the variables showing considerable variation. Finally, the system reaches equilibrium with a relatively high number of declining industries and a low number of new enterprises. Because the economic conditions depend upon the ratios of the types of businesses, the equilibrium condition is referred to by Forrester as the *stagnation phase*. In this phase, both employment opportunities and housing facilities for the population have minimum values.

Much of the urban dynamics study was devoted to a consideration of how government policies would affect an area which had reached equilibrium conditions. Certain programs which had been implemented by the federal government were evaluated and, on the basis of this model, found to be detrimental. New programs were suggested and, using this model, shown to be beneficial.

"Urban Dynamics" was published during a period when there was a great deal of discussion regarding the "urban problem." It raised much criticism and controversy caused to a large extent by the comments on past government programs and recommended new programs. A number of articles in reference [9] demonstrate the wide range of assessments and extensions of this work.

The basic problem of the urban dynamics model is its verification. As a scientific study, it is inadequate because it completely omitted step 4, an experimental test of the hypothesis. While it is true that a controlled experimental test of urban growth patterns is not possible, it is not true that testing by observation is impossible. Some efforts were made by other researchers to compare actual historical growth patterns with the urban dynamics model, but these efforts were not successful in either establishing or disproving the model and have not continued. The probable reason for this is that in the development of the model, the requirement for its verification was ignored.

In complex socioeconomic systems, it will never be possible to carry out the laboratory-type experiments that are so effective in the physical sciences. For these systems, the available data will be observations of uncontrolled system

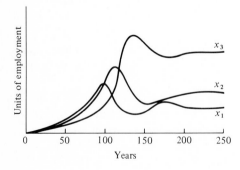

Figure 10.2 Urban dynamics simulation results; business sector variables.

behavior. This means that the verification of hypotheses (or models) will usually involve philosophical arguments and will always be less convincing than results in the physical sciences. However, some forms of validation are possible and must be achieved in order to establish results which can be generally accepted.

Much of the criticism of the urban dynamics model was related to the philosophical basis of the model and to the fact that so many aspects of urban development were not included. While it is true that the recommended policies overlooked many significant social considerations, the fact that the model was simplified and based on intuitive concepts of human behavior and economic processes is not a valid objection. If this model were to be capable of predicting certain aspects of urban growth with even fair precision, it would represent a substantial advance in the understanding of this process and would be of practical benefit in many activities. However, even if it is a good predictive model, it is not adequate, by itself, for determining governmental policies because cities involve far more than just the factors included in this model.

10.2.2 Nonexperimental Research

The development and validation of models for relationships where laboratory-type experiments cannot be conducted is not a new field of study. Social scientists have recognized this need for a long time and have developed some useful methods for dealing with problems of this type. However, simulation technology has developed from a basis of physical science and engineering with an emphasis on dynamic models. This is a different type of model than that used in most areas of the social sciences. The areas of social science with the most appropriate work related to simulation modeling are known as *econometrics* and *mathematical sociology*. The standard types of statistical analysis are not very effective in nonexperimental research.

In simulations, it is desirable and often necessary to have causal models. *Causal models* are those which represent the effects on some variables caused by changes in other variables. These models may be contrasted with what are known as *forecasting models*, which can be obtained from statistical correlation. The difference between causal and forecasting models can be illustrated by considering the computer job-input-rate model developed in Sec. 7.3. That is a forecasting model which would be useful as long as the system varies in the same manner as it did when the observations were made. The function of that model was to provide an input rate for the simulation of a computer system. If we assume that the purpose of the simulation is to investigate methods of improving service to the user, such as faster completion of a program, then the limitation of this forecasting model becomes evident. It is well known that, for the specific system considered, improved service would result in increased demand. Thus, to completely evaluate the effect of improvements to the computer system, the input-rate model should include the effect caused by improved service.

In nonexperimental research, it is not possible to establish cause-and-effect relationships simply by using statistical correlations. It is necessary to make assumptions based on an understanding of the system, not simply based on measurements of the system. Measurements are useful in testing these assumptions but are not adequate by themselves. There is no well-defined procedure for specifying causal models of this type, but we will consider one example which should help in understanding the nature of work in this area.

The example that follows is from a study done by a group at Battelle Memorial Institute [4] on economic growth in the Susquehanna River Basin. This study utilized the same modeling approach as was used in the urban dynamics study. However, the Battelle study considered a specific real system and was intended to be used for a specific purpose. The basic scheme of the study was to develop a regional model containing demographic, economic, and water-usage sectors and to estimate the parameters of this model for each of eight regions in the river basin area. The objective of the study was to predict the relative future development of these regions in order to aid the planning efforts of a group of utility companies which serve this area.

The specific example we will consider is the manner in which the equations for predicting future changes in region relative wages were developed. It was assumed in this study that future growth of an industry in a particular region would depend upon the relative costs for that industry in the region as compared with costs in the other regions. The relative wage in a region is defined as the average industry wage in the region divided by the average nationwide wage in that industry, and is a major component of the industry's costs.

The basic hypothesis used in this study was that local relative manufacturing wages will increase faster where

1. The local labor markets are tight.
2. There are fewer workers available from nearby rural farm areas.
3. High-paying industries tend to predominate in the region.

In order to test this hypothesis, the following variables were defined:

x_1 = the change in the average wage for production workers in an area during a specific period for a particular category of industry
x_2 = the ratio of the total nonagricultural employment in an area to the total population, less the rural farm population, of that area
x_3 = the ratio of the rural farm population to the total population for an area
x_4 = the average wage for all production workers in an area

Variables x_2, x_3, and x_4 correspond to the hypothesized effects 1, 2, and 3, respectively.

The hypothesis was actually tested by using the 50 United States as the regional areas, data from the 1960 census, and regression analysis to an equation of the following form for several categories of industry.

$$x_1 = a + bx_2 + cx_3 + dx_4$$

where a, b, c, and d are coefficients determined from the regression analysis. From this analysis, for the primary metals industry category, the only statistically significant variable was x_4. This result implies that, of the effects assumed in the hypothesis, only the third, i.e., the general or overall average wage, directly affects the wage increase in this particular industry.

The result that the availability of workers does not affect the average wage increase did not agree with the intuitive understanding of economic developments. So additional study of this relationship was carried out. The Simon-Blalock method of causal analysis [1, 11] was used to consider alternate causal models. The first such model considered can be represented by the simple arrow diagram of Fig. 10.3, which indicates that x_3 affects x_2, x_2 affects x_4, and x_4 affects x_1. This model assumes that the variables x_2 and x_3 do have an effect on x_1, but indirectly, through variable x_4. In this procedure, the adequacy of a model is tested by using the empirical correlation coefficients. If predicted correlations implied by a model are not in reasonable agreement with the actual correlations among the variables in the model, then the model is rejected.

The correlation coefficients among these variables, using 1960 data for the states, in the primary metals industry group are

$$r_{12} = + .194$$

$$r_{13} = - .226$$

$$r_{14} = + .566$$

$$r_{23} = - .314$$

$$r_{24} = + .311$$

$$r_{34} = - .394$$

The model of Fig. 10.3 can be represented by the equations:

$$x_1 = a_1 + b_1 x_4 + e_1$$

$$x_4 = a_4 + b_4 x_2 + e_4$$

$$x_2 = a_2 + b_2 x_3 + e_3$$

where the a's and b's are constants, and the e's are assumed to be normally distributed random values which are independent of any of the x_i variables. Now, if we determine the constants in these equations using the given data, the corre-

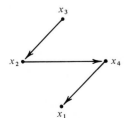

Figure 10.3 Causal model 1.

lation between x_1 and x_4 will be $r_{14} = +.566$. Similarly, the correlation between x_2 and x_4 will be $r_{24} = +.311$. But this means that the model implies that the correlation between x_1 and x_2 should be $r_{24} \times r_{14} = (+.566)(+.311) = +.176$. This result is reasonably close to the observed correlation $r_{12} = +.194$; however, the implied correlations between x_1 and x_3 and between x_3 and x_4 are not in reasonable agreement with the actual correlations, so this model is rejected.

The results from the first model suggest that a direct effect of x_3 on x_4 is needed to match the correlation data. Adding this effect gives the model shown in Fig. 10.4, which does give implied correlations reasonably close to the observed correlations r_{12} and r_{13}.

The result that x_3, the percent of the population which is rural farm, has a direct effect on both the urban employment ratio x_2 and the average wage x_4 suggests that this factor be considered more closely. The concept contained in the hypothesis is that workers on rural farms in an area are potentially available for urban employment in the area. However, the workers' availability will depend on how well they are doing on the farm. Thus, it seems reasonable that the number of farm workers available would be related to the number of low-income farms. For this reason, another variable was introduced into the model,

x_5 = the ratio of the number of low-income farms to the total population in an area

The observed correlations between this variable and the others were

$$r_{15} = -.41$$
$$r_{25} = -.575$$
$$r_{35} = +.731$$
$$r_{45} = -.592$$

Using this data leads to the consideration of the causal model shown in Fig. 10.5, which fits all the correlation data remarkably well. The implication of this model is that migration to the cities from low-income farms affects the average wage of production workers in an area but that a tight labor in the area's cities does not.

Models of this type can be used to develop the differential equations of a dynamic model. This was the approach used in the Susquehanna River Basin study and produced a model which was much more convincing than the urban dynamics model which simply used hypotheses of effects and assigned values which seemed reasonable to the model builders.

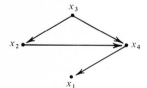

Figure 10.4 Causal model 2.

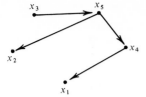

Figure 10.5 Causal model 3.

The weakness of this approach is that it assumes observed relationships will continue to be the same in the future as they were in the past. An interesting fact related to this point is that in the Susquehanna study the textile industry group did not fit a wage-increase causal model similar to the above model for the primary metals industry. It was the only industry group of those tested which did not. It was noted that during the period for which observation data was collected, there was a change in the federal minimum wage law. This law would have had the greatest effect on the lowest wage levels, which were in the textile industry, and was suspected to have operated to cancel the effects being analyzed. This case illustrates the need for including discrete events in the causal model which will, of course, increase the complexity of the modeling task.

This example should convey the idea that developing causal models for systems where controlled experimentation is not possible is a difficult and complex problem. Statistical analysis can only reject some models, but cannot fully validate any. Confidence in such a model must ultimately be based on confidence in the theory or hypothesis used to establish the model structure. In view of this, it is important to be careful in how the results from such a model are used or interpreted.

It may seem that this discussion of modeling has overemphasized the idea of considering systems which are not subject to experimentation. It is true that in the past most simulation activity has been related to systems where experimental research is possible, and these studies are where the greatest success has been achieved. However, there is great interest in systems not subject to experiments, and there are certain indications that this is the area where simulation has its greatest potential value.

10.3 TRENDS IN SIMULATION

There has been a trend toward extending simulation studies beyond the range of experimentally verifiable results. There are two major reasons for this. The first reason is a natural development of enlarging the scope of any problem which can be successfully solved. In terms of systems theory, this can be thought of as resulting from the fact that any system is, in the real world, part of a larger system. Very often, the critical aspects of the larger system involve economics and human behavior. This would be the case if we were to enlarge the scope of the checkout counter, inventory system, and elevator examples that were considered in Chaps. 2 and 4.

The second major reason for simulating systems not subject to experimentation is simply the interest in and importance of many systems of this type. When first exposed to the problems and limitations of nonexperimental research, many people feel that it is not worthwhile to develop models of highly questionable validity and/or those which cannot be scientifically established. However, there are arguments to support such studies. The main basis for these contentions is that modeling and simulations are the best alternatives available.

In applying the method of simulation to practical problems, we are in essence predicting the future. To do this beyond established scientific theory is not really possible. But, in order to assess the effect of any present action on future developments, it is necessary to predict those future developments. Thus, when a decision is made with respect to some economic, political, or environmental action, that decision is based on a prediction of future effects. Often this type of prediction is not made on any formal basis but rather is based on personal opinions. If these opinions are formed by persons with expert knowledge and experience in the problem area, they may well be the best predictions possible. However, it is not unusual for different experts to recommend different decisions.

When there is controversy as to the proper action to take, it is worthwhile to devote efforts to determine whether or not these differences in opinion are simply due to a difference in information as to the consequence of the action. It is important to recognize that these differences in opinion are not necessarily due to different information but rather to differences in interpretation as to the meaning of the information available. Moreover, even if there is agreement as to the probable effects of an action, there may be differences in goals and in values attached to the effects which will cause different opinions as to the appropriate action to take. Nevertheless, in these situations it is useful to provide all the pertinent information that is available in a form which can be understood by all the participants involved in the decision. This may resolve some conflicts or may reveal the correct basis for the difference in opinion.

In complex systems a simulation model can be a very effective way of presenting a large number of relationships and data values in a manner that is relatively easy to understand. This is the role in which some people believe simulation can make its greatest contribution. It is true that in most situations, the better a problem is understood, the more likely that effective solutions to the problem can be agreed upon. This leads to the idea that simulation, by providing greater understanding, can produce better decisions in policy questions related to economic and social systems. The criticism of this idea is based on the fact that simulation models are biased in that some effects are easily included in such models but others are difficult or even impossible to include. There is some degree of validity in the viewpoint that the concepts conveyed by a model are primarily the concepts held by the modeler.

The point of the above discussion is that the use of simulation with nonexperimentally verifiable systems can be justified, but that such efforts are also subject to well-justified criticism. Because of this situation, there have been numerous simulation projects which have produced more controversy than understanding [6, 14].

The philosophical shortcomings and potential dangers to society of the systems theory approach has been discussed by Lilienfeld [7]. His position is that the scientific approach to social systems is too narrow and tends to ignore much of the knowledge available from humanistic studies. Although his arguments are well supported, he does recognize that the scientific method is certainly applicable to aspects of society, though not to the whole of social activity.

There is a middle ground between the two opposing points of view regarding the application of the systems approach to social questions. That is to use a simulation-type approach only when considering specific and limited problems where results are produced which can, to some degree, be validated. This suggests that models should be developed in an evolutionary manner, i.e., extending an accepted model by relatively small steps in any new study. But to achieve acceptance of any model, it is necessary that validation procedures can be carried out by individuals or groups, independent of those which developed the model. This seems to be the obstacle which, at the present time, is preventing noticeable progress toward developing models for systems not subject to experimentation. The simulation studies in this area appear to be carried out without proper consideration of what other studies have been done previously or of how the present study can be validated and extended.

Thus, what is needed to increase the utility of simulation in these new areas is a cooperative effort that will enable workers to use and add to the work accomplished by others. This is, of course, the type of process which has been used in the physical sciences. The lack of such a procedure in the simulation area may be due to several factors. One major reason is that in nonexperimental research there is no standard approach to the problem of validation. Another reason is the separation of the simulation subject area and the subject areas of the various applications of simulation. There are valuable techniques which are generally applicable to simulations but are not widely known to specialists in many fields of study. So specialists in simulation can contribute to studies in many areas. But it is not likely that an effective simulation can be achieved without specialized knowledge in the area of application. Cooperative-type efforts are needed but appear to be rare.

Despite its limitations, simulation has been an effective tool in numerous applications. Its use continues to grow, and progress is being made in building a foundation for a science of simulation. It is a powerful tool, and its effects can be quite profound. But its ultimate value will depend not primarily on the capabilities of the tool but on how we choose to use it.

10.4 BACKGROUND AND REFERENCES

For those interested in computer-based modeling and simulation, there is an extensive and varied literature available. Much of this material appears in publications primarily devoted to specialized interests and often requires a knowledge of the area in order to follow the presentations. There are two periodicals devoted to the general subject of simulation which can be used to follow current trends and interests among a large number of simulation practitioners. These are the monthly journal *Simulation* published by the Society for Computer Simulation, and *Simuletter* published quarterly by the Special Interest Group on Simulation of the Association for Computing Machinery. Both of these publications include editorial comment, informal communications to professionals in the field, and announcements of events, as well as technical articles.

Technical articles related to simulation appear in many different periodicals and special publications. The most convenient guide to these sources is provided by various abstracting services. One such service which is widely available is the monthly "Computing Reviews" publication of the Association for Computing Machinery. This journal includes the category, simulation and modeling, and covers most of the computer-related technical literature in the English language.

Often simulation-related articles published in archive journals are condensed summaries of the studies reported and do not contain detailed descriptions of the models and programs used. In some cases, this material is available in reports issued by the company or agency which carried out the study. Many reports of this type are available from the National Technical Information Service of the U.S. Department of Commerce. This is a central source for the public sale of reports from all United States government-sponsored research and development projects and includes other selected technical documents.

REFERENCES

1. Blalock, H. M.: "Causal Inferences in Nonexperimental Research," University of North Carolina Press, Chapel Nill, N.C., 1964.
2. Churchman, C. W., R. L. Ackoff, and E. L. Arnoff: "Introduction to Operations Research," Wiley, New York, 1957.
3. Forrester, J. W.: "Urban Dynamics," MIT Press, Cambridge, Mass., 1969.
4. Hamilton, H. R., S. E. Goldstone, J. W. Milliman, A. L. Pugh, III, E. R. Roberts, and A. Zellner: "Systems Simulation for Regional Analysis, An Application to River Basin Planning," MIT Press, Cambridge, Mass., 1969.
5. Hamming, R. W.: "Numerical Methods for Scientists and Engineers," McGraw-Hill, New York, 1962.
6. House, P. W.: "The Developing Forecasting Hoax," *Simulation*, vol. 29, no. 5, pp. 139–141, November 1977.
7. Lilienfeld, R.: "The Rise of Systems Theory, An Ideological Analysis," Wiley, New York, 1978.
8. Moder, J. J., and S. E. Elmaghraly (eds.): "Handbook of Operations Research: Models and Applications," vol. 2, Van Nostrand Reinhold, New York, 1978.
9. Sage, A. P. (ed.): "Urban Dynamics: Extensions and Reflections," *IEEE Transactions on Systems, Man and Cybernetics*, vol. SMC-2, no. 2, April 1972.
10. Shannon, C. E., and W. Weaver: "The Mathematical Theory of Information," University of Illinois Press, Urbana, 1949.
11. Simon, H. A.: "Spurious Correlations: A Causal Interpretation," *Journal of the American Statistical Association*, vol. 49, pp. 467–479, 1954.
12. Von Bertalanffy, L.: "General Systems Theory: Foundations, Developments, Applications," Braziller, New York, 1968.
13. Von Neumann, J., and O. Morgenstern: "Theory of Games and Economic Behavior," Princeton University Press, New Jersey, 1944.
14. Watt, K. E. F.: "Why Won't Anyone Believe Us?" *Simulation*, vol. 28, no. 1, pp. 1–3, January 1977.
15. Wiener, N.: "Cybernetics," 2d ed., MIT Press and Wiley, New York, 1961.

AN INTRODUCTION TO PL/I
FOR FORTRAN PROGRAMMERS

FORTRAN was one of the earliest programming languages developed and, in many respects, the most successful. It is the most widely accepted higher-level language in use for scientific, or more accurately, mathematically oriented programming. The best feature of this language is its balance between generality and efficiency for algebraic-type computations. Various extensions to the language have added features which enhance its effectiveness and exploit the capabilities of modern computer equipment. However, much of the popularity of FORTRAN is owed to its simplicity.

PL/I is a more recently developed language and was designed to provide programming capabilities for a wider variety of users and applications than FORTRAN. A number of features are included in PL/I which are particularly useful in programming simulations. Moreover, because simulation programs often become very large and complex, all the additional capabilities of PL/I are potentially of value in this type of application.

In this text, the programs are written in PL/I, except for those in Chap. 5. This language was chosen primarily because certain functions may be programmed more conveniently than if written in FORTRAN and because programs may be more concise and readable than in FORTRAN. However, the programs have been written so that the reader who is familiar with any version of FORTRAN or a similar language can easily follow them. In this appendix, certain characteristics of the PL/I language needed for this purpose are presented.

A limited subset of PL/I is considered here. This subset is essentially the equivalent of FORTRAN. That is, we consider only the differences between a FORTRAN program and the equivalent program written in PL/I. Some additional features of the PL/I language are covered in Chap. 4. While this material covers only a few of the many features included in PL/I, it should indicate the nature of the advantages offered by this language for simulation programming.

A.1 PROGRAM FORMATS IN PL/I

Statements in PL/I may be written in free format and are not affected by card or line boundaries. The end of a statement is denoted by a semicolon. If a statement must be referred to, a name, rather than a number, is used. The statement name, called a *label*, precedes the statement and is separated from the statement by a colon. For example, the FORTRAN statements

$$1 \ A = B + C$$
$$D = E - F$$

could be written in PL/I as

ONE: $A = B + C$; $D = E - F$;

For card input, PL/I statements can use only columns 2 through 72. PL/I does not ignore blanks, as most versions of FORTRAN do, so blanks cannot be embedded in names. But, between names and operators, any number of blanks may be used and statements may continue for as many cards or lines as needed.

Comments may be included in any position where blanks are allowed and are enclosed in brackets/* ... */. For example,

ONE: /* THIS STATEMENT HAS THE LABEL 'ONE' */ $A = B + C$;

illustrates the use of a comment within a PL/I statement.

Programs begin with a PROCEDURE statement, and a main program in which execution is initiated contains the keywords OPTIONS(MAIN). Thus, a main program named EXAMPLE would start with the statement:

EXAMPLE: PROCEDURE OPTIONS(MAIN);

The conclusion of a program is denoted by an END statement which may or may not include the program name. For the program EXAMPLE, this could be

END EXAMPLE;

As in FORTRAN, the first character of a name used in a PL/I program must be an alphabetic character. The remaining characters, if any, may be alphabetic, numeric, or the special break character___. In PL/I, the characters $, @, and # are considered to be alphabetic characters. The language definition limits the length of a name to 31 characters; implementations may make further restrictions. The programs in this text were developed for an implementation which restricts names which are used outside a procedure to a maximum length of seven characters. This is why the program of Chap. 2 uses SCHEDUL and CUSTOME rather than SCHEDULE and CUSTOMER.

Since there are a greater variety of operations available, PL/I contains many more keywords than FORTRAN. However, in PL/I keywords are not reserved. That is, keywords such as IF may be used as a variable name or statement label, even in a program which also contains IF as a keyword. This is an example of the features included in PL/I that enable use of the language without complete knowledge of its specifications.

A.2 DATA TYPES

PL/I provides a wider range of data types than FORTRAN and gives the user the ability to declare in detail the way in which arithmetic data shall be stored and used in computation. However, if this level of detailed control is not desired, it may be omitted and standard forms will be assumed.

The attributes of a variable are specified in PL/I by the DECLARE statement, which combines the functions of the various specification statements of FORTRAN. The scale of arithmetic variables in PL/I is either fixed point or floating point and is denoted in the DECLARE statement as FIXED or FLOAT. For example, the statement

DECLARE A FIXED, B FLOAT;

defines A as an integer and B as a floating-point number. Since no additional specifications were provided, other attributes of these variables will assume default values. This will result in the same type of floating-point variable as does the FORTRAN statement

REAL B

or the FORTRAN default specification for the variable B. The PL/I fixed-point variable A will be the same type variable as would be specified by the FORTRAN statement

INTEGER A

except that the default precision in PL/I is 15 binary bits while the standard FORTRAN IV precision for integers is 31 binary bits. The PL/I variable A may be defined to have this same precision by the statement

DECLARE A FIXED BINARY(31);

Any variable in a PL/I program that is not specified in a DECLARE statement will default to a floating-point variable unless its name begins with one of the letters I through N. In this case, it will default to an integer. Thus, the default specification in PL/I is the same as in FORTRAN except for the range of the integers.

An array may be specified by including subscripts following the array name in a DECLARE statement. Thus,

DECLARE C(5,5) FLOAT , D(10) FIXED BINARY(31);

is equivalent to the FORTRAN specification statements

DIMENSION C(5, 5)
INTEGER D(10)

In PL/I, both the upper and lower limits of a subscript can be specified, in contrast with FORTRAN, where the lower limit is always 1. For example,

DECLARE E(0:4,-2:2) FLOAT;

defines E as a 5×5 array whose first element is identified as $E(0, -2)$ and whose last element is $E(4, 2)$.

Initial values may be assigned to variables at the start of program execution by using the DATA statement in FORTRAN. In PL/I, these values are included in the DECLARE statement. The statement

DECLARE A FIXED BINARY(31) INITIAL(0), B FLOAT INITIAL(3.14);

would assign the value 0 to A and the value 3.14 to B. Also, the statement

DECLARE F(5) FLOAT INITIAL(1.2,3.4,5.6,7.8,9.0);

will assign the value 1.2 to F(1), 3.4 to F(2), and so on.

The FORTRAN functions of COMMON and EQUIVALENCE have been replaced in PL/I. The PL/I specification EXTERNAL serves much the same purpose as COMMON, but the method of storage allocation is different. This is discussed in Chap. 4. The PL/I specifications DEFINED or CELL are used to replace EQUIVALENCE. These specifications are included in the DECLARE statement. The principle of the DECLARE statement is that all the attributes of a variable should be specified in a single statement.

The format of the DECLARE statement is flexible. Variables may be grouped within parentheses and the order of specifications is immaterial. Also, abbreviations may be used, such as DCL for DECLARE and BIN for BINARY.

A.3 ASSIGNMENT STATEMENTS

Arithmetic expressions specify the computations to be performed. In nearly all cases, a PL/I expression that is an exact copy of a FORTRAN expression will have precisely the same meaning algebraically. For example, the expression

$$X(I) = Y(I)*Z/(U + V*(W - 1.))$$

evaluates the same series of operations in FORTRAN and PL/I and assigns a value to X(I).

However, PL/I includes many more data types then FORTRAN and allows much greater freedom in combining types in expressions. Because of this, PL/I has much more detailed rules for specifying the sequence in which operations are carried out and for the order and method of conversion from one kind of variable to another.

There are some additional assignment statement options in PL/I that are at times useful. In PL/I, an assignment statement may have several variables on the left-hand side, all of which would be assigned the value of the expression. For example,

$$I, J, K = 5*M;$$

assigns the value of 5*M to each of the variables I, J, and K.

In PL/I, whole arrays may be used as variables within an expression. The interpretation of an array name appearing in a statement is that the statement is to be performed repetitively, using each element of the array in turn. If two or more arrays are used in an expression, the arrays must have identical dimensions and identical upper and lower bounds. As an example of array statements, given the DECLARE statement

$$DECLARE\ (A(10,10),B(10,10),C(10,10))\ FLOAT;$$

the PL/I statement

$$A = B + C;$$

is equivalent to the FORTRAN program segment

```
    DO 5 I = 1,10
    DO 5 J = 1,10
  5 A(I,J) = B(I,J) + C(I,J)
```

Also, scalars may be used in array expressions. The PL/I statement

$$A = 0.5*B + 3.6;$$

is equivalent to the FORTRAN segment

```
    DO 7 I = 1,10
    DO 7 J = 1,10
  7 A(I,J) = 0.5*B(I,J) + 3.6
```

In addition to allowing a whole array to be used in an expression, PL/I permits the programmer to specify a part of an array. If the asterisk symbol * appears as a subscript, the expression is to be evaluated for all values of the subscript. For example, using the array A declared above, the PL/I statement

$$A(I,*) = A(I,*) + A(J,*);$$

would add the *j*th row of a matrix to the *i*th row. In FORTRAN this would require the loop

```
    DO 9 K = 1,10
  9 A(I,K) = A(I,K) + A(J,K)
```

When the asterisk notation is used in an expression, the dimensions of the resulting arrays must be identical. To illustrate this, given the statement

$$DECLARE \ (X(2,3),Y(3)) \ FLOAT;$$

the following is a valid assignment statement:

$$X(2,*) = 2.5*Y + X(1,*);$$

and is equivalent to the FORTRAN statements

```
     DO 11 I = 1,3
  11 X(2,I) = 2.5*Y(I) + X(1,I)
```

A.4 CONTROL STATEMENTS

The three principal control statements of FORTRAN, GO TO, IF, and DO, are also used in PL/I. But the form of the statements has been changed to remove some of the restrictions of FORTRAN and to improve their power and clarity.

The unconditional "GO TO n" of FORTRAN is the same in PL/I except that n is a label name rather than a number. The computed and assigned forms of GO TO are accomplished in PL/I using a new type of variable called the *label variable*. These forms have not been used in the programs of this text.

In PL/I there is one basic form of the IF statement:

$$IF \ comparison \ expression \ THEN \ statement_1; \ ELSE \ statement_2;$$

The comparison expression is of the form

$$value_1 \ relational \ operator \ value_2$$

where $value_1$ and $value_2$ may be constants, variables, or expressions. The relational operators are the same as in FORTRAN IV, except that the symbols used are different. The following lists show PL/I symbols and their equivalents in FORTRAN IV.

PL/I	FORTRAN IV
=	.EQ.
<	.LT.
>	.GT.
¬ =	.NE.
< =	.LE.
> =	.GE.
¬ <	.GE.
¬ >	.LE.

When the comparison expression is true, statement$_1$ is executed but not statement$_2$. If the comparison expression is not true, statement$_2$ is executed but not statement$_1$. The clause 'ELSE statement$_2$;' may be omitted from the IF statement. This is equivalent to having a statement$_2$ which does nothing.

An example of a PL/I IF statement is

IF A > 7.6 THEN B = X + Y; ELSE B = X − Y;

This is equivalent to the FORTRAN program segment

```
IF(A .GT. 7.6) GO TO 4
B = X − Y
GO TO 5
4 B = X + Y
5 ...
```

The statements following the keywords THEN or ELSE may be IF statements. This nesting of IF statements can be continued to several levels if desired. In these cases the outermost IF statement may or may not have an associated ELSE clause. But every inner IF must have an associated ELSE clause when any IF statement at a higher level requires an associated ELSE clause. This can be a null ELSE, written as

ELSE;

which does not require the execution of any computer operation.

Often it is desired to execute more than one statement within the THEN or ELSE clauses. This can be accomplished by using one form of the DO statement. If a group of statements are bracketed together by using the statements DO; and END;, they will all be carried out. For example, the PL/I statements

IF A > 7.6 THEN DO; B = X + Y; C = Z + 2.5; END:
ELSE DO; B = X − Y; C = Z + 5.2; END;

are equivalent to the FORTRAN program segment

```
IF (A .GT. 7.6) GO TO 4
B = X − Y
C = Z + 5.2
GO TO 5
4 B = X + Y
  C = Z + 2.5
5 ...
```

The word DO by itself can be considered to specify a DO loop with only one iteration. The word END is used to terminate DO loops and other groups of statements. It is not the same as the END statement in FORTRAN.

In PL/I, DO loops with iterations are similar to those in FORTRAN. The most obvious differences are illustrated by the following example. The PL/I statements

```
DO I = 1 TO 9 BY 2; X(I) = 0;
DO J = 1 TO 5; X(I) = X(I) + Y(J);
END; K = K + 1; END;
```

are equivalent to the FORTRAN statements

```
    DO 25 I = 1,9,2
    X(I) = 0.
    DO 20 J = 1,5
 20 X(I) = X(I) + Y(J)
 25 K = K + 1
```

That is, in PL/I the last statement in a loop is not referred to in the DO statement, and the words TO and BY are used rather than commas. Other differences are that in PL/I the initial value, limiting value, and increment for the counter variable may be negative, nonintegers, or expressions. Also, the use of the counter variable is much less restricted.

Another important form of the DO loop in PL/I is with the WHILE clause. The form for this type of statement is

```
DO WHILE (comparison expression);
```

The comparison expression is similar to that in an IF statement. At the beginning of the loop execution, this comparison is made; if it is true, the loop is executed and then control returned to the DO statement for the next comparison. For example, the PL/I statements

```
DO WHILE (C > 120); A = B + C; B = C + A; C = A + B;
END;
```

are equivalent to the FORTRAN statements

```
30  IF (C .LE. 120.) GO TO 80
    A = B + C
    B = C + A
    C = A + B
    GO TO 30
80 ...
```

The WHILE clause offers opportunities for endless loops during program execution. It is recommended that a counter variable be used with a WHILE clause. The PL/I statements

```
CHECK = 0; DO I = 1 TO 100 WHILE(CHECK > = 0);
CHECK = X(I); END;
```

will examine the elements of array X, starting with X(1) and continuing in order until finding a negative value or until after X(100) is assigned to CHECK.

The comparison expressions used with the IF statement and WHILE clause can be compound-logical expressions with the symbol & denoting the logical AND operation, and the symbol | denoting the logical OR operation.

A.5 SUBPROGRAMS

The subroutine facilities in FORTRAN are essential for writing efficient large programs. In PL/I the same type of capability is provided but with some changes. The format for subprograms in PL/I is consistent with the rest of the language. The FORTRAN statement

```
SUBROUTINE ABE(X,Y)
```

becomes the PL/I statement

```
ABE: PROCEDURE(X,Y);
```

That is, every subprogram is a procedure and its name appears as a label. The last statement of a procedure is END;. Control is returned to the calling procedure by a RETURN or an END statement.

A subroutine subprogram is executed by a CALL statement, such as

```
CALL ABE(R, S);
```

This statement would cause the procedure ABE to be executed with the addresses of variables R and S substituted for the addresses of the subroutine parameters X and Y, respectively.

The manner in which variables of the CALL statement and parameters of the subprograms are related is somewhat different in PL/I than in FORTRAN. The only effect of this, in converting FORTRAN programs to PL/I programs, is that constants cannot be used in the variable list of the CALL statement. Thus, the FORTRAN call statement

CALL ABE(5.0,T)

would require the following PL/I statements in an equivalent program

D = 5.0; CALL ABE(D,T);

where D may be any dummy variable that has the same specification as the subroutine argument X.

The only difference between a subroutine and a function subprogram in PL/I is that the word RETURN in a function subprogram is followed by an expression enclosed in parentheses. The value of the expression is the value returned by the function.

An example of a procedure used as a function is

DEG_RAD: PROCEDURE(R);
RETURN(R*.01745329); END;

This function would be used in a statement such as

RADX = DEG_RAD(DEGX);

to convert from degrees to radians.

A significant feature of PL/I program structures is that subprogram procedures may be contained in other procedures. These internal procedures are not compiled separately and may refer to variables used in the program within which it is nested without using an argument list or other means of passing arguments. The arithmetic statement function of FORTRAN is a limited version of this capability.

External procedures in PL/I may be compiled separately, as are function and subroutine subprograms in FORTRAN. Multiple entries to PL/I procedures are provided by the ENTRY statement. Such entry points may have different lists of parameters from that of the main entry.

A.6 INPUT/OUTPUT

The facilities in PL/I for the input and output of data to and from the main computer memory are far more extensive than those of FORTRAN. PL/I has the capability of transferring data between memory and auxiliary storage without checking and conversion, which is similar to that available in the COBOL language. This provides an important advantage of greater execution efficiency for programs requiring large amounts of data transfers. However, PL/I also provides facilities for the type of input and output operations normally used in FORTRAN.

The edit-directed input/output statements in PL/I come closest to FORTRAN input/output. The form of this type statement for input is

GET EDIT (data list) (format);

and for output is

PUT EDIT (data list) (format);

Each item in the data list is matched with an item in the format, as in FORTRAN. The format does appear in the GET and PUT statements, but this may be a reference to a separate, or remote, FORMAT statement.

The notation used in PL/I formats is slightly different from that in FORTRAN. But the main difference is that in PL/I the format type refers only to the appearance of the data on the external medium, whereas in FORTRAN a format type specifies conversion between one internal form and one external form. For example, an F format type in FORTRAN specifies conversion between internal floating point and external fixed point, with a printed decimal point. In PL/I, F format may be used with any internal data; externally, the data appears in the same form as the F format output in FORTRAN.

Examples of edit-directed input/output statements are the following. The PL/I input statement

GET EDIT (A, B, C) (F (7, 2), X (3), 2 F(3));

would be used to read fixed-point input data from the first seven columns of a data card and assign this value to A. Three spaces would be skipped, and then two fixed-point numbers with widths of three spaces each would be read and the value assigned to B and C in turn. The PL/I output statement

PUT EDIT ('X = ', X, 'Y = ', Y)(SKIP(2), A, F(7, 2), SKIP, A, F(5, 1));

would cause the printer to skip two lines and then print

X = 1234.56
Y = 789.0

assuming these values were stored in variables X and Y.

List-directed input in PL/I provides a method for reading data without specifying its format. The input statement

GET LIST(A, B, C);

causes three items to be read from an input stream and assigns the values in turn to A, B, and C. In this type input, the data items are separated by a comma and/or one or more blanks. The output statement

PUT LIST(X, Y, Z);

will cause the values of X, Y, and Z to be printed out using a standard, implementation-dependent format.

The elements of PL/I described here are a very limited set of features and options available in this language. But it includes all the differences between PL/I and FORTRAN used in the program of Chap. 2. In addition, these rules are sufficient to write FORTRAN-like programs in PL/I.

SOME JCL ROUTINES

In order to construct and use the type of programming system developed in Chap. 4, it is necessary to employ certain facilities that are usually provided by a computer's operating system. The functions required for this purpose are considered in this appendix. These are illustrated by examples of Job Control Language (JCL) routines for use with the IBM System 360/370 OS/VS operating system.

B.1 INCLUDING STORED OBJECT-MODULE SUBPROGRAMS

The exercises of Chap. 2 assume that the subprograms included in the chapter have been compiled and stored in an on-line data set. In order to use these object modules with a modified version of the main procedure for this example program, the following input card deck may be used:

```
//EXFIRST   JOB   ACCOUNT#,' PROGRAMMERS NAME ',CLASS=J,TIME=(0,30)
//    EXEC   PL1LFCLG
//PL1L.SYSIN   DD    *
 FIRST: PROCEDURE OPTIONS(MAIN);
     :
     :    (OTHER CARDS OF FIRST)
     :
 END FIRST;
/*
//LKED.SYSIN   DD    *
   INCLUDE SUBS(SCHED,ARRIVE,DEPART,OPEN,GENRND,GENARIV)
   INCLUDE SUBS(GENCOC,STAT,OUTPUT)
//LKED.SUBS   DD   DSNAME=D.PLSIMLIB.C,DISP=SHR,UNIT=3350,VOL=SER=UOK210
//GO.SYSIN   DD    *
  :
  :    (DATA CARDS, IF ANY)
  :
/*
//
```

This job uses the system procedure PL1LFCLG to compile, link-edit, and execute the program FIRST. The standard JCL statements required with this procedure are included in the deck. Additional JCL cards used to include the object modules are the two DD-type statements named LKED.SYSIN and LKED.SUBS. The LKED.SYSIN statement causes the system linkage-editor program to read in the INCLUDE control cards which specify the members of a data set designated as SUBS that are to be available during the linkage-editor stage. These members are the subprograms and are identified by the procedure name. The JCL statement LKED.SUBS defines the data set which contains the subprograms as one named D.PLSIMLIB.C that is stored on a type 3350 disk with the serial number UOK210.

Data cards and the GO.SYSIN card would be needed only if the new version of the procedure FIRST contained a GET-type statement.

If any of the subprograms need to be changed, these alterations may be included after the procedure FIRST, and preceded by a PROCESS card. For example,

```
    :
 END FIRST;
*PROCESS;
 SCHED: PROCEDURE(LS,MS);
    :
 END SCHED;
/*
    :
```

could be used to include a modified version of the procedure SCHED in the program. In this case, the corresponding procedure name, SCHED, may be omitted from the INCLUDE statement.

The JCL used to include some other set of subprograms in object-module form could be similar to the above. Only the name and location of the data set containing the modules and the names of the procedures need be changed.

B.2 BUILDING OBJECT-MODULE DATA SETS

Before subprograms may be included in a program, as shown above, they must first be placed in a data set in the appropriate form. To build a data set of this type, a program is needed that will compile a procedure written in PL/I, referred to as a *source module*, and store the resulting object module in the data set.

The listing on the top of page 301 includes an in-stream procedure called ADDSUB which can be used to accomplish this task under system 360/370 OS/VS. This example illustrates how the in-stream procedure can be used to build a data set for the object modules of the inventory system simulation program.

This in-stream procedure executes the system PL/I compiler program IEMAA and stores the output in a data set defined by the SYSLIN DD statement. For this example, the data set containing the object modules is named D.PLSIMLIB.EX1. This same in-stream procedure was used to build the data set D.PLSIMLIB.C which contains the subprograms for the program FIRST and the data set D.PLSIMLIB.B which contains the procedures described in Secs. 4.1.1 and 4.1.3.

```
//BUILDOMS   JOB   ACCOUNT#,' PROGRAMMERS NAME ',CLASS=J,TIME=(0,30)
//ADDSUB   PROC   LET=B,MEMB=XXX,NOL=OLD
//PL1L   EXEC   PGM=IEMAA,REGION=192K
//SYSPRINT   DD   SYSOUT=A
//SYSLIN   DD   DSNAME=D.PLSIMLIB.&LET(&MEMB),DISP=(&NOL,KEEP),
//   DCB=(RECFM=FB,LRECL=80,BLKSIZE=2960),SPACE=(TRK,(5,1,3)),
//   UNIT=3350,VOL=SER=UOK210
//SYSUT1   DD   DSN=&SYSUT1,UNIT=SYSDA,SPACE=(CYL,(1,1))
//SYSUT3   DD   DSN=&SYSUT3,UNIT=SYSDA,SPACE=(CYL,(1,1))
//   PEND
//STEP1   EXEC   ADDSUB,LET=EX1,MEMB=SALE,NOL=NEW
//PL1L.SYSIN   DD   *
 SALE: PROCEDURE;   /*SELL ONE UNIT*/
   :
   :
 END SALE;
/*
//STEP2   EXEC   ADDSUB,LET=EX1,MEMB=INITIAL
//PL1L.SYSIN   DD   *
 INITIAL: PROCEDURE;
   :
   :
 END INITIAL;
/*
//
```

There is no restriction on the number of execution steps in a program of this type, so it can be used to add one object module to a data set or all the modules.

The symbolic parameter NOL is set equal to NEW only when a data set is first created. At all other times, the default value, OLD, is used. If an object module needs to be changed, the new version is added to the data set using the same member (MEMB) name. The last version of any member will be the version retrieved from the data set.

B.3 USING THE PREPROCESSOR OPTION

For procedures which use the preprocessor option of the PL/I compiler, a slightly different in-stream procedure must be used. The following listing shows how the object module for the procedure CONTROL may be added to data set D.PL-SIMLIB.EX1. This example assumes that the preprocessor library is stored in the data set named D.PLSIMLIB.A.

```
//BUILDOMS   JOB   ACCOUNT#,' PROGRAMMERS NAME ',CLASS=J,TIME=(0,30)
//ADDSUBM   PROC   LET=B,MEMB=XXX,NOL=OLD
//PL1L   EXEC   PGM=IEMAA,REGION=192K,PARM='MACRO'
//SYSPRINT   DD   SYSOUT=A
//SYSLIN   DD   DSNAME=D.PLSIMLIB.&LET(&MEMB),DISP=(&NOL,KEEP),
//   DCB=(RECFM=FB,LRECL=80,BLKSIZE=2960),SPACE=(TRK,(5,1,3),
//   UNIT=3350,VOL=SER=UOK210
//SYSUT1   DD   DSN=&SYSUT1,UNIT=SYSDA,SPACE=(CYL,(1,1))
//SYSUT3   DD   DSN=&SYSUT3,UNIT=SYSDA,SPACE=(CYL,(1,1))
//SYSLIB   DD   DSNAME=D.PLSIMLIB.A,DISP=SHR,UNIT=3350,VOL=SER=UOK210
//   PEND
//STEP5   EXEC   ADDSUBM,LET=EX1,MEMB=CONTROL
//PL1L.SYSIN   DD   *
 %DECLARE (EVENT1,EVENT2,EVENT3) CHARACTER;
 %EVENT1 = 'SALE';   %EVENT2 = 'INVTORY';   %EVENT3 = 'RECEIVE';
 %DECLARE (J,L) FIXED;   %J = 5;   %L = 3;
 %INCLUDE CONTROL;
/*
//
```

Both of the in-stream procedures ADDSUB and ADDSUBM can be included in one program if desired. All in-stream procedures must precede any execution step in a program. Depending on local installation rules, the in-stream procedures may be included as system procedures by cataloging them.

B.4 EXECUTING PROCEDURES THAT USE THE PREPROCESSOR

The method for executing a PL/I program which uses subprograms in object module form has been shown above. If the PL/I procedures require the use of the preprocessor, the parameter 'MACRO' must be passed to the compiler program and the preprocessor library data set must be defined. The following example illustrates how the main procedure for the inventory control program and a subprogram named STAT may be compiled using the preprocessor facilities. The example also shows how the general routines stored in D.PLSIMBIB.B and the subprograms for this example, stored in D.PLSIMLIB.EX1, may be included in the program when it is executed. These LKED statements illustrate how more than one data set may be included in a data-definition (DD) type JCL statement.

```
//EXONE    JOB   ACCOUNT#,' PROGRAMMERS NAME ',CLASS=J,TIME=(0,30)
//     EXEC PL1LFCLG,PARM='MACRO'
//PL1L.SYSLIB   DD   DSNAME=D.PLSIMLIB.A,DISP=SHR,UNIT=3350,VOL=SER=UOK210
//PL1L.SYSIN   DD   *
 INVENEX: PROCEDURE OPTIONS(MAIN);
    :
    :
 END INVENEX;
*PROCESS('MACRO');
 STAT: PROCEDURE;
    :
    :
 END STAT;
/*
//LKED.SYSIN   DD   *
   INCLUDE SUBS(INITLST,ADDTO,GETTOP,FINDELE,RND,RNEXP,RNNORM)
   INCLUDE SUBS(SALE,INITIAL,OUTPUT,CONTROL)
//LKED.SUBS   DD   DSNAME=D.PLSIMLIB.B,DISP=SHR,UNIT=3350,VOL=SER=UOK210
//          DD   DSNAME=D.PLSIMLIB.EX1,DISP=SHR,UNIT=3350,VOL=SER=UOK210
/*
//
```

B.5 ADDING MEMBERS TO THE PREPROCESSOR LIBRARY

The members of the preprocessor library, stored in the data set named D.PL-SIMLIB.A, are card-image files. The following example illustrates one method for adding a member to this data set. In this case, the member is named DCLSEED.

```
//ADDTEXT   JOB   ACCOUNT#,' PROGRAMMERS NAME ',CLASS=J,TIME=(0,30)
//     EXEC   PL1LFCLG
//PL1L.SYSIN   DD   *
 NEWMEMB: PROCEDURE OPTIONS(MAIN);
   DCL IN FILE RECORD SEQUENTIAL INPUT,
       OUT FILE RECORD SEQUENTIAL OUTPUT,
       LINE CHAR(80) BASED(A);
     OPEN FILE(IN), FILE(OUT);
     ON ENDFILE(IN) GO TO FINISH;
   LOOP:
     READ FILE(IN) SET(A);
     WRITE FILE(OUT) FROM (LINE);
     PUT EDIT(LINE)(SKIP,A);
     GO TO LOOP;
   FINISH:
     CLOSE FILE(IN), FILE(OUT);
 END NEWMEMB;
/*
//GO.OUT   DD   DSNAME=D.PLSIMLIB.A(DCLSEED),DISP=OLD,
//     UNIT=3350,VOL=SER=UOK210
//GO.IN   DD   *
   DCL SEED(8) FIXED BINARY(31) EXTERNAL INITIAL(1956987325,1156987325,
   1908986925,1508586121,1468582113,1472622913,1480662953,1521070957);
/*
//
```

B.6 USING A PRIVATE LIBRARY OF PROGRAMS

After a simulation program has been thoroughly checked out, it may be stored as a load module and, when needed, executed directly. A procedure for creating a library of this type and inserting the inventory control simulation program is shown below.

```
//GENPGMS   JOB   ACCOUNT#,' PROGRAMMERS NAME ',CLASS=J,TIME=(0,30)
//JOBLIB    DD   DSNAME=D.PLSIMLIB.PGMS,DISP=(NEW,CATLG),
//     DCB=(RECFM=FB,BLKSIZE=2960,LRECL=80),SPACE=(TRK,(5,1)),
//     UNIT=3350,VOL=SER=UOK210
//STEP1     EXEC  PL1LFCL
//PL1L.SYSIN   DD   *
 INVENEX: PROCEDURE OPTIONS(MAIN);
   :
   :
 END INVENEX;
/*
//LKED.SYSLMOD   DD   DSNAME=D.PLSIMLIB.PGMS(EXONE),DISP=OLD,
//     VOL=REF=*.JOBLIB
//LKED.SYSIN   DD   *
   INCLUDE SUBS(INITLST,ADDTO,GETTOP,FINDELE,RND,RNEXP,RNNORM)
   INCLUDE SUBS(SALE,INITIAL,STAT,OUTPUT,CONTROL)
//LKED.SUBS   DD   DSNAME=D.PLSIMLIB.B,DISP=SHR,UNIT=3350,VOL=SER=UOK210
//     DD   DSNAME=D.PLSIMLIB.EX1,DISP=SHR,UNIT=3350,VOL=SER=UOK210
/*
//
```

This procedure uses the JOBLIB DD statement and places the name of this data set and its members in the computer system catalog. Once the data set is created, the additional parameters are not necessary. That is, to add another program to this data set requires only

//JOBLIB DD DSNAME = D.PLSIMLIB.PGMS,DISP = OLD

to define the JOBLIB data set.

In order to execute the program stored by the above procedure, the following program can be used.

```
//STOCK   JOB   ACCOUNT#,' PROGRAMMERS NAME ',CLASS=J,TIME=(0,30)
//JOBLIB   DD   DSNAME=D.PLSIMLIB.PGMS,DISP=OLD
//STEP1   EXEC  PGM=EXONE
//SYSPRINT   DD   SYSOUT=A
//SYSIN   DD   *
   :
   :   (DATA CARDS, IF REQUIRED)
   :
/*
//
```

The routines presented in this appendix provide the primary job control language required with the system 360/370 OS/VS. Local installation rules for naming and maintaining data sets may require minor changes. In order to use the programming system developed in Chap. 4 with other computers and/or other operating systems, routines should be developed that accomplish similar operations.

STATISTICAL TABLES

Table C.1 The standard normal density and distribution

$$f(x) = \frac{1}{\sqrt{2\pi}}\, e^{-x^2/2} \qquad F(x) = \int_{-\infty}^{x} f(t)\, dt$$

$$f(-x) = f(x) \qquad F(-x) = 1 - F(x)$$

x	$f(x)$	$F(x)$	x	$f(x)$	$F(x)$
.0	.3989	.5000	1.8	.0790	.9641
.1	.3970	.5398	1.9	.0656	.9713
.2	.3910	.5793	2.0	.0540	.9772
.3	.3814	.6179	2.1	.0440	.9821
.4	.3683	.6554	2.2	.0355	.9861
.5	.3521	.6915	2.3	.0283	.9893
.6	.3332	.7257	2.4	.0224	.9918
.7	.3123	.7580	2.5	.0175	.9938
.8	.2897	.7881	2.6	.0136	.9953
.9	.2661	.8159	2.7	.0104	.9965
1.0	.2420	.8413	2.8	.0079	.9974
1.1	.2179	.8643	2.9	0060	.9981
1.2	.1942	.8849	3.0	.0044	.9987
1.3	.1714	.9032	3.1	.0033	.9990
1.4	.1497	.9192	3.2	.0024	.9993
1.5	.1295	.9332	3.3	.0017	.9995
1.6	.1109	.9452	3.4	.0012	.9997
1.7	.0940	.9554	3.5	.0009	.9998

x	1.282	1.645	1.960	2.326	2.576	3.090
$F(x)$	.90	.95	.975	.99	.995	.999

Table C.2 The student's t distribution

The values t_v in this table are such that $F(t_v) = P$ where F is the student's t cumulative distribution. Thus the P values represent fractile points for the student's t distribution having v degrees of freedom. For two-sided confidence interval calculations, with confidence level $1 - \alpha$ and sample size n, $P = 1 - \alpha/2$ and $v = n - 1$. For a one-sided confidence interval calculation, with confidence level $1 - \alpha$ and sample size n, $P = 1 - \alpha$ and $v = n - 1$.

			P		
v	0.75	.90	.95	.975	.99
3	.765	1.638	2.353	3.182	4.541
4	.741	1.533	2.132	2.776	3.747
5	.727	1.476	2.015	2.571	3.365
6	.718	1.440	1.943	2.447	3.143
7	.711	1.415	1.895	2.365	2.998
8	.706	1.397	1.860	2.306	2.896
9	.703	1.383	1.833	2.262	2.821
10	.700	1.372	1.812	2.228	2.764
15	.691	1.341	1.753	2.131	2.602
20	.687	1.325	1.725	2.086	2.528
30	.683	1.310	1.697	2.042	2.457
60	.679	1.296	1.671	2.000	2.390
∞	.674	1.282	1.645	1.960	2.326

Table C.3 The chi-square distribution

The values u in this table are such that $F(u) = P$ where F is the chi-square cumulative distribution with k degrees of freedom. Thus, for example, a random variable having the chi-square distribution with 5 degrees of freedom has a 10 percent probability of being greater than 9.24, a 10 percent probability of being less than 1.61, and an 80 percent probability of having a value in the range from 1.61 to 9.24.

			P			
k	.10	.25	.50	.75	.90	.99
3	.584	1.21	2.37	4.11	6.25	11.3
4	1.06	1.92	3.36	5.39	7.78	13.3
5	1.61	2.67	4.35	6.63	9.24	15.1
6	2.20	3.45	5.35	7.84	10.6	16.8
7	2.83	4.25	6.35	9.04	12.0	18.5
8	3.49	5.07	7.34	10.2	13.4	20.1
9	4.17	5.90	8.34	11.4	14.7	21.7
10	4.87	6.74	9.34	12.5	16.0	23.2
12	6.30	8.44	11.3	14.8	18.5	26.2
14	7.79	10.2	13.3	17.1	21.1	29.1
16	9.31	11.9	15.3	19.4	23.5	32.0
18	10.9	13.7	17.3	21.6	26.0	34.8
20	12.4	15.5	19.3	23.8	28.4	37.6
30	20.6	24.5	29.3	34.8	40.3	50.9
40	28.9	33.7	39.3	45.6	51.8	63.7
50	37.6	43.0	49.3	56.3	63.2	76.2

Table C.4 The *F* distribution

The values *w* in this table are such that $F(w) = P$, where F is the F cumulative distribution with m and n degrees of freedom in the numerator and denominator, respectively.

m	*n*	.90	.95	.99	*m*	*n*	.90	.95	.99
			P					P	
2	2	9.0	19.0	99.0	10	2	9.39	19.4	99.4
	3	5.46	9.55	30.8		3	5.23	8.79	27.2
	4	4.32	6.94	18.0		4	3.92	5.96	14.5
	5	3.78	5.79	13.3		5	3.30	4.74	10.1
	10	2.92	4.10	7.56		10	2.32	2.98	4.85
	20	2.59	3.49	5.85		20	1.94	2.35	3.37
	30	2.49	3.32	5.39		30	1.82	2.16	2.98
	∞	2.30	3.00	4.61		∞	1.60	1.83	2.32
3	2	9.16	19.2	99.2	20	2	9.44	19.5	99.4
	3	5.39	9.28	29.5		3	5.18	8.66	26.7
	4	4.19	6.59	16.7		4	3.84	5.80	14.0
	5	3.62	5.41	12.1		5	3.21	4.56	9.55
	10	2.73	3.71	6.55		10	2.20	2.77	4.41
	20	2.38	3.10	4.94		20	1.79	2.12	2.94
	30	2.28	2.92	4.51		30	1.67	1.93	2.55
	∞	2.08	2.60	3.78		∞	1.42	1.57	1.88
4	2	9.24	19.2	99.2	30	2	9.46	19.5	99.5
	3	5.34	9.12	28.7		3	5.17	8.62	26.5
	4	4.11	6.39	16.0		4	3.82	5.75	13.8
	5	3.52	5.19	11.4		5	3.17	4.50	9.38
	10	2.61	3.48	5.99		10	2.15	2.70	4.25
	20	2.25	2.87	4.43		20	1.74	2.04	2.78
	30	2.14	2.69	4.02		30	1.61	1.84	2.39
	∞	1.94	2.37	3.32		∞	1.34	1.46	1.70
5	2	9.29	19.3	99.3	∞	2	9.49	19.5	99.5
	3	5.31	9.01	28.2		3	5.13	8.53	26.1
	4	4.05	6.26	15.5		4	3.76	5.63	13.5
	5	3.45	5.05	11.0		5	3.11	4.37	9.02
	10	2.52	3.33	5.64		10	2.06	2.54	3.91
	20	2.16	2.71	4.10		20	1.61	1.84	2.42
	30	2.05	2.53	3.70		30	1.46	1.62	2.01
	∞	1.85	2.21	3.02		∞	1.00	1.00	1.00

Table C.5 Kolmogorov-Smirnov acceptance limits

This table gives acceptance limits $K_{n,\alpha}$ for the Kolmogorov-Smirnov test statistic D. For sample size n and significance level α, the hypothesis that the samples came from the assumed distribution is rejected if $D > K_{n,\alpha}$; otherwise the hypothesis is accepted.

	α			
n	.20	.10	.05	.01
3	.56	.64	.71	.83
4	.49	.56	.62	.73
5	.45	.51	.56	.67
6	.41	.47	.52	.62
7	.38	.44	.49	.58
8	.36	.41	.46	.54
9	.34	.39	.43	.51
10	.32	.37	.41	.49
15	.27	.30	.34	.40
20	.23	.26	.29	.35
25	.21	.24	.26	.32
30	.19	.22	.24	.29
35	.18	.21	.23	.27
>35	$\dfrac{1.07}{\sqrt{n}}$	$\dfrac{1.22}{\sqrt{n}}$	$\dfrac{1.36}{\sqrt{n}}$	$\dfrac{1.63}{\sqrt{n}}$

D

GENERATING RANDOM NUMBERS

The generation of random numbers is an essential element in the simulation of stochastic models. For simulations implemented on general-purpose digital computers, this means that program segments are required that are able to produce an acceptable approximation to random behavior.

One method for doing this is illustrated in the program of Sec. 2.2 and is discussed more fully in Sec. 3.3. This procedure consists of using a multiplicative congruential generator to obtain approximations to independent samples from a uniform distribution and using these values with an inverse transformation operation in order to generate independent samples from nonuniform distributions. While this approach is intuitively reasonable and may be used in practice, it is not necessarily the best method. There are other, more sophisticated, techniques which are preferable in many situations.

A great deal of study has been devoted to the subject of generating random numbers on digital computers. There is an extensive list of publications relating to this subject [11], and many alternative methods have been developed for this purpose. The reasons for using other methods is to obtain closer approximation to random behavior and to reduce the number of computer operations needed.

In this appendix, some of the currently utilized procedures for generating random numbers will be considered. Our objective here is to introduce some extensions and alternative approaches to the basic method of Sec. 3.3, not to attempt the development of elaborate random-number generating facilities. Many facilities of this type have been developed and are available in software packages [4].

D.1 NONRANDOM CHARACTERISTICS

The primary motivation for seeking improved random-number generators is to avoid nonrandom characteristics. The simplified example of a multiplicative congruential generator shown in Fig. 2.7 may be used to illustrate one type of nonrandom behavior which has been encountered. In that example, the following sequence of numbers was produced:

$$1, 37, 25, 29, 49, 21, 9, 13, 33, 5, 57, 61, 17, 53, 41, 45, 1, \ldots$$

The 16 numbers of this sequence, which occur before it starts repeating, provide a rough approximation to a uniformly distributed random sequence in the range between 0 and 64. Although this is a very limited sequence, it is nearly uniform and does appear to be independent. At least the correlation coefficients for this sequence do not indicate any dependence. But, if this sequence of numbers were used to generate points in a plane, the eight points would be as shown in Fig. D.1 and would have the order indicated. That is, the first point is (1, 37), the second (25, 29), etc.

The points in Fig. D.1 are very nicely distributed in the rectangular area but, obviously, these points are not random. How this pattern, or *nonrandom property*, would affect simulation results depends on the specific simulation, but clearly the assumption of random points is not valid for this sequence.

Studies have shown that for any multiplicative congruential random-number generator, there are relationships between pairs in the generated sequences somewhat similar to that of Fig. D.1 [2]. Such relationships can easily be avoided if they are known. For example, if random points are needed, two different random-number streams may be used to produce the two coordinates. But there is always the danger that unexpected nonrandom characteristics will occur and not be recognized.

It is not possible to assure that any deterministic process such as a computer-implemented algorithm will produce a sequence without any nonrandom characteristics. But procedures have been devised and tested that are better in this

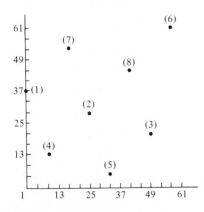

Figure D.1 Plot of points obtained using the sequence of values from the 6-bit random-number generator as coordinates.

respect than the most easily implemented algorithms and better than many other procedures that have been used widely in practice.

D.2 GENERATING UNIFORM VARIATES

As in the method of Sec. 3.3, the primary step in all practical random-number generating techniques is to obtain uniformly distributed variates. The currently popular algorithms for this task use some variation of the congruential method first discussed by Lehmer [7]. The general form of the mixed congruential generators may be represented by the equation

$$x_{n+1} = \alpha x_n + c \qquad \mod m \qquad (1)$$

where c represents a constant value added to the product of the multiplier α and the preceding random value x_n. Here the modulus m is an integer but not necessarily equal to 2^k, where k is the number of bits used to represent the values of x.

One advantage of the mixed congruential generator is that by the proper choice of parameters, a full-period generator may be obtained. That is, the x_i take on all integer values from 0 to $m - 1$ before repeating. In particular, if

$$m = 2^k$$

for a k-bit word length in a binary computer and $\alpha = 8t - 3$ for some integer value t, then if c is relatively prime to m, the sequence of x values generated by use of Eq. (1) will be full period.

This form does provide more random numbers than a similar generator with c equal to 0. But a more practical advantage is that the seed value for a sequence is not restricted to only odd numbers. This is helpful in avoiding one type of user error which often occurs.

A full-cycle sequence can also be achieved by using an m which is equal not to 2^k but rather is the largest prime number less than 2^k. With this condition and c equal to 0, the sequence generated includes the integers from 1 to $m - 1$ inclusive.

A number of theoretical studies have considered the problem of determining the proper choice of values for the parameters α, c, and m of the mixed congruential generator [5]. Several sets of values have been experimentally investigated and used in practice [2]. These efforts have resulted in generators which are closer to a truly random generator than the simplest implementations, but there is no one form which has been accepted as the best.

While these more sophisticated methods may provide greater confidence in simulation results, it must be remembered that any particular sub-sequence from any type of generator may have very different characteristics from those of the complete sequence. For this reason, it is important that the sequence of values actually used in a simulation be tested.

These alternate methods do require added computational operations, compared with the simple algorithm used in Fig. 4.13. Since uniform random numbers are used many times in most simulations, it is desirable that the program for generating these numbers be computationally efficient. But computational efficiency is dependent on the hardware configuration and operating system for any specific computer. This means that the best programs for implementing a uniform random-number generator are the ones that most effectively utilize the capabilities of a specific machine. Thus, different methods and programs have been developed for use with different computers.

Most computer centers have access to subroutine-type programs for generating random numbers that have been developed for their machines. These programs may differ in terms of efficiency, convenience of use, and statistical properties of the output. These routines usually represent the result of considerable programming and testing efforts. Because of this, they are often preferred for simulation programming.

D.3 THE LLRANDOM GENERATOR

As an example of a uniform random-number generator which is widely used, we will briefly describe the LLRANDOM routine which is provided in the IMSL software package for the IBM System 360/370 computers. This routine was originally devised and tested by Lewis, Goodman, and Miller [8]. An efficient implementation was developed later by Learmonth and Lewis [6].

This routine uses the recursion relation

$$x_{i+1} = 16,807x_i \qquad \mathrm{mod}\ 2^{31} - 1$$

There are 31 bits available for computation in the 32-bit general registers of the IBM System 360/370 computers, since one bit is effectively a sign bit. In this case, the largest prime number less than 2^{31} happens to be $2^{31} - 1$ and 16,807 is a positive primative root of $2^{31} - 1$. Thus, this generator can produce a sequence of numbers with a full cycle of length $2^{31} - 1$.

Since this generator uses a modulus which is not equal to 2^{32} or 2^{31}, it is not possible to simply use overflow to accomplish the modulo operation. This operation may be accomplished by dividing the product $16,807x_i$ by $2^{31} - 1$. However, there are more efficient ways to implement this operation, and greater efficiency can be achieved using facilities available in assembler language.

The random numbers generated by this method were extensively tested for uniformity and independence. It was found experimentally that these parameters gave much better results than almost all of many other values that were investigated. This implies that a random-number generator must be carefully chosen to assure that it produces a close approximation to truly random numbers.

D.4 TESTING UNIFORM VARIATES

As discussed in Sec. 3.3, in order to verify that a generator output sequence is random, it is necessary to verify that the values are uniform and serially independent. The chi-square goodness-of-fit test illustrated in Sec. 3.3 is a convenient and effective method of testing for uniformity and is the most commonly used method in practice. However, serial independence is often tested by other methods than the correlation test described in that section. There are a large number of such tests that have been devised [5]. Here we will consider two of the most popular tests of this type: the "runs" test and Good's serial test. Both of these procedures are included in the IMSL software package [4].

In a sequence of numbers x_i, a run upward of length k is defined to be the occurrence of k consecutive numbers, where each successive number is larger than the preceding number. Thus, in the sequence

$$\overline{1, \ \overline{37, \ \underline{25,}} \ 29, \ \overline{49,} \ \underline{21, \ 9,}} \ 13, \ 33, \ \underline{5,} \ 57, \ \overline{61,} \ \underline{17,} \ 53, \ \underline{41,} \ 45$$

where runs up are overscored and runs down are underscored, there are 11 runs of lengths 1, 1, 2, 2, 2, 1, 2, 1, 1, 1, 1, in that order. Thus, this sequence of 16 supposably random numbers has seven runs of length 1 and four runs of length 2.

The expected number of runs of length k in a sequence of n independent numbers is given by [12]:

$$E_k = \frac{2[(k^2 + 3k + 1)n - (k^3 + 3k^2 - k - 4)]}{(k + 3)!}$$

Using this relationship, a chi-square test, as that in Sec. 7.1, provides a check for independence.

Another form of the runs test [8] is often used. For large n, the expected number of runs of length k is

$$E_k = \frac{2[(n - k - 2)(k^2 + 3k + 1)]}{(k + 3)!}$$

and the expected number of runs of all lengths is

$$\frac{2n - 7}{3}$$

Since the expected number of runs of length k decreases rapidly with increasing k, the expected value of all runs larger than some k is used. For example, the expected number of runs of length 8 and greater is

$$E_8 = \frac{2n - 7}{3} - \sum_{i=1}^{7} E_i$$

For a series of n numbers, let R_i be the number of runs of length i, for i from 1 to 7, and R_8 equal the number of runs of length greater than 7. Then if

$$U_1 = \sum_{i=1}^{8} \frac{(R_i - x_i)^2}{x_i}$$

where

$$x_i = E_i\left(\sum_{j=1}^{8} R_j\right) \Big/ [(2_n - 7)/3]$$

the statistic U_1 has the chi-square distribution with approximately 7 degrees of freedom if the series of numbers are independent.

Good's serial test is, in a sense, a test of the independence between x_{j-1} and x_j. In this procedure, the range of the values in the sequence is divided into k equally spaced subintervals. Then, the number of times, n_{ij}, that a value x_p in the ith interval is followed by x_{p+1} in the jth interval is calculated for all values of i and j from 1 to k. For example, using the sequence of 16 values given above, let k equal 4, then the numbers 1, 5, 9, and 13 are in interval 1. Thus, the value for n_{11} is equal to 1 since x_7 (9) is followed by x_8 (13). Moreover, n_{12} equals 0, n_{13} equals 2, and n_{14} equals 1.

Good shows in [3] that if

$$n_i = \sum_{j=1}^{k} n_{ij}$$

then

$$U_2 = \left(\frac{k^2}{n}\right) \sum_{i=1}^{k} \sum_{j=1}^{k} \left(n_{ij} - \frac{n}{k^2}\right)^2 - \left(\frac{k}{n}\right) \sum_{i=1}^{k} \left(n_i - \frac{n}{k}\right)^2$$

has approximately the chi-square distribution with $k(k-1)$ degrees of freedom.

If the statistic U_2 is calculated for the sequence of 16 values given above, with k equal to 4, we find that

$$U_2 = 6$$

From Table C.3, the probability that a chi-square-distributed value with 12 degrees of freedom would be greater than 6.3 is found to be 90 percent. Thus, this result indicates that for the example sequence the dependence between successive elements is less than would be expected. The usual procedure is to not reject the hypothesis of independence unless the probability of exceeding the value computed for the statistic is small.

D.5 SAMPLING FROM TABLES

The table look-up procedure can be used to transform uniformly distributed random variates to any other specified distribution. For distributions having theoretical models or formulas, particular features of the formulas may be exploited to obtain more efficient and more convenient methods. For empirical distributions, the table look-up procedure is usually the most effective method. However, the basic table look-up procedure, illustrated in Figs. 2.8 and 2.9, can be made more efficient.

Consider the case of generating variates with the discrete density function shown in Fig. D.2. A subprocedure to generate these variates, using the table look-up method, is also shown in Fig. D.2. One general method for improving the efficiency of this program is to reduce the expected number of times the DO loop and the IF statement are executed. This may be accomplished, in this

```
DVGEN: PROCEDURE(I) RETURNS(FLOAT);
  DCL D(4,2) FLOAT STATIC INITIAL(.1,4,.4,5,.8,6,1,7);
    U = RND(I);
    DO J = 1 TO 4;   IF U < D(J,1) THEN
      DO;   X = D(J,2);   RETURN(X);   END;
    END;
END DVGEN;
```

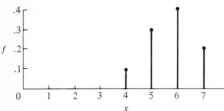

Figure D.2 A specific discrete distribution and procedure to generate a corresponding random variate.

example, by simply changing the declare statement to

DCL D(4,2) FLOAT STATIC INITIAL(.4,6,.7,5,.9,7,1,4);

This modification minimizes the average number of operations by testing for the most likely event first, then for the second most likely event, and so on. This method is applicable to all discrete table distributions.

Another method can be used to reduce the number of operations required for this type problem but does usually require increased storage space. This technique is illustrated by the procedure listed in Fig. D.3 for generating random variates with the distribution shown in Fig. D.2. In this case, the array S contains a sufficient number of entries to provide the proper relative frequency for the output values. If the original probabilities were specified to two decimal places, S would need 100 elements, and if these probabilities were given to three decimal places, 1000 elements would be required.

These two approaches to improving the efficiency of the table look-up procedure can also be applied to the case of continuous variates. To illustrate this, we consider the density function and corresponding distribution shown in Fig. D.4. A typical table look-up procedure for generating random variates with this distribution is also shown in Fig. D.4. The expected number of DO loop executions in this procedure can be reduced in a similar manner as the discrete case above. For the continuous distribution example, this may be accomplished by changing the F-array declaration and the interpolation formula in the procedure of Fig. D.4 as follows:

DCL F(5, 3) FLOAT STATIC INITIAL(0, 6, 7, .4, 5, 6, .7, 7, 8, .9, 4, 5, 1, 0, 0);
X = F(J, 2) + (F(J, 3) − F(J, 2))*(U − F(J, 1))/(F(J + 1, 1) − F(J, 1));

```
ADVGEN: PROCEDURE(I) RETURNS(FLOAT);
  DCL S(10) FLOAT STATIC INITIAL(4,5,5,5,6,6,6,6,7,7);
    U = RND(I);
    IU = 10.*U + 1.;
    X - S(IU);
    RETURN(X);
END ADVGEN;
```

Figure D.3 Alternate procedure for generating discrete random variates.

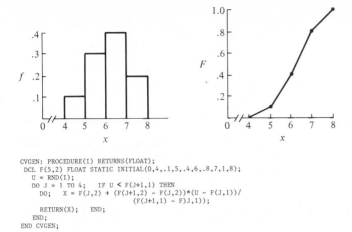

```
CVGEN: PROCEDURE(I) RETURNS(FLOAT);
 DCL F(5,2) FLOAT STATIC INITIAL(0,4,.1,5,.4,6,.8,7,1,8);
  U = RND(I);
  DO J = 1 TO 4;   IF U < F(J+1,1) THEN
    DO;   X = F(J,2) + (F(J+1,2) - F(J,2))*(U - F(J,1))/
                      (F(J+1,1) - F)J,1));
    RETURN(X);   END;
  END;
END CVGEN;
```

Figure D.4 A continuous distribution example.

This modification does require added storage space but will reduce the average number of operations needed to generate this random variate.

The method illustrated in Fig. D.3 is used with a continuous distribution in the procedure of Fig. D.5. This subprocedure will produce random variates with the distribution of the example of Fig. D.4. The S-array values are specified somewhat differently from in the discrete case in order to simplify the required interpolation. Note that in this procedure a second uniform variate, V, is used for interpolation. This is used since the first uniform variate is not independent of the interval in which interpolation is to be carried out. However, this second uniform variate can be eliminated by using the first few bits of U to specify the interval and the remaining bits of U for the interpolation.

The advantage to be gained by using either of the two modifications considered here depends on the specific case to which they may be applied. If the computer time spent in executing such random-variate generation is significant, then the gain achieved may be significant. These modifications do provide examples of how even very straightforward operations involved in random-number generation can be improved.

D.6 TRANSFORMS FOR SOME USEFUL DISTRIBUTIONS

Very sophisticated procedures have been developed for generating random variates from many standard distributions. But at times, it is helpful to be able to conveniently program a routine to produce such variates. This section presents several relationships which provide methods for generating variates with the chi-square, Erlang, F, and student's t distributions. These methods may be used when more efficient approaches are not readily available and the development of

```
ACVGEN: PROCEDURE(I) RETURNS(FLOAT);
  DCL S(11) FLOAT STATIC INITIAL(4,5,5.33,5.67,6,6.25,6.5,6.75,7,
                                 7.5,8);
    U = RND(I);    V = RND(I);
    IU = 10.*U + 1.;
    X = S(IU) + V*(S(IU+1) - S(IU));
    RETURN(X);
END ACVGEN;
```

Figure D.5 Alternate procedure for generating continuous random variates.

such software is not justified. In particular, these forms may be useful with the exercises and examples in this textbook.

As discussed in Sec. 3.2.2, if

$$Y = X_1^2 + X_2^2 + \cdots + X_n^2$$

where $X_1, X_2, \ldots, X_n$ are independent random variables with the standard normal distribution, then Y has the chi-square distribution with n degrees of freedom. It is also true that if

$$X_1 = (-2 \ln u_1)^{1/2} \cos 2\pi u_2$$

and

$$X_2 = (-2 \ln u_1)^{1/2} \sin 2\pi u_2$$

where u_1 and u_2 are independent random variates distributed uniformly on $[0, 1]$, then X_1 and X_2 are independent random variables with the standard normal distribution. Thus, if

$$Y = -2 \ln u_1$$

then Y has a chi-square distribution with 2 degrees of freedom. More generally, if $u_1, u_2, \ldots, u_n$ are independent and uniformly distributed on $[0, 1]$, then

$$Y = -2 \ln (u_1 \cdot u_2 \cdot \cdots \cdot u_n) \tag{1}$$

has a chi-square distribution with $2n$ degrees of freedom. Also, if X has the standard normal distribution and Y is obtained from (1), then if

$$Z = Y + X^2 \tag{2}$$

Z has a chi-square distribution with $m = 2n + 1$ degrees of freedom. Equations (1) and (2) may be used to generate chi-square random variates with any degree of freedom.

The Erlang distribution is related to the chi-square distribution. Specifically, if the Erlang parameters λ and m equal $1/2$ and $n/2$, respectively, then this distribution becomes the chi-square distribution with n degrees of freedom. In general, if $u_1, u_2, \ldots, u_m$ are independent random variables, each having the uniform distribution on $[0, 1]$, then

$$E = -\frac{1}{\lambda} \ln (u_1 \cdot u_2 \cdot \cdots \cdot u_m) \tag{3}$$

is an Erlang variate with parameters λ and m.

The F distribution is the probability distribution of the ratio of the sum of the squares of random normal variates. If Z_1 and Z_2 are random variates with the chi-square distribution with m and n degrees of freedom, respectively, then if

$$F = \frac{Z_1/m}{Z_2/n} \tag{4}$$

the variate F will have the F distribution with m and n degrees of freedom. Thus an F-distributed variate may be generated by combining two chi-square-distributed variates.

The student's t distribution is the probability distribution of the ratio of a standard normal and chi-square variate. If Z is a random variate with the chi-square distribution with m degrees of freedom and X is a random variate with the standard normal distribution, then

$$T = \frac{X}{(Z/m)^{1/2}} \tag{5}$$

will produce a variate T having the student's distribution with m degrees of freedom.

These relationships provide easily programmable methods for generating variates from a few commonly used statistical distributions. Many other relationships of this type, for a large number of distributions, may be found in the literature [11].

D.7 A FAST PROCEDURE FOR GENERATING NORMAL RANDOM NUMBERS

As an example of the methods developed for efficient generation of standard distributions, we will consider a procedure created by Marsaglia, MacLaren, and Bray [10]. This procedure for generating variates from a standard normal distribution and a similar one for exponential variates [9] are generally regarded as the most efficient methods presently available [1].

The basic approach of this method is to represent the normal distribution density function as the sum of three density functions:

$$f(x) = .9578 f_1(x) + .0395 f_2(x) + .0027 f_3(x)$$

Then with probability .9578, generate a random variable with density f_1; with probability .0395, generate a random variable with density f_2; and with probability .0027, generate a random variable with density f_3.

The density function f_1 is a rectangular approximation to the standard normal density function in the range $0 < x < 3$. Random variables from this density function are generated using the same principle as that of the procedure in Fig. D.5. However, the actual implementation uses modifications not available in high-level programming languages to speed the computation. The table used to define the rectangles (similar to the array S in Fig. D.5) is carefully selected to achieve a balance between storage requirements and the accuracy of the approximation to the normal density function. This part of the procedure executes very fast and is used for almost 96 percent of all random numbers generated.

The density function f_2 is the difference between the rectangular approximation and the true normal density function in the range $0 < x < 3$. It consists of a series of wedge-shaped segments, one for each rectangle. A special technique is used for generating samples from the "wedge" function which is efficient although not as fast as the method used with f_1. Samples from f_2 are only needed for less than 4 percent of the variates generated.

The density function f_3 represents the tail of the standard normal distribution, where $x > 3$. Samples from this density function are obtained using transformation techniques similar to the ones indicated in the previous section. This is not a fast computation, but since it is only used for about 1 out of every 400 variates, it does not appreciably increase the expected variate generation time.

The details of this procedure [10] provide a good example of the ingenuity that has been used in developing efficient computer algorithms for random-number generation.

REFERENCES

1. Ahrens, J. H., and U. Dieter: Computer Methods for Sampling from the Exponential and Normal Distributions, *Comm. ACM*, vol. 15, no. 10, pp. 873–882, October 1972.
2. Fishman, G. S.: "Principles of Discrete Event Simulation," Wiley, New York, 1978.
3. Good, I. J.: The Serial Test for Sampling Numbers and Other Tests for Randomness, *Proc. Camb. Phil. Soc.*, vol. 49, pp. 276–284, 1953.
4. International Mathematical and Statistical Libraries, Inc.: "Reference Manual," IMSL LIB2-0006, Houston, Tex., 1977.
5. Knuth, D. C.: "The Art of Computer Programming: Seminumerical Algorithms," vol. 2, Addison-Wesley, Reading, Mass., 1969.
6. Learmonth, G. P., and P. A. W. Lewis: "Random Number Generator Package LLRANDOM," NPS 55 LW 73061 A, Naval Postgraduate School, Monterey, Calif., 1973.
7. Lehmer, D. H.: "Mathematical Methods in Large-Scale Computing Units," *Ann. Comp. Lab.*, Harvard University, vol. 26, pp. 141–146, 1951.
8. Lewis, P. A. W., A. S. Goodman, and J. M. Miller: "A Pseudo-Random Number Generator for the System/360," *IBM Systems J.*, vol. 8, no. 2, pp. 136–145, 1969.
9. MacLaren, M. D., G. Marsaglia, and T. A. Bray: "A Fast Procedure for Generating Exponential Random Variables," *Comm. ACM*, vol. 7, no. 5, pp. 298–300, May 1964.
10. Marsaglia, G., M. D. MacLaren, and T. A. Bray: "A Fast Procedure for Generating Normal Random Variables," *Comm. ACM*, vol. 7, no. 1, pp. 4–10, January 1964.
11. Nance, R., and C. Overstreet: "Bibliography on Random Number Generation," *Comm. Rev.*, vol. 13, pp. 495–508, 1972.
12. Newman, T. G., and P. L. Odell: "The Generation of Random Variates," Hafner, New York, 1971.

INDEX